Irony on Occasion

Irony on Occasion

**From Schlegel and Kierkegaard
to Derrida and de Man**

Kevin Newmark

FORDHAM UNIVERSITY PRESS

NEW YORK 2012

Fordham University Press has no responsibility for the persis-
tence or accuracy of URLs for external or third-party Internet
websites referred to in this publication and does not guarantee
that any content on such websites is, or will remain, accurate or
appropriate.

Fordham University Press also publishes its books in a variety of
electronic formats. Some content that appears in print may not be
available in electronic books.

Library of Congress Cataloging-in-Publication Data

Newmark, Kevin, 1951–
    Irony on occasion : from Schlegel and Kierkegaard to Derrida
and de Man / Kevin Newmark. — 1st ed.
        p. cm.
    Includes bibliographical references and index.
    ISBN 978-0-8232-4012-8 (cloth : alk. paper) —
ISBN 978-0-8232-4013-5 (pbk. : alk. paper)   1. Irony in literature. 2. Irony.   3. Literature—Philosophy.   4. Philosophy in
literature.   5. Romanticism.   6. Deconstruction.   7. Criticism.
8. Literature, Modern—History and criticism—Theory, etc.
I. Title.   II. Title: Schlegel and Kierkegaard to Derrida and
de Man.
    PN56.I65N49 2012
    809'.918—dc23

                                                    2011037021

Printed in the United States of America

14 13 12   5 4 3 2 1

First edition

CONTENTS

ACKNOWLEDGMENTS

Many of the people I never met, it goes without saying, played a crucial role
in the elaboration of this book. A number of colleagues and students with
whom I have worked or crossed paths at lectures, conferences, and in class-
rooms have contributed in ways that would be difficult to circumscribe with
precision. Others have helped more directly. Over the years, Dick Macksey
provided regular access to the pages of *MLN* with easy-going yet gracious
benevolence. Hillis Miller, who was the first to suggest I write a book on
irony, was also among those who most recently encouraged me to publish
one. Still others—Birgit Baldwin, Pat de Man, Ted Fraser, Georgia Albert,
François Raffoul, Madeleine Dobie, Wayne Klein, Ora Avni, Matilda Bruck-
ner, Jonathan Ree, Scott Carpenter, Luca Pes, Michael Syrotinski, Lawrence
Kritzman, Jonathan Culler, Mark O'Connor, Ronald Mendoza-de Jesús, Va-
nessa Rumble, Jon Stewart, Martin McQuillan, Patsy de Man, Lindsay Waters, Werner Hamacher, Ethan Wells, Liz Rottenberg, Ann Miller, Helen
Tartar—generously provided me with specific occasions to think and write a
little more about irony. An abiding fascination with literature and philosophy,
as distinct from any scholarly pretensions, made it nearly inevitable that I
would one day encounter irony in the work of Paul de Man and Jacques Derrida. A happy coincidence permitted me to discover their writings by having
them as teachers over the course of several all-too-short years. For a longer
period of time now, I have benefitted from the intellectual friendship offered
me by Cathy Caruth, Ellen Burt—who gave me a nudge at a key moment—
and Andrzej Warminski, who has been an uninterrupted force of dialogue. At
home—provided one bears in mind that "home" is more likely than not the
first thing that will have been irremediably altered whenever irony makes its
abode there—at home, then, I have been singularly blessed by having been

taken only slightly more seriously than my work by Hannah, Paul, Helen, and, of course, Moses and Seamus. Unless, unbeknownst to me, it was the other way around. To each and all I am infinitely indebted.

As far as institutions go, I am grateful for the support I received on various occasions from both Yale University and Boston College. A special word of thanks is due to David Quigley, Dean of Arts and Sciences at Boston College, for the alacrity with which he helped to arrange a subsidy for the preparation of an index. Early versions of some chapters have appeared in print; permission to publish later versions here is gratefully acknowledged. Chapter 1 originally appeared as "L'Absolu littéraire: Friedrich Schlegel and the Myth of Irony," *MLN* 107:5 (December 1992). An earlier version of chapter 2 was published as "Taking Kierkegaard Apart," *diacritics* 17:1 (spring 1987). Chapter 3 appeared as "Secret Agents: After Kierkegaard's Subject," *MLN* 112:5 (December 1997). An earlier version of chapter 5 was published as "Between Hegel and Kierkegaard: The Space of Translation," *Genre* 16:4 (winter 1983), and the chapter is published by permission of the University of Oklahoma. Chapter 6 appeared originally as "Nietzsche, Deconstruction, and the Truth of History," *Graduate Faculty Philosophy Journal of the New School for Social Research* 15:2 (fall 1991). An earlier version of chapter 8 was published as "Practically Impossible: Jean Paulhan and Post-Romantic Irony," *parallax* 9 (October–December 1998). Chapter 9 was published as "On Parole: Blanchot, Saussure, Paulhan," *Yale French Studies* 106 (December 2004). An earlier version of chapter 10, titled "Deconstruction," appeared in *The Columbia History of Twentieth-Century French Thought*, edited by Lawrence D. Kritzman with the assistance of Brian Reilly and with translations by Malcolm DeBevoise, copyright © 2006 Columbia University Press; the chapter is published here by permission of the Press. Chapter 11 appeared originally as "Bewildering: Paul de Man, Poetry, Politics," *MLN* 124:5 (December 2009).

Without the occasion, nothing really happens, and yet the occasion has no part in what happens.

—SØREN KIERKEGAARD

Gibs auf!

Es war sehr früh am Morgen, die Straßen rein und leer, ich ging zum Bahn-
hof. Als ich eine Turmuhr mit meiner Uhr verglich, sah ich, daß es schon viel
später war, als ich geglaubt hatte, ich mußte mich sehr beeilen, der Schrecken
über diese Entdeckung ließ mich im Weg unsicher werden, ich kannte mich
in dieser Stadt noch nicht sehr gut aus, glücklicherweise war ein Schutzmann
in der Nähe, ich lief zu ihm und fragte ihn atemlos nach dem Weg. Er lächelte
und sagte: "Von mir willst du den Weg erfahren?" "Ja," sagte ich, "da ich ihn
selbst nicht finden kann." "Gibs auf, gibs auf," sagte er und wandte sich mit
einem großen Schwunge ab, so wie Leute, die mit ihrem Lachen allein sein
wollen.

— F R A N Z   K A F K A

Give it up!

It was very early in the morning, the streets clean and empty, I was on my way to the train station. As I compared the tower clock with my watch, I realized it was already much later than I had thought, I had to hurry, the shock of this discovery made me feel unsure about the way, I didn't yet know this town very well, luckily there was a policeman nearby, I ran up to him and out of breath asked him the way. He smiled and said: "From me you want to learn the way?" "Yes," I said, "since I can't find it myself." "Give it up, give it up," he said and suddenly swung himself away, like people who like to be alone with their laughter.

— FRANZ KAFKA

Introduction: *Irony on Occasion*

Εἰδὲ ὁ ὀφθαλμός σου ὁ δεξιὸς σκανδαλίζει σε, ἔξελε αὐτὸν καὶ βάλε ἀπὸ . . .
Wenn aber dein rechtes Auge dir Anlaß zur Sünde gibt, so reiß es aus und wirf es weg . . .
Si ton œil droit est pour toi une occasion de chute, arrache-le et jette-le loin . . .
And if your right eye proves an occasion of falling to you, tear it out and cast it away . . .

— MATTHEW 5:29[1]

If it is true that a book can always be traced back to an occasion from which it must have started out, then the initial occasion for writing this book was not exactly irony. The chapter that was written earliest and which therefore stands more or less at its source is entitled *"Fear and Trembling"*—an essay that in the first instance ought to be about faith. It may well be, of course, that the book in its entirety is about the unexpected ways in which irony and faith are indissociable. At any rate, the faith that first occasioned the chapter on Kierkegaard's *Fear and Trembling* can be traced back to an aside that Paul de Man made during a seminar he was conducting at Yale in the spring of 1980, and which was devoted to Hegel's *Lectures on Aesthetics*. Interrupting his commentary on a passage in Hegel's *Encyclopedia*, de Man paused for a moment and began to speak about Kierkegaard. Kierkegaard, he said, took issue with Hegel's conception of language, took issue with the idea that language must function solely and exclusively as a means for expressing the generality of thought. And then de Man mentioned *Fear and Trembling* as a sustained attempt on the part of Kierkegaard to contest Hegel's conception of the dialectical relationship between thought, language, and subjectivity.[2] But he went on to add a rather curious comment, or at least at the time it seemed curious to me, as well as detached from the principal topic at hand. He began to talk about the ram that Abraham saw as he looked up just after the angel commanded him to stop his raised arm and the knife it held from coming down on Isaac's throat. If I remember correctly, it was at that point that de Man said that he had always been intrigued by the role played by the ram in this story, and he concluded his digression by suggesting that one day it would be worth someone's trouble to read the story of Abraham and Isaac from the point of view of the ram! The comment seemed motivated at the time by the desire to generate a laugh, and it did—so that would be one sense in which the initial occasion for this book actually did have something to do with irony. But on that occasion I must have also believed somehow that what de Man said about the ram was not merely ironic, or that the irony in his remark lay somewhere else, and was not just prompted by the desire to produce the laugh that, as a teacher, one is always anxious to secure in the course of a demanding seminar.

The following year, in spring 1981, I attended the seminar Jacques Derrida was giving in Paris, and for my contribution I delivered an exposé on *Fear and Trembling* that largely concerned itself with the relationship between Hegel and Kierkegaard. But it didn't mention the ram. I was fortunate enough to be offered the opportunity in 1983 to publish a version of that exposé; that version didn't mention the ram either. So I took the occasion of rewriting that essay for this book so that I could finally say something about the ram in Kierkegaard's text—which also means that the chapter on *Fear and Trembling* represents not only the initial occasion but also the most recent occasion for this book. All of which suggests that it would be of far more interest and relevance here, in the introduction, to discuss the concept of the "occasion" than to rehash one after the other the many and various occasions on which I just happened to begin writing the essays that comprise the book as it now stands. That said, there is no reason to conceal the fact—which no doubt also goes without saying—that this book is of a highly occasional nature, and the essays that form the basis for its chapters were without exception written originally for occasions having nothing whatsoever to do with this book—having to do instead with particular authors, critics, theoretical issues, or even occasions.[3] Except that they were all written with the romantic and postromantic concept of irony in mind. A better way to approach an introduction to this particular book might therefore be to ask: what does the concept of the occasion have to do with the concept of irony?

At least in that respect some genuine headway could be made—though probably not within a mere introduction—since for any number of legitimate reasons, irony can never be anything but occasional. The best thing that has been written about the occasion is by Kierkegaard—not so surprising, since he also wrote some of the best things on irony—and it is entitled, oddly enough, "The First Love."[4] One can already gain some sense of Kierkegaard's insight into the occasion by reading the little note that precedes his essay, since in it he reveals that the essay that one is about to read was actually intended to be published somewhere else, on a different occasion. To think about the occasion, then, is necessarily to think about accidents and how they happen, and how they change things that were supposed to be different from the way they actually turned out; "Anyone who has ever had leanings toward productivity," Kierkegaard writes, "has certainly also noticed that it is a little accidental external circumstance that becomes the *occasion* for the actual producing" (*EO* 1:233). While it would certainly be worthwhile—somewhere else and on another occasion—to read carefully what Kierkegaard had to say about the occasion, or *Anledningen* in Danish, on this particular occasion it might be somewhat more efficient to forget about Kierkegaard for a moment and consider more closely the way we say *occasion* in our own language, that is, in English.

Occasion, as one is liable to remark as soon as one stops to think about it, is related in a crucial but indeterminate sense to the word *cause*. What might occasion and cause have in common? To what extent can occasion and cause be traced back to the same thing, or the same root? It just so happens that the etymology of cause is itself *causa*, or thing. To reflect on a cause is to seek the thing, *la chose*, the *res, die Sache*, that lies at the origin of something else—for instance, the reason that lies behind, or the thing that stands under and thus provides the grounds for, something else—say, the writing of a certain book, whether it be on irony or not. But when Heidegger thinks about cause, or *Ursache*, he asks that we resist stopping with the noun, *causa*, and proposes instead that we think *causa* in its relation to the verb *cadere*, to fall. To think about cause and causality, Heidegger says, is to consider that which brings it about that something falls out as a result in such and such a way.[5] To the extent that one of the chapters of this book, chapter 9, "On Parole," is actually about the power and limits of etymology, it would probably not be entirely appropriate here, in the introduction, to take the etymology of *occasion* at face value or as the grounds of anything but a few brief and very preliminary remarks.

Nonetheless, it may be worth noting that by thinking both *causa* and causality as indissociable from *cadere*, Heidegger also reopens the way for thinking the relation between causality and the occasion in a most original fashion. For Heidegger, the occasion would no longer remain of secondary or derivative importance with respect to the privilege that is regularly accorded to the concept of a causal ground, or "thing." On the contrary, Heidegger's entire effort is aimed at displacing the priority of the self-enclosed "case," "thing" or "matter" that is explicitly designated by the Latin word *causa*, and which is also implied in the German word for cause—*Ur-Sache*—by paying close attention to the verbal stem at work in the two German words commonly used for occasion, *Anlaß* and *Veranlassung* ("QT" 9–13; "FT" 14–17). By focusing on the way *Anlaß* and *Veranlassung* are derived from the verbs *an-lassen* and *ver-an-lassen*—to allow something to begin or to happen, to get things going, to set something in motion or release it on its way—Heidegger invites us to consider the way in which the word *aition*, which the Greeks used in place of what we call "causality," is actually much closer in tenor to the German words for occasion than it is to terms like *causa, cause, Kausalität,* or *Ursache.* He then cites a key passage from the *Symposium* in which Plato uses the term *aition*, which Heidegger immediately translates as *Veranlassung*, or occasion. The passage in question, 205 b, is the one in which Diotima reminds Socrates that every *aitia*—every *Veranlassung*, or occasion—for whatever passes from out of not being into being is *poiesis*, and Heidegger uses the passage to propose that *poiesis* be translated as *Her-vor-bringen*, or "bringing forth" ("QT" 10; "FT" 15). For Heidegger, then, the occasion, *Anlaß* or *Veranlassung*, is no unified thing, *chose, Sache,* or cause; rather, it is a complex set of circumstances thanks to which alone whatever was not already there is allowed to come about, become manifest, and therefore to happen.

Far from accrediting the priority of the "thing" in thinking causality, Heidegger turns the traditional concept on its head by making the cause depend on the occasion, insofar as it is the occasion that allows whatever lies in concealment—that which is hidden in our ordinary thinking of causality, for starters—to come forth into the open and begin to occur at all. In this way, Heidegger attempts to rehabilitate the concept of the occasion and disclose it as the essence of what, since the Greeks, has been translated—and thus covered over—by a Latinized conception of causality: "We now give the word *ver-an-lassen*—to occasion," writes Heidegger, "a wider meaning so that it can name the essence of what the Greeks thought as causality [*das Wesen der griechisch gedachten Kausalität*]" ("QT" 10; "FT" 14). Moreover, by thinking the occasion—*Anlaß* and *Veranlassung*—as *Her-vor-bringen*, bringing forth and, especially, bringing forth out of concealment, Heidegger is able to make the crucial link between occasion and truth, or *Wahrheit* as *Aletheia* ("QT" 11–12; "FT" 15–16). The concealed truth of what we usually think as causality, suggests Heidegger, is in fact the *occasion*, provided we are able to begin thinking the occasion through the German word *Veranlassung* as that which—in *poiesis* or *techné*—originally sets, or better, sends us on our way and, ultimately, toward our historical destiny, or *Geschick* ("QT" 24–32; "FT" 28–36). Heidegger's gesture with respect to cause and occasion is nothing if not provocative, since it appears to unsettle the ground, or *Sache*, that we all-too-casually associate with causality. It puts causality into motion and then replaces it within the history of being that is *occasioned* by the disclosure of truth, or *A-letheia*, in both *poiesis* and *techné*. But to the extent that this movement is cautioned at every point by a thinking of *Aletheia* as historical destiny, or *Geschick*, one begins to suspect that Heidegger's interpretation of the occasion—as compelling as it is—ultimately has very little to do with Kierkegaard and his irony, since it unsettles the ground of causality only in order to establish it on an even more secure ontological footing. What has happened here with the radically *accidental* element that Kierkegaard always associates with the occasion and its disruptively ironic effects?[6] As Kierkegaard himself points out—anticipating in this way not only Heidegger's reception of his little essay but also a good many others—the occasion, like irony, is equivocal to the utmost degree. The occasion is neither exactly like nor is it wholly unlike causality; rather, it is simultaneously, though unreliably and therefore deceptively, both like and unlike causality. For this reason, according to Kierkegaard, the occasion could never be simply dismissed, as it was by Carl Schmitt, for instance in his interpretation of German romanticism; nor could it be successfully transformed into a remedy for the far-reaching philosophical problems of which it is always a symptom, which is more or less what Heidegger attempted to do with it. "The occasion," Kierkegaard writes, "always has this equivocal character, and it is of no more use to want to deny this, to want to free oneself from this thorn in the flesh, than to want to place the occasion on the throne. . . . It is very easy, however, to go astray in this manner, and frequently it is the best of minds that do so" (*EO* 1:237).

Whether or not it is a mere coincidence, the term *occasion*—as opposed now to *cause*—is regularly associated not just with the etymological root *cadere*, as Heidegger's commentary suggests; it also and unavoidably evokes etymological relationships with words like *occidere*, *ob-cadere*, and *ad-cadere*. And these words—all of which also contain references to falling: falling down, falling away, and falling upon—belong without fail to a constellation in which *chance* plays an essential role. The *occasion* necessarily includes a semantic shading that places it closer to the *aleatory* forces of chance, luck, and accident than could ever be the case for the concept that is by tradition linked to the term *cause*. Whatever else it is, then, an occasion is also a cause that is somewhat more accidental, incidental, and random in nature than a strict cause would be. And what is important to retain for the purposes of this book is that accidents do indeed *happen*; they are in no way mere fictions. A true "cause," on the other hand, and as Heidegger well knew— a *thing* that could be identified once and for all as the ultimate root of the matter—well, that may be something of a heuristic fiction, in the sense that it may be impossible ever to pin down and know such a cause, absolutely, in all its complexity, and without further ado or qualification. Such a cause would, at least up to or beyond a certain point, always have to be taken on faith. But an accident is another matter; it is not a fiction of that sort—for who would deny that accidents befall us everywhere and all the time, with great regularity, and to the exclusion of nearly everything else, if one could still put it that way?

It is no doubt for this reason that the Church—for which such concepts as *cause* and *occasion* might be expected to hold special importance—attempts to distinguish between two types of occasion whenever it is a question of how sin takes place. The root "cause" of sinfulness as such would be internal—call it human nature as it exists universally after the original fall. The "occasion," on the other hand, refers to the actual circumstances in which individuals always find themselves implicated and thus subject to discrete failure as a result of having to make specific choices or decisions. There exist, then, proximate and remote occasions of sin, a key distinction in which it is the distance to "causality" that makes all the difference. A proximate occasion of sin is barely distinguishable from a concept of strict causality—and therefore such proximate occasions are to be avoided whenever possible, since one can know, predict, and calculate with a reasonable degree of probability which effects will ensue from them. A firm determination of the occasion as proximate would have to be of only limited pertinence in this context, since it would leave very little if anything open to that which, in history as distinct from pure science, must remain unforeseeable as the future. A remote occasion of sin, on the other hand, is one that preserves within it an inherently accidental and unpredictable factor, since one never knows in advance just how things will turn out when it is encountered—surprises can always happen here. Kierkegaard insisted that we know we are taking historical reality seriously as soon as we begin talking about sin. Nietzsche suggested as much with respect to causality. In both cases, one rediscovers the dilemma Kant faced in having to move from the first to the second *Critique*, from pure to practical reason, in other words, from a discourse of causality to one of free will.[7] It should therefore come as no surprise that the question of the occasion and of irony will have to correspond to the place occupied in Kant's system by the third *Critique*. To some extent, then, the "last" chapter of this book, which deals with the aesthetic in Kant, could also be legitimately considered its "first," since without the complications bequeathed to the philosophical tradition by Kant's third *Critique*, the writings of Schlegel, Kierkegaard, Nietzsche, and Mann would all be deprived of one of the more decisive occasions for their own occurrence.

At any rate, these overly sketchy remarks concerning the way the occasion surfaces in a fragment of Kierkegaard's *Either/Or*, in Heidegger's interrogation of causality, and within theological considerations about sin suggest in their own way that it may in fact be the "accident" that provides the most conclusive link between irony and the occasion. It could just be that the occasion will forever be associated with irony to the precise extent that it is impossible to think irony without thinking the accident in all its richness and complexity. To some extent, then, the title *Irony on Occasion* could be taken to mean something like "irony on irony," since both irony and the occasion are intimately related to the accidental. And this book is also constructed that way: one incidental occasion of irony after the other, in other words, one isolated instance of irony on top of another, one accidental chapter following the one before it. But on another level, the book means to be slightly more serious than that. For the occasion—and especially the occasional and incidental aspect of the occasion—also suggests something quite particular, some specific set of circumstances that can be localized and referred to with a considerable degree of precision and accuracy—such as, for instance, the seminars of Paul de Man and Jacques Derrida to which I referred earlier by means of dates and places as well as of proper names. And that is another very legitimate reason why irony will be forever inseparable from the occasion. Because irony all by itself is not easy to locate, to determine, to define and to control; it always has a way of slipping away from whatever means of observation, verification, and oversight one tries to apply to it. It may therefore be thanks only and exclusively to the occasion that we will ever be granted access to irony.

For if Kierkegaard knew what he was talking about—and this book places a good deal of faith in Kierkegaard—it is as difficult to "see" irony itself, alone and in all its singularity, as it would be to depict an elf wearing a hat that makes him invisible.[8] One reason for this is that irony, in itself, is *nothing*. How one understands this "nothing" can of course vary a great deal, and it can be approached by many different and sometimes incompatible paths. But one relatively straightforward point of agreement might be best reached by emphasizing—in the long, if not infinite, wake of German romanticism—the negativity that seems inherent to every true instance of irony. The negativity of irony has need of something else on which it might produce its negative effects. That would be the occasion for irony. If irony happens, then it can happen only on occasion, only by means of an occasion thanks to which its negativity is allowed in this or that singular manner to exercise itself ironically. This also means that a book that claims to be about irony always runs a very distinct danger of losing its subject precisely by trying to observe it—identify it, define it, interpret it, explain it, understand it—too directly. To write a book on irony—or rather, to allow irony to occasion a book—is necessarily to write obliquely and on all kinds of other topics: topics that are more or less, now and then, here and there, literary, philosophical, religious, political, ethical, personal, interpersonal, and cultural in nature.

For instance, to take some concrete examples, the negativity of irony may emerge from an examination of the attempt by Philippe Lacoue-Labarthe and Jean-Luc Nancy to furnish for once a properly philosophical understanding of the German romantics. Or it could issue from an analysis of Kierkegaard's treatment of Abraham and his religious faith. Ironic negativity can occur on the occasion of considering how the word *deconstruction* is itself an example of what Jacques Derrida calls deconstruction, or even what he says calls for deconstruction. If irony cannot appear directly, on its own, then one should not be overly surprised if an aphorism by Nietzsche on *Verstellung*, or dissimulation, were to provide it with a most propitious occasion on which to take place. Or, if irony tends to occasion interruption, deflection, and digression, it might be of interest to see what happens when Paul de Man treats the philosophical category of the aesthetic as a necessary but problematic passage, connection, or articulation between epistemology and politics, or knowledge and action. And if irony is associated with Socrates for good reason, and Socrates is considered in his function as a teacher, then education—in all its manifold aspects—may just be one of the most frequent and decisive occasions on which irony occurs. This is not to deny, of course, that irony can also crop up on the occasion of its being referred to overtly and directly by those who, as we say, should know what they are talking about. But in that case, the negativity in question may occasion a different kind of irony than the one that we were expecting or even promised. Thus, in the case of Thomas Mann, an encounter with irony becomes strictly unavoidable—both as a theme in his critical writings and as a determining element within his fiction. But there is no guarantee that in the particular case of Thomas Mann, the well-informed and even expert theoretician of irony's negativity will not himself fall prey on occasion to the negativity that is inscribed in the ironic techniques deployed in his own literary texts.

The example of Thomas Mann, moreover, is a telling one, since it raises the question of how one might justifiably establish the constellation of oc- casions on which irony could be documented to occur in its diverse guises. Just how seriously is the accidental nature of the occasion to be taken here? If irony is "itself" occasional and therefore utterly accidental in nature, should the contents of a book on irony, or occasioned by irony, display no order- ing principles whatsoever? This book, at least, does not, I hope, engage that question directly. For there would be little reason to exclude from a serious consideration of irony any of the authors and texts chosen for inclusion in this book—their appearance in a book on irony should, as it were, speak for itself. More problematic—and to the point—would be to pose the question the other way around: which authors and texts that do *not* appear in this book should by right have been included? That question reveals the way that this book—whether I like it or not, whether I acknowledge it or not—actually conforms to a relatively traditional and therefore respectable conception of the history of modern irony as it has been treated in philosophy and litera- ture: from German romanticism through its aftermath in French thought and writing in the twentieth century. Even the coda, on J. M. Coetzee, can be connected back to this tradition by way of its intertextual inscription of certain vestiges of German romanticism that are to be found within English romantic poetry. But if that is the case, what exactly is the principle of selec- tion that governs these chapters, and how comprehensively or accurately does this book convey the history of the concept and technique of irony from Ger- man romanticism onward?

One could perhaps argue that the principle of selection is roughly syn- ecdochal in nature; that is, the book may not include everybody who should be included, but it does include a good number of the most significant and exemplary of the texts and authors who "made irony their business," so to speak. Granted, there is nothing in the book on Solger, Tieck, or Novalis. But texts by those authors could easily be treated in the context of what is said here about Schlegel and Kierkegaard. The writings of Thomas Mann are, for better or worse, made to stand in for a very large number of texts that could be chosen to exemplify a certain type of modern and postmodern engagement with irony. More difficult to ignore or explain—at least as I see it—is the absence of writers of fiction in German who are by no means taken care of by the chapter on Thomas Mann, such as Heinrich von Kleist and Franz Kafka. It would be entirely inadequate to include Kafka by way of an epigraph and Kleist by way of a footnote in a book on irony, but that is what I have done. Also, the crucial articulation from German to French texts is handled here in a manner that is none too smooth; or, it would be more honest to say that it is simply missing. Considering the way that Coetzee's novel reanimates a romantic concept of irony by reinscribing certain Byronic elements within its own narrative plot, one is entitled—or even obligated—to ask about how, exactly, the concept and rhetoric of irony is deployed within nineteenth-century French texts. But that question appears to be left wholly untouched here, except by way of some fleeting references in the chapters on Nietzsche, Paulhan, Blanchot, Derrida, and de Man. How can one treat the concept of irony in theory and literature without mentioning Baudelaire, Mallarmé, or behind them, Edgar Allan Poe?

Putting the question in this manner, moreover, helps to disclose the way that the long shadow of Walter Benjamin falls over the entirety of this book. "The book we have just considered," Maurice Blanchot once wondered in reference to a book on irony he had just read, "is that really the work that must be read? Isn't it rather only the appearance? Would it not be there merely to conceal ironically another essay, more difficult and more dangerous, whose shadows and ambition one can only surmise?"[9] From the perspective of its author, *this* book is to some degree only the shadowy appearance, or *Schein*, that would serve to conceal a deferred encounter with Walter Benjamin. For it is of course the writings of Walter Benjamin that mark the point of articulation between German romanticism and its most fruitful aftermath in the twentieth century, and especially in the twentieth century of French thought and writing. Mentioning him here provides the occasion for correcting slightly a potential misunderstanding that always creeps into the discussion as soon as one uses the term *history* in relation to irony. To suggest, as I have just done, that this book conforms to a relatively traditional model of history and in particular to the history of the concept of irony as it has been elaborated since the end of the eighteenth century is also to forget or erase what was said earlier here about the *occasion* and the accidental nature that it necessarily shares with irony.

In short—and to put it rather bluntly—there can be no history of irony, because irony is the condition of possibility for history. That is what Walter Benjamin has taught us by reading the concept of irony in German romanticism and then extending that reading in all directions through his study of allegory in both the baroque *Trauerspiel* and Baudelaire's poetry. Once one allows a metaphysics of "cause" and "causality" to be interrupted and forever displaced by what actually happens on occasion, and therefore only by accident, then *irony* will always suggest itself as one term among others to name this interruption—that is history. The principle of selection here cannot, then, be synecdochal except in the most superficial and misleading of senses. The principle of selection must be occasional in the very precise sense that it cannot be made sufficiently causal; it is not therefore part of any possible whole, and that would still be true even if all the relevant authors and texts could somehow manage to appear between the covers of just one book. The occasion marks the fall of causality, and the first casualty of such a fall is the unified concept of the "thing"—subject, object, project—that would otherwise stand behind, beneath, or above whatever truly happens only in very singular and therefore occasional circumstances. We call *irony* that which always befalls on occasion—in other words, that which can happen only without its having been anticipated, predicted, or calculated in advance of its own random occurrence and effects. Irony, on occasion and by accident, is historical because it interrupts the reign of a formal causality that would otherwise be machinelike in its imperviousness to anything other than its own predetermined and crushing movement.

To recall one more time, and in conclusion, Kierkegaard—for it is never good to forget too long about Kierkegaard whenever the occasion calls for irony—irony is like a dash in history; but what exactly is a dash?[10] In Danish, the word for dash is *Tankestreg*, proximate in meaning and form to the German word *Gedankenstrich*. Now it can hardly be considered a coincidence that the German thinker who is most famous for his use of dashes—*Gedankenstriche*—turns out to be Nietzsche. However, it is perhaps less well known that Nietzsche also left behind a marginal but endlessly suggestive gloss on how the *Gedankenstrich* operates in his own writing, an annotation that puts him very close to the way Kierkegaard conceives of the *Tankestreg* in his book on irony. Writing to his sister Elisabeth in May of 1885 from Venice of all places, Nietzsche says; "Alles, was ich bisher geschrieben habe, ist Vordergrund; für mich selber geht es erst immer mit den Gedankenstrichen los."[11] This is certainly not an easy affirmation to translate, much less to comprehend, but after acknowledging that everything he has written up to this point is to be considered "foreground," Nietzsche then goes on to say that, at least as far as he is concerned, things, or more precisely, "it," only really gets going with the dashes—"mit den Gedankenstrichen." What is *it?* And how is it related to what Kierkegaard says about irony being like a dash—*en Tankestreg*—in world history? Could it be that Nietzsche is taking advantage of the occasion, ironically as it were, to play with the word *Gedankenstrich,* a word that, like *Tankestreg* in Danish, refers at one and the same time to the typographical mark of punctuation—the dash—designated by this name and to the "thought-line," the "stroke of thought" that the word spells out with its own letters in both German and Danish? The dash in Kierkegaard and Nietzsche—*Tankestreg* and *Gedankenstrich*—however obliquely and silently, relates this particular mark that occasionally punctuates writing to thought. The dash in Kierkegaard and Nietzsche can therefore be considered writing's own thought-mark. But how are we to understand this? It might be construed to mean that the dash marks the place where thought used to be—in Socrates or in Nietzsche, for example—but is no longer present in writing. Or, it could mean that the written mark is where the thought of Socrates or of Nietzsche now resides, if we only knew how to get at it, to read and thus seize hold of it as such. Or, it could mean that—for Socrates, Kierkegaard, Nietzsche, and the rest of us as well—thought is for right now missing there, but might eventually be made to appear: a space left open for thought to come. It could even mean that this line strikes thought and runs it through, indicating the place where thought itself has been stricken and ruled out for good. However it is drawn, then, the dash in writing's punctuation can always be translated as a peculiar stroke of thought. Irony, though, as Kierkegaard points out in reference to Socrates and as Nietzsche implies in referring to his own writ-ing, is not merely like a dash—irony is therefore no ordinary stroke, line, or writing of thought. Rather, irony for Socrates, Kierkegaard, and Nietzsche is like a dash that marks the spot where "it"—writing, thought, history—first gets going and is always set loose. Irony would be like the writing of thought in history—though a writing of thought into history only as a dash, an inter-ruption, and, paradoxically enough, a setting loose that is, first of all as well as always, a pause. Irony—like the dash—punctuates history by first drawing a line, a stroke of thought, that also always leaves its mark on history. Or, perhaps a better way to put it would be: irony, on occasion, draws a stroke of thought that leaves its mark as history.

PART ONE

Romantic Irony

ONE

Friedrich Schlegel and the Myth of Irony

> Es ist gleich tödlich für den Geist, ein System zu haben, und keins zu haben.
>
> — FRIEDRICH SCHLEGEL

The peculiar status of irony within the literary and philosophical tradition is perhaps best illustrated by the vexing questions that always hover over its founder and chief exemplar, Socrates. Was Socrates a model pedagogue or a seducer and corrupter of innocent youth? Was his method of rigorous ignorance a path leading to negative knowledge or an abyssal spiraling of rhetorical tricks? Was his stubborn insistence on interpersonal questioning and dialogue a form of urbanity or the egotistical undermining of any genuinely sociopolitical form of community? Was his death sentence an unacknowledged confession of moral and intellectual bankruptcy in Greece or a necessary step in the unfolding of Western thought? These questions assume their most acute form in the epoch of German romanticism—that is, in the constellation of texts signed by Schlegel, Hegel, Kierkegaard, and several others—precisely because they will have been repeated there in a way that has left an indelible mark on our own thinking about literature, philosophy, and political history. Reading these texts will therefore always entail the difficulty of determining exactly what the question of irony is about, and how, as well as how far, such a question can be taken seriously.

For instance: was Friedrich Schlegel a genuine philosopher or a mere *littérateur*, a dilettante, or worse, a *farceur*, an intellectual practical joker, a pretentiously literate buffoon? In a perceptive essay about some of the more controversial issues surfacing in discussions about literature, literary theory, and philosophy at the turn of the last century, Schlegel was once wittily referred to as a "playboy philosopher."[1] Such a characterization pretty much sums up the way he has been considered, and dismissed, by most serious philosophers ever since he received his first shellacking at the hands of Hegel. To call Schlegel a "playboy" philosopher, moreover, serves above all to highlight the ludic element of "play" that precedes the age and gender specification of "boy"—though of course neither sexual difference nor the accusation of immaturity is without pertinence whenever irony becomes a subject for serious discussion. Primarily at issue in Schlegel is the nonsystematic mode in which his speculative writings relate to what is perhaps philosophy's principal object and motivation, truth. Is irony the name for a specific kind of philosophical truth, say, its masked appearance in more or less playful form; or is irony rather play as sheer dissimulation, deception, and ultimately the distortion and even destruction of truth? This question, because it states the issue in terms of truth and its manifestation in a subsidiary, and in this case, veiled form, also serves to remind us that irony is a term that always marks the encounter and potential tension between literature and philosophy, or truth and tropes. Irony, that is, always seems to confront us with the very serious question of the precise way in which literature's constitutive dimension of tropological play, or rhetoric, is related to philosophical determinations of meaning, knowledge, and truth.

Schlegel himself, moreover, went out of his way on more than one occasion to draw attention to the appeal and even inevitability of such an encounter between literature and philosophy. One of his more laconic and well-known formulations in this regard reads: "The whole history of modern poetry is a continuous commentary on the short text of philosophy: every art should become science, and every science should become art; poetry and philosophy should be united" (*Lyceum Fragment* 115).[2] This is all well and good, of course, but as we know—notwithstanding Keats's happy version of this commonplace—such encounters between poetry and philosophy, or between truth and tropes, always run the risk of having their constituents rub each other the wrong way. The solicitation of literature by philosophy can always become a simple invitation to trouble, as the saying goes, especially if it is not taken seriously enough, or, as may be the case with Friedrich Schlegel, if it is taken so seriously that it no longer leaves the limit between the serious and the nonserious in its proper place. Another of his fragments, this one published posthumously, just happens to read: "Critique of Philosophy = Philology of Philosophy, that is one and the same.—Since philosophy has criticized so very much, in fact has criticized just about everything under the sun, it certainly ought to be able to stand a little criticism itself" (*PF* 228; *KA* 18:40).[3] And so it is perhaps high time to subject philosophical truth to a critique by philology or literature, and to do this for once seriously enough not to take the limits of philosophy's own playfulness for granted.

The basic contours of such a critique are cogently sketched out by Philippe Lacoue-Labarthe and Jean-Luc Nancy in what remains today the best general presentation and analysis of the relation between literature and philosophy as it is articulated in German romanticism, *L'Absolu littéraire* (*The Literary Absolute*).[4] Unquestionably one of the more vigilant and successful efforts of recent European philosophy to criticize itself by taking up the challenge of literature, *L'Absolu littéraire*—the literary absolute, or the absolutely literary, depending on how one chooses to read the uncanniness of the French title— offers a privileged approach to the enigmatic place occupied within German romanticism by Friedrich Schlegel and his irony. It is precisely in this spirit that Lacoue-Labarthe and Nancy state clearly and right from the start of their presentation:

> It is imperative that [romanticism] be accounted for *philosophically*, that it be articulated with the philosophical itself, for in its fundamental provenance and consequences, it is philosophical through and through. . . . [R]omanticism is rigorously comprehensible (or even accessible) only on a philosophical basis, in its proper and in fact unique (in other words, entirely new) articulation with the philosophical. . . . In other words, if romanticism is approachable, it is approachable only by means of the "philosophical path." (*LA* 28–29)

As things turn out, however, Lacoue-Labarthe and Nancy immediately recognize that the philosophical path invoked here will have to negotiate as well the "eruption," or interruption, produced along its length by "the question of literature": "[Romanticism] introduces, within the philosophical, a distance from the philosophical, a distortion and a deviation [une distortion et un écartement]" (29). Might it not also be true that this distortion, this deviation, or turning aside from the straight path that philosophy would otherwise be free to pursue, also names, albeit by the roundabout figure of periphrasis, the eruption, or interruption, of irony within romanticism?

In another well-known posthumous fragment, Schlegel himself under-scored the relation between irony and the sudden eruption that serves to disrupt or interrupt the movement of a straight line, by linking it to the dramatic procedure whereby the chorus interrupts and intervenes in the sequential unfolding of a Greek tragedy: "Irony," Schlegel once wrote, "is a permanent parabasis" (*PF* 668; *KA* 18:85). But to judge at least from the explicit references by Lacoue-Labarthe and Nancy in *The Literary Absolute*, irony does not constitute a major crux of their argument about the kind of deviation introduced into the philosophical path by the question of literature, nor do they devote to the term *irony*, as they do to the romantic theorizing of fragments, religion, poetry, and criticism, a sustained and differentiated commentary. Still, it would not be entirely true, or even fair, to claim that romantic irony is simply overlooked by Lacoue-Labarthe and Nancy. There can be little doubt that a good deal of *The Literary Absolute* is itself written "ironically," at least from a stylistic perspective. Perhaps even more to the point, however, there are several key passages of the book in which the romantic concept and use of irony is invoked and analyzed. Nonetheless, it remains true that the most telling reference to irony to be found in *The Literary Absolute* is not made in direct reference to Schlegel but rather in connection with Socrates and the *subjective* mastery he always maintains within the Platonic dialogues. In this regard, Schlegel merely emulates Socrates, though without managing ever to match him. Such an interpretation conforms to the most classic understanding of Schlegel's work—proposed by both Hegel and Kierkegaard—as a belated and watered-down version of the legitimate Socratic project to found subjective consciousness on firm ground. Lacoue-Labarthe and Nancy write: "Socrates . . . has always represented the anticipatory incarnation or prototype of the Subject itself. . . . The reason for this, in Schlegel's case at least, is that Socrates . . . is what could be called the subject of irony . . . which is the exchange of form and truth or . . . of poetry and philosophy. . . . Irony is precisely this: the very power of reflection or infinite reflexivity" (*LA* 86). To the extent that irony is principally thematized by Lacoue-Labarthe and Nancy as this anticipation of self-conscious exchange, or infinite reflexivity, between "form and truth, or poetry and philosophy," rather than as their mutual disruption, irony is necessarily denied the privileged status they willingly attribute to "writing" as it will have been articulated and theorized in the aftermath of romanticism by both Maurice Blanchot and Jacques Derrida.

It could be, of course, that in this respect Lacoue-Labarthe and Nancy are simply taking at face value—always a dubious maneuver when irony is in the offing—suggestions made by the two German critics who have most influenced the writing of *The Literary Absolute* and the place of Schlegel within it: Walter Benjamin and Peter Szondi. In his dissertation, *The Concept of Art Criticism in German Romanticism*, Benjamin points out that Schlegel, in part because he lacked "sufficient logical force" to do otherwise, had a confusing habit of substituting different names for his systematic concepts, making it difficult if not finally useless to attempt to find in his writings a clear definition of such terms as "irony, religion, or history."[5] And Peter Szondi is even more straightforward on this point. In an essay called "Friedrich Schlegel and Romantic Irony," which Lacoue-Labarthe and Nancy are familiar with and cite, Szondi, very close to the end of his discussion of irony, has this surprising comment to make: "So far we have sought to discover the presuppositions of romantic irony *without naming the concept and without attempting to define it.* For it was our hope that in this way we might *resist the temptation* to which so many scholars have succumbed."[6] Irony, it seems, at least for the properly philosophical discourse, is something of a temptation to be resisted, and it is therefore best written about when it is neither "named" nor "defined." As a grounding principle for a general theory of hermeneutics, this would be a very interesting idea to pursue: you can be sure that irony has ceased to be a serious topic of philosophical inquiry as soon as it is named as such. More germane to the point at hand, though, would be to ask the following question of *The Literary Absolute*: What, precisely, happens to a reading of Schlegel and German romanticism when the ironic dimension of their legacy to modernity is not tackled directly and at length? What happens, that is, when the temptation to name and define irony in a philosophically rigorous manner is in fact avoided? Is the philosophical admonition to avoid speaking of irony not itself ironic? Can the suggestion that one resist irony be followed without falling prey to an even greater irony, that is, the irony of taking one's own philosophical discourse *too* seriously?

In order to suggest a possible response to this question, it will be helpful to examine in some detail how Lacoue-Labarthe and Nancy eventually deploy the fundamental and invaluable insight which their philosophical treatment of romanticism enables them to reach. What finally sets *The Literary Absolute* apart from almost every other study devoted to its subject is the recognition that, prior to any determination of either the specifically literary or philosophical element within German romanticism, the constitutive *relation* between philosophy and literature must become an object of critical analysis in its own right. "Romanticism," Lacoue-Labarthe and Nancy therefore remind us, "is neither mere 'literature' . . . nor simply a 'theory of literature.' . . . Rather, it is *theory itself as literature* or, in other words, literature producing itself as it produces its own theory" (*LA* 12). But perhaps this indispensable insight is more suited to formulation (and therefore to formalization and repetition) than it would be to negotiating the actual pitfalls involved in any genuine critical analysis and understanding of a given text, romantic or not, ironic or not. What, precisely, does it mean for literature and philosophy when literature begins to produce itself as it produces its own theory, that is, when theory assumes the necessary burden of being at one and the same time theoretical and "literary"?

One thing it certainly does *not* mean, insist Lacoue-Labarthe and Nancy, is that we should be led astray by the "rather feeble" point of view adopted by Mme de Staël on the relation of literature and philosophy in German romanticism. When theory becomes literary, it does not simply dispense with philosophical rigor; on the contrary. Mme de Staël, who in this respect helped to found what Lacoue-Labarthe and Nancy also call a long tradition of "ignorance" and "critical unintelligence" on the subject, wondered if great writers "needed metaphysics" to be great, and eventually she became a bit impatient with "philosophical systems that are applied to literature."[7] It is this impatience with the philosophical aspect of romantic literature that Lacoue-Labarthe and Nancy finally identify with a refusal to read the texts in question, and that they characterize as Mme de Staël's typical "resistance to theory [la résistance au théorique]" (*LA* 12–13). Only by fully recognizing that romanticism is "*theory itself as literature* or, in other words, literature producing itself as it produces its own theory" would it be possible to come into contact with the *absolu littéraire* by which Lacoue-Labarthe and Nancy rightly characterize Schlegel and the romanticism he helped to articulate. But would it then suffice to suggest, along with Lacoue-Labarthe and Nancy, that such a formula for the literary absolute that is simultaneously absolutely literary is also equivalent to the philosophico-literary program announced in Schlegel's *Lyceum Fragment* 115, which quite simply calls for "poetry and philosophy to be united [vereinigt]" without further ado? And if, as a result of acknowledging this reciprocal ideal of unity for literature and theory, it were possible to overcome for once the kind of *superficial* resistance to theory practiced by Mme de Staël and her academic heritage, would it then follow that such a book as *The Literary Absolute* could itself complete the "*properly* philosophical study of romanticism" (*LA* 13) it in fact helps to initiate?

Certain "literary theoreticians," not that distant from Lacoue-Labarthe and Nancy in terms of their textual interests and approach, have pointed to a kind of "resistance to theory" that cannot simply be overcome once and for all by an act of critical recognition and vigilance on the part of the philosophical commentator on literature. At issue, for instance, in Paul de Man's writings on the relation between literature and theory is the peculiar suggestion that, beyond the necessarily theoretical, or philosophical, vigilance required for any genuine reading of a literary text, there still remains an insurmountable obstacle to the critical analysis and understanding that such vigilance could alone make possible. "Nothing," de Man says with a bit of irony of his own, "can overcome the resistance to theory since theory *is* itself this resistance."[8] What can de Man mean when he says that this self-reflexive resistance to theory, which he also calls a "resistance to reading," *cannot* be overcome? And, further, what specific effects would the impossibility of overcoming the resistance to theory have on a "properly philosophical" reading of Friedrich Schlegel?

On the one hand, and very much like the romantic *absolu littéraire* named and theorized by Lacoue-Labarthe and Nancy, de Man's model of literary theory can be said to be neither simply literature nor purely a theory of literature, but is rather made up of both theory and literature at once. For de Man, then, literary theory refers to *both* the rhetorical awareness, sometimes called "close reading," that allows access to the specifically linguistic dimension constitutive of any text *as* text, *and* the systematic transformation of this dimension into a universal logic of philosophical meaning and truth. Literary theory, for de Man as for Friedrich Schlegel, is literature as theory; it is literature's own production of an absolute theory at the same time that it reproduces itself absolutely. But on the other hand, and in ever so slight distinction from Lacoue-Labarthe's and Nancy's avowed project of achieving a properly philosophical description and understanding of this *absolu littéraire*, it is precisely the systematic theorization of the literary structure of any text whatsoever that de Man says is always and necessarily "resisted" in a way that nothing could hope to overcome. According to de Man, the actual specificity of the literary, figural, or ultimately, rhetorical, element in the text is what always resists theoretical and philosophical systematization. And, conversely, the necessarily systematic aspect of all theoretical exposition is what eventually threatens to erase any given literary specificity by transposing it into a generalizable law of philosophy. It is in this very particular sense—and not as a result of some will to paradox or obfuscation—that de Man's resistance can be said to be a built-in constituent of "literary theory." Schlegel himself had already said something quite similar about this ironic resistance to theory in literature; it's just that we usually resist reading that as well: "It is equally deadly for the mind to have a system as not to have one. So we'll just have to learn to combine the two" (*Athenaeum Fragment* 53, *PF* 24; *KA* 2:173). Taken in conjunction, the two terms of the textual relation—literature/theory, systematic/nonsystematic, poetry/philosophy, like the *absolu littéraire* they disclose, moreover—always designate a necessarily philosophical task whose ultimate possibility is radically suspended by the very nature of its literary object.

If it is true, then, that romanticism names the movement in which literature produces itself as it produces its own theory, then it must be granted by the same token that no genuine access could ever be had to this moment by economizing on either the systematically theoretical or the specifically rhetorical dimension that by definition resist *each other* in their mutual production of what we call romanticism. To the extent that any analysis aims at and could actually achieve a "properly philosophical" exposition of romanticism, it would necessarily engage in a systematic avoidance of the very literary dimension it sets out to document and understand. By an ironic twist that at this point would have very little to do with subjective mastery, caprice, or jest, the theoretical resistance to romanticism's *absolu littéraire* would be most redoubtable precisely at the moment it claimed to describe the systematic distortion and undoing of the philosophical discourse actually brought about by romantic literature.

What now remains to be determined with somewhat more precision is what an absolutely "literary theoretical" or "systematically nonsystematic" reading of Schlegel's romanticism would consist in, were it not to fall prey immediately to a theoretical reduction of the literary elements comprising its object of analysis. Such a determination could not itself be reduced to a mere description of literary theory, but would have to include an actual example of the literary element that is to be—but that ultimately also resists being— fully theorized. But how do we actually *give* a literary example without merely describing it, representing it, and thus resisting it philosophically?[9] The question brings us back to Lacoue-Labarthe's and Nancy's philosophical description and understanding of the "romantic genre par excellence, the fragment" (*LA* 40). The fragment exemplifies the philosophical logic of romanticism it serves both to constitute and interrupt, or fragment. Lacoue-Labarthe and

Nancy themselves gloss this logic: "Each fragment stands for itself and for that from which it is detached. Totality is the fragment itself in its completed individuality" (44). And this remark leads to a recognition in the same paragraph that "fragments are definitions of the fragment." In other words, fragments are both examples of particular fragments (literature) as well as formalized descriptions of the fragment in general (theory). Fragments are therefore the *mise en abyme* of the fragmentation that they always exemplify, abyssally, as both theory and literature.

Now this recognition leads, in *The Literary Absolute*, to a certain tension. On the one hand, the totalizing tendency of the logic of the fragment—simultaneously literary fragment and theoretical definition of the fragment—is clearly distinguished from what the authors understand to be the "disseminating" effect of more contemporary examples of literary theory, examples that no doubt possess the advantage of no longer being "romantic." Unlike the operation of "writing" referred specifically to Maurice Blanchot or Jacques Derrida, then, "the romantic fragment, far from being the dispersion or the shattering of the work into play, inscribes its plurality as the exergue of the total, infinite work. . . . Fragmentation is not, then, a dissemination" (*LA* 48, 49). On the other hand, as mere exergue, romanticism never seems quite able to achieve the totalization of the literary absolute it represents to itself in the mode of the fragment. It turns out that the otherwise fertile plurality of the fragment might be disseminating after all: "Within the romantic work, there is interruption and dissemination of the romantic work. . . . [T]he fragment closes and interrupts itself at the same point" (57).

If we go on to ask where, exactly, this disseminating character of the literary fragment would begin to manifest itself in a way that would no longer be theoretically or philosophically totalizable, we meet with the following enigma in *The Literary Absolute*: "there is interruption and dissemination of the romantic work, though this in fact is not *readable* in the work itself, even and especially by privileging the fragment" (*LA* 57). What can Lacoue-Labarthe and Nancy mean when they say that the radical fragmentation that actually traverses and undermines the totalizing logic of romantic writing is not "readable" in the fragment itself, or on the level of the fragment? It may ultimately mean simply that the "interruption and dissemination of the romantic work" is not readable in the romantic work because it is not philosophically stated in all clarity there. What is readable *in* a literary work is what is *written* there philosophically, and therefore what is *readable* in the romantic work of literature is not the dissemination that is written, or better, that is *writing* in the philosophical texts of both Blanchot and Derrida—and, we can surmise, in the writing of Lacoue-Labarthe and Nancy. It may be, then, that Lacoue-Labarthe and Nancy themselves never question the underlying principle of semantic coherency that they assume to govern any properly philosophical reading of romanticism's theory of literary writing. And this philosophical fidelity to a principle of semantic determination—which is not necessarily shared in exactly the same way by either Blanchot or Derrida—is in fact readable in the way Lacoue-Labarthe and Nancy, despite their unerring theoretical formulations of the disarticulating and disseminating logic of the example, still identify the actual writing and reading of the romantic fragments with the capacity of such writing to signify and be intelligible in an unproblematic, even if multiplicitous and finally self-contradictory way.

For the romantics, according to *The Literary Absolute*, fragmentary writing is not just an effect of happenstance, the character of a text that for contingent reasons remains unfinished, a mere draft. Rather, the romantic fragment constitutes itself as a particular genre with its very own aims: it implies a type of writing that functions "as a determinate and deliberate *statement* [comme *propos* detérminé et délibéré] assuming or transfiguring the accidental and involuntary aspects of fragmentation" (*LA* 41). As such, the romantic fragment also becomes "the very method . . . suitable for access to the truth" (45). Taken together, the fragment's statement and method would therefore constitute a *mimologics* of truth: "The exposition cannot unfold on the basis of a principle or foundation because the 'foundation' that fragmentation presupposes consists precisely in the fragmentary totality, in its *organicity*. The fragment thus constitutes the most 'mimological' writing conceivable for the individual's organicity" (44). Because the truth of the individual romantic work or subject must be formed through an infinite process of auto-production, the ultimate form of the subject or work can be given *only* in a fragment of the necessarily incomplete and progressive totality at which it always aims.[10] In this way, the motif of the fragment would respond to and even mirror, on the level of its incomplete formal articulation, the philosophical meaning of incompletion it is always already oriented toward. Following a path traced out by Gérard Genette in his book *Mimologiques*,[11] Lacoue-Labarthe and Nancy ultimately rely for their understanding of the romantic fragment on just such a mimetic principle of identity and analogy—even if this understanding eventually leads to a theoretical statement of its own collapse and dissolution.

Is it not precisely because Lacoue-Labarthe and Nancy never actually question their own capacity to read and understand the romantic fragment according to a mimologically determined principle of meaning that they must insist that the dissemination, or radical interruption, of philosophical speculation engaged in our own day by Blanchot and Derrida is *not* readable on the level of the romantic fragment? Is this not also the reason they go on to make the claim about there being "interruption and dissemination of the romantic work, though this in fact is not readable in the work itself. . . . Rather, according to another term of Blanchot, it is readable in the unworking [désoeuvrement], *never named, and still less thought*, that insinuates itself throughout the interstices of the romantic work" (*LA* 57; emphasis added)? An entirely correct theoretical statement, that there is something in the romantic project of the fragment that exceeds and radically suspends a thinking of identity based on a mediation with nonidentity, leads to a conclusion and a reading practice with respect to the texts themselves that goes entirely counter to the literary truth of the very same statement. For it remains to be seen whether it is not precisely at the level of the literary examples deployed in and around the act of naming that romantic writing could be said to inscribe a textual interruption exceeding itself at every point, and this time beyond the reach of any theoretical conceptualization. In this case, *irony* might just turn out to be one of the most rigorous ways to name a "readability" so resistant to theoretical formulation that it would necessarily remain hidden or dissimulated with respect to any properly philosophical understanding of Schlegel's text.[12]

Such a dissimulated readability, moreover, can be traced in Schlegel's text whenever it confronts the perplexing power of the name, as it does, for instance, in his "Rede über die Mythologie" (published in English as "Talk on Mythology"), where Schlegel addresses the essentially historical challenge that is always posed to any self-consciousness of modernity. If romanticism is to become an example of such a modern self-consciousness, Schlegel acknowledges, it will have to occur through the production of what he calls "a new mythology."[13] The slogan has become as well known, one might almost say as notorious, as anything else Schlegel ever wrote: "We have no mythology," he says at the beginning of the text; "but," he immediately adds, "we are close to getting one, or rather, it is high time we set to work together to produce one" ("Talk," *DP* 81). And this, of course, is where the merely academic topic of romantic "literary theory" takes a surprising and dramatic turn toward the more compelling questions of referential history and politics. For it does not take an overly active imagination, on the contrary, to see that the production of the "new mythology" called for by Schlegel at Jena in 1800 is not just an aesthetic—that is, a formal and epistemological—ideal. Rather, as both Lacoue-Labarthe and Nancy have subsequently helped to demonstrate with more perspicuity and force than nearly anyone else, the German romantic reflection on "myth" cannot be separated from its profound implication in aesthetic, philosophical, and political developments that extend well into and even beyond the twentieth century, and that sometimes involve the most disastrous consequences.

In this respect it is of no small significance that the treatment of Schlegel and Jena romanticism undertaken by *The Literary Absolute* was followed by the publication in 1986 of Jean-Luc Nancy's *La Communauté désoeuvrée* (*The Inoperative Community*, 1991), and by the publication, in 1987 and 2002 respectively, of Philippe Lacoue-Labarthe's *La Fiction du politique: Heidegger, l'art et la politique* (*Heidegger, Art, and Politics: The Fiction of the Political*, 1990) and his *Heidegger, la politique du poème* (*Heidegger and the Politics of Poetry*, 2007).[14] All three of these texts can be read as legitimately extending the study of romantic motifs inaugurated by the earlier book into a far-reaching analysis of their legacy for more recent thought and politics. Reading them together helps to situate more accurately the event of German romanticism within the larger context of our own era and to identify the seminal place occupied within it by the writings of Friedrich Schlegel. An attentive reading of the analyses of Lacoue-Labarthe and Nancy that chart the inextricable links between art, philosophy, and politics still characterizing our own relation to Jena romanticism makes it difficult, moreover, merely to dismiss Schlegel as a brilliant but finally rather idiosyncratic and inconsequential thinker.[15] If German romanticism is to be taken seriously at all, then it must be understood in terms of the historical and political implications that necessarily follow from its literary and philosophical components. And this also means that we must be willing to confront Schlegel's version of the *absolu littéraire*, of literature producing itself as it produces its own theory, with the fateful transposition that this model will undergo in twentieth-century Germany to a total and totalizing vision of history and politics. The formal model of auto-production Lacoue-Labarthe and Nancy trace back, in *The Literary Absolute*, to early German romanticism is thus shown by their later work to be coterminous with a political model of auto-production that eventually made common cause with the totalitarianism of National Socialism in the 1930s.

Auto-production, as the word is used by Lacoue-Labarthe and Nancy, is therefore to be understood in terms of an all-encompassing model of autopoiesis. It is the self-forming production of an aesthetic *Bild*—form, figure, or image—as well as its articulation with a social *Bildung*, or cultural matrix, in which all such figures, including the production of the quotidian itself, would always have their appointed place. The resulting specular relationship between individual sensuous forms and the intellectual or spiritual community such forms constitute together would ensure by the same token the ultimate unity or *identity* of self, community, and State—though always in contradistinction to those foreign elements remaining recalcitrant to this mimetological identity. Thus, the word *fiction* in the title of Lacoue-Labarthe's book on art and politics designates the originary operation of making, inventing, or fashioning, prior to its further implication in epistemological determinations of truth and falsehood. For this reason too, the *art* of self-fashioning that according to *Heidegger, Art, and Politics: The Fiction of the Political* will eventually govern the entire Nazi model is dubbed by Lacoue-Labarthe *national aestheticism*. By tracing out the brief but significant alignment in 1933–34 of Heidegger's thought with the National Socialist state, Lacoue-Labarthe is able to suggest the common strands of aestheticism and nationalism that made such an accommodation possible in the first place. In the final analysis, he is able to point out, the specific configuration of art, politics, and philosophy that allowed Heidegger to make common cause with National Socialism, however briefly and in however differentiated and qualified a manner, must be understood in the historical context of a much older pattern, one "that would be impossible not to identify with the romantic model of Jena" (*Fiction*, 13–14; *La Fiction*, 29). And this reference to the model of romanticism developed at Jena is then placed in apposition to Lacoue-Labarthe's contention that, however contrary in appearance, the entire collection of "motifs" serving to organize Heidegger's thought even after 1934 ends up by producing its own "new mythology." At bottom, according to a number of the most incisive analyses of Lacoue-Labarthe, it would be the common ideal of creating just such a "new mythology" that is shared, however distinctively, by Heidegger, National Socialism, and the Jena romanticism in which Friedrich Schlegel occupies a crucial place.[16] A clear statement of Lacoue-Labarthe's orientation—which perhaps does not entirely do justice to Heidegger's text, much less to Schlegel's—can be found near the middle of *The Fiction of the Political*. Summarizing the most important motifs—art, language, and myth—that constitute Heidegger's conception of History (and as a result, his politics), Lacoue-Labarthe anchors them with one sweeping gesture in what he calls "a longstanding German tradition that originated in the Jena of Schiller (and not of Goethe)—the Schlegel brothers and Hölderlin, Schelling and to some extent the 'young Hegel'" (*Fiction*, 56–57; *La Fiction*, 88–89). And he takes this remark one further step by adding that this particular tradition—for all intents and purposes, the romantic tradition that includes Schlegel, but also passes through Wagner and Nietzsche—"ended up by imposing itself and, under various aspects, dominating in any case the Germany that remained unresistant to the 'movement' of the thirties" (*Fiction*, 57; *La Fiction*, 89).

Now it is clear that Lacoue-Labarthe, while loosely associating in this way the thought of Jena romanticism with a broad tradition of "national aestheticism" that proved ultimately unrecalcitrant to the actual fact of National Socialism in Germany, is *not* suggesting that all the proper names implicated in this context can be read and understood in the same reductive way with respect to twentieth-century ideology and politics. The inclusion here of the name Hölderlin, in fact, should give us pause, since both Lacoue-Labarthe and Nancy have on a number of occasions gone out of their way to distinguish between Hölderlin's poetics and the "main stream" of German romantic literary theory with which they are contemporary.[17] Even the reference to a "new mythology" is not necessarily meant to designate Friedrich Schlegel alone. For the phrase *new mythology* also occurs, and well before Schlegel's "Talk on Mythology," in the text titled "Earliest System-Program of German Idealism," a text whose authorship is difficult to determine with precision, but which emerged from the same general romantic context that included Hegel, Schelling, and Hölderlin.[18] Before ideas can have any genuine interest for "the people," this prototypical text reads, they must be made aesthetic, that is, "mythological." And it concludes with the kind of reflexive imagery characteristic of early romanticism by claiming that "mythology must become philosophy in order to render the people reasonable; philosophy must become mythology so that philosophers can be made sensuously perceptible— and then alone will eternal unity reign." Such a chiasmatic exchange between reason and sensuous appearance, philosophy and mythology, the thinker and the people, is in fact reminiscent of Schlegel's *Lyceum Fragment* on poetry and philosophy with which we began. Similar examples could easily be found in Schelling, Hegel, and Schiller as well. But this fact alone is not an adequate substitute for a genuine reading of any of the texts signed by these authors. The question here is not to document the general fate of a philosophical concept of myth whose formalization as a concept remains to be accounted for and cannot therefore be taken for granted in any given text. Rather, what matters first of all in this context is to test whether and to what extent a reading of Schlegel's own "Talk on Mythology," and of its necessary implication in his theory of irony, can in fact be called "resistant" with respect to the philosophical concept of a "tradition" that would in this specific case lead back to Schelling and Schiller and forward to Wagner and to the overtly political ideologues of national aestheticism.[19] The proximity of Schlegel's text to the motifs of all the new mythologies with which we have become in the meantime only too familiar is obvious and massive. It cannot simply be overlooked or discounted. But, on the other hand, the stakes of the discussion—from now on political and historical as well as literary and philosophical—are enormous. They are certainly imposing enough to warrant a return to Schlegel's own text before subscribing once and for all to the commonplace that is recirculated about it without comment by Lacoue-Labarthe and Nancy: "The *Dialogue*'s 'Talk on Mythology' is virtually a pure distillate of Schelling" (*LA* 93).

As is well known, Schlegel's new mythology is oriented toward the possibility of giving a name and a form to the highest of poetic powers, the productive power or force of what, as constitutive of the spiritual, is also called the most sacred. "Should the power to inspire that is indeed Poetry forever split itself to pieces [Soll die Kraft der Begeisterung auch in der Poesie sich immerfort einzeln versplittern]," the discourse begins by asking, "ultimately and alone falling mute [endlich einsam verstummen]? Should the holiest [Soll das höchste Heilige] always remain *nameless and formless* [immer *namenlos und formlos* bleiben], left in darkness to chance [im Dunkel dem Zufall überlassen]?" ("Talk," *DP* 81; *KA* 2:311–12).[20] The question that relates both name and form to the poetic powers of spiritualization, moreover, is soon qualified here by another, quite singular, term, *Bildungen*: "[I]s there an art worthy of the name [gibt es wohl eine Kunst, die den Namen verdient], if it does not have the force [wenn diese nicht die Gewalt hat] . . . to inspire beautiful formations [die schönen Bildungen] in accordance with its necessary caprice [nach ihrer notwendigen Willkür]?" The typically Schlegelian insistence on bringing together the necessary with the arbitrary in the romantic conception of art—*Willkür* naming a mode of freedom, often enough associated with *irony*, that is as random as it is peremptory—serves to reinforce the possibility that "darkness" (*der Dunkel*) and "chance" (*der Zufall*) are not themselves simply contingent or accidental factors when it comes to the poetic constitution of both names and forms. For the potentially random nature of every name and form precipitates out at the instant the German word *Bildungen* appears in the text, since in this one form is condensed the entire program of "Talk on Mythology." Such a mythological program would entail the production of sensuous figures, or *Bilder*, susceptible of forming a new spiritual community for Germans, of organizing its disparate members according to determinate shapes and thus allowing them to grow and develop into their own identity, their unity as a culture or a people properly speaking.[21] The new mythology would therefore be that which "the modern poet" ("der moderne Dichter") must work to bring about so that the orders of the aesthetic (as *Bild*) and the sociopolitical (as a comprehensive model of culture, or *Bildung*) might come together and ultimately meet. To some extent, then, the question that opens the text is whether the link that binds the aesthetic image to the unfolding of a given cultural and political community—in other words, that which ties *das Bild* to *die Bildung*—will be able to find "mythological" forms and names adequate to the task, so that their encounter would no longer risk being left to, or in, the darkness of chance.

This question is not, however, entirely rhetorical, not entirely a literary device used by Schlegel simply to anticipate the philosophical response that will have been provided by the remainder of the "Talk on Mythology," much less by its subsequent readers. Or, rather, if the question of the name and the peculiar mode of chance and darkness in which it is first allowed to appear in this text *is* rhetorical, it would be so in a way that could not be neatly reduced to theoretical exposition and understanding. For, despite the apparent resolution that is reached in the talk on mythology that follows, this question is first introduced as a direct challenge or a summons to ask questions ("will ich Euch auffordern, Euch selbst zu fragen")—and therefore it cannot be dismissed as not being a "real" question without reducing the entire text to naught. Once such a questioning attitude is granted in all its radicality, moreover, a quite unexpected answer insinuates itself into the "Talk": "If what is highest, the Ideal, is in fact not susceptible to determinate formation [absichtlichen Bildung], then let us *give up* any claim to a free art of ideas [so läßt uns nur gleich jeden Anspruch auf irgendeine frei Ideenkunst *aufgeben*], which would then be merely *an empty name* [*ein leerer Name*]" (*DP* 86; *KA* 2:318; emphasis added). In other words, Schlegel's text stakes the entire project of romanticism—this free art of ideas (*freie Ideenkunst*) that might once again coordinate literature and theory, poetry and philosophy—on the possibility of a kind of naming that would simultaneously be a determinate form and a formation, a *Bild* and a *Bildung*. But with the very same gesture his text also names and thus introduces a threat that is immediately posed to this task *by* the name, that is, the possibility of a kind of naming whose relation to form and formation would remain curiously indeterminable, or empty. At the beginning of the text, the question is whether art can become a force for name- and form-giving. But later in the text it becomes apparent that names and forms may themselves turn out to be "empty," mere simulacra of the art of forming and naming. This means that the originary power to name must itself have a name, but this naming power on which all else rests might very well remain "empty," that is, a name that is profoundly *unabsichtlich, ungebildet*, and thus incapable of any respectable formation or *Bildung*.

Of course, it can always be argued that the reference at this particular moment to the "empty name" is itself gratuitous and unintentional, and therefore it might have absolutely nothing whatsoever to do with the text's original question of giving a name and a form to poetic force. The second reference to the name could thus be considered a mere accident within the context of the essay taken as a whole, and to draw attention to it in this way would serve only to display one's own lack of culture, refinement, or *Bildung*. But then it is precisely the challenge of determining the very status of the name on the basis of the necessary distinction between chance (*Zufall*) and intention (*Absicht*) that is at issue here in the formation of a new mythology.[22] This kind of potentially frivolous accident, then, the textual slip that transforms the challenge of the "nameless art" into the radical threat of an "empty name," far from resolving the tension, exacerbates it even further.

At this point, moreover, the second reference to the name, this time not just "missing" (*namenlos*) but empty (*ein leerer Name*), actually does serve to interrupt the text's own movement. The interruption concerns a grammatical decision about the status of the example now given for a "free art of ideas." That is, it interrupts the possibility of our understanding without hesitation the very particular name, "Mythology," around which the entire discourse is supposed to have been organized. "If what is highest of all is in fact susceptible to no determinate formation whatsoever," Schlegel writes, "then let us give up [aufgeben] any claim to a free art of ideas [Ideenkunst], which would then merely be an empty name. *Mythology* is such a work of art" ("Talk," *DP* 86; *KA* 2:318; emphasis added). Mythology then, *is* the exemplary name for a free art of ideas, and that much at least should be abundantly clear. But whether the form and formation of this name for a free art of ideas, "mythology," could itself ever be fully determined according to a logic of intention or of accident is not to be decided lightly. Just what is mythology an example of here? In other words, determined only by the demonstrative qualification, "*such* a work," does mythology have as its grammatical antecedent the promise of "determinate formation" or the threat of the "empty name"? Is mythology the name *as* determinate form for all poetic force, and therefore a substantial and free art of ideas in its own right; or is mythology an art of ideas only insofar as it is actually nothing but an empty name? (In which case we would do well to *give up* making any important claims on it—aesthetic and philosophical, much less social and political.)

According to one of the oldest and most compelling philosophical distinctions, Schlegel, wittingly or not, thus places the question of romantic "mythology" within a highly volatile relation. On the one hand, mythology names a mode of historical and collective auto-formation and knowledge. But, on the other hand, mythology also designates a tool of deception or self-deception that, as the very stuff of mystification and ideology, can have no serious claim (*Anspruch*) to epistemological or historical legitimacy. Myth has the power to fashion; but does it fashion self-identity or self-deception? As we have seen, the grammar of Schlegel's text, at this particular point in any case, does not allow us to decide the outcome of this tension in favor of one of its two sides over the other. At least it does not do so without obligating us at the very same time to have recourse to a kind of authorial intention, or *Absicht*, over the formation of meaning that is in fact the point of contention, and thus foreclosed as a possible solution, in the text itself. There can as yet be no question of saying that Schlegel actually *meant* this but rather *said* that; nor can we safely assume that this or that aspect of the writing represents the "thought" or "unthought" portion of his discourse. Rather, all we can legitimately say is that it is precisely the enigma of this dilemma that is named in Schlegel's writing by the word *mythology*. It could therefore only be by a *more* extended reading of how the text actually initiates and develops the formation of this particular example—*mythology* as the name for "*such* a work of art"— that we might ever hope to approach this text with anything like the critical rigor necessary for Schlegel to have written it in the first place.

The "Talk on Mythology," as we have seen, opens on the opposition between poetry and knowledge, individual activity and universal understanding. Throughout the *Dialogue on Poetry*, in fact, this distinction will also correspond to the assumption of a historically determinable schema in which antiquity, as an age of prereflective harmony, will be opposed to modernity, as an age of negativity and division that, so far at least, has been unable to produce anything but isolated moments of poetic and philosophic achievement. The argument of Ludovico, the main speaker in the "Talk on Mythology," responds once again to the received opinion that the modern age must learn to demonstrate its capacity to unite the two antithetical tendencies of poetic creativity and theoretical organization into a higher unity. For, unless works can be produced in which the specifically poetic force of each new creation is also provided with a firm basis, there can be no hope of ever advancing beyond the stage of what Schlegel, in *Über das Studium der griechischen Poesie* (*On the Study of Greek Poetry*), calls "the purposelessness and lawlessness of the whole of modern poetry."[23] Modern poetry, he goes on to say in that text, "is like a sea of warring forces in which the particles of dissolved beauty, the fragments of shattered art, clash in a confused and gloomy mixture . . . a chaos" (*Study*, 21; *KA* 1:223–24). With the question of mythology, then, we are brought to the very heart of romanticism's projection of a poetic work capable of producing itself as it produces its own philosophical theory; in other words, to the heart of Lacoue-Labarthe's and Nancy's *absolu littéraire*.

Now the romantic project of this literary absolute, as can be remarked yet again in the stated aim of the "Talk," to overcome the originary *formlessness* of poetic force, is also the project of literature's universal formation, and even formalization. As Lacoue-Labarthe and Nancy point out in *The Literary Absolute*—and as is confirmed by Lacoue-Labarthe's *Heidegger, Art, and Politics: The Fiction of the Political*—the romantic concept of "formation," or *Bildung*, "is the place of intersection for shaping and molding, art and culture, education and sociality—and in the end, for history and figuration" (*LA* 36). And this is also why, at least in principle, Lacoue-Labarthe and Nancy have little difficulty linking Schlegel's, and beyond him, romanticism's "theory of literature" with an "aesthetico-political" program whose continuation and effects reach well into the "national aestheticism" of Nazi Germany. The power to name, and thus to form, is by the same token not only part of any given State; it actually accounts for its very possibility. The *Bild*, which starts out from purely formal considerations about naming and the kind of poetic activity that makes it possible, by necessity ends up implicated in the formation of State power. "The artist should no more wish to rule than to serve," Schlegel starts a fragment that becomes glaringly clear on this point: "He can only form [bilden], do nothing but form [bilden], and so can do nothing for the State but form [bilden] those who lead and those who serve. " (*Ideas* 54, *PF* 99; *KA* 2:261). The "nothing" that only the artist can accomplish is that nothing out of which alone the State can eventually become something.

At stake in the name *mythology*, then, would always be the possibility of passing out from the lawless chaos of disjointed particles of beauty, from the discrete poetic *Bilder* produced by transitory and therefore accidental forces, to a systematic process of historical and political organization, formation, and universality, that is, to the comprehensive order of *Bildung* itself. In the early essay *On the Study of Greek Poetry*, and immediately after bemoaning the merely scattered images of poetic power offered by present-day art, Schlegel had indeed already identified this as the crucial problem for romanticism: "If it were only possible to clarify modern poetry's principle of *Bildung*, then perhaps it would not be so difficult to work from there toward the actual fulfillment of its task. . . . *Bildung* is the very essence of human being" (*KA* 1:224, 229). The same principle and task is again specified in the "Talk on Mythology," though this time, as we have seen, in the paradoxical and interrogative mode that allows the rest of the "Talk" to unfold, if not to come entirely undone: "Is there an art worthy of the name that does not have the power . . . to breathe life into its beautiful *Bildungen* in accordance with its necessary arbitrariness [nach ihrer notwendigen Willkür]?" ("Talk," *DP* 81). To be truly worthy of its name, Schlegel will conclude, art must be capable of producing a new mythology, one that would be able to harness the arbitrary nature of its poetic force to a systematic exposition and development, in order finally to achieve that "artfully ordered confusion and charming symmetry of contradictions" (86) toward which the entire *Dialogue* is oriented.[24]

Nonetheless, the actual formation of the name *mythology* in the "Talk" reserves some unexpected twists for the smooth articulation of the politico-aesthetic ideal to which it constantly alludes. For instance, Schlegel insists that the necessity of form-giving must eventually face up to the disturbing possibility of bringing forth a result that, because it would be purely accidental or arbitrary, could not be brought back to a determination on the basis of an organic and self-conscious model of intentionality. What would it mean, Schlegel therefore goes on to consider, to beget only the lifeless image of an empty name? In this text, where the metaphor of poetic force is continually supplied by the biological process of procreation, it could only mean incurring the risk of giving birth to the still form of a corpse. This is because it is always possible that the godlike principle, or soul, of spiritual life (*Bildung*) would somehow remain absent from its outward manifestations (*Bilder*): "And isn't this soft reflection of the Godhead in man the true soul, the enkindling spark of all poetry?—Mere representation [das blosse Darstellen] . . . or artificial forms [die künstlichen Formen] in themselves amount to nothing. . . . That is only the visible, external body, and should the soul be missing, then indeed it would leave only the dead corpse of poetry [der tote Leichnam der Poesie]" ("Talk," *DP* 85; *KA* 2:318).

It is precisely as a preventative to ward off the threat of such a stillborn corpse that the actual example of "mythology" is brought forth in the "Talk." "Mythology has one great advantage," Schlegel has Ludovico say; "it allows what otherwise would be in constant flight from consciousness to be apprehended bodily-spiritually [sinnlich geistig], and held fast, like the soul in the surrounding body, through which it glimmers before our eyes and speaks to our ears" ("Talk," *DP* 85; *KA* 2:318). Mythology is thus the bodying force of a name that would prevent the sheer power of the poetic act from going nameless and formless, and thus from remaining forever inaccessible to our eyes and ears, as well as to our understanding. It would be a kind of name that, far from being an empty body, would not only be capable of containing our own soul, but would further ensure our capacity to apprehend this soul *sinnlich geistig*. In other words, Schlegel's "mythology" names the possibility of a transcendental coordination of the senses (*sinnliche Bilder*) and the mind (*geistige Bildung*). And the particular bodily-spiritual form of the soul that is put back into circulation at this point of the text is that of a glimmering *light*. In the new mythology named by Schlegel, the soul would shine, and through its shining it would prove that it is not absent from the body, prove, in fact, that the body it shines through is not an empty form, that is, a mere corpse. This form, or *Bild*, that is being shaped, or *gebildet*, throughout the "Talk," is, of course, the very myth of philosophy: the phenomenal intuition of a light that would ultimately guarantee the intelligibility of divine truth in thought as well as being. As Schlegel finally declares through his own stand-in Ludovico, and in a barely disguised revision of Genesis 1:1–4: "Be worthy of the greatness of the age and the fog will lift from your eyes; there will be light before you. . . . Then would the empty chatter stop and man . . . would understand the earth and the sun. That is what I mean by the new mythology" ("Talk," *DP* 88; *KA* 2:322).

However, the transition to this exalted pronouncement takes one last detour in Schlegel's text. Immediately after naming mythology the principle of coordination capable of appropriating the solar body of light to a spiritual process of (self-)understanding, Schlegel points out that this living synthesis of mind and body, this mimetologics, or budding "national aestheticism," is still not quite alive *enough*. At this point, the entire edifice the "Talk" has built around the mythological unity of image and meaning begins to wobble, if not topple altogether. For mythology, which names precisely this specular system of sensuous *Bild* and spiritual *Bildung*, or of poetry and philosophy, cannot,

says Schlegel, endure all by itself. In order to be maintained it constantly requires the support of *another* principle of light and life, one that would exist
beyond all the self-reflexive categories operative so far: "nor can a mythology
subsist [bestehen] without a highly original and inimitable element [ohne ein
erstes Ursprüngliches und Unnachahmliches], something that is absolutely
irreducible [was schlechthin unauflöslich ist], something that after all transformations [was nach allen Umbildungen] still allows its primal nature and
force to shimmer through [noch die alte Natur und Kraft durchschimmern
läßt]" ("Talk," *DP* 86; *KA* 2:319). This passage confirms that the "soul" living
on in the name of its own "mythology," the primal force sustaining all the
mythological constructions of the text, cannot itself be construed or understood strictly *as* an image, that is, on the basis of a *Bild* properly speaking. The
actual force that allows the body and soul to be held together in "mythology,"
according to Schlegel's own words here, becomes accessible only "nach allen Umbildungen," that is, only after—which is always also only before, *ein
erstes Ursprüngliches*—and therefore once and for all *beyond* all the analogical
transformations of *Bild und Bildung* on which its own descriptions are necessarily based. This means that no image, illustration, figure, example—that is,
myth—in the text could ever give sufficient access to the mythic force it depends upon and refers to, since this force would itself be absolutely inimitable
and irreducible (*unauflöslich und unnachahmlich*). And it further means that
each of the key terms the "Talk" relies upon to describe its true subject—
the "soul," "light," or "spark" of mythology—is necessarily inadequate to the
precise extent that it names what by definition cannot be understood. That is,
each of these terms, in its own irreducible and inimitable manner, names precisely that which cannot be *imitated* by and so *reduced to* the kinds of analogical
images, figures, or *Bilder* that are required by every act of comprehension.
Whatever original light still glimmers through the "Talk" can therefore be
said to *shine* there only insofar as it is not itself the adequate sensuous appearance, or *Schein*, of anything else beyond it.[25] In other words, such a *Schein*
could be said to *shine* or even *shimmer* through all that appears, but for the
same reason, it could never simply shine forth and therefore appear itself as
any kind of phenomenal *Erscheinung*, since it is the condition of possibility of
all appearance.

What is this inimitable and irreducible light that still shimmers beyond or
behind all the visible, that is to say, "readable" forms, formations, and transformations of poetic and philosophical thought in Schlegel's text? Schlegel

himself couldn't have been clearer in his response to this question: "nor can a mythology endure without something most original and inimitable, which is absolutely irreducible, which after all transformations still lets its primal nature and power to shimmer through, in which naïve profundity lets the shine [den Schein] of error and madness, or of foolishness and stupidity to shimmer through" ("Talk," *DP* 86; *KA* 2:319). All translators, including Lacoue-Labarthe and Nancy moreover, have a great deal of trouble with this passage, since a literal rendering of its *Schein* would so radically challenge the basic task of philological and philosophical understanding upon which their own writing ultimately depends. For the passage actually posits a radical break between the origins (*die alte Natur und Kraft*) and ends or endings (*alle Umbildungen*) of any promise—in other words, of any myth of understanding, including its own.[26] What is truly astonishing in this passage, however, is *not* the overt reference to "madness"—no matter how eye-catching that happens to be—but rather the silent inscription of the word *Schein* at this particular place in the text. For how can *Schein*, the word par excellence for aesthetic representation, appear precisely when the mimetological link constituting the entire series of *Schein* and *Wesen*, appearance and essence, body and soul, form and substance, light and truth, literature and theory, nature and history, has been undone at its very source by a power that remains inassimilable to all these related versions of the same transformational logic? At this moment, then, *Schein* can no longer be said to designate anything but its own peculiar madness and stupidity—no matter how these words are translated—since what could be more blindly foolish than to continue calling an absolutely inimitable and irreducible force by the word *Schein*?

The structure of this madness is very curious indeed. On the one hand, Schlegel insists that the union promised in mythology of poetry and philosophy could never itself subsist without a more original force that he names "madness." On the other hand, by going on to call this madness itself a *Schein*, his own text also implies that in spite of the true nature of this mad force, it always tends to re-engender precisely the same transformational system of *Bild* and *Bildung* to which it by necessity remains irreducible. What Schlegel calls *mythology* turns out to be another version of what Paul de Man, in his later work, tended to call *ideology*: a resistance to reading, and thus to understanding, that is actually occasioned by the kind of theoretical formalization required to begin reading, and thus understanding, any text in the first place. In the case of both Schlegel and de Man, the literary (or mythic) text demands a philosophical (or critical) reading that is self-resistant; the imperative to read produces an aberrant motion of self-fragmentation or of mutual interruption that has no choice but to go forward. The theory, or logic, or mytho-ideo-logic that would systematize literary specificity—in other words, any given textual example—is always interrupted by it; but the particular examples that must be given in order to illustrate the resulting fragmentation also find a way of generalizing themselves into a systematic formulation, however anomalous such formal systems have just been shown to be. The interruption of theory by literature, or of mimo-, mytho-, or ideologic by the untranslatable *Schein* of madness, or the disruption of each and every *Bild(ung)* by the empty name, must be fragmented, or interrupted in its turn, by the ensuing statement of its own "truth," and so on and so forth. And nothing, Schlegel seems to be saying, can stop this endless process of permanent interruption. At least, this is what he can now be understood to have been saying in that most self-resisting definition of irony that he ever gave: "Irony is a permanent parabasis—" (*PF* 668; *KA* 18:85). The truth is that irony is a philosophical force of questioning that interrupts the possibility of fully saturating, and therefore understanding, the poetic field of *Bildungen* to which it also necessarily belongs. But this philosophical truth can be reached only by means of the very textual examples it nonetheless requires us to understand and thus reformulate anew, to the second degree. Irony is therefore this self-resisting— that is, infinitely though nonreflexively *repetitive*—truth about the literary structure of all possible philosophical meaning.

What is it, finally, in the "Talk on Mythology" that best exemplifies this truth about the endless alternation between philosophical formulation and its interruption by the ironic structure of all poetry? The question takes us back to the "empty name" in which, according to Schlegel, the potential for mythological constructions (*schöne Bildungen*) would no longer be underwritten by any intention whatsoever. Of all the philosophical transformations that occur in the text, none is more sustained or imposing than the one that, as we have seen, would ultimately relate the mythological image (*Bild*) to a systematic capacity for self-formulation (*Bildung*) through the mediating process of poetic activity (*bilden, umbilden, anbilden*). Beyond all these transformations (*nach allen Umbildungen*) of one and the same name, *Bild*, there is no denying the absolutely inimitable and idiomatic—that is, irreducibly mad—force that shines through each of them. This originary force is able to bring all the names of this mythic constellation together in Schlegel's own text only because of the unconditionally arbitrary links formed by what he refers to as an "indirect mythology," and which includes a "constant exchange of enthusiasm and irony that lives even in the smallest members of the whole" ("Talk," *DP* 86; *KA* 2:319). Such an ironic dispersion of all poetic "enthusiasm" into its "smallest members" *b–i–l–d* does indeed constitute a wholly inimitable *Schein* in Schlegel's text, and it must also remain forever recalcitrant to an original intention that would still be accessible in any theoretically verifiable mode.

It may seem farfetched, naïve, or even arbitrary to associate Schlegel's concept of irony in this way with what is sometimes, though often misleadingly, referred to as "the play of the letter."[27] But it is this ironic law of the letter—at one and the same time arbitrary *and* binding, as Saussure will later put it, echoing in his own way Schlegel's characterization of Socratic irony in *Lyceum Fragment* 108—that is nonetheless inscribed as the secret legacy of Schlegel's text. Thus, and on the threshold of the dialogue in which the "Talk on Mythology" will unfold, Schlegel insists: "Wherever living spirit appears bound up in a formed letter, there is art, there is a secret remains, material to overcome, tools to work with, an outline and laws for carrying it out" ("Talk," *DP* 60). But this is not only a general theoretical statement about the production and use of alphabetic letters that just happens to name the semiotic principle in its barest possible formulation. It is also an exemplary deployment of those very elements the text will later put to work in carrying out its own mythological construction of romanticism: "Wo irgend lebendiger Geist in einem ge*bild*eten Buchstaben gebunden er*schein*t, da ist Kunst, da ist Absonderung, Stoff zu überwinden, Werkzeuge zu gebrauchen, ein Entwurf und Gesetze der Behandlung" (*KA* 2:290). In this case, the romantic project announced, described, and executed follows a law of fragmentation—the originary *Absonderung* (generation and sundering, or secretion and detachment) of blank letters (*b–i–l–d*) that will eventually appear (*scheinen*) in the construction (*Gebilde*) of a teleological development of living spirit (*geistige Bildung*).

Fragmentation here, though, is not only a sketch, finished or unfinished, to construct meaningful images—of oneself or of one's own intellectual or political community. It is also the necessary play, that is, the law of the accident, that can always undo the systematic coherency of all such projects in the name of its own letters. Schlegel's text on the possibility of a properly "romantic" mythology, then, is not merely, or univocally, the enthusiastic construction of a universal philosophy of literature that would eventually converge with a totalizing, and potentially totalitarian, national aestheticism. It is, in addition, a more sober and therefore prosaic reminder about the literal forces that work through and serve to interrupt such mythic constructions before they ever get off the ground. That Schlegel was finally led to exemplify the enigmatic structure of this myth by reference to an originary form of *madness* should in no way be considered a mystification, and therefore a flight from, the very real threat that is always posed by it. On the contrary, only by designating in this way the permanent parabasis, or irony, that forever and again disrupts the mythological unity of literature and philosophy would it become possible to begin reading it in its true light, or *Schein*.

TWO

Taking Kierkegaard Apart: *The Concept of Irony*

The basic crux of a reading of Kierkegaard remains the same today as it was when he was first being widely read and discussed in Europe during the early twentieth century: how to understand his theory and technique of indirect communication. It is only by neglecting the centrifugal force exerted by this question on his entire *oeuvre* that it is possible to underestimate or misconstrue the importance of Kierkegaard's place in the current scene of critical intellectual debate. The issue is not so much to historicize the question and then attempt to choose sides between all the different "Kierkegaards" who have been proposed to our consideration over the past hundred years. Rather, no matter how, where, or when one reads Kierkegaard, it will always be necessary to return yet again to the following inescapable challenge: how to read a mode of writing premised on the impossibility of the subject's expressing the truth of its own thought directly. "Everything subjective," Kierkegaard warns in an especially direct formulation of the problem, ". . . eludes a direct form of expression, is an essential secret."[1] Every possible understanding, every past as well as future hermeneutics of this text—as a unique instance of literary style and inventiveness, philosophical interrogation, personal belief, desire, or ethicopolitical act—must pass first through the epistemological challenge posed to reading by the rhetorical dimension of its self-acknowledged indirection, which puts all of Kierkegaard's writing "under a vow of silence"—*under Tausheds Løfte*, so to speak (*Concluding*, 66; *SKS* 7:78).

Sylviane Agacinski, whose encounter with Kierkegaard took place partly by way of her early interest in the work of Gilles Deleuze, partly by way of Maurice Blanchot's suggestive remarks about Kierkegaard's *Journals*, and partly by way of Jacques Derrida's deconstruction of writing as presence, deserves credit for having written the first full-length book that attempts to match Kierkegaard's own rhetorical self-awareness while charting an interpretative path that would lead from his theory of language as indirect communication to its deployment in his texts, in other words, to the singular engagement that Kierkegaard's writing transacts with philosophy, religion, sexuality, economics, and politics. With a clear recognition that the most critical test for any understanding of Kierkegaard's theory of language as indirect communication is offered by his Magister thesis, published in translation as *The Concept of Irony*, Agacinski begins her book *Aparté: Conceptions and Deaths of Søren Kierkegaard* with a long chapter devoted to that text's many interconnecting strands—strands that will later be developed and reworked throughout Kierkegaard's other texts.[2] Not only is the thesis on irony the text from which all the others "originate" in straightforwardly genetic terms—it is his first major published work—but more importantly, it is the one text expressly "about" how language has to operate as indirect communication before it can be "about" anything else. Irony, for Kierkegaard, first of all names this always possible discrepancy between what an expression says and what it means—a potential divergence between *logos* and *lexis* without which no language would be conceivable as such. The possibility of language is therefore always already dependent on the possibility of irony as this originary discrepancy, or indirection, even if, though only on occasion, it "succeeds," more or less, now and then, here and there, in overcoming it. There can in fact be no communication that is not in the first place indirect: either in the sense that it *is* ironic and thus intentionally exploits the discrepancy between sign and meaning directly; or else in the sense that it is *not* ironic and thus somehow manages to pass, indirectly as it were, "around" the discrepancy between sign and meaning that would otherwise always thwart its operation.

It is for this reason that *The Concept of Irony* is at the origin of Kierkegaard's writing in a sense that cannot be merely genetic or historical in any ordinary manner, since everything that Kierkegaard will go on to write will have had its necessary starting point in this interrogation of irony and the linguistic indirection peculiar to it. Indeed, maintaining the philosophical coherence of such fundamental concepts as genesis and history is precisely what is at stake as soon as the question of irony is addressed in a serious way. What is irony? Where does it come from? That is, how exactly does irony occur, and once it occurs, how far does it go, or how long does it last? Where, and how, in the final analysis, does it leave us in its wake? How is it possible, in other words, to speak directly about the shape and limits of an event—if irony is one, properly speaking—that always takes place only indirectly? Agacinski's reading of Kierkegaard re-enacts these questions from the very beginning in a way that is as subtle and duplicitous as the "origins" of irony itself.

But, how, on the other hand, could one ever avoid speaking directly about the irony that threatens to turn every direct question of origins and ends aside from its aim? Or, rather, one *can* easily avoid speaking about irony directly—and in fact we have no choice but to do so always and everywhere, simply for the sake of ever saying anything "serious" at all. But that in no way ensures that we always remain immune from irony and its powers of indirection. And first of all, it doesn't mean we remain immune from a most distressing paradox: if, for the sake of seriousness, one goes out of one's way *not* to speak directly about irony, then how exactly can one be entirely sure that one's own seriousness *is* "genuine," that is, that it has not somehow already been affected by an insidious ironic indirection about which one chose, or thought one chose, not to speak, or perhaps not even to think directly? If philosophy is to acquire, conserve, or regain true seriousness, then sooner or later it will be compelled to address directly the possibility of its own exposure to ironic indirection. It is therefore *only* by confronting the indirection of irony directly that philosophy could in fact ever "demonstrate," in good faith and therefore in a truly serious fashion, that it is not somehow already there, or at least on its way toward, where indirection, as irony, is always to be found lying in wait for it. And it is precisely in the name of this most philosophically serious and therefore unavoidable prerequisite that Agacinski's first chapter constantly dwells on the place that irony will have been assigned by philosophy itself; in particular, on the place irony will have been assigned by the most systematic model of philosophical seriousness articulated to date—in other words, by Hegel.

Of course, in this respect, as well as in several others, Agacinski is doing no more, and no less, than repeating a gesture inaugurated by Kierkegaard himself. If the title of Kierkegaard's thesis, *The Concept of Irony, with Constant*

Reference to Socrates (*Om Begrebet Ironi med stadigt Hensyn til Socrates*), implies that the author will be directly concerned with Socrates, then it may come as something of a surprise to note just how often references to Hegel "interrupt" what the title promises as a continuous, *stadigt*, and therefore uninterrupted consideration of the Greek thinker's irony. Or, if the title is read, perhaps as it should be, as promising a direct reflection on irony as a philosophical *concept*, as distinguished, say, from a self-conscious subjective or literary technique instantiated by either Socrates or Plato, then this conceptual program is immediately—and constantly—at risk of being interrupted by all the subsidiary references to Socrates and his preconceptual, because merely ironic, treatment of the philosophical Idea. Either way, the challenge is to maintain a serious philosophical reflection on the subject at hand, irony—whether in its properly conceptual or in its conversationally subjective form. And this means that Hegel's own confrontation with Socrates—and his irony—will have to be the subject of both Kierkegaard's thesis and Agacinski's reading of it.

Now inside the historical framework of Western philosophy, according to Hegel, the indirection that is characteristic of irony in the merely casual sense will always have to appear as a more "serious" moment of negativity as well. This negative moment, as is illustrated in exemplary manner by the case of Socrates and his famous "ignorance," can also be identified with the subject's acceding to self-consciousness. "Irony is indeed the first and most abstract determination of subjectivity," Kierkegaard summarizes, "and with this we have arrived at Socrates" (*CI* 281). Irony, as negativity, characterizes the coming to consciousness of subjectivity through the subject's original capacity to turn away from—and therefore to negate—all else, including its own propensity for error as natural consciousness. Irony is a serious philosophical attitude to the extent that it, like Socrates, dares to call into question its own pretense to know how things stand. No longer restricted to a classical understanding of the so-called rhetorical difference between what is said and what is meant by a knowing subject whose own understanding of what it is saying is always taken for granted, the concept of romantic irony demands along with Socrates that one first of all critically examine any claim to knowledge.

When, with Friedrich Schlegel, irony becomes a term for this type of serious philosophical reflection, it thus also always names the possibility that it is precisely the speaking subject who understands least of all the actual meaning of what is being said in its name and through its agency. Schlegel said this in his own inimitable fashion in the course of his essay entitled, appropriately enough, "Über die Unverständlichkeit" ("On Incomprehensibility"): "[I]t often enough happens that words understand themselves better than those by whom they are used."[3] Socratic irony—which by the display of its own ignorance leads indirectly to the disclosure of the ignorance of others as well—is of paramount interest first of all to Schlegel, and then to Hegel and Kierkegaard after him, because it asks seriously about the limits of all accepted knowledge, and especially that of the speaking subject. However, from a strictly philosophical point of view, such a moment of self-conscious negativity can possess any positive interest and importance only insofar as it enters into a historical process that exceeds the self and its own consciousness. Irony would thus coincide with the freedom of subjective thought to isolate itself as a question in its own right, and to subject its claim to knowledge to critical examination by "ironizing" it. At the same time, as *self*-consciousness reflection, the ironic consciousness always manifests itself as the particular and individual in opposition to the universal. For Hegel, irony is a necessary—but also necessarily deficient—negative moment: in coming to know itself as the freedom of self-reflection, the ironic subject remains too particular, and therefore capricious, in its philosophical comportment. Ultimately, such a subject must learn to accept objective limits for itself so as to prepare for an affirmative content integrating its limited particularity with the unlimited universality of the Idea. In this way alone, and always according to Hegel's reading, irony can become a fundamental category in the evolution of philosophical thought leading from Socrates to the German romantics (Schlegel, Tieck, Solger). The passage from Socratic to romantic irony would therefore take place by way of a negative dialectic in which increasing levels of self-conscious subjectivity would lead toward the "absolute freedom" claimed by the German thinkers on irony—though for Hegel such "ironic" freedom remains not only negative, it is also always vain, or "empty," insofar as it still lacks the genuine earnestness and thus solidity with which Hegel's System intends to provide it.

From a purely formal perspective, then, Hegel identifies the ironic moment with a disparity that might best be described in terms of the inverted relation characterizing the two modes of "indirection" through which the rhetorical figures of ellipsis and hyperbole always operate: Socrates in his modesty stakes "too little" a claim on subjectivity, whereas the self-complacent romantics exhibit "too much" of it. But this formal discrepancy remains a problem for philosophy only so long as it fails to include the mediating agency of a diachronic movement. Once the ironic point of view has been recognized as being merely one element within a more encompassing process of historical

transitions, it ceases to be threatening for a dialectic of increasingly objecti-
fied subjectivity, or self-negating Spirit. In this case, Socrates did *not yet* know
that the negativity of his subjectivity would become part of a larger development and history, while the romantics have somehow *already* forgotten that
the negativity of their subjectivity is only part of a history that exceeds them.
From the standpoint of history, there is very little difference between the two,
since in each case, and in a manner appropriate to the particular moment, the
indirection of ironic negativity actually prefigures the means with which history will be able to overcome this negativity: by freeing Socrates a bit more
from the ignorance with which he mistakenly limits his subjectivity, and by
limiting a bit more the illusory freedom the romantics claim for theirs. From
the standpoint of history, irony's negativity is always one-sided and *prema-
ture*.[4] For Hegel, the very one-sidedness of irony will always have implied a
positive complement that, no matter what the historical period in question,
can follow on its heels and cancel its indirection by turning it back to the
direction—in both senses of the term—established by history.

To some extent, this perspective will also hold true for Kierkegaard, whose
thesis on irony closely parallels Hegel's treatment. What Kierkegaard, after
Hegel, calls "the world historical validity of irony" is put to use in the thesis to
organize and explain the crucial passage in its own development from an analysis of Socrates' nascent and rather tentative subjective irony to an analysis of
the overly self-indulgent subjectivity flaunted by the theoreticians of irony in
the wake of Fichte. But whereas Hegel appears to vacillate in his evaluations
of these two discrete "moments" by referring rather "haphazardly"—at least
according to a critique that Kierkegaard will advance in a subtle but continuous manner throughout the thesis—sometimes to a positive Socrates (who
would be nonironic) and sometimes to a negative Socrates (who would be
ironic), and by referring sometimes to a positive romantic irony (exemplified
by Solger, who died too young to have written what would have surely completed his philosophical development) and sometimes to a negative romantic
irony (exemplified by Schlegel, whose writings exceeded every limit set by
decency as well as philosophy), Kierkegaard's thesis aims to achieve a higher
level of systematic consistency. One of Kierkegaard's main objectives is therefore to throw Hegel's own value judgments into greater relief and to help
them become more decisive, to separate once and forever the positive from
the negative, the serious from the nonserious, with total clarity and precision.
In this respect, one effect of the thesis is to make Kierkegaard appear—or
to make him appear to want to appear—even more Hegelian than Hegel

himself.[5] The fact that Kierkegaard's history of subjectivity in the thesis takes the form of a unilateral process of decline—at least with respect to irony— thus allows for the possibility of differentiating Socratic from romantic irony unequivocally in terms of their respective positive and negative values, thus correcting some of the ambiguity, equivocation, or indirection implied by Hegel's own model of irony's history. Kierkegaard's less "haphazard," and thus more systematic, version of the decline of irony throughout history will therefore allow the thesis to distinguish in a more definitive fashion between a "good" and a "bad" irony. Such a scheme of historical values is what in fact accounts for the way Kierkegaard's thesis will always insist on its own capacity to recognize and assimilate to its (Hegelian) perspective a timely irony of the past (Socrates) while rejecting without appeal an untimely irony of the present (the romantics).

It follows that in order for irony to be judged "good," its negativity—like Socrates' questions—has to be "timely" in a very precise sense; that is, it has to correspond to the needs of the historical moment in which it originates. In the case of Socrates, this meant that the empty substantiality of the Greeks was *ready* to be negated and replaced by the dawning subjectivity provided by Socrates and ironic interrogations. Otherwise, were this not the case, then the negativity of subjective play would be merely gratuitous and of no "use" whatsoever, like the arbitrary playfulness of the romantics that empties objectivity of its content without being geared toward replacing the void it creates with any ideal positivity of its own. Here is one of Kierkegaard's clearest formulations of this necessarily dialectical conception of subjective irony: "To the extent that [Socratic] irony is world historically justified, the emancipation of subjectivity takes place in the service of the Idea, even though the ironic subject is not clearly conscious of this. This is the genial quality of an irony that is warranted. As for an unwarranted irony, it may be said that whosoever shall save his life shall lose it. But whether irony is warranted or not can only be adjudicated by history" (*CI* 280). In this way, all of irony's negativity can be put in its rightful place, assigned its necessarily past—which is to say, surpassed—moment in history (Socrates), or else once and for all deprived of any place whatsoever (the romantics).

This would be one way of understanding the concluding chapter of the thesis, "Irony as a Mastered Moment: The Truth of Irony." History functions here as the accumulation of individual layers of consciousness, a means of ordering from a higher perspective the negativity of subjectivity's irony in order to reduce the "more or less"—the ellipses and hyperboles—of various stages to a synthesis that can ultimately provide the "truth" or "mastery" of a philosophical thesis about the developmental process of all subjective self-consciousness. Philosophically speaking, and to return to our point of departure, we could say that Kierkegaard's theory of indirect communication results in this way from his theory of subjectivity, which, in turn, is a dialectical theory of mediated, that is, *historical* negativity. The sequential narration, or "history" of this negativity—whether it is conceived in philosophical, theological, psychoanalytical, or even political terms—also includes the promise of its eventual sublation. From this perspective, it would be perfectly legitimate—not to say illuminating—to read Kierkegaard's own evolution as a writer from *The Concept of Irony* to *The Point of View* as a particular version of the gradual unfolding of all subjectivity; an experimental process of authorship that begins after the academic thesis by speaking playfully in a language of indirection or irony (and is as a consequence riddled with the subterfuge and pseudonymity implied by it), though only in order to advance by stages to the positivity of a self that freely speaks in and takes responsibility for his own name, even if in this name he also accepts the risk of suffering religious martyrdom for the sake of his age.

All of this is more or less straightforward, and more or less readily legible in the texts of both Hegel and Kierkegaard. So by titling the first section of her book "Irony as a Subject?" Agacinski seems to place herself within the same tradition of philosophic inquiry to which Hegel and Kierkegaard themselves belonged, and in which the question of irony has always been linked in this way to the negativity that the self-conscious subject must appropriate for itself in order to inaugurate the infinite process of thought's unfolding freedom. "Irony as a Subject?" then, could be taken to ask about the kind of subjectivity that always depends upon and then results from the philosophical exercise of irony. The section title could almost be translated, "*Who* is the subject that is constituted out of irony?" with the obvious answer being "Socrates"— in other words, the first and exemplary subject of Western philosophy. But Agacinski adds to this heading a note that deflects the question in a somewhat different direction by having it ask first about the academic context in which Kierkegaard's thesis originally appeared. As an institutionalized act of *language* that is recognized—that is, legitimated—only insofar as it adopts the recognizable form of propositions or statements that are supposed to mean what they say in a straightforward and proper manner, Kierkegaard's thesis has first of all as its "subject," irony—and that subject has to be taken into account before the thesis can ever be understood to broach (much less explicate, interrogate, or resolve) the question of ironic "subjectivity" in the history of Western philosophy beginning with Socrates. Rather than asking about the properly philosophical relation that obtains between irony and subjectivity—that is, between irony and the subjectivity of the first subject who occurs in Western thought as Socrates—the title redirects itself by way of a note that appears beneath the main text, and so it actually poses this simpler but less overtly philosophical question: "Is irony a fit *subject* for a *thesis*?" To ask about the conditions in which subjectivity can come to consciousness through irony is one thing, but who cares about a list of possible thesis subjects at the University of Copenhagen in 1841? Nonetheless, Agacinski's question is intriguing, and potentially disruptive. For the footnote subtly shifts the question of ironic "subjectivity" from its necessary relation to consciousness and history toward a supplementary consideration of the way that philosophical discourse is itself always subject to the shifting conventions, or contexts, that govern the authority of its own language, contextual conventions that alone are capable of certifying it as serious philosophical reflection in the first place.

By the time the footnote—a mere appendage to the main body of the text—has been reattached to the question asked in the heading, the concept of the "subject" has therefore expanded considerably. It now refers not only to the existential category that is to be determined by a philosophical theory of historical self-consciousness; it also refers to the way that no serious thesis—philosophical, personal, political, economic, or other—can ever be advanced without first passing by way of a formalized code, or *grammar*, in which any given subject—or predicate—must itself be determinable as "serious" or not. Rereading the title this way, it becomes difficult to avoid noticing an effect that could only be ascribed to Agacinski's own irony. A question that seems on the surface to ask about the all-important relationship between irony and subjectivity discloses a submerged level at which what is really in question is the relation between thought and language, between consciousness and grammar, or between the power of philosophical reflection and the power of sheer convention, or law. What Agacinski does at the threshold of her book—and then throughout the book with increasing insistence—is to repeat Kierkegaard's question about whether irony, considered before all else as a possible deflection of any given convention, any law established to ensure serious communication, could ever be made compatible with a philosophical thesis that necessarily posits and therefore depends upon maintaining the seriousness of its own conventionality. "The difficulty here encountered," writes Kierkegaard, "is essentially that irony in a strict sense can never set forth a thesis"

(*CI* 286). But to *repeat*—at least according to the singularly unconventional, and therefore *ironic* twist that Kierkegaard will later give to that same term in the text titled *Repetition*—does not at all mean to say the same thing, either. For example, in the version of the dilemma as it is articulated by Agacinski, the term *thesis* now refers not (just) to the discourse of Socrates—considered as the dawning moment of Western self-consciousness—but rather, or in addition, to the institutionalized form of Kierkegaard's dissertation. What Agacinski does by repeating Kierkegaard's affirmation that irony cannot posit a thesis is to suggest that Kierkegaard's own thesis on the subject of irony may not actually *be* a thesis. When irony becomes the subject of a philosophical thesis, Agacinski insinuates, then the philosophical thesis may become in its turn subject to irony. The "thesis" surely continues to say things, but no longer according to the laws of philosophical grammar. The "subject" may still be irony, but its meaning, as it is now repeated outside the laws of philosophy, may no longer be subject to anything but its own deviant grammar. Irony is a kind of language that speaks without obeying the laws dictated to it by philosophical meaning. The question of irony as a subject thus runs the risk of turning the thesis, and not just the academic one signed by Kierkegaard, into something else altogether.

In this case, the subject, irony, would no longer be governed by the constraints of either self-consciousness or history; it would still have to do with self-consciousness and history, but now this relation would be governed only by the potential discrepancy between whatever language as *grammar* (subject, predicate, attribute) is able to say and its intended *meaning* (thesis, proposition, statement) as philosophical thought. What would it mean, the first heading of *Aparté* seems to ask or to say, for the subject of a proposition (say, "Kierkegaard is a fit subject for a thesis") to be *irony*, to *be* ironic; that is, what would it mean for the "subject" of a statement, or a question, not to be as earnest and directly intelligible as the conventions established for ensuring the seriousness of philosophical thought would always demand of it? The question seems to ask whether irony is a fit subject for a thesis, but if the "subject" of its own language is ironic—"Is *irony* a fit subject?"—then how can such an instance of interrogative language hope to know exactly *what* it means by asking such a question? Would not the "meaning" of any proposition or question necessarily be threatened by the possibility of its being predicated upon a subject that was, from one end to the other, "ironic"? And how could we ever determine with certainty which subjects are ironic ("irony," "Kierkegaard," "Socrates," etc.), and which are not ("earnestness," "Hegel," "Plato," etc.)? Kierkegaard's thesis, once again, is an inevitable example of this dilemma. For the answer it proposes is that the duly appointed university "authorities" ultimately *decided* that irony was a fit subject for a thesis, and that that philosophical thesis on irony was to be taken as serious. Only once they had determined—in other words, ruled—on those two questions, according to their own laws rather than according to the rather peculiar grammar of Kierkegaard's thesis, were they free to determine whether or not Kierkegaard had actually understood anything about the relation between irony and the philosophical constitution of subjectivity and its truth.

In its most general form, the same question can be asked in this way: if the relationship between a grammatical subject and the proposition in which it appears can always be one of irony, then how can we ever be sure that grammar (for instance, the "subject") and the meaning (or the "thesis") can be made truly compatible, can be made to coincide in a direct way that allows for no further doubt? We know, for instance, at least since Hegel, that irony *is* a serious subject for philosophy, and considered as the source of self-consciousness since Socrates, it is therefore one of the most meaningful subjects of philosophy. But in addition to the story of irony's (subjective) place within philosophical discourse that is hinted at by the first (philosophical) paragraphs of *Aparté*, there is also what we might now call the rhetorical question of the heading: "Irony as the subject of a thesis?"—in other words, "You must be kidding." And this *rhetorization* of the heading also points to the possibility that *any* proposition, serious or not, insofar as it is necessarily predicated on a purely grammatical subject that can always be "irony," may also be condemned to not knowing with absolute assurance whether it is or is not ironic—that is, to not knowing whether its own "subject" will always obey the laws and conventions of its "own" intended meaning.

The distinction Agacinski brings into focus here is one between *consciousness* and *discourse*, or between philosophy and its language; or to return to the terms used above, between what a text says and the particular way, within any given language, it must say it. It may be true that subjectivity, considered solely in terms of self-consciousness, requires a moment of negativity that will itself be negated in the process of its self-development, and that this moment can, conveniently and legitimately, be referred to from a philosophical point of view as *irony*. As long as we restrict ourselves to asking about this irony in terms of consciousness, we may rely on a dialectical process like that of history to resolve the negativity involved in the individual ironic moments by ultimately organizing them into a totality in which they become bounded and therefore understandable. But once we begin to ask about the status of a *subject* that cannot *a priori* be determined on the basis of consciousness— and this is true of every grammatical subject of every conceivable proposition or thesis, and a fortiori of every thesis involving the self-consciousness of subjectivity—then we have left such assurances behind once and forever. And if philosophical models of self-consciousness and its history can always be shown to depend on theses that must themselves have recourse to such grammatical subjects, then it will be necessary to reassess our understanding of subjectivity and its history through an understanding of grammar, rather than the other way around. Such would be one of the most far-reaching theses dissimulated within Kierkegaard's own thesis on irony. No doubt the question of Socrates' history and the extent of his self-consciousness always remains an interesting and possibly fruitful subject for philosophical reflection. But a far different method of analysis would be required to address the status of the grammatical subjects that allow for such propositions to be stated— "Socrates," "Kierkegaard," or "Irony"—since these "subjects" can obviously not be considered to have either consciousness or the kind of history that goes along with all consciousness. That irony could in this manner name both a negatively subjective moment within the history of self-consciousness (Socrates or Kierkegaard, for instance) and the grammatical structure that puts into question the articulation of any subject ("irony") and its predicates (meaning conceived of as the possibility of a *serious* "thesis") would also be "ironic"—though in this case the term threatens to lose its usefulness as a term for understanding anything beyond its own aberrant operation. For these two mutually exclusive meanings of irony enter into a self-obliterating relationship between the self-as-consciousness and the self as grammatical case, and so the (rhetorical) question that begins by asking about irony as a "subject" makes it forever impossible to decide whether irony is what allows for consciousness to come into being as such, or what prevents it from ever establishing itself on firm ground.

At any rate, one of the places where these questions resurface in a more developed fashion in Agacinski's reading of *The Concept of Irony* is the point at which she turns to a particularly compelling example that Kierkegaard introduces into his own text to characterize the negativity and indirection adhering to irony. "There is an engraving that portrays the grave of Napoleon," writes Kierkegaard; "two large trees overshadow the grave. There is nothing else to be seen in the picture, and the immediate spectator will see no more. Between these two trees, however, is an empty space, and as the eye traces out its contours Napoleon himself suddenly appears out of the nothingness" (*CI* 56; *SKS* 1:80–81). Appearing coincidentally within the dismissive presentation of Xenophon's Socrates, this brief sketch, or skit, is itself like the engraving of Napoleon it describes, and it contains all the elements of a radical and comprehensive theory of irony, of which Kierkegaard's entire authorship can be considered but one long extension. We should recall that, in its context, what is at issue is not merely "seeing" the head of Napoleon, or rather not seeing this shape as "mere" head. Kierkegaard prefaces the reference to the engraving by saying, "Allow me to illustrate my meaning through an image [ved et Billede]," and so it should be clear that he does not tell us the story of the head for its own sake, but rather as a means for us to use our heads in order to understand his meaning more easily. Napoleon's head becomes a *figure* for what, in this case, just happens to be the difficulty involved in understanding the meaning hidden in the ironic words of Socrates. In order to tell us that there is no direct access to what is or is not in Socrates' head, Kierkegaard avoids telling us directly what is in *his*, Kierkegaard's, own head; instead he tells the story of another head, also mute, that of Napoleon.

This moment in *The Concept of Irony* thus employs indirect communication in presenting Socrates as a subject for serious philosophical reflection, and in this particular instance, the ironic negativity that is inherent to the Socratic method of questioning also provides a convenient means for determining the kind of subjectivity Socrates actually possesses. Taken together, then, the elements of the engraving and the use to which they are put by the thesis on irony provide a virtual emblem for the entire Kierkegaardian project. Kierkegaard wants us to "see," that is to *understand*, that seeing the head of Napoleon emerge from the empty space of nothingness in the engraving can be considered as a figure for "hearing" or understanding the meaning of Socratic irony, or indirection. The appearance of subjectivity, clearly marked in the making-visible of Napoleon's head, is thus linked metaphorically not only with the initial subjective negativity associated by Hegel with Socratic irony, but also with the possibility of mastering this irony retrospectively through an act of understanding: "Napoleon himself suddenly appears out of the nothingness . . . It is the same with Socrates' replies. As one sees the trees, so one hears his discourse; as the trees are trees, so his words mean exactly what they sound like. There is not a single syllable to give any hint of another interpretation, just as there is not a single brush stroke to suggest Napoleon. Yet it is this empty space, this nothingness, that conceals what is most important. As in nature we find examples of places so curiously situated that those who stand nearest the speaker cannot hear him, but only those who stand at a fixed point often at a great distance; so also with Socrates' replies when one recalls that in this case *to hear* is identical with *understanding*, not to hear with *misunderstanding*" (*CI* 56–57; *SKS* 1:81; emphasis added).

Irony would be like such an engraving, or rather irony would occupy the place that is empty in the engraving, the empty space from which the head of Napoleon pops up without anyone's having noticed. Inside a picture, irony has to occupy the empty space, the space in which a picture could no longer or not yet be said to be a true picture, truly representing something. Irony, with respect to every mode of representation, is just an empty space; though, ironically enough, it is an empty space within the model of representation that is itself capable of revealing *more* picture and more *subjective* picture: the head of Napoleon. Drawing on Jacques Derrida's trenchant critique of representation in *La Dissémination*, Agacinski points out that the metaphor of painting, the image, or the engraving in this case, has always been used to characterize the mimetic relationship between thought and idea that is crucial to Western metaphysics.[6] Some mode of imitation or analogy is what guarantees a relationship of adequation between presence and representation and allows the particular kind of recognition necessary to the philosophical discourse of truth to take place. But, Kierkegaard tells us by way of the indirect figure of the Napoleonic head, the relationship between the words of Socrates and the "idea" he is trying to communicate is not one of resemblance or mimesis. This is Socrates' irony, and insofar as it is an *empty* space, insofar as there is literally *nothing* there, it tears or interrupts the process of painting, representation, perception, mimesis, or any metaphorical exchanges based on resemblance. Irony does not imitate anything, it is not part of the metaphysical system of mimesis, and yet, it is out of this empty space *within* the metaphysical system of mimesis that the image of the subject—Napoleon—bursts forth. Irony is not mimetic, but it seems capable of producing mimesis as an aftereffect. Irony is also not primarily subjective; if anything, it is more like the death of the subject, since it first hovers over the *grave* in this engraving. The story of the engraving tells us—though only indirectly—that irony is not mimesis, but that mimesis emerges out of irony; that irony is not subjective, but that subjectivity appears in the wake of irony; and finally, that the only access we have to understanding irony is through both mimesis and subjectivity, that is, through the mimetic "like" of analogy and the "Napoleonic" figure of subjectivity, since here we are told by Kierkegaard that irony is "like" an empty picture of "Napoleon." How are we to understand such an ironic process?

Perhaps we should look again at this curious picture; or, since irony is not mimetic, not painterly or representational, perhaps we should not so much *look* at it as one looks at an image, but should rather try to *read* it as one reads a text, for instance the text of Socratic irony. We should recall, in fact, that *as* a figure, the painting of Napoleon is itself originally a substitute for a text. The painting or engraving, Kierkegaard tells us, is a figure for Socrates' own *words.* Is there any place in this engraving where its own status as a figure for language as text, as distinguished from painting or figure, can be said to have been engraved or inscribed? In fact, language as text—as what has to be *read* rather than to be experienced as an empirical perception or intuition—is precisely what has been occulted in Kierkegaard's narrative depiction of this textual image. For there *is* something to be read in the empty space, and it is something akin to the proper name, *Napoleon.* As a marker that stands in for what is no longer simply present as such, the grave in the engraving must also, however minimally, function as an inscription. Engraved on the tombstone, the inscription is that of the proper name, and in this case, as on any grave, the proper name, visible or not, is that which spells out the death of the subject's empirical subjectivity—in this case, Napoleon. No longer there in living flesh, Napoleon can appear in the empty space of his engraved grave only as a ghostly figure that hovers above this final resting place. It is in this space, then, above the inscription of subjectivity's death that is necessarily implied by the inscription of a grave, that irony works to produce an afterimage of subjectivity. But is the image of Napoleon that appears after his empirical death a mode of philosophical idealization, a giving up of sensuous immediacy that permits access to the ideal realm of philosophical thought? Or, as Kierkegaard puts it, can the irony that prepares or produces such an engraved image still be said to function "in the service of the Idea"?

The status of language as inscription rather than as representation, or in slightly different terms, the relationship of language to both the proper name and self-consciousness, returns in the last section of Agacinski's chapter, called "The Serious Side of the Thesis: The Defense" (*Aparté,* 72). The section opens with a citation of the first heading, "Irony as a Subject?" Is it merely a coincidence that the section that will discuss the general "citationality" of inscription is itself introduced by a citation that repeats the earlier question in which the subject as thought was distinguished from the subject as grammar? Is there a link between the displacement of subjectivity by mechanical laws of grammar and the law of iterability that, as Jacques Derrida has demonstrated, applies to all writing, to all language as a system of repeatable signs rather

than of self-enclosed images?[27] Could this "link" have something to do with
irony? "The possibility of writing," Agacinski will write a little later in this
section, "is also the possibility of irony: it is the possibility of detachment"
(*Aparté*, 76). The inscription or writing on the grave *is* irony then, insofar as it
performs the same interruption of mimetic, that is, self-evident, connections
between mind and nature as does irony. And to the extent that all writing is
ironic, that is, nonmimetic and dependent on the machinelike codes of grammatical subjects and predicates to signify the appearance of self-conscious
subjectivity, it is also, and by necessity, indirect. Kierkegaard's special theory
of indirect communication, it turns out, is also a general theory of language
as irony.

What makes such a theory of language a theory of *indirect* communication is that, unlike the faithful image of Napoleon that will eventually appear
between the trees, the inscription of the name cannot be *seen* here, anymore
than it is literally possible to "see" or "hear" the irony of Socrates that Kierkegaard is attempting to portray here with an image. To the extent that it does
not represent or imitate, all writing constitutes itself as an "empty space" in
every image, or picture. As such, a name must be *read* rather than perceived
directly by the eye, or ear, or hand; that is, it must first be placed within an
arbitrary but infinitely repeatable—that is, recognizable—code, or grammar.
But from the moment the self, as name, must depend on the systematic but
merely formal laws of a grammar, it also must give up any illusion of speaking
exclusively for itself, speaking directly in its very own voice, and so it must
hand itself over or entrust itself to a process of production and recognition
that is mechanical rather than self- conscious. This is why, within language
conceived as a system of notation, it is never possible to determine without
remainder the exact extent to which the "subject" of enunciation is a mind
or a machine; that is, to what precise extent it is the "citation" of a merely
grammatical, rhetorical, or ironical "self" rather than a fully self-conscious
thinking subject. Writing as inscription, insofar as it requires the mechanical
underpinnings of a grammar, is itself the question of "irony as meaningful
subject," the locus of the possible disarticulation of grammar and consciousness, and therefore the coming apart of the subject as self-consciousness. The
turn toward language as a system of inscription, as an engraving of names
rather than, say, a representation of trees, is an *aparté*, a turn away from a
metaphorical chain of resemblances between mind and matter in which it
would always be possible to determine exactly what one is seeing or hearing.
Writing, then, is always the engraving of a tombstone, since within language

conceived as inscription the appearance of the subject—as name—must also coincide with its disappearance, or death, as sheer presence. To cite Agacinski herself, whenever we are faced with writing, as with irony, it is never possible to exclude the possibility "that the subject would not be thinking whatever it is it is arguing" (*Aparté*, 75–76).

What is the status of a subject that argues (a thesis) without thinking? Such a subject would seem to be the grammatical epitaph for self-consciousness itself, since it could continue to exist as subject independently of its own thought or consciousness. It is the grammatical subject cut off or disconnected from the meaningful propositions it just happens to be pronouncing. Yet this is not, as the saying goes, the end of the story. The ironic subject could never on its own account for the fact that the picture, the image, the entire metaphorical chain of subjective attributes suggested by the appearance of "Napoleon himself" actually does occur here: "Napoleon himself suddenly appears out of the nothingness, and now it is impossible to make him disappear. The eye that has once seen him now goes on seeing him with an almost anxiety-ridden necessity" (*CI* 56; *SKS* 1:81). What the eye sees when it looks at Napoleon is *itself*, though in the image of the other, Napoleon in this case. It sees itself as the reflexive image of a metaphorical resemblance between inside and outside, the object seen and the self-conscious subject seeing, and thus understanding it. For after all, Kierkegaard's image is meant to enable each and every thinking subject to understand its own relation to the concept of Western subjectivity as it entered world history in the person of Socrates and his irony. In this scene of self-recognition, the philosophical figure of Napoleon reflects the gaze of Narcissus, and so it is no wonder that the eye that has once seen itself in this commanding image will continue to look for it with a necessity born of anxiousness (*med en næsten ængstende Nødvendighed*). It is only at this moment when the self can recognize itself as an image of subjective consciousness—as either Napoleon or Socrates—rather than a mere inscription that it can begin to enjoy the self-conscious freedom that is traditionally, if somewhat hastily, associated with ironic subjectivity. Kierkegaard himself speaks in this regard of the ironist's "enjoyment" at being able to direct all of his activity back into himself at every moment: "the ironist moves proudly as one terminated in himself—enjoying" (*CI* 176; *SKS* 1:198). The pleasurable intoxication attributed to the ironist is not to be found in the mute name inscribed on a tomb, but rather in the heady *freedom* to find himself again and again in a Socratic-Napoleonic image of his own making and at his own pleasure.[8]

However, there remains something curious about this passage, and it is not the fact that the self would look repeatedly for itself with something akin to anxiety, since such a reaction is easily explained from the perspective of a subjective consciousness concerned with its own relation to death, especially when faced with the image of a graveyard. But that the look would occur by *necessity* (*Nødvendighed*) is somewhat surprising, since, like the arbitrary but systematic element in the grammatical "I," the force of necessity shifts the act of self-reflection away from the self-willing subject and once again turns it toward a machinelike repetition. For this reason, it would not be legitimate to equate the image of Napoleon appearing over the grave of the empirical subject with the philosophical "subject" of Idealism, Hegelian or other. To say that the subject looks for itself "by necessity," or that it is "impossible" for the subject to make the image of itself disappear (or appear), is also to say that this subject is not really a subject in any truly philosophical sense of the term, since such a subject would have no power over what it repeats with near obsession. No doubt the image of the Napoleonic Self occurs on the far side of the grammatical reduction of the subject, but it cannot be said for this reason alone that this new image of subjectivity is any less mechanical than the nonmimetic and citational "subject" of grammar from which it issues. What *is* different at this stage, though, is that this "subject" does not read itself accurately as the insuperable interference between name and thought, but instead *mistakes* itself for Napoleon! To be reduced to looking for oneself in the guise of a grammatical case would be bad enough, but to be such a grammatical subject and then entertain Napoleonic delusions of grandeur would be the height of irony.

However, it is precisely out of such a place, "out of the nothingness," as Kierkegaard's image puts it, that the "necessity" of Napoleon's image will appear: "Napoleon himself suddenly appears *out of the nothingness*, and now it is *impossible* to make him disappear. The eye that has once seen him now goes on seeing him with an almost anxiety-ridden necessity." The necessity referred to here differs from the "necessity" associated with natural causes and effects, since it is precisely the natural, mimetic order that is interrupted by the ironic nothingness in the engraving. Irony, as the empty space of nothingness, as the nonmimetic inscription of a name on the tomb, makes the subjective appearance of Napoleon possible, but at the same time it prevents the subject from getting itself (or its image) under control. The ironic subject would be as powerless to generate the Napoleonic image as it is subsequently to be rid of it, and the "necessity" that makes this self look for itself again obeys the same mechanical laws that made the self see itself in the first place. What is this strange power in irony that produces a subjectivity so deluded that it thinks it sees itself whenever it stares into the blank space of inscription, so deluded that it affirms its absolute freedom at the very moment it falls under the sway of blind and mechanical necessity?

An answer to this question can be glimpsed at the moment Kierkegaard finally addresses the limits of Socrates' irony. The discussion crystallizes around the element of negativity at the core of the Socratic method. What was the true status of the claim to ignorance that made all of Socrates' questioning possible in the first place? Were the assurances of Socrates that he knew nothing given in earnest, or was he merely being ironic? How far was Socrates *serious* about his own ignorance? What hangs in the balance is nothing less than the possibility of philosophy itself being able to take irony "seriously," being able to determine for the sake of its own seriousness whether irony as a philosophical category is "serious" or irredeemably "ironic." Socrates apparently knew at least *that* he was ignorant. However, such a knowledge is not, according to Kierkegaard, a knowledge *of* something, so it has no positive content. And for the same reason, the Socratic claim to ignorance that is itself serious cannot be in its turn taken seriously without a remainder. "To this extent," Kierkegaard concludes, "his ignorance is both to be taken seriously and not to be taken seriously, and upon this point Socrates is to be maintained" (*CI* 286; *SKS* 1:306).

What accounts for this aporia between seriousness and nonseriousness on which Socrates is to be kept suspended would be a further extension of the linguistic complication between the subject as grammar and the subject as meaning (or proposition, thesis) that makes all language indirect in Kierkegaard's sense. Here, the discrepancy is best characterized as one that splits language between its function as *meaning* (a thesis) and its function as *act* (a power). "The difficulty here encountered," says Kierkegaard on the same page, "is essentially that irony in a strict sense can never set forth a *thesis* [at Ironien i strængere Forstand aldrig kan opstille en *Sætning*]"; nonetheless, he is quick to add, "the ironist must always *posit* something, but what he posits in this way is nothingness [Ironikeren altid ponere Noget, men det, han saaledes ponerer, er Intet]" (*CI* 286; *SKS* 1:306). The ironist speaks, then, but not according to the conventions of philosophy, that is, in the language of meaningful theses. Rather, he speaks the language of force or imposition, the "positing" power of language as an arbitrary act prior to any philosophical determination of its meaning. What the ironist posits in this way is nothingness, or since irony *is* nothingness, what irony posits when it posits nothingness is itself *as* nothingness. But what must be kept in mind here is that since the language of positing is radically discontinuous with the language of meaning—as thesis, or *Sætning*—the necessary gesture on the part of the self to understand the meaning of such a positing (of itself) will have to be aberrant. This moment, which is the necessary moment of (self)-reading that allows any text to come into being as text, occurs in Kierkegaard's own text when Socrates, as irony, says, "I am ignorant," which amounts to his trying to *say* that the language he speaks is not *saying* something, either positive or negative, but saying *nothing*, that is, *positing*—though a peculiar nothingness. And by making use here of the word *ponere*—an affected term for positing that is borrowed by Danish directly from the Latin language—Kierkegaard underlines just how foreign positing always has to remain with respect to the meaning of one's own language. Furthermore, since this "nothing" of positing is in no way assimilable to the conventional affirmations or negations of meaningful theses, it is precisely when Socrates (ironically) says that he knows nothing that we (mistakenly) believe we know "what" he is actually saying. The irony here is the blind positing of the self as nothingness—"I am ignorant"—that necessarily ends up taking on the appearance of the self as something positive—"I am Socrates." In the mimetic imagery of the engraving of Napoleon, such a moment occurs when the nothingness of positing the name on the grave produces the aberrant thesis or image of Napoleonic subjectivity, albeit in the negative, though still symmetrical, form of its natural death.[9]

Irony, then, is an attribute of neither the empirical nor the ideal self, but rather of a linguistic self that is neither one nor the other, and yet is both at once. It is the positing of the self as an empty inscription or name, and only in the wake of such an ironic subject will empirical and ideal selves be able to retrace their own shadowy features from it. Kierkegaard himself could not be clearer on this score when he later compares the Christian to the ironist. The scenario resembles in an uncanny way the earlier image of the engraving and the distinction in it between the ironic inscription of the tomb and the mimetic and subjective figure of Napoleon that suddenly appears out of its blank nothingness. In this version, the Christian—whose life, according to Kierkegaard's analysis, can become meaningful only in the sacrificial space left by Christ's empty tomb—assumes the shape of Napoleonic subjectivity, since it is the Christian who finally takes the nothingness of irony "seriously," thus despairing of the ironic self in order to allow a new self to be produced poetically by God.

What is it that determines this poetic production of the Christian's subjective individuality, to which Kierkegaard also refers as a self-enclosed form, a plastic shape or figure, *en plastisk Skikkelse* (*CI* 297; *SKS* 1:316)? It is nothing other than the power to confer meaning upon words, to allow them to acquire shape and figure by suppressing the knowledge that they are originally the *disjecta membra* of (ironic) inscription: "The man who allows himself to be poetically produced also has a determinate given context [en bestemt givet Sammenhæng] into which he must fit, and so he does not become a word without meaning for having been deprived of its connections [bliver saaledes ikke et Ord uden Mening, fordi det er revet ud af sin Forbindelse]. But for the ironist this context, which allows for everything to hang together [Men for Ironikeren har denne Sammenhæng], which he would say only hangs things up and gets in the way [dette hvad han vilde kalde Paahæng], has no validity . . . he not only poetically produces himself but his environment as well. The ironist is reserved and stands aloof; he lets mankind pass before him, as did Adam the animals, and finds no companionship for himself" (*CI* 299–300; *SKS* 1:318). The scene, whether political (Napoleon returning from exile) or religious (the seriousness of the New Testament vs. Adam's ironic aloofness), is always a scene that covers over the grave of language by producing meaningful connections where there may in fact be none; or, at least, where none can be verified without further ado. Irony, the positing power belonging originally to all language, is the inscription of a word— "without meaning for having been deprived of its connections"—even when that word, like Adam, names itself "man." What is free, arbitrary, and powerful in irony, and what Kierkegaard will also refer to in the same section as irony's "sheer possibility," is therefore not some sort of subject or subjective will; rather, it is the random coming apart, the chance disconnections of words and letters from any transcendentally determined context.

Ironically enough, Kierkegaard's own text inscribes such a random coming apart of a word at the very instant it names irony as the arbitrary power to undo all meaningful contexts. It undoes the particular "context" (*Sammenhæng,* or "hanging together") of its own argument by disconnecting what hangs together in the philosophical content of the word *Sammenhæng,* leaving behind only the tangle of letters in which the serious meaning of the Christian risks being hung up, and therefore interfered with, when irony has its say in the word *Paahæng.* Playing on its accidental proximity to *Sammenhæng,* Kierkegaard uses the Danish word *Paahæng* (which means "accessory" or "encumbrance," or idiomatically, an unwelcome "hanger-on"), which also names a kind of "hanging." But the hanging of the ironist—which he calls a *Paahæng*—is not like the hanging of the Christian—who allows himself to hang together [sammen] and become gathered into a meaningful context, or *Sammenhæng*. Appended to [paa] the Christian's *Sammenhæng*, the ironist's *Paahæng* is a mere suspension. The preposition "at," or "on," unlike the gathering power of the adverb "together," provides no contextual integration or articulation; it is a foreign element as unnecessary as it is unwelcome. What remains, however, and what this example also goes on to illustrate, is how the "sheer possibility" of ironic interruption is then suppressed in its turn by a subject that survives such "disconnections" by recontextualizing them as moments in a sequential narrative of self-consciousness. The recontextualization of ironic disruptions occurs here when the relation of the ironist to the rest of the world is compared to the way Adam stands aloof from and posits the names for all the animals that pass before him. If the ironist can ultimately be compared to Adam in this way, then he can also be made to fit into a very familiar context (*Sammenhæng*), indeed. This is the context of the Christian typology in which the Old Testament has validity only insofar as it prefigures and effaces itself before the coming of the New Testament—a context in which the free play of the signifier *hanging* now acquires the supplemental value of Christ's sacrifice on the cross. With this gesture, Kierkegaard completes and reverses the philosophical history of irony from Socrates to Schlegel by reinscribing it within the salvational narrative in which Adam's fall will eventually have been redeemed by Christ's elevation and hanging on the cross. And from this moment on, eschewing any affinity for Hegel's secularized model of dialectical history, Kierkegaard will begin his highly original meditation on precisely those religious motifs that offer the most resistance to the Hegelian concept of mediation. These motifs, repeating the philosophical concept of mediation only by interrupting and thus forever displacing it, will include paradox, passion, anxiety, faith, the instant, and repetition itself.

It is only by taking such occasions of ironic disruption "seriously," moreover, only by reconnecting their accidental occurrence to "a determinate given context" [en bestemt givet Sammenhæng], that any discourse still able to account for self-consciousness—and chief among them, the discourses of philosophy and religion—could ever provide itself with an image (*et Billede*) for its own meaning, however aberrant such images would in the process turn out to be.[10] Kierkegaard's willingness to recognize and accept this obligation always and again to reinscribe the ironic disruption otherwise is nicely exemplified in the crucial distinction his thesis ultimately draws in characterizing

the "twofold" nature of the relation between subjectivity and historical actuality (*den historiske Virkelighed*). The actuality of subjectivity, Kierkegaard will
insist, must therefore be understood as both a "gift" that is not to be refused
and a "task" that is to be realized (*CI* 293–97; *SKS* 1:312–16). Kierkegaard
makes it clear that in the movement from "gift" to "task" resides the essential
historical continuity, or context, linking the past (which is necessarily given)
to the future (which demands to be accomplished). And this movement is also
analogous to the one that passes from the randomness of ironic imposition
(a kind of gift) to the serious responsibility (or task) of philosophical and/or
religious theses. Now what allows for such a passage to get underway in the
first place, though it remains occulted in the English translation of the text,
has little to do with either philosophy or religion considered as meaningful
and meaning-producing discourses.

What relates *gift* to *task* in Danish, and what therefore allows the freedom or gratuitousness of the *gift* of subjective actuality to shade without tension into the necessity of the *task* for which such actuality is destined—or in
slightly different terms, what allows the instantaneous sprites of irony to be
reconnected with the mediations of historical development—is once again
due to, or made "necessary" by, the arbitrary breaking loose of words from
their determinate meanings or contexts. The passage from irony to history,
or irony to philosophy, or irony to religion—which remains the burden of the
entire thesis on irony—is itself irreducibly *ironic* here insofar as it exploits the
untranslatable—and so unsublatable—play between the Danish words *Gave*
(gift) and *Opgave* (task).[11] The "link" that holds the two concepts of gift and
task together in the same context of associations relies first of all on an effect
of the letter and not on the meaning of the words. Such an association of
the two syllables—what Kierkegaard himself calls the "double mode [dobbelt
Maade]" in which *Gave/Op-gave* are related to each other—remains foreign
to the "meanings" the two words ought to possess in the determinate context
of either philosophy or religion—as distinct from the more "poetic" context
in which their syllables so obviously "echo" each other—as is made clear by
their translation into the unrelated pair of English words *gift* and *task*, or the
French pair *don* and *tâche*. The "double"—or duplicitous—manner in which
they are related to each other in Danish can thus appear only on condition
that the words as meaningful wholes are pried apart and set free in the play of
their syllables.[12] In order for the recuperative process of history to function
effectively in the thesis—in part dialectical with its Hegelian perspective, in
part religious with Kierkegaard's growing dissatisfaction with and displace-

ment of Hegel—the gratuitous nature of irony (the gift) has to be sacrificed. But the meaning of the word that makes such a sacrifice necessary, *task*, also has a particular shape in Danish, *Opgave*, that makes this same sacrifice impossible. Irony thus re-enters the system at the very moment the seriousness of the task—the meaning of historical actuality—was supposed to do away with it, since such a task (*Opgave*) is itself given by the play of the word's own syllables: the imposition of a sacrifice, a command to "give up" (*give op*) the arbitrariness of the gift (*Gave*). However, it is logically inconsistent to believe in this way that one might sacrifice arbitrariness in such an arbitrary manner. Like the aporia between Socrates' seriousness and his unseriousness, the aporia between *Opgave* as meaningful thesis (task) and *Opgave* as arbitrary positing (*give op Gaven*, "give *up* the gift," or what would amount to almost the same thing, *give Op-gaven*, "give the task") remains forever impossible to mediate.[13] Nonetheless, like the engraving of Napoleon, such a purely "poetic" aporia cannot prevent itself from taking on the necessarily misleading appearance that it will eventually acquire within both philosophical thought and religious belief.

What Kierkegaard does when he goes on to retrace the movement leading from *Gave* to *Opgave* as though it were conceivable in terms of a temporal and sequential model of "upbringing, education or formation" that evolves, like the "seeds" of a plant, from past (gift) to future (task) (*CI* 297; *SKS* 1:316), or what we do when we read such a story as the unfolding of a hermeneutic process of understanding and self-understanding, is to *impose* in turn a meaningful narrative pattern on an ironic provocation that once and forever will resist, and therefore interrupt, every such imposition, or positing, of meaning. All that is lacking in Sylviane Agacinski's path-breaking treatment of Kierkegaard is a more sustained analysis of the kind of inevitability with which these fallacious hermeneutic readings continue to occur in the wake of ironic disruption no matter how fallacious they are shown to be. The indirection of irony always seems to occasion a narrative recuperation that serves to redirect and prolong the underlying ironic disturbance in ever new directions, and these altered paths of interruption demand to be methodically followed and interrogated. To some extent, Agacinski's own lapidary style, her commitment to the *aparté* as a highly effective stylistic device as well as an object of critical analysis, may ultimately turn her writing aside from such a task. Two of the most serious readers of irony in the twentieth century, Walter Benjamin and Paul de Man, were led in their work to "progress" from an interest in the *aparté* of irony to a preoccupation with allegory. To the degree that al-

legory would be inconceivable without an extension of the ironic moment—
for example, the sudden appearance of the Napoleonic, Socratic, or Christian
image—along a figural line of indeterminate length, it might fruitfully be
juxtaposed to the way mythology functions and comes apart in the writing
of Friedrich Schlegel. Allegory would thus name the altered—and therefore
profoundly unpredictable—course that irony's indirection always takes when
it is given a fresh impetus—call it *history* for want of a better term. History, it
would appear, is the jolt that is occasioned when the hermeneutic imperative
takes on the task of reading and therefore understanding any given moment
of ironic disruption. In terms of Kierkegaard's authorship, *The Concept of Irony*
would therefore mark the locus of just such an inaugural impetus, one that
then occasions an allegorical extension of irony in all his other writings.

THREE

Modernity Interrupted: Kierkegaard's Antigone

Every so often, and driven by a slightly different critical impulse in each case, a new collection of scholarly essays dedicated to the writings of Søren Kierkegaard appears.[1] One can hardly doubt the enduring importance of Kierkegaard for literary, philosophical, and religious study, yet identifying this significance with any genuine precision, much less consensus, has proven to be a task as elusive as it is repetitive. At stake always seems to be the same issue of what, finally, can be learned from Kierkegaard. And, of course, nothing could be more appropriate to the production of disciplinary criticism and scholarship than asking what, exactly, its object of study is still capable of teaching us. There is something odd and potentially unsettling, though, about devoting an academic study to such an author as Kierkegaard, for one immediately encounters Kierkegaard's own virulent resistance to academic endeavors to which publications like this one necessarily contribute, whether they like it or not, whether they admit it or not. Indeed, it is difficult to know just how to proceed with a thinker who considered academics in general to be "a pack of robbers who, in the guise of serving the idea, betray its true servants and confuse the people, all for the sake of paltry earthly advantage."[2] As a teacher, then, Kierkegaard hardly invites us to become students of his writings in an orthodox manner, for he bequeaths to us professional commentators a legacy resembling a curse far more than a blessing: "Were there no hell, it would have to be created in order to punish the professors, whose crimes are such that they are barely punishable in this world" (*Journals*, 3:653). The prospect of immediately becoming a thieving money-grubber, a betrayer of ideas, a source of confusion for the common reader—well, that doesn't really constitute much of an incentive to write about Kierkegaard, does it?

And then there is another side to Kierkegaard's resistance to commentary. Even if one somehow manages to avoid the hellish tendencies of the professors, an ideal not in itself inconceivable and surely worthy of our best efforts, there is still no guarantee that the results would ever satisfy the desire to pierce the innermost secrets contained by his texts. In another *Journals* entry that has not failed to produce precisely the type of exegetic divinations that it both foretells and dooms to failure, Kierkegaard assures us that "no one will find in my writings the slightest information (this is my consolation) about what really filled my life" (*Journals*, 5:226). That Kierkegaard, who definitely did write, and wrote quite a bit about himself at that, finds this outcome a "consolation" suggests that the real reason for reading his writing, whatever secrets he might have left to teach us about, has little or nothing to do with providing us with information or positive knowledge about what he at least felt really filled his life.

This rather inauspicious beginning, though, offers at least two possible insights with respect to how *not* to write about Kierkegaard. These two common recipes for failure in reading Kierkegaard would therefore be 1) looking for information about Kierkegaard himself; and 2) using Kierkegaard's texts as a pretext for pedagogical purposes. But what exactly does that leave? If one cannot read Kierkegaard in order to learn something about Kierkegaard—since, ultimately, there is no means of piercing the secret into which he has now disappeared; and one cannot read Kierkegaard in order to teach others about anything—since in so doing one would only confuse people and betray the very ideas one pretends to be writing about—then what can one possibly do when one reads Kierkegaard and then writes about it?

To take a hint from Kierkegaard, one can perhaps only ask oneself over and over again the very same question, which is also the question about what kind of truth, beyond mere information, one can ever learn at all—about Kierkegaard, about others, about oneself. The book that states this question most directly is, of course, *Philosophical Fragments*: "How far does the truth admit of being learned? With this question let us begin."³ The inaugural difficulty that each of Kierkegaard's texts begins with anew is characterized in this way: "one cannot seek for what one knows, and it seems equally impossible to seek for what one does not know. For what is known cannot be sought, since it is known; and what is not known cannot be sought, for in that case one would not even know what to seek" (*PF* 11). In the very first place, then, we can learn from Kierkegaard that learning anything whatsoever about the truth is itself a very complicated process strewn with pitfalls. The possibility of learning the truth about anything should never be taken for granted, let alone used as a pretext for trying to teach others something about it.

This, though, is a truth that seems at first of rather modest, if not barren, proportions, and so it is with some difficulty that we can imagine just how far it is likely to take us. Theodor W. Adorno, one of the best among the first serious commentators on Kierkegaard in Europe, was particularly sensitive to this aspect of his writings, especially the so-called religious ones. Adorno, who himself wrote with great succinctness, was quick to notice how loquacious, even "boring and painful," Kierkegaard is able to become, always talking only about the same thing. "Verbosity is the danger of all Kierkegaard's writings," Adorno points out with some justification; "it is the verbosity of an interminable monologue that continually repeats itself, without any real articulation."⁴ Such a recognition on Adorno's part certainly does not prevent him from saying some of the most perspicacious and relevant things that have ever been said about Kierkegaard.

When Adorno speaks of the three spheres of existence in Kierkegaard, for instance—the aesthetic, the ethical, the religious—he does not, like so many other interpreters, reduce them to a simplistic formula for mapping out some of the more obvious regions in which all human subjects necessarily, though with more or less awareness and success, operate in their day-to-day activities. Adorno's own book on Kierkegaard is predicated upon the essential insight that the three spheres do not provide direct access to representative subjective determinations. Rather, they constitute three different, but mutually dependent, modes of interpretation with which the subject is confronted, rather than modes of conduct that can simply be adopted through direct experience.⁵ That the truth content involved here has to do in each case with how any given subject is able to interpret its own existence returns us to the original question of what can be learned from Kierkegaard's writing. The deepest mystery concerns how the self could ever come to discover anything about itself that it doesn't already know. The existential spheres or stages along life's way, at least in the way they are treated by Adorno, offer us a semiology rather than a phenomenology of subjective truth. They do not describe the various types of empirical behavior that would simply manifest in existence the hidden truth of a given subject's inner essence. Rather, they construct a series of coded references in which the path leading the self from the enigma of signs to the interpretation of its own meaning, or from its existence to its truth, must be followed in a most indirect and thus secretive manner.

It is a commonplace of Kierkegaard studies that one cannot begin to understand his writings without taking into account the peculiarity of their relation to Hegel. But this does not mean that this relationship is not itself coded, and therefore secretive in its own way. It would therefore hardly suffice merely to document, from an objective position of observation presumed to be outside the fray, as it were, the individual points of contact and separation between the two.[6] Kierkegaard did not choose to argue with Hegel in the ordinary sense in which one's choice of an opponent or ally is always at least in part contingent and based on local circumstances and preferences. Kierkegaard understood, more clearly than most, that Hegel's true importance lay in the way his writings still provide the fullest exposition of the capacities and limits of Western philosophical thought. Kierkegaard must be given credit in this regard, since he is among the few who realize that Hegel's philosophy, whatever else, constitutes an absolutely inevitable point of departure for his own writings as well as everyone else's, provided only that they take the philosophical demand for truth seriously in the first place.

One of the curious, but perhaps entirely predictable, effects of the history of philosophy, and even of history itself, since Hegel has been the tendency to forget just how omnipresent the presuppositions and conclusions of his thought still tend to be in our own understanding of the way things work whenever philosophical, ethical, or even political issues are considered in a logically consistent manner. This was the case even when, in the first half of the twentieth century, the reception of Kierkegaard actually was new enough to seem exciting, and Kierkegaard was often heralded as providing an attractive alternative to certain elements in Hegel's philosophy that then seemed *démodés* or even disagreeable. But it is more than ever the case today, when the urgency surrounding so many modes of analysis, critique, and behavior serves only to mask the philosophical principles on which they are founded. The urgency itself is real enough. However, to the extent that such urgency often discourages more detailed and thoughtful analysis in favor of a perceived necessity to speak and act immediately to avert or dispel crisis, it can also just as often result in the rather unfortunate consequence that we remain inadequately informed about precisely those ways in which we still understand things according to philosophical concepts worked out most systematically by Hegel. This risk—whose name is empiricism—is especially present when we think we are far beyond and different from Hegel and the philosophical concerns that animated his thought.

And so it doesn't make much sense to treat the relation of Kierkegaard to Hegel as a merely historical problem, except to the extent that we recognize that the history of our own thought cannot even be said to begin until we confront seriously those elements in the philosophy of Hegel that are ineluctable for any thought in the first place. Only then might we go on to take the measure of those elements in Kierkegaard's response to Hegel's philosophy that could make a decisive impact upon it. In a word, Kierkegaard's response to Hegel has to do with the way that he gave to subjective existence a valence that continually resists the systematic coherence of all thought, but in such a way that such resistance is always also predicated on recognizing the legitimacy of precisely that which it must ultimately resist.

Kierkegaard understood that Hegel's own thought was exemplary to the extent that it provides an unrivaled conceptualization of the systematic and dialectical character of any thinking. However, he also understood, if we can still use that word in this sense, that there was something else—and he called this *existence*—that always prevented the systematic thrust of the Hegelian dialectic from fulfilling itself and achieving closure without remainder. Kierkegaard granted to Hegel the possibility of arriving at objective truth only through systematic thought. But he also insisted upon the subjective truth that was a necessary corollary of actual existence, for even objective truth has to enter existence, if it is ever to occur at all. The vehicle by which truth enters existence, Kierkegaard called the *subject*. Kierkegaard himself was fond of putting his relation to Hegel in the form of a recurrent joke. Hegel would be right in everything he ever said about truth and the dialectical understanding particular to it, at least from the objective point of view of the ideal system. But from the point of view of subjective reality, well, he was absolutely wrong, or at least wrong about the Absolute. The actuality of existence, the coming into being of truth in the only way it can in the first place occur—that in no way can be governed by the logical system of objective truths that only follows from it.[7] A straightforward reading of Hegel suggests that reason and history must ultimately be able to converge with each other. There is even a short text by Hegel called "Reason in History," which also implies that history is enclosed in reason. Hegel also wrote books with such titles as *Philosophy of History* and *History of Philosophy*, which also suggest that the relation between thought and actuality are symmetrical and neatly reversible. For Kierkegaard, though, things are not like that at all, and everything he wrote exhibited the discrepancy—as distinct from the convergence—that he found between philosophy and history, between the logic of reason and the actuality of existence. He could find this, however, only after taking Hegel seriously in the first place.

It is the site of this discrepancy that Kierkegaard identified with the truth of subjectivity, a jagged mode of truth whose existential signs are most available to us in everyday affects such as guilt, anxiety, and despair. Kierkegaard analyzes such moods, to which subjectivity is itself subject as such, in great detail in his writings. Thinkers as opposed to each other as Heidegger and Adorno both noticed that Kierkegaard would be far less interesting to us if all he did was provide a phenomenology of these subjective affects. To what extent Kierkegaard himself, or anyone else for that matter, exhibits or suffers from guilt, anxiety, or despair is therefore not of primary importance here. Kierkegaard's own writings, in fact, can often seem quite lighthearted and merry in discussing such seemingly depressing moods. Rather, subjective existence is constituted in such a way as to be primordially susceptible to these affects, and their philosophical significance consists in the precise ways that their possibility discloses a nonconvergence between reason and history, or between objective and subjective truth, in Kierkegaard's terms. But to say in this way, as Kierkegaard actually does, that there is a radical discrepancy, or separation, between objective and subjective truth, between history and philosophy—is that not also to suggest that actual existence is not and cannot ever be made fully compatible with thinking, cannot, ultimately, become reasonable, and therefore that existence remains to some extent an arbitrary, if not wildly capricious, affair? To point out every now and then that the real is not always rational is quite a different thing, for instance, than to declare in this manner that actual existence is and must remain, at least on some level, fundamentally alien to all thought. "The systematic Idea," Kierkegaard tells us, "is the subject-object, the unity of thought and being. Existence, on the other hand, is their separation [Adskillelse]. . . [I]t has brought about, and brings about, a spacing between subject and object, thought and being [den har spatieret og spatierer Subjektet fra Objektet, Tanken fra Væren]" (*Postscript*, 112). We should in all honesty be willing to admit what a shocking, and potentially irresponsible, thing it is for Kierkegaard to think the separation of being and thought in the first place, not to mention his writing it down so that it can be repeated over and over again for others to see. This is one secret he ought surely to have kept to himself.

Scandalous ideas like this, though, are easily enough said: existence separates thought and being; thinking and acting are incompatible. Can such statements even be said to come close to shocking us these days? On the one hand, the empirical discrepancy between thought and being has become one of the most familiar of all experiences. It governs our worst fears of powerlessness and vulnerability as well as, often enough, our secret complicities with them as soon as we are given the opportunity to exercise our own power. On the other hand, to say that the discrepancy between thought and action is not just an empirical fact of life, to be parried or domesticated to whatever extent possible, but that it is instead constitutive of subjective truth as such—now that seems disheartening to the point of becoming incendiary, at least considered from a sociopolitical perspective. Kierkegaard is not often read in this manner, though nothing would prevent it. The overtly religious dimension of his texts, which return obsessively to such conventionally reassuring, if somewhat unpleasant, topics as sin, guilt, and despair, seems to have sheltered Kierkegaard from the suspicion of what otherwise might become a radically demoralizing, if not amoralizing, reading.

Nonetheless, Kierkegaard himself always made an effort in his texts to draw attention to the way in which they *should* occasion either scandal or folly for our understanding. Perhaps there is a way that we have become cushioned from the shock of Kierkegaard's text, though not, as is too easy to assume, because the very real difficulties of contemporary existence make things so much more complex and urgent than they ever could have been for Kierkegaard, tucked away in nineteenth-century Copenhagen. Perhaps it is our own unacknowledged but unshakable faith in Hegel that accounts for this. It may be more difficult than we imagine to put in question a mode of dialectical thinking that implicitly promises to link thought and being, all counterexamples notwithstanding, and that by the same token prevents us from taking more seriously what Kierkegaard, as opposed to Hegel, actually says in his texts. For example, in *Fear and Trembling*, before beginning to examine the way existence comes to fragment thought and being for Abraham, Kierkegaard tells the story of someone who listens to a sermon on the Biblical story, the hypothesis of such a listener functioning as an allegorical figure for the reader of Kierkegaard's own text. Unlike the official preacher and the rest of the congregation, this one person takes Abraham's plight seriously for once. "The most terrifying, the most profound, tragic and comic misunderstanding is very close at hand," Kierkegaard insists; "the person goes home, wants to do just as Abraham did, for the son, after all, is the best."[8] Of course, "to do just as Abraham did" is a periphrasis that names the father's willingness to carry out an order to put his only son to death. The most terrifying misunderstanding Kierkegaard refers to, then, would be the risk that someone hearing such a story would actually consider imitating Abraham, and as a result would begin preparations for administering death to their very own child.

An unthinkable possibility, Kierkegaard acknowledges, at least for the preacher and all the others in the assemblage, whose very orthodoxy is set up to exclude any such radical challenge to common sense. Abraham's story is strictly unassimilable to such a community, Kierkegaard suggests. Only to the extent that the story is prevented from having any bearing on actual existence, in other words, only to the extent that it is relegated to a past so distant as to become safely aestheticized as a mere story or parable, can it even still be "heard" today. The absurdity of Abraham's situation is to be understood metaphorically rather than literally, and therefore deprived of the very challenge that it offers to all understanding—one simply doesn't *do* that anymore. Indeed, faced with a contemporary example of the same existential dilemma—and there are, unfortunately, all too many even to mention one—the institutionalized community must immediately disown a deeper affinity to it: "You despicable person, you scum of society, what devil has so possessed you that you want to murder your son" (*FT* 28).[9] What would be a more common, a more reasonable and finally understandable response to the abominable idea of taking Abraham's "sacrifice" to heart?

But, Kierkegaard almost immediately adds, it would be *only* on condition of precisely such a risk—the risk of a folly and scandal no less susceptible to dialectical recuperation than a literal case of infanticide—that one should even speak of Abraham and the discrepancy between thought and actuality that his story exemplifies: "Is it possible to speak unreservedly about Abraham without running the risk that some individual will become unbalanced and do the same thing? If I dare not [run precisely this risk], I will say nothing at all about Abraham" (*FT* 31). In fact, the bad faith of the institutionalized reception of Abraham—and *a fortiori* of Kierkegaard—is evident in the unwillingness of that response to recognize that the risk of radical misunderstanding is no different in this case than in all the others patterned upon it. With respect to the separation of thought and existence that characterizes subjective truth as such, there can be no privileged standpoint of certitude and safety: "We recite the whole story in clichés," Kierkegaard complains, pointing out at the same time: "What is omitted from Abraham's story is the anxiety. . . . What if he himself is distraught, what if he had made a mistake. . . . Was it such a simple matter not to make a mistake?" (*FT* 28, 61, 66). For Kierkegaard, radical fallibility, the utter failure of understanding, and the potential for committing a mortal error is what determines the separation of being and thought in the first place. The potential for the most profound referential misunderstanding therefore becomes the condition—the necessary risk—for existence to occur at all. The danger to which Abraham is exposed, according to Kierkegaard, is not just an unfortunate and merely contingent accident: it is the threat of deadly misapprehension or incomprehension, and it has to be possible at every moment in order for anything to happen at all.

It seems, then, that the so-called absurd dimension of Kierkegaard's thought is not to be taken lightly. The scandal, folly, shock, and paradox that characterize his oblique relation to the dialectic of reason that—at least on the most superficial and thematic level of his text—is articulated in Hegel's philosophy cannot be domesticated by reading them in a purely metaphorical register, since Kierkegaard himself provides ample evidence of their unpredictable potential to recur as actual referential forces in everyday life. While it is not strictly necessary to suffer from the empirical symptoms of anxiety, guilt, or despair in order to read Kierkegaard effectively, to do so would certainly be more relevant than reading him without ever experiencing a flutter or a twinge. Such symptoms might even constitute a first appropriate response to his suggestion that our own day-to-day "sacrifices" of epistemological and ethical duty are not nearly as foreign to Abraham and Isaac as we are wont to think.

Still, the risk of complacency in reading everything in Kierkegaard as though it were merely figural might ultimately be preferable to the danger of taking his thought and writings just literally enough to justify all kinds of recklessly subjectivistic modes of thinking and behavior. Emmanuel Lévinas seems to regard Kierkegaard's insistence on subjective truth as inwardness from such a perspective, and he is therefore highly suspicious of it. Linking Kierkegaard's "taste for scandal" to a certain "cult of ardor and passion," Lévinas identifies in Kierkegaard's concept of existence "a kind of irresponsibility, and a germ of disintegration."[10] Lévinas should be credited for being one of the few to take Kierkegaard seriously enough to see clearly the very real risk of subjectivism and violence that is inscribed in all of his texts, a risk that at the very least has to be acknowledged before it can be confronted, much less parried. However, Lévinas is rather quick to go from recognizing in Kierkegaard a risk that, after all, accrues to any genuine decision and any real act, to characterizing his writings as "irresponsible"—unless such irresponsibility would itself be unavoidable as soon as one writes responsibly about subjectivity's actuality. In his willingness to write about the necessary risk incurred by "existence," Kierkegaard acknowledges and accepts responsibility for the possibility of subsequent misunderstanding that inheres to it; he does not thereby become directly responsible for all specific examples of misunderstanding that can or do actually occur in its wake.

For to say that there is a radical separation between thought and being is not automatically to suggest a straightforward alternative between, on the one hand, a pietistic flight from being into abstract reflection and, on the other, a pure and simple rejection of thought in favor of subjective caprice. In scrutinizing the separation that thwarts every identity of subject and object, or thought and being, Kierkegaard is very careful to add: "It does not by any means follow that existence is thoughtless" (*Postscript*, 112). What can we learn from Kierkegaard about this highly paradoxical idea that existence, which produces subjective truth through its very separation of being and thought, need not by the same token be merely thoughtless?

In a lecture entitled "Kierkegaard and Evil," Paul Ricoeur initiates a partial response to this question.[11] To the extent that human finitude, freedom, and evil exist, he says, they necessarily escape the philosophical strategies of systematic thought that otherwise would be able to comprehend and thereby eliminate them as anything more than ideal categories. But Kierkegaard's writing about those elements in existence that—from the point of view of comprehending thought—can only be called paradoxical, absurd, or offensive is something far different from a simple proclamation of irrationalism: "We should not say that Kierkegaard delights in the irrational. . . . [I]t is important to understand how Kierkegaard himself thought in the face of the irrational, the absurd. For he did not proclaim; he thought" ("KE" 317, 314). Merely to proclaim existence absurd would itself be a rather irrational and irresponsible act that managed to take neither philosophy nor existence very seriously in the final analysis. And Kierkegaard, whatever one knows about his so-called ironic style, remained a very serious thinker of existence. His writing is motivated *not* by the affirmation that existence is a meaningless void, but rather by the recognition that everything in existence, including meaning itself, is constantly at risk of becoming a meaningless void.

The problem for Kierkegaard is therefore the following: how to avoid the complacent and self-deluding philosophical belief that all existence is susceptible to objective and rational understanding (and, eventually, justification), without falling into the symmetrical and equally deluded trap of subjective willfulness? What is therefore of the most enduring importance in the thought of Kierkegaard is the way his writings attempt to approach, confront, and reflect upon the *limits* of reason and understanding in actual existence. Kierkegaard's work is not the place to find justification for the simple disappearance and replacement of reason by something else, least of all by the illusionistic motives of self-interest and desire.[12] For how could one even know exactly what one really desired, much less find it, without first taking the trouble to learn as much as possible exactly what one *is*?

We can now identify with more precision what Kierkegaard still has to teach us. The question of what can be learned is always disclosed as an operation that can only be conducted by the self in search of its own truth. But this truth of subjective existence is produced by the repetitive shocks through which the self discovers itself again and again as nothing but the gap between thought and being, as the nonidentity of subject and object. To come back to Adorno's comment, one can readily admit the potentially loquacious, boring, even painful nature of such repetitions—the ones detailed in Kierkegaard's own text as well as the ones performed by readings like this one—provided one is willing as well to recognize that they are in some sense inevitable. Moreover, as Adorno himself also recognized, concealed within such tiresome abstractions are much more concrete truths about all kinds of realities. The truly critical elements of Kierkegaard's thought can therefore turn out to be every bit as objective and social as they at first appear to be exclusively subjective and inward. Kierkegaard's insistence on the *self* is thus always implicated in an indirect insistence on the *other* as well.

Demonstrating this, however, represents no small challenge, and as such it remains the task of future readings of Kierkegaard. Even with some of the necessary preliminaries about subjective truth out of the way, an encounter with actual examples of Kierkegaard's literary, philosophical, and religious production still leaves the impression of an endlessly provocative but rather abstruse, ingeniously topical, but cranky and inconclusive collection of scraps or fragments. On the one hand, beyond the question of the self, one finds abundant references to other difficult but equally important philosophical concepts, and such references are almost always made with originality and daring. But, just as often, one can't help coming away with a doubly disappointing conclusion: not only has one not really understood Kierkegaard's text; in addition—or instead—what one has understood makes Kierkegaard's own conclusions appear slightly off the mark, or even retrograde.

Kierkegaard's brilliantly perceptive book on irony, *The Concept of Irony: With Constant Reference to Socrates*,[13] would be a case in point, though more dramatic examples could be found in his treatment of less recondite and academic subjects. For instance, there are alluring places where Kierkegaard embarks upon an examination of conventional social, religious, political, and even sexual concepts and comportments. After all, how could any consideration of the self achieve coherence if it failed to take seriously these fundamental modes of its existence? It would be difficult to deny, however, that at first glance his most incisive political commentaries, to take but one of these topics, seem to go in the direction of a dubious complacency regarding absolutist and undemocratic forms of authority and power. Perhaps even more difficult to accept without qualification would be Kierkegaard's recurrent references to the way every subject is implicated in the play of sexual difference and politics. No concept of the self can be separated from a thinking of sexual difference, and Kierkegaard's self is certainly no exception.

The theme of romantic love is illustrated in several texts, usually based on a conventional distinction, taken straight from the code of chivalry, between the active male protagonist and a passive female accompanist, such as in "The Diary of the Seducer," or *Repetition*. And there is the overtly metaphorical use of sexual difference to characterize and advance philosophical arguments, such as the opening to *The Concept of Irony*, where Kierkegaard playfully recasts the Hegelian relation between philosophical observation and the phenomenon to be observed and conceptualized as an interpersonal scene of seduction and domination: "it is fitting for the phenomenon, which as such is always *foeminini generis*, to surrender to the stronger on account of its feminine nature" (*CI* 47). However sorry such affirmations appear on the level of sexual politics, to the extent that the actual subject under discussion is not sexual difference per se but something very different, for which commonplaces of sexual difference furnish a ready and merely approximate analogy, it becomes impossible ultimately to decide whether recourse to such gender stereotypes is itself conventional, and therefore contingent, or on the contrary an essential feature of Kierkegaard's thought.

Even in texts where the question of sexual difference is confronted directly, such as *The Concept of Anxiety*, to take one important example, the contextual apparatus can become so entangled as to render definitive judgments highly risky and open to misunderstanding. On the one hand, Kierkegaard goes out of his way to promise an entirely new approach to the subject: "The whole question of the significance of the sexual . . . has undeniably been answered poorly until now."[14] For Kierkegaard, the concept of anxiety is itself unthinkable outside a consideration of original sin, and any consideration of this type of sin—a constituent characteristic of human finitude that has little to do with actual behavior in the first instance—must take sexual difference and sexuality into account from the outset. Anxiety is possible only from the moment consciousness becomes aware of its finitude, finitude also being indissociable from the body and the sexual difference expressed through it. On the other hand, Kierkegaard will also mention his intention to develop at more length later in the book "in what sense woman is the weaker sex, as it is commonly said of her, and also that anxiety belongs to her more than to man" (*CA* 47). And when Kierkegaard does return to this topic in a subsequent chapter, he will indeed expound upon several commonplaces associated, empirically as well as conceptually, with women. "That woman is more sensuous than man," Kierkegaard assures us, "appears at once in her physical structure" (*CA* 64). Modestly eschewing a more detailed pursuit of just how this difference would become apparent physiologically, Kierkegaard instead develops the concept from an aesthetic and then an ethical perspective. From the point of view of aesthetics, woman would be conceived as a "beautiful" silence; from that of ethics, she would be "procreative" fidelity. "Venus is essentially just as beautiful when she is represented as sleeping," Kierkegaard tells us, "perhaps more so, yet the sleeping state is the expression for the absence of spirit. . . . [S]ilence is not only women's greatest wisdom but also her highest beauty. . . . Viewed ethically, woman culminates in procreation. . . . Although it is also true that the husband's desire is for the wife, his life does not culminate in this desire, unless his life is wretched or lost" (*CA* 65, 66). No doubt, such a woman would have to do a great deal of sleeping indeed in order not to end up even more wretched and lost than such a man.

Still, the very facility with which we find such examples of an ideologically tired conception of sexual difference within a philosophical analysis that is in other essential respects incompatible with them should give us pause. In the case of Kierkegaard's discourse on sexuality, for instance, it is too easy to isolate those fragments of his texts that are readily understood, and then assimilate them to more general but equally familiar concepts taken from the larger tradition. Afterwards, it would be a simple matter of attempting to legitimate them, or to demystify them, depending on one's own taste in such matters. Far more difficult, but also more to the point of beginning to respond to the actual significance of the sexual within a general economy of subjectivity, would be to notice and develop the ways in which Kierkegaard's discourse on sexuality (or on religion, politics, or literary and philosophical productivity, for that matter) rests upon principles that risk upsetting and thus altering any conventional comprehension of it. The situation is in fact akin to the one that pits Hegel—with his emphasis on the objectivity of the System—against Kierkegaard—with his emphasis on the subjectivity of the Individual. In some respects, Kierkegaard's text is to Hegel's as Kierkegaard's conception of "woman" is to Kierkegaard's conception of "man." Or, better, if Kierkegaard teaches that the concept of systematic objectivity required by all thought depends in the final analysis on subjectivity in order to enter historical actuality in the first place, then there can be no simple relationship between man and woman as existential categories.

Thus, it is undeniable that many of Kierkegaard's most predictable and indefensible anthropological musings about the masculine/feminine relationship are grounded in his own very real and empirical *fear*: of being misunderstood and distorted in the first place, and then, of actual politics, sexuality, and women in the second. The philosophical arguments in which these musings are found, however, begin precisely where such empirical fears reach their limit. It is not his life, but each of Kierkegaard's writings, that begins anew in a kind of "fear and trembling" that is oddly *fearless* in proceeding to the outermost limits of its various "thought experiments."[15] We should be careful not to reduplicate unnecessarily the empirical Kierkegaard's fearfulness when we are ourselves confronted in his texts by paradoxical, absurd, or radically ironic conceptualizations requiring of our thought a fearlessness it is rarely able to exhibit all on its own.

For instance, in the case of sexual difference, the entire argument hinges upon the traditional concept of Adam's original sin, but in such a way that Kierkegaard's inflection of the Biblical text produces a difference that makes each one of the terms slightly unrecognizable in its turn. Adam is the first man, but what characterizes him as such in the creation narrative is his relation to Eve and their implication in a sin of subjective awareness at the "origin" of all subsequent human "derivation." What Kierkegaard refers to as "the secret of the first" is therefore an oxymoronic principle of derivation that is actually original to the entire race (*CA* 30). What remains an impenetrable secret is how the concept of the origin can be made accessible to thought only in the form of a derivation, a secret which doesn't make the desire to grasp this origin any the less powerful. On the contrary; the secret turns out to be what produces history as an infinite, and infinitely frustrated, task of disclosure. For Kierkegaard, then, sexuality would be a knot in which subjective consciousness, sexual difference as consciousness of the other, and human history as radical finitude are all inextricably named and simultaneously put into unstoppable motion. As Kierkegaard repeats over and again, at the beginning of the race, capable of appearing only with "the suddenness of the enigmatic," is Adam. But it is also the case that this particular enigma named Adam cannot be recounted, much less understood, outside his paradoxical relation to the entire race, which is also to say, his relation to Eve in the very first place. The secret originality of Adam's story is the way it can be unraveled only in its sexual derivation from Eve and the social history they engender together: "Adam is the first man. He is at once himself and the race. . . . He is himself and the race. Therefore that which explains Adam also explains the race and vice versa" (*CA* 29). The term that stands between Adam and the race in this formulation, and without which neither the race nor Adam would ever become comprehensible, is of course Eve.

As innocence, as sleeping or dreaming spirit before it awakens to its own difference as spirit, Adam already names Eve, albeit unknowingly, or in the deflection of an anxious ignorance that both names and conceals sexual difference as such. In Kierkegaard's reading of the Biblical narrative, sleep is not just an anesthetic applied to Adam in order to create Eve from one of his ribs: sleep is the entire existential category that Adam inhabits before his awakening to Eve is posited through sexual difference, hers as well as his. "In innocence," Kierkegaard says, "Adam as spirit was a dreaming spirit. . . . In the moment spirit posits itself, it posits the synthesis, but in order to posit the synthesis it must first pervade it in all its difference, and the ultimate point of sensuous difference is the sexual" (*CA* 49). The Biblical text, along with its entire exegetic tradition, is itself a *fact* of history that Kierkegaard refuses to reduce to the status of a mere fiction or myth. However, he insists on reading them in such a way that Adam must now be understood simultaneously as himself and as his other, as becoming a self only by passing through his own sexual difference in his relation to Eve.

Thus, one could not begin to understand, much less demystify, something like Kierkegaard's concept of sexual difference without first being able to account for the way in which whatever is eventually said about women is also to be understood as man's own original possibility, and vice versa. Man enters history as a woman: the incomprehensibility of the proposition must constitute an endless object for reflection or else become a new temptation of the serpent, who—according to the same text—has always "tempted writers to be clever" (*CA* 48). To the extent that the concept of anxiety names a necessary awakening to the derived and therefore enigmatic status of every generation of human subjectivity—as an individual as well as a member of a given group, that is, of every single difference—the concept of woman also names not only the origin of Adam's own sexual, and therefore derived, awakening, but also the possibility of generating his subsequent history from that point on. In the course of her commentary on sexual difference in Kierkegaard, Sylviane Agacinski characterizes the necessarily gendered aspect of this situation as "a constitutional bisexuality," one of whose principal effects would be the futile attempt to define and therefore separate masculine and feminine traits from each other.[16] There is, in the first instance, no self that is either male or female, since the self can awaken—in other words, begin to exist consciously—only as a result of finding itself in a relationship partaking of both feminine and masculine elements.

That the question—of the self, of sexual difference, and finally of all human history—is itself generated in contradiction, or generates an ongoing contradiction within itself because it is able to isolate and refer to one element in the relation only by its deflection and derivation through all the others, Kierkegaard himself, his own conventional and ideological discourse notwithstanding, saw clearly. "At every moment [I ethvert Øieblik]," he has no trouble admitting, "the individual is both itself and the race. This is man's perfection viewed as a state. It is also a contradiction [en Modsigelse], but a contradiction is always the expression of a task [men en Modsigelse er altid Udtryk for en Opgave], and a task is movement [men en Opgave er Bevægelse]. . . . First in sexuality is the synthesis posited as a contradiction, but like every contradiction it is also a task, the history of which begins at that same moment [Først i det Sexuelle er Synthesen sat som Modsigelse, men tillige, som enhver Modsigelse, som Opgave, hvis Historie i samme Øieblik begynder]" (*CA* 28, 49; *SKS* 4:335, 354). The individual has a history or, better, engenders the movement of a history, in the instant that sexual difference is assumed as a task rather than a simple given. The task, as always for Kierkegaard, is the recognition of the truth of subjectivity, but the truth of this subjectivity is also always derived, like sexual difference, from a given relation of the self to the other.[17]

Another name Kierkegaard uses to characterize the situation is *passion*. Passion, though, is not an easy thing—concept, term, experience—to grasp in Kierkegaard. It signifies at one and the same time, scandalously, the exemplary story of self-sacrificing love recounted in Christ's passion *as well as* the natural power of the self's erotic inclination and desire. Passion thus names infinity's sacrifice of itself in finitude, its bearing witness to finitude's infinite potential beyond itself, and finitude's own desire for itself, its will to lose itself in and as its own or another finitude. As such, Kierkegaard's passion is, like his concepts of anxiety or despair, indicative of a most peculiar kind of synthesis between consciousness and the body. A synthesis continuously interrupted, passion would be a "synthesis" of consciousness and body always available only in contradiction with itself, and thus always engaged in surpassing itself wherever it truly exists.[18] But passion also appears in a particular idiom—*passio* in Latin, *Leidenschaft* in German, *Lidenskab* in Danish—and the particularity of the word enriches and complicates the situation a great deal in Kierkegaard's texts. In the word for *passion*, Kierkegaard hears and repeats, by way of etymological relays, the *passivity* of a suffering that he attributes to the passion of both self-sacrifice and erotic inclination.[19] The truth of subjectivity is ultimately this truth of its suffering, of its passivity, and of its vulnerability with respect to another, even if this other at first seems only like another self, or a self divided. *Passion* is therefore always another word for the way in which the self endures the openness of a wound. But however *passive* passion is, in the sense of its enduring a suffering that is necessarily occasioned by a collision with its other, it is also necessary, according to Kierkegaard, to recognize how *active* passion must be in order to sustain to the end the passage of this shock. The wound that passion opens is always passive to the extent that it can only be inflicted upon the subject from outside the self's own limits. But this vulnerability to the outside can also be freely assumed by the subject, can become a mode of suffering activity, or patience, on the part of the subject. Kierkegaard's *passion* therefore lies beyond any strictly philosophical understanding of the founding distinction between active and passive, agent and patient, and thus intention and accident, since it also names the place where the presumed distinction between self and other is eclipsed by their mutual implication and undoing.

Whether it is Christ's passion that entails his suffering and sacrifice on the cross, or the self's passion for itself or another in the erotic mode of longing or belonging, or the passion of the intellect to discover and assimilate whatever lies beyond it, passion always names the paradox of its own undoing: "one should not think slightingly of the paradoxical; for the paradox is the source of the thinker's passion, and the thinker without a paradox is like a lover without feeling: a paltry mediocrity. But the highest pitch of every passion is always the will to its own downfall" (*PF* 46). It is for this reason that the *Philosophical Fragments* can begin with only one thought, that of the ultimate downfall of the self in its own death: "I stand ready to risk my own life. . . . I have only my life, and the instant a difficulty offers I put it into play. . . . [F]or my partner is the thought of death" (*PF* 6–7). The final truth of subjectivity, always dependent for its very existence upon the force of its passion for the other, is not just its patient suffering; it is as well its active willingness to encounter the thought of its own death.

But what could it mean for the subject to think its own death? In other words, what can we, whose passion is thought, still learn from Kierkegaard, if all he eventually teaches us about the truth of subjectivity is the necessity of thinking our own death and dissolution, which also names the undoing or the disaster of all thought?[20] The question is no longer adequate to the occasion of its enunciation. For, as an incommensurable difference that for once cannot even be questioned, death exceeds the question-and-answer structure of thought at every point. Death is what makes asking and answering questions possible, but death is itself never a real question or answer to anything. As soon as thought would grasp death in its passion it would by the same token reduce this radical difference to itself once again. And the same goes for any passion through which the self is truly opened to something else, whether in the mode of epistemological, religious, or erotic passion. From one perspective, Kierkegaard's text always appears poised in this way between the same dreary alternatives: either the subject deceives itself by refusing the thought of its own death, and thereby lacks the passion necessary to pass into actual existence in the first place; or else the subject embraces in its passion the thought of its own death, and thereby necessarily reduces the otherness of death to a philosophical equivalent whose claim to mastery is the biggest deception of all. Either way, the wound of death is closed upon itself and makes no real difference to the self. Whether one accepts the thought of one's death, or one refuses the thought of one's death, one will regret it either way, since

but will, God

in neither case will it ever be possible to encounter the actual difference death has to make in one's own existence.[21] Or else again—and here would lie the truly Kierkegaardian alternative—no longer assimilable to the question-and-answer structure of a pedagogical dialogue or a philosophical dialectic, passion turns into something altogether different: faith.

In this context, Kierkegaard's use of the word *faith* can only be called ironic. The one thing the self must do in order to pass into existence is to endure and embrace—in passion—the thought of its own death. But this the self either will not or cannot do on its own, as a self-identical subject; that is, it cannot do it unless the self is given, from elsewhere as it were, the occasion to open itself to the absolute alterity of death in an act, an event, of faith. Faith, though, as an operation of subjective belief rather than a calculation of objective knowledge, understanding, or reason, is itself inconceivable outside the very first-person paradigm it also excludes: *I* believe, says faith. There can be no faith outside the speaking subject who is its agent, but the self who begins to speak in this way always becomes the agent of its own passion, downfall, and death. In passion and death, I believe, and so I always say my belief in my own death out loud before all others. Such belief, despite its necessary reliance on the first person singular, in no way can be said to originate in the subject who speaks it. Rather, it is the subject that is subjected to and consequently always paradoxically free to believe and answer for—or doubt and refuse—precisely the one event that is by definition beyond its own ability to control or know for sure: death.

Faith is thus a mode of witnessing, in the sense of testifying before others about the truth of an event that could never be demonstrated beyond the shadow of a doubt. Faith certifies the singular event of its own belief; it speaks aloud and gives its word to others about something to which it alone is privy, and that therefore might otherwise disappear without a trace. Without itself ever being the ultimate source of the secret truth for which it must vouch, faith becomes a potential source for the continued possibility of such truth to speak, even if this also means at the same time and for the same reason that this truth can always endure aberrantly as indirection, misperception, distortion and dissimulation, or even genuine deception. Faith is therefore the shadow that stands between certitude and doubt, the belief that continues to speak about certitude in the face of all possible doubt.

In Kierkegaard, the hidden event that lies in this way beyond the mastery of any subject, the shadowy secret to which the subject constantly bears witness in its faith, is the rapport between the self and its absolutely other, that

is to say, the wound of death conditioning the self in its relation to everything else. Faith is the way the subject relates to, or testifies to—rather than
knows, fears, flees, understands, embraces or negotiates with—its own death
in its relation to others. In faith the subject must say "I" (believe), but what
the I actually does when it speaks in this way before all others is attest to the
originary experience of its own demise. What can only be called ironic here
is that Kierkegaard designates the concept of faith—the necessity that the
"I" bear witness in its own name to a secret it alone, in its absolute singularity, possesses—as the sole means of access the subject will ever have to its
own dissolution and death. The only way the self can relate to its own death,
which is also the condition of its passing into existence, is for it not to disappear entirely in silence, but rather to continue to speak to others in a certain
way.[22] To call this situation ironic, however, merely serves to beg the question until we have secured a stable meaning for the philosophical concept of
irony. But it was precisely such a concept that *The Concept of Irony*, by speaking
about it in a certain way, forever altered and placed beyond all philosophical
conceptualization. Like faith, irony in Kierkegaard also names, in its own
concealed way, the obligation that the subject bear witness to its own undoing
in order to exist in the first place. The enigmatic figure Kierkegaard uses in
Philosophical Fragments to convey this irony of faith is *autopsy*: "for the believer
is always in possession of the *autopsy* of faith; he does not see through the
eyes of another, and he sees only what every believer sees—with the eyes of
faith."[23] Faith functions as a kind of eye witnessing; or rather, faith, since it
is a discourse of belief and not in any way a "perception," always testifies in a
hypothetical mode, *as if* it had actually seen something with its very own eyes,
in an autopsy. Faith testifies to whatever can no longer be there to be seen
firsthand with any eyes, and is thus always at risk of eluding us altogether.
Faith is a mode of testimony that not only enacts its own belief but also asks
to be believed, taken at its word, or credited by others in its turn.

But since what the subject always swears in faith to have "seen" for itself
is also its own passion and fall, its opening unto the absolutely other that
can never simply be witnessed as such by the self, faith is also a speaking
that must, in the *other* sense of autopsy, give retrospective testimony before
others about its passing away. In faith's autopsy, the I speaks of its encounter
with absolute otherness, speaks of this collision in such a way that the I is
no longer there as an integral self, and so finally speaks of itself only as another, in the third person. The reason it would no longer suffice to call such
a characterization of faith "ironic," at least not in the colloquial, rhetorical,

or even properly philosophical sense of the term, is that Kierkegaard had already in his thesis, and despite his own intentions, also acknowledged that in irony, too, one ultimately bears witness to one's own demise. With respect to the speaking subject, Kierkegaard concedes midway through *The Concept of Irony*, irony severs consciousness from itself, compelling the subject to speak meta-ironically, from beyond its own grave, as it were: "the ironic nothing is that deathly stillness in which irony appears again and haunts [Ironien gaaer igjen og spøger] (this last word taken wholly ambiguously as both a haunting and a jesting)" (*CI* 275; *SKS* 1:296).[24] The last word, whether it be given to irony or to faith in Kierkegaard, and no matter how playfully (or piously) the expression can be taken, will always return to haunt the subject whose death continues all the same to speak through it.

One of the most extraordinary examples of such a subject is Kierkegaard's Antigone, whose sketch appears in the first volume of *Either/Or*.[25] Although the text is very short—it is a fragment of a fragment, in fact—it deserves extensive analysis. The text on Antigone occupies a position of privilege in Kierkegaard's writing, since it provides a critical transition between his thesis on irony, which proposes to analyze Socrates as the classic model for self-conscious subjectivity in Western philosophy, and his later books, such as *Fear and Trembling*, *Philosophical Fragments*, and *The Concept of Anxiety*, where the truth of subjectivity is embodied in Judeo-Christian figures. Kierkegaard's Antigone is in this way the matrix out of which philosophy's ironic subject can be reborn in the mode of religious subjectivity and faith. Or, rather, Antigone names the rearticulation of a certain concept of irony with a highly idiosyncratic and unorthodox reading—Kierkegaard's *repetition*—of Christianity.[26] Kierkegaard's Antigone will thus remain barely recognizable as the familiar figure of an older tradition. Uprooted into a "modernity" that Kierkegaard carefully insists *has not yet arrived*, this Antigone recollects far less for us the Greek context to which she originally belonged than she announces, and even preempts, some of the radically new features that will later be attributed by Kierkegaard to Adam, Abraham, and the Christian par excellence.

Like Adam, Antigone will be haunted for Kierkegaard by an anxiety whose sorrowful character must be appropriated in an originary mode of guilt and sin, inherited in this case from the house of Oedipus. Like Abraham, Antigone will also be subject to a law of absolute silence; through a faithfulness that remains secret, both Abraham and Antigone separate themselves definitively from all living beings.[27] And, according to the narrator of this peculiar little text, whose own identity is designated, and therefore also concealed, by the initial *A*, the essential difference—or "break"—that serves to distinguish the "modernity" of this Antigone-always-yet-to-come from all other ancient or modern tragic figures, past and present, consists in her mode of "self-consciousness." This Antigone is a figure for the truth to the extent that each and every aspect of her "activity" (*Handlen*) will have to issue from a fully self-conscious and reflective mode of subjectivity. For according to the narrator, A, what has until now always eluded the self-consciousness of the ancients *as well as* the merely contemporary moderns, and what will bring his—or is it really *her?*—Antigone so much closer to a future Abraham and Adam than to her ancient Greek kin, will be the particular mode of her *suffering.* A fully self-conscious suffering, or *Liden*, then, will have to mark the secret truth of subjectivity's activity, or *Handlen*, in modernity. But is such a unique concatenation of action and suffering—of activity and passivity (*Handlen og Liden*)—not also the moment in which Antigone's unspeakable pain and anxiety begin to reflect, in advance as it were, what Kierkegaard will later characterize, in the *Fragments* for example, as the religious subject's necessary *passion?* What A will finally call in this text Antigone's "extraordinary passion [overordentlig Lidenskab]" is not her passion alone, moreover, but the passion of the exemplary Christian as well.

Now, this text on Antigone, "The Ancient Tragic Reflected in the Modern Tragic," is not just a fragment in the ordinary sense of the word. It is subtitled "A Venture in Fragmentary Endeavor," it describes its subject as the fragmentation, the crucial *break* occurring in the historical development of the tragic, and it also interrupts itself in the middle of the first part of its exposition, digressing at length upon its stated aim to indulge in "fragmentary pursuit" at the expense of "coherency." So the text on Antigone is not only a tiny fragment considered within the total context of the first volume of *Either/Or*, it also arrests the development of its two principal subjects in order to reflect—to the second degree as it were—upon the fragmentary nature of its own genre, and it ends by shattering into at least three disparate parts. It comprises a reflection on antique tragedy and the kind of modern tragedy that has been produced to date, a reflection on a modern tragedy that is yet to come, and the actual interruption of both of these reflections by the narrator, who self-consciously reflects upon his own writing of this text at precisely the moment where the first reflection should be joined to the second reflection. Curiously enough, it seems that the more the text reflects upon its stated subject, the more it breaks off into fragments of reflection. Reflecting upon the fragmentation inherent to the historical development of the tragic, Kierkegaard's text can only interrupt itself in a series of unfinished digressions. Just what kind of secret pact joins the truth of subjectivity, which is always characterized by Kierkegaard as a fully self-conscious mode of reflection, to this strange economy of fragmentation, which is also an economy of passion?

Among the different ways the Danish word *Reflex* functions in the essay's title, "Det Antike Tragiskes Reflex I det Moderne Tragiske," there occurs a very particular reflection between Antigone's "extraordinary passion" and a brief comment made earlier by the narrator. The comment is not, however, about ancient tragedy at all. A mentions in passing that there exists a level of passion—an activity reflected fully in passivity, and vice-versa—that defies the aesthetic dimension of tragedy. Such passion would place the tragic beyond aesthetics altogether: The identity of an absolute activity and an absolute passivity [Identiteten af en absolut Handlen og en absolut Liden] is beyond the powers of the aesthetic. . . . In the life of Christ there is this identity, for his suffering or passivity is absolute, since its activity is absolutely free, and his activity is absolute passivity or suffering, since it is absolute obedience" ("Tragic," *EO* 1:150; *SKS* 2:149). How, exactly, is Christ's passion reflected, across the narrator's interruption on fragmentation, in the extraordinary passion of this Antigone-yet-to-come?

Mysteriously. Passion that defies aesthetics defies as well representation. And such passion can be reflected only mysteriously, in the mode of a secret shared by Christ and Antigone. The ultimate truth of subjectivity, its secret passion, can therefore be disclosed only in the fragments of the narrator's interruption of the philosophical exposition on tragedy, since such a secret is not susceptible to exposure by philosophy. This secret, which is their passion, is also what lends meaning to their life: "Perhaps nothing ennobles a person so much as keeping a secret. It gives a person's whole life a significance [en Betydning]" ("Tragic," *EO* 1:157; *SKS* 2:155). Kierkegaard's Antigone is such a person, or rather, the secret she keeps in her passion also makes her into such a person, gives to her a meaning that otherwise she could not have. Linked in this way to Christ, Antigone is called a "bride of God," keeping for the absolute Other a secret about what it means to be a human subject in the first place. According to A, this secret that keeps Antigone separate from all others, the secret to which she sacrifices *as well as* owes her life, is not in fact *her* secret at all: it is a secret she has inherited from another, Oedipus: "At an early age, before she had reached maturity, dark hints of this horrible secret had momentarily gripped her soul. . . . How she found out is extraneous" (1:154). The secret that one always inherits from and keeps for another is thus another

name for one's passion. Antigone accepts as her own activity this secret that
has been received in the first place from the other, passively.

Here, as well as in other texts by Kierkegaard, subjectivity's secret passion is also referred to as a mode of indebtedness or *guilt*. It is a "suffering"
or "passivity" that not only endures the weight of its burden (*lider derunder*),
but also "participates" in it actively ("men baerer Skylden med, particiferer i
denne"; "Tragic," *EO* 1:159; *SKS* 2:158). What is so peculiar about the secret
Antigone owes her father Oedipus, which she keeps for him alone and which
in turn also keeps her separate, secret, from everyone else, is that even the one
who has given it to her does not seem to know exactly in what it consists. Or,
at the very least, he cannot be said to know exactly what is being concealed by
the secret he will eventually share with her. The secret that binds Antigone
actively to her father, the one from whom, passively, she has inherited her
own life as well as its secret meaning, is something that they "share" without
knowing it. Their bond is not just the "secret"; secret as well is the bond
of their passion that, in uniting them, also escapes all positive knowledge:
"Antigone knows everything; yet within this knowledge there is still a nonknowledge. . . . [A]bout one thing, she does not know, and that is whether or
not the father himself knew" (1:161).

Whether or not the father knew, he passes on to the child the burden of
this secret, and the child, according to the text, becomes a subject in her own
right only by accepting the weight of this incomplete and therefore fragmented knowledge about her relation to someone else. She can be herself
only by carrying the burden of another, and the exact content of that burden,
measured as both guilt and indebtedness, can never be made fully known
to her. Strangely enough, though—through an extra twist, or reflection, of
sexual difference—she now becomes not just a subject as child, but a subject
as *mother*. Compared at one point to the "bride of God," Kierkegaard's Antigone appears primarily as the daughter of Oedipus, but she is also sister to a
dead brother, Polyneices, and beloved of still another, Haemon. Nonetheless,
at a crucial moment of the essay, the burden she carries transforms her into a
mother, a *virgin* mother in fact: "she is *virgo mater*; she carries her secret under
her heart, concealed and hidden. . . . *She knows no man*" ("Tragic," *EO* 1:158;
emphasis added). The family relationships in this text, each of them redou-
bled by specific elements of sexual difference, are, as always in Kierkegaard,
exceedingly complex. Nonetheless, given that one of the stated objectives of
the essay is to illustrate "the dialectic that connects the individual to the family" so that "the individual sees the inherited characteristics as a component

of its truth" (1:160), one should not gloss over them lightly. The reference to the virgin mother, for instance, is also a reference to the Virgin Mary, the earlier reference to Christ's passion reflected yet again in Antigone's passion, which also becomes a displaced version of Mary's passion beginning with the Annunciation. Still, there is another sense in which the phrase "she knows no man" should be read—it is not simply a question of sexual virginity here. In the passion of her secret, Antigone is separated in an essential way from *every* living being, no matter what their gender or relationship to her: "she feels alien to humankind" (1:161).[28]

But how can a mother, even a virgin mother, remain alien to those very ones she brings into the world, her own children? Because such a mother, conceived herself from a secret inheritance and conceiving in turn a new child from out of this secret self, always gives birth to another secret.[29] The child is a secret, whose own birth coincides with a radical separation from the parent. The separation is what can be said to "join" parent and child in their shared secret, and by the same token it fractures whatever sense of autonomy each might otherwise believe could have been theirs. At least, this seems to be the mysterious story that is told, or rather acted out, by the narrator, A, in the space of the interruption that occurs between the first and second parts of the essay, that is, between the ancient tragic that is no longer there, and the modern tragic that has not yet occurred in the figure of Antigone.

Antigone, of course, doesn't just name the daughter of Oedipus in the ancient tragedy; she will also have been the child of the parent and narrator, A, who is going to produce her in this very essay: "She is my work. . . . She is my creation, her thoughts are my thoughts. . . . I put words into her mouth" ("Tragic," *EO* 1:153). And in keeping with a certain tradition of authorial identity, A even alludes with pride to the "*paternal* prejudice" he feels in considering his new child, Antigone (1:162). On the other hand, A's recourse to a rhetoric of authority at precisely the moment Antigone makes her appearance in the text also testifies to a more profound and original uncertainty on his—or *her*—part about occupying the "paternal" position claimed.[30] In fact, A states unequivocally at another point, whatever chance remains for a "rebirth" (*Gjenfødelse*) of ancient tragedy in modernity, it remains only by reason of the individual's relation to the family and race, and this relation or tie (*Forbindelse*) must pass through the specificity of the mother's body: ". . . a rebirth, not only in the spiritual sense but in the finite sense of the womb [Modersliv]" (1:159; *SKS* 2:158). It may indeed be true, as A says of Antigone, that the "father is always in her thoughts" (1:161), but it is also the case that *this* thought, of the father, must function as the secret place in which Antigone becomes a virgin mother and gives birth in her turn: "Her father is always in her thoughts, but how—that is her painful secret."

In those thoughts of the father resounds an echo, a reflection and a repetition, of the way A had already claimed to have given birth to Antigone with his/her own thoughts in the first place: "She is my creation, her thoughts are my thoughts" ("Tragic," *EO* 1:153). A is the "father" of Antigone and gives her his thoughts; and so, of course, the father has to be constantly in her thoughts. But *how*, that is her painful secret, as well as his, it turns out. For in the most peculiar twist of all, A him/herself will be reborn through the creation of Antigone's secret, reborn out of *her* thoughts, though reborn in the mode of a new secret for him and her both. After recognizing the need in modernity for renewal and rebirth (*Fornyelse og Gjenfødelse*), A introduces Antigone and immediately confuses all the family and gender roles. Gone once and for all is the possibility of telling the difference between mother and father, parent and child, self and other, active and passive, masculine and feminine, agent and patient. The moment Antigone comes into the world, it becomes impossible for A to say with certainty who gave birth to whom, to say for sure which is which or who speaks for whom, and so it becomes all the more hopelessly urgent for A to stake a claim to legal ownership: "She is my creation, her thoughts are my thoughts, and yet it is as if in a night of love I had rested with her, as if she had confided, entrusted to me a deep secret. . . . I put words into her mouth, and yet it seems to me as if I abused her trust or confidence. . . . She is my property, she is my lawful property, and yet at times it is as if I had cunningly crept into her confidence and trust, as if I always had to look behind me for her; and yet it is the reverse, she is always in front of me" (1:153). The passage makes it impossible to decide precisely where the secret originates, or whose trust would be abused in sharing such a possession. Nevertheless, in their common passion both self and other work together, though perhaps without knowing it, to produce a renewal and rebirth in the text.

The truth of the subject in Kierkegaard is therefore the law of this secret, a secret always shared between self and other, though shared in such a way, abusively, that it remains hidden in front whenever one looks behind for it, and vice versa. Neither self nor other can ever have full access to its own origin or end in the secret sharing of both. As a law of property that is also a law of both trust and abused trust (*Fortrolighed, misbrugte Fortrolighed*; *SKS* 2: 152)— that is, at bottom, *faith* (*Tro*)—this truth of subjectivity is always susceptible to the most wayward interpretations, manipulations, and misunderstandings.

That is, when all is said and done, it is always susceptible to *irony*. Nothing can stop this irony, Kierkegaard teaches us, since irony is the nothingness that always returns to jest and haunt. Even in Antigone's piety, in her trust, and faith, there is always the nonknowledge that can come back to haunt her as an ultimate inheritance from the other as father, or mother, or brother, or sister, or lover. That too is her secret, the very knowledge that what she now knows can never be shared with another; she knows no man and can be known by none. This secret is precisely the nonknowledge—of self and other—that lies in what can never be sufficiently revealed, as knowledge or as teaching, much less in writing. Which is another way of naming her secret: death.

What Antigone, the modern subject yet to come, knows without being able to say or teach directly, is a secret about death: "our Antigone's life, on the other hand, is essentially at an end. . . . She, too, although alive, is in another sense dead; her life is quiet and concealed" ("Tragic," *EO* 1:156–57). This is the secret she keeps for another, the debt she owes and that alone will make her into a self in the first place. It is also the secret in which the other keeps her. The secret that always keeps her, that keeps her from herself as well as from all others, quietly, is the death that is always shared with another. Shared, not in the sense of a revelation or disclosure, but rather shared by entering into the other's death, as an always returning impossibility that quietly haunts the living self, who can therefore share it only incompletely and in an unfinished mode.

And this, ultimately, is what Kierkegaard teaches in each of his texts, if it still makes any sense to call that teaching. This is the reason the narrator of this text, A, speaks only to and of those who are dedicated to "fragmentary pursuit." Those to whom the text is addressed do not form a community, a family, or a race. They are not members of some group that would be fragmented in the sense of currently experiencing the deprivation of a greater whole or totality to which they might at some other point have belonged in the past, or may belong in the future. They are, all together and each alone, fragmented in the much more original and definitive sense that what they share is nothing other than this secret death—quietly concealed. And so the narrator coins a term for speaking, or writing, to all those who come together only in the shared secrecy offered by death: *Symparanekrōmenoi*.[31]

The ones to whom A addresses this text, however, are not on that account any the less lively or living; indeed, they seem to be flourishing. At each and every Friday meeting, in fact, the entire company of these entombed ones (*Begravne*) undergoes renewal and rebirth (*Fornyelse og Gjenfødelse*). But the initiation into this indefinitely repeated encounter among the dead, no matter how closely it remains tied to certain mysteries, certain secrets, will not resemble familiar rituals of resurrection and salvation. Rather, acts of renewal and re-birth are predicated here on a mode of thought (*Tankegang*) that the narrator calls, again using a Greek word that, if not a neologism, is still rather bizarre in this context, *anakoluthiske*: "The art, then, is to produce . . . anacoluthic thought" ("Tragic," *EO* 1:152; *SKS* 2:151) *Anacoluthon* is a technical term of rhetoric; it names the interruption of one syntactical pattern, one grammatical construction by another before the first is allowed to complete itself. Like so much else in this text, it is a deviation, a rupture or a break within an overall movement that could otherwise be integrated into one system of meaning. In part, the word is perfectly suited to its context, since A indulges himself at this particular moment in a stylistic feat which the editors call a "periodic tour de force" (1:629), a continuous series of intricately interwoven subordinating clauses whose accumulated meaning denies the human possibility of ever achieving the kind of coherency that is so delicately achieved by its own grammar. In other words, the "anacoluthon" that is illustrated by this very passage would be the interruption of its rhetorical "coherence," or syntactic integrity, by the philosophical thesis of "fragmentation" articulated through it.

But the true interest of the anacoluthon here lies elsewhere.[32] What hangs in the balance of the anacoluthon is the potential of any given subject to construct itself meaningfully without exposing itself at the same instant to the threat of ceaseless distraction. In the case of Kierkegaard's text, we have seen how "Antigone" functions as the name for an anacoluthon that keeps her from ever coinciding with her own destiny—since the only thing she knows about her own origin is a secret that is now aggravated rather than appeased by its broken reflection, that is, its ungovernable dispersal, in a modernity that is always to come. The truth of Antigone's subjectivity, whatever else it is, is also that of such an anacoluthon. To the extent that she must recognize her truth in an ineradicable debt to an inaccessible other, Antigone's future can be constructed only by a detour through this hidden inheritance. But as a result of this construction of self that is also permanently interrupted through the other's secret, her coherency as a subject will become only increasingly fragmented.

Understood in this way, anacoluthon also names the interruption of subjectivity by its encounter with the wholly other: death. A company of the dead, *Symparanekrōmenoi* is by definition beholden for each renewal to the anacoluthic mode of thought—the thought of death being nothing but a thought of interruption, though an interruption that cannot itself be thought through to its completion, and thus always a secret remains. That is why the narrator of this text, A, specifies that the art of the *Symparanekrōmenoi* consists in producing a very particular kind of writing. A writing of the dead for the dead, for the constant renewal of the dead by the dead, such writing is always dedicated to the secret subject, the subject of the secret that lives only by returning to a thought of the dead, or a thinking that death always interrupts before it arrives at its appointed end or hour. Such writing, according to A, can be nothing but *posthumous*, no matter how alive its author; or, better, the more alive and lively the author, the more renewed and reborn, the more the writing will be posthumous: "Our society requires a renewal and a rebirth at every single meeting and to that end requires that its intrinsic activity be rejuvenated [forynges] by a new characterization of its productivity. Let us, then, designate our purpose as a venture in fragmentary endeavor or the art of writing posthumous papers [Lader os da betegne vor Tendens som Forsøg i den fragmentariske Stræben eller i den Kunst at skrive efterladte Papirer; posthumous papers, papers left behind]" ("Tragic," *EO* 1:152; *SKS* 2:151). To go on living by commemorating anew the dead and, especially, the dead that make the subject itself more and more alive to its unfathomable debt to the dead—that is no doubt what Kierkegaard would have left behind to be read in each of his texts. But it is readable there only in the mode of a proliferating secret, an anacoluthic flight of thought, interrupted and therefore concealed in its very unfolding, before it could ever manifest itself clearly, coherently, completely. And so it is also always prevented from becoming the finished construction of a perfectly autonomous and self-conscious subject—hence the need to leave it behind always again . . . only for others. But as papers left behind, posthumous writings are also, according to A, unfinished in another sense as well: they are untidy, negligent, indolent, careless and even slipshod in their relation to every path of thought (Tankegang). "Consequently, I will call what is being produced among us property left behind [Efterladenskab], or rather, artistic property left behind [kunstnerisk Efterladenskab]; negligence [Efterladenhed], indolence I will call the genius we commend" (*EO* 1:153; *SKS* 2:151–52). What Kierkegaard so artfully left behind will remain forever fragmented between the broken parts of these two Danish words, *Efterladenskab* and *Efterladenhed*, the first of which speaks of things that have been made only to be left behind, posthumous property, inheritance, estate; the second of which speaks of things that have been done only slovenly, perhaps in an inexcusably neglectful or distracted and careless manner. What does it mean,

Kierkegaard is asking, to leave behind for others precisely that which one has failed to accomplish, or to inherit from someone else a cache of papers that have been left unfinished and perhaps unfinishable? If his own posthumous writings can still teach anything, it would be that the secret of such an impossible legacy is always there for the taking.

Reading Kierkegaard: To Keep Intact the Secret

Taking another look at the way someone like Sylviane Agacinski reads Kierkegaard would be of considerable interest for a number of reasons. First of all, it helps to disclose the way that major philosophical writers such as Kierkegaard seem to engender in their wake at least two very different, perhaps incompatible, types of intellectual reception. On the one hand, there is the relatively coherent and self-contained body of scholarship around which a given community of academic specialists constitute themselves as both the members and the custodians. In the world of academe, it is easy enough to recognize the contours of a domain called "Kierkegaard studies," just as one refers in analogous fashion to Kant studies, Hegel studies, and even Nietzsche studies. What is always a bit surprising to notice in the case of Kierkegaard and Nietzsche, of course, is the ease and effectiveness with which an academic community of scholars is able to appropriate for itself figures whose own impact on institutionalized forms of philosophical inquiry stems in large measure from their indirect and highly equivocal relations to it. Or, rather, such impact stems directly from their position *outside* the academy—an outsider status that should be understood both in terms of their not finally belonging to any academic institution and in terms of the way their writings tend to put into question the very theoretical foundations upon which such institutions are erected and seek to endure. To judge by the number as well as by the kind of references made to her work within the community of Kierkegaard studies—but to judge as well by the near-total absence of reference in Agacinski's work to any Kierkegaard scholars—Agacinski should not in the first place be considered a member of it. This fact, if indeed it is one, remains of less interest in itself than for the way it would suggest a second kind of reception for Kierkegaard. A highly original and important book such as Agacinski's *Aparté*,[1] especially when reconsidered more than thirty years after its publication, suggests just how difficult it is for a given community of academic specialists to assimilate to itself those approaches to Kierkegaard's by-now "canonical" writings that do not in any way contribute to its own conservation as a scholarly establishment.

Another way to frame the same issue would be to return to those doubts Kierkegaard himself expressed concerning the degree to which anything relating to "the truth" actually admits of being learned.[2] As odd—and potentially arrogant—as it sounds, such a proposition nonetheless seems to lead to an ineluctable conclusion. If, as Kierkegaard suggests in *Philosophical Fragments*, there is a fundamental discrepancy between what he calls "truth" and "learning"—the goal toward which all scholarship is necessarily directed—then the reception of a figure such as Kierkegaard is bound to split into a community of academic scholars on one side and, on the other, those readings of Kierkegaard that, in the name of getting at the "truth" inscribed in his writings, eventually diverge from sanctioned methods of scholarly and pedagogical efficiency. It would be rather naïve, of course, to believe that one could simply bypass scholarly methods and techniques altogether; for only by acquiring the necessary competence to read Kierkegaard according to such standards could one reach the point in his texts where the category of understanding is no longer adequate to them. The task of reading Kierkegaard for the sake of the "truth" would then consist, at least in part, in encountering his writings in a different mode, one that would afford the most chance of remaining recalcitrant—or resistant—to whatever built-in resistance to the truth the academic community of Kierkegaard specialists must exhibit in order to establish themselves as a community in the first place. *Aparté*, then, would not just be the title of Agacinski's main contribution to reading

Kierkegaard; it would also name the position of self-imposed distance and separation that this reading of Kierkegaard stakes out for itself and then occupies with respect to any canonical reception of his texts.

And since *separation*, as distinct from a dialectical impulse toward mediation and integration, is precisely the motif that characterizes so much of what Kierkegaard wrote, it may by the same token offer a promising first step in determining which readings of Kierkegaard best resist assimilation to the most conventional methods of interpreting and understanding his work. But if it is true that Agacinski succeeds in reaching a level of Kierkegaard's text where what is at stake is no longer a matter of mere scholarship and knowledge but becomes instead a question of the "truth" as Kierkegaard himself used that term, that certainly does not mean that she alone has managed to keep her writing on Kierkegaard separate—or apart—from the didactic constraints under which all teaching and learning must take place. Nor should it be taken to mean that there is nothing didactically effective and therefore potentially learnable from her writings. In fact, rather than employing this most conventional of didactic techniques, that of clearly and neatly dividing the reception of Kierkegaard along two easily identifiable and mutually exclusive lines—as I have just done—a more judicious beginning might, for the sake of argument, ask about another kind of separation, or *aparté*, that reaches even further. Such an *aparté* might no longer allow for maintaining in univocal fashion a hard and fast line between "truth" and "scholarship," nor, as a consequence, the hypothetical line cleanly separating the "merely" academic and didactic readings of Kierkegaard from those that offer decisive resistance to them. In this case, taking another look at Agacinski's reading of Kierkegaard can also help to determine whether and to what extent she has been able to keep intact her separation from conventional methods of understanding in her own writing.

A possible means for undertaking such an assessment would be by first retracing Agacinski's affinity with another reader of Kierkegaard who seems to have made even less of a mark on Kierkegaard studies than Agacinski herself, and then taking stock, not only of certain features of *Aparté* itself, but also of three essays on Kierkegaard that Agacinski wrote in the years after the publication of *Aparté* in 1977. It was in December of 1941, a year before Albert Camus published his *Myth of Sisyphus* and nearly two years before Jean-Paul Sartre published *Being and Nothingness*, that Maurice Blanchot wrote a short piece published in the *Journal des débats* called "Le 'Journal' de Kierkegaard."[3] It would obviously make little sense to place the beginning of what has in the meantime become fashionable to call "postmodernity" *before* the avowedly "modern times"[4] of French existentialism—which always claimed Kierkegaard as one of its own intellectual antecedents, moreover—but an argument could be made for considering this essay by Blanchot as one of the very first and most forceful encroachments upon a reception of Kierkegaard that would remain subservient to the didactic aims required by philosophical, theological, and literary criticism, and, for that matter, to the historical models of "modernity" and "postmodernity" which such disciplinary studies also tend to foster. In any case, it is this little-referred-to article by Blanchot that has clearly left an indelible mark on Agacinski's approach to Kierkegaard. "Like his entire authorship," Blanchot writes there, "Kierkegaard's *Journal* is dominated by the two figures upon which this extraordinary mind never abandoned its meditation, that of his father, a profoundly religious man whose later years were dogged by the memory of a double fault, and that of his fiancée, Regine Olsen, with whom he broke off his engagement after only a year. Revolving around these two images, his thought would search incessantly for itself, eventually extracting from them an entire world, the tragic response to a truly unintelligible universe" ("Journal," 25). A brief overview of Sylviane Agacinski's interpretation of Kierkegaard should thus begin by emphasizing the way she inherits from Blanchot precisely the concerns that he singles out for attention in this axiomatic portrait of the *Journal*'s author.

For Agacinski, Kierkegaard's writing first of all was and will remain a creative reaction that emerges from his contact with a world of *unintelligibility*; more specifically, it is a response to the peculiarly unintelligible forces that impinged upon his whole existence through the burden placed on him by the memory of the father, Michael Pedersen Kierkegaard, and the broken promise to his fiancée, Regine Olsen. The summons issued to him through the father's authority on one side, the obligation he felt to sacrifice the beloved on the other, combined, according to Agacinski, following in the steps of Blanchot, to provide Kierkegaard with an uninterrupted source of reflection for his own writing. What Kierkegaard had to but could not quite comprehend, what he fervently believed in without ever fully piercing, was the secret link that could have explained how, exactly, the painful memory of the father was connected to the perceived need to break with the fiancée.[5]

Put in terms of the two types of discourse most readily available to Kierkegaard for exploring this enigma through writing—which writing, always according to Blanchot and Agacinski, would eventually constitute the entirety of Kierkegaard's *universe*—his authorship was as though destined to take

place between the poles of Hegel's philosophical speculation on the one hand
and Abraham's religious faith on the other. What accounts for Kierkegaard's
irresistible attraction to these two figures is the way that, in both cases, the
possibility of moving forward, of entering into history in order to build a
genuine future there can be realized only by confronting and engaging with
a dynamic force of *negativity*. For Hegel, this means the dialectical negativity
that must look death in the face for the sake of what is absolute in thought,
and for Abraham, it means the religious negativity of a faith that must, for the
sake of life itself, sacrifice absolutely what is nearest and dearest in life. It is the
experience of this unrelieved tension between the negativity of thought and
the negativity of faith that nourished Kierkegaard's own authorship and that
orients the critical interest in Kierkegaard for both Agacinski and Blanchot.
However, as Blanchot also spells out in his short treatment of Kierkegaard,
to the negativity that is proper to thought and the negativity that is proper to
faith, Kierkegaard would be compelled to add a third mode of negativity, one
that may be related to both of the others without in the end being proper to
either of them: the negativity of *language* ("Journal," 28). It is no secret that
the idiom in which Kierkegaard created his written world is neither the dialectical exposition of philosophical thought nor the pure silence or invisibility
that should characterize the true knight of faith. Rather, his idiom is that of
a "poet" whose mode of language is necessarily one of "indirect communication" and in whose element philosophical and religious truth may appear
only "sequestered," or "incognito," like the pseudonymous authorship with
which his own signature remains forever indissociable.[6] It is for this reason
that Blanchot, immediately after claiming that Kierkegaard's most faithful
thought is dedicated to his father and to Regine, subtly indicates the one and
only mode in which such a commitment could ultimately become legible: in
the form of *images* whose own relation to reality will have been always already
displaced through the imaginative faculty of the poet from whom alone such
forms can issue.

Now, if it is exclusively in the indirect mode of images that Regine and the
father are allowed to enter and be kept in Kierkegaard's writing, then it will
be inevitable that, in order even to begin to assess and understand the meaning of their place there, it will become at some point necessary to develop
protocols of reading that are themselves geared specifically to the creation
and decipherment of poetic imagery. Readings of Kierkegaard that proceed
along disciplinary lines tend in the final analysis to presuppose that his writings could be treated as though they were, in essence, examples of philosophi-

cal, religious, sociohistorical, or autobiographical discourse, and that by the same token they can be effectively interpreted and understood as arguments, disquisitions, opinions, or disclosures; in short, as various kinds of *statements*. Agacinski, meanwhile, exhibits in nearly everything she writes a fidelity to the poetic and therefore literary dimensions in which each of these discourses— philosophical, religious, sociopolitical, and autobiographical—is actually carried out. Nonetheless, it would be an error to believe that Agacinski's attentiveness to what one could thus call the *rhetorical* dimension of Kierkegaard's writing precludes a serious engagement with all those other concerns. On the contrary, a truly serious consideration of Kierkegaard's signal contributions to philosophy, religion, history, and psychoanalysis could never afford simply to ignore or efface the fact that such contributions are themselves, always to a degree that remains to be determined, the result of a stylistic indirection whose effects are never negligible; nor are they reducible to disciplinary models of understanding that could be considered independently of their specifically linguistic constitution—even when the discipline in question would be named "literature."[7] In Kierkegaard, the faculty of the imagination is never simply in the service of philosophy, or any other circumscribable field or intention for that matter; the relation between the image and what it serves both to disclose and to conceal is finer and more unsettling than a straightforward equivalence between figure and concept, or sign and meaning.

A relevant case in point is exemplified by a lecture Agacinski delivered in Copenhagen not long after the publication of *Aparté*, entitled "La Philosophie à l'affiche" (When Philosophy Appears on a Signpost).[8] Taking her cue from a short aphorism found in the Diapsalmata of the first volume of *Either/ Or*, Agacinski demonstrates how Kierkegaard himself never lost sight of the curious manner in which philosophy depends on specifically linguistic factors and functions that it remains incapable of mastering completely. "What philosophers say about reality," the aphorism reads, "is often as disappointing as what one reads on a sign in a secondhand shop [*Marchandiser*]: 'Pressing Done Here.' If someone actually brought his clothes to be pressed, though, he would be deceived; for the sign is merely for sale."[9] The aphorism, Agacinski has no difficulty showing, points up the way that language always possesses a performative function that, operating in addition or next to its constative and cognitive dimensions, also serves to open up a rhetorical space that generates its own complexities and complications, some of which may indeed turn out to be wholly incompatible with its semantic and referential functions. Long before the British philosopher J. L. Austin reminded us of the problems posed by "performative utterances," Kierkegaard's analysis and use of indirect communication served as a cogent warning about the way such language can do things with the truth-value of the words it must use to convey its philosophical, theological, psychoanalytical, and sociopolitical content; things that no philosophy, theology, political science, or psychoanalysis could all on its own ever fully know, much less restate with unequivocal certainty.

The fact that Kierkegaard's witty aphorism just happens to take "reality" or "actuality" (*Virkelighed*) as its own target is yet another sign of what remains forever at stake in the performative function of language. For the *reality* of thought, faith, the self, or the state is precisely what such regional discourses as philosophy, theology, psychoanalysis, and political science will always need to claim as their principal justification as well as their ultimate and proper objects of study. However, to the extent that every "reality" must as such be susceptible to leaving a trace of its own existence in the world, no reality whatsoever will ever be wholly exempt from the potential displacements and "deceptions" brought into play by the properly linguistic, that is, "secondhand" context in which alone such a reality can first of all be registered and preserved as a trace. To go on from there in Kierkegaard's doubly pseudonymous text to suggest—as the aphorism penned by A and edited by Victor Eremita actually does—that one of these possible displacements will involve the economic *profit* to be gained by whatever individual or group is able to establish and then maintain proprietary control over this unruly context is by the same token to expose to critical analysis another layer of self-interest that makes the incentive for deceit all the more redoubtable and difficult to govern. Every sign, no matter where it is posted, can thus always and for a variety of ulterior motives serve to conceal precisely that reality that it also claims to communicate, though necessarily only by indirection, ruse, or pretense. "Reality" is not only a fundamentally hermeneutic issue of determining the limits of truth and illusion with all possible scholarly precision; it is in truth also a performative field of competing rhetorical forces, each vying with all the others to acquire and then keep the rights to assign reality's meaning a fixed place and a fixed value (or price) that would be anything but "rhetorical" in the common sense of the term.

For these same reasons, Agacinski's reading of this one fragment itself becomes an indirect figure for *Either/Or* as a whole, if not for Kierkegaard's entire authorship. But before assuming that such a figure would be just another example of synecdochal totalization, wherein an individual part promises, and rather economically at that, to grant access to the whole of meaning in which every other meaningful part can also eventually be subsumed, we should re-member the radically fragmented nature of this particular particle. For this fragment—which by itself indicates the way in which the meaning of "real-ity" and the means by which the reality of this meaning must be signaled can always and over and over again part ways—operates as a figure for the whole only to the extent that it also reveals the concealed manner in which the whole is constantly and anew coming apart. Thus it is, for instance, that the papers among which the Diapsalmata in fact had to be "found" before they could be published in this volume, though under a pseudonym randomly chosen by someone else—a certain Victor Eremita, the editor of the papers, whose aptitude for hiding is also signaled by the hermetic nature of his name—were themselves the "secret" contents of a writing desk. Now this writing desk, which is called a *Secretair* in Danish, was purchased by the editor, as distinct from the "author" of the papers, by Victor Eremita, then, rather than A, in a secondhand shop, *en Marchandiser*; and he acquired the writing desk without the slightest idea that it contained secret contents (*EO* 1:4–6; *SKS* 2:vi–ix). It is therefore not just the "sign" of philosophical reality deposited in the fragment of the Diapsalmata that has been uprooted from its proper site and that is henceforward used "merchandise" put on sale to whoever can afford to "pay," in other words *speak* or account for it. Rather, that single fragment, the Diapsalmata, the Papers of A, *Either/Or*, Kierkegaard's authorship as such—they *all* end up advertising or performing a meaning that is forever fractured to the precise extent that none of them can ever hope to arrest and therefore master or own the very meaning that they themselves put into play anew.

In fact, Victor Eremita himself "discovered" the hidden contents of the secretary only when they accidentally spilled out as it cracked open under the violent blow he administered when he decided to force it open with a hatchet. This "lucky blow" that revealed the concealed papers that Victor is now publishing occurred because he wasn't using the desk for writing at all, but rather as a hiding place for his money. When the drawer containing the money would not open the way it was supposed to, Victor lost his tem-per and "opened" the desk with an ax, but in the process he also exposed to view the mysterious papers that had been secretly deposited in the *Secretair* by someone else. That so many twists and turns, so many chance happen-ings, so many deviations from original intention to actual meaning, so much impatience and even violence would have to be involved simply to gain ac-cess to these papers—who would now dare to claim to pierce the meaning of their secret writing with any measure of assurance? Every new claim to break into the secret of their true value will only repeat the original exposure of the hidden cracks thanks to which Victor Eremita glimpsed an even more deeply buried reality contained within the *Secretair*. "For in the most rigorous sense," Victor concludes before deciding to publish his surprising discovery, "these papers, as is ordinarily said of all printed matter, are silent" (*EO* 1:12; *SKS* 2:xvi–xvii). Silent, of course, not in the trivial sense that they say nothing whatsoever—but in the much more profound sense that Socrates famously complained about in Plato's "Phaedrus" with respect to all writing. The papers published in *Either/Or* will continue to speak to whomever listens, that is, to whomever reads them. But they can do so only at the price of wandering further and further away from the lost and anonymous source of their actual "authority."

The "reality" of philosophical truth, religious faith, socioeconomic conditions, or the innermost self can as a consequence never be made accessible to thought beyond the reach of all rhetorical complication and deflection. In each and every case where such truth is at issue, the corresponding realities must always at least in part be treated as derived and therefore "secondhand" products—what in French would be referred to as *produits d'occasion*, articles of undetermined value that have somehow become detached from any "proper" site, or home. The force of the "occasion," that which makes all these realities secondhand and used products from the start, is of course the very particular displacement they must undergo in order to appear—for the very first time—in the "original" version of any given language. "Reality," Kierkegaard—or at least Kierkegaard's pseudonymous stand-ins—remind(s) us, is never made available to us except on what one might call an "occasional" basis. It is always only on the occasion of linguistic devices specific to this or that particular language—each of which is exceptional in this or that individual respect by comparison to all the "comparable" but nonidentical devices available to any other language—that we could ever hope to obtain any purchase on reality. Such "occasions" as are offered on a case-by-case basis, in this or that context or market, would therefore remain utterly unique and by the same token perfectly unreproducible anywhere else—despite the fact that they can never be prevented, on the contrary, from actually taking place elsewhere, though never in exactly the same way. Each "occasion" on which reality can be said to occur, then, always remains in some sense sealed within the secret compartment of some secondhand *Secretair*, which can always be sold and broken into yet again. Tied in an indisputable manner to the specific "occasions" on which alone such realities can occur, they defy their translation into all other idioms, or occasions, even and especially when, like the Danish word *Marchandiser*, moreover, they have actually been negotiated from somewhere else—in this case through a lateral transaction from French to Danish. Paradoxically enough, it is precisely the always secondhand and therefore occasional nature of these verbal commodities that constitutes their efficacy and durability as genuine material realities, as well as their unstoppable potential to lead us astray when they appear as written images within Kierkegaard's writings.

Considered from this perspective, the book called *Aparté* remains Agacinski's most important and sustained examination of the quasi-totality of Kierkegaard's writings. In the wake of her extended analysis of Kierkegaard's thesis *The Concept of Irony*, Agacinski explores the way philosophical, rhetorical, and personal indirection functions throughout Kierkegaard's *oeuvre* both to solicit and to frustrate traditional models of interpretation and understanding. In addition to the nearly fifty pages she devotes to *The Concept of Irony*, she offers incisive readings of *Philosophical Fragments, Fear and Trembling, The Concept of Anxiety, Repetition, Prefaces, The Point of View*, and the *Journals*. Other texts—such as *Either/Or, Stages on Life's Way, Concluding Unscientific Postscript, The Instant, Training in Christianity, Two Minor Ethico-Religious Treatises, Edifying Discourses*—are also referred to on occasion for the light they shed on Agacinski's main objects of study. While the book helps to establish Agacinski's place alongside some of the most innovative readers of Kierkegaard in the twentieth century, it also suggests the way that this place has itself become something of a problem for Kierkegaard scholarship. It does so both in terms of the indirection with which it has been treated by specialists of Kierkegaard since its publication and in terms of the indirection with which it treats, or does not treat, these scholars. Why, one should ask, does Agacinski go out of her way to eschew a direct engagement with earlier readings of Kierkegaard—her debt to Blanchot's reading of Kierkegaard constituting the one exception in this regard? Why does Agacinski write as though the originality of her own reading practice were itself something of a private matter? In other words, is there anything that would indicate that the *aparté* within Kierkegaard's writing necessitates her turning away, her stepping aside, *aparté*, from all those readings of Kierkegaard whose attention to the linguistic complications of his texts remains subservient in the final analysis to extratextual considerations? It could be that Agacinski's silence in this regard serves in its own way to displace pre-existing protocols that have been developed by the most canonical methods of philosophy, religion, political economy, literary criticism, and psychoanalysis in reading Kierkegaard. It could be that Agacinski's writing implies by omission that we must begin reading again from scratch, by taking stock of the way that Kierkegaard's writings contain the power to alter once and for all the languages of philosophy, religion, aesthetics, psychoanalysis, and political science in unpredictable and radically new ways.

There could be no better way to begin an answer to this question than to consider the particular manner in which Agacinski will broach the one question that no legitimate reading of Kierkegaard can afford to ignore: how is one to treat the category of *existence* in Kierkegaard's thought? If existence is in Kierkegaard the bottom line, the first and last word, this in no way implies that we have yet understood what is meant by existence in his writing, least of all, for instance, when we have succeeded in attaching the sempiternal adjective *existentialist* to his name in one form or another. The task that Agacinski has first of all set herself in *Aparté* is therefore to examine with care the philosophical and religious concepts of existence as Kierkegaard inherits and reworks them in dialogue with both Hegel and the main texts of the Biblical tradition. On the other hand, though—and this aspect is so intimately connected with the conceptual process that it threatens along the way to become indistinguishable from it—there is the actual "existence" of Kierkegaard as it was uniquely experienced by him and then forever inscribed indirectly in his writing through the twin figures of his father and Regine. It is at this point, moreover, that the concept and experience of *existence* together form an inextricable knot with what one could call the birth of the *image* in Kierkegaard's writing. For what will have to happen if the experience of one's own existence can become philosophically conceivable to the subject it alone will have constituted only *retrospectively*, if the singularity of subjective experience must somehow fade away into the generality of thought before it can be said to exist philosophically in the full sense of the term? This question constitutes the running debate in which Kierkegaard will engage with Hegel throughout his writings, always insisting that Hegel's conception of thought economizes unfairly on the individual existence in which it must somehow remain rooted. As a result, and precisely in order to wrest subjective existence away from the mummified state in which philosophical thought is obliged to place it simply in order to preserve it, Kierkegaard will always have recourse to reconceiving his existence, over and over again, in the oblique particularity of images whose effectiveness lies precisely in their capacity to resist such philosophical conceptualization. The *aparté* is therefore itself just such an image that Agacinski borrows from the theater in order to stage in her own writing those images that will have been engendered by Kierkegaard himself to resist the philosophical reduction of subjective existence to a merely objective concept or content.

At least one of the meanings of *Repetition*, whose subtitle is "A Venture in Experimental [*Experimenterende*] Psychology," will have to recall the rather curious experience of the self or psyche that is entailed in such *apartés*.[10] Possessing on its own no direct means of access to its inmost reality, subjective existence will therefore have to *experience* itself by *experimenting* with derivative reflections in which it must repeat and thus seek to recover itself, as if in an echo chamber. The most originary experience of the self is in this way always also a theatrical experiment, a representation in which subjective existence undergoes the unthinkable ordeal of having to find itself only in the deflected image of the other.[11] Every new image, as we are reminded at the Berlin Königstädter Theater that opens up in the middle of *Repetition*, thus becomes a turning aside from the philosophical tendency to drain existence of its actuality. But the price paid for entering into this private theater of the *aparté* is that experience "itself" ultimately appears as an endless succession of "exceptional" roles for which no original, and no definitive escape, can from now on ever be found. The origin and end of all the *apartés* thus remains forever concealed, cut off from the one whose very identity consists in performing them. Each role effectively inaugurates a new conception of subjective existence in its absolute particularity, but, as also becomes legible in *Repetition*—itself nothing but an increasingly digressive set of examples written to illustrate the kind of resistance that subjective existence must repeatedly offer to universalizing concepts such as, recollection, interiorization, and mediation—subjective existence, or one's "self," as it is called by one of the book's two abysally specular figures, is born to itself at the very same moment that it "keeps something inward, as a secret that it cannot explain" (*Repetition*, 229; *SKS* 4:153). Even the image of a religious point of view that would, presumably, at some extreme point of development, no longer require any merely aesthetic images in which to project itself will have to occur as yet one more role that is both experimented with and thus "experienced" in Kierkegaard's text, though like all the others, always only indirectly, incompletely, and therefore inadequately.

In Kierkegaard's writing, it is precisely the innermost depth of subjective existence that remains most inexplicably secret *to* the self. At this depth of self-secrecy, it would no longer make any sense even to attempt to establish a priority either for the "private" figures of father and fiancée or for the "universal" figures of God and Abraham that are all inscribed there as impossible figures for the exceptional experience of existence. Rather, *Kierkegaard* is itself the proper name for that originality wherein the exception and the universal have no meaning outside their hyperbolically differential and therefore mutually obliterating relation to one another. It would be just as legitimate in this case to suppose that Kierkegaard was compelled to invent the inexplicable relationship to his father and the equally inexplicable rupture of his relationship to Regine in order to provide himself with a particularly apt poetical image for the secrecy of all subjective existence, as it would be to continue to imagine that somewhere behind all of his philosophical and religious texts on the subject there stand concealed yet empirically verifiable autobiographical experiences that would one day be capable of illuminating them. To the degree that the self in Kierkegaard keeps a secret that it cannot explain, *period*, it will only ever be able to re-experience its own existence through the unintelligible touch of the other, in other words, as a mere *image*. The father and Regine are of course the readiest images at Kierkegaard's disposal for exploring such a touch—but each and every image, inasmuch as it inaugurates a genuine *aparté* within the secret depths of the self, will repeat this unintelligibility even as the self attempts with every stroke of the pen to use the image to touch and thereby regain hold over it.

What Kierkegaard constantly sought in the written images of his father and Regine was therefore most definitely *not* a faithful portrait of his father's or of Regine's existence. It was rather the displaced image of *himself*, and more particularly, the exceptional nature of that self whose "own" existence was in the first place unintelligible to itself as a strict consequence of its having been experienced most profoundly as an inexplicable secret. But what exactly is an "experience" that is in such a manner not experienced directly by the subject? In conformity with the way Kierkegaard was to develop the images of the father and Regine, such an experience will have to acquire certain general characteristics, and these characteristics will have to alter a philosophical understanding not only of the self, but of the wider context—of time and space—in which the experience of the self (and other) is rooted. When existence is experienced by the self only as the inheritance of a secret passed down from the parent, and a secret that, for the very same reason, can never be shared, that is, revealed as such even to the most intimate and trusted other, or fiancé(e), by necessity every conceivable understanding of history will be affected. For history is a philosophical concept that depends in the first and last instance upon a more stable and organic understanding of experience than is granted to it by Kierkegaard. What kind of history can result from an experience that can never become *present* to itself but can only ever be compulsively rehearsed in its very inaccessibility? Should one still call *history* that which challenges or even precludes the concepts of presence and process, disclosure and progress, cause and effect, concepts without which the most recognizable models of history would have to founder? These are questions Agacinski first broached in *Aparté* when she interrogated the more-than-curious status of temporality as it is modified by Kierkegaard's reworking of "original sin" in *The Concept of Anxiety*.[12] However, the full magnitude of the impact that Kierkegaard's characterization of original sin as "retrogressive" will eventually make, not just on the religiously teleological history of Christianity, but also, and especially, on every model of history as such, becomes apparent only in the second lecture Agacinski delivered in Copenhagen during the fall of 1981, entitled "Le Savoir absolu d'Antigone" (The Absolute Knowledge of Antigone).

Commenting mainly on another short text from the first volume of *Either/ Or*, "The Tragic in Ancient Drama Reflected in the Tragic in Modern Drama," Agacinski will develop the ways in which the experience of subjectivity as treated by Kierkegaard moves counter to the entire modern tradition, from Descartes to Hegel. According to Agacinski, that tradition, at least in its most massive and consistent development, thinks the subject on the basis of ever-ascending levels of self-presence and self-consciousness. Kierkegaard, however, displaces this emphasis on self-reflexive presence toward an acknowledgement of the always belated structure of what he—or, rather, the anonymous author of "The Tragic in Ancient Drama"—terms a *re-flex*. It is from within the confines of such a re-flex, or "echo," that every subject, originally conceived as "child," can ultimately know itself historically only by learning what it has already inherited through vestiges left behind from "other" members of the same family. In this way, Kierkegaard offers a wholly alternate model for history itself, since no generation is able to do anything more than "repeat" all the generations that have preceded it. If, for Hegel, the child is conceived as that which allows the parent, through its simple negation in the next generation, to return to itself in the future unfolding of higher and higher layers of self-consciousness, in Kierkegaard the child becomes the locus where the parent's own lack of self-consciousness is somehow handed down as an impenetrable secret that must be forever and otherwise reconceived anew.

Put in terms of a historical framework, Kierkegaard's insistence on identity as a secret legacy that can only repeat what was already missing from an earlier stage will prevent the concept of "modernity" from achieving any genuine dialectical coherence or closure. A heritage is in this respect by definition secret, moreover, to the degree that, like a dowry, it has always already been accumulated without one's direct participation, and it becomes operative only at the moment that it alters unpredictably and irreversibly the future course of the one upon whom it is finally bestowed. For Kierkegaard, then, and in distinction to the historical pattern of overcoming and development that is the thematic engine of Hegel's *Aesthetics* (the specific text that Kierkegaard takes as his target in the lecture-essay on modernity), the mode of self-consciousness that characterizes "modernity" cannot be represented as an increased level of self-awareness, and in no way does that self-consciousness constitute an advance over antiquity. The more the modern subject becomes self-aware, in fact, the more it suffers from the knowledge of the secret legacy it carries without being able either to reveal or explain it—least of all to itself. The concept of history in Kierkegaard involves self-awareness all right, but it is a self-awareness that does not proceed by way of a simple reflection of its own consciousness. Rather, history can be said to occur as modernity only at the moment when its subject rediscovers for itself, and thus repeats in a *bent* mode, as a re-*flex*—flex, *flectere*, to bend, to twist, to fold—that which, as antiquity, has always already taken place elsewhere. Not that modernity could, by a symmetrical reversal, be considered for the same reasons a *decrease* in self-awareness by comparison to an antiquity in which self-consciousness would at its origin have been more fully present to itself. As is already abundantly clear in the exemplary case of Oedipus, for instance, ancient subjectivity can be termed "tragic" only and precisely to the degree that its consciousness of self has always been, from the start, radically deficient, or "blind." By the time Oedipus understands anything about what he has already occasioned, it is over and done, and he is therefore in the curious condition of having "inherited" this legacy of subjective nonunderstanding from "himself." The historical model of modernity that is operative in Kierkegaard's text must therefore be characterized as having no identity other than that of providing antiquity with a disintegrating "echo" of itself: a repetition whose own diffuseness serves only to bring out the way the "original" was already lacking something essential.

Hence, according to Agacinski's suggestion, Kierkegaard's strategic choice of Antigone for embodying the most legitimate subject of a tragic modernity that in its very incompletion, as a necessarily "posthumous" echo of antiquity, will also always remain provisional and therefore "yet to come." For Antigone, as she reappears in Kierkegaard's text, is exceedingly well placed to function as an image for the tragic "re-flex" of antiquity in today's modernity. Already in Sophocles, the parents' legacy is necessarily reflected in the child's destiny—Ismene reminds her sister at one point in the play of the crimes that have been committed by Oedipus and Jocasta. But in the ancient tragedy this hereditary blindness does not itself and as such become a subject for Antigone's self-reflection, which remains focused on her own objective act of defiance aimed at Creon for the sake of what she owes her dead brother, Polyneices. What the ancient Antigone would need to be "modern" in Kierkegaard's sense is for her to become aware of herself not simply as the one who in her own terms defies the present rule of Creon, but rather as the one who, on behalf of her father, Oedipus, carries forward a legacy of blindness more ancient than herself or her brother. The movement of history that is suggested here, if it is one, does not occur in such a way that the blind heritage of Oedipus would in any way be resolved or dispelled by its self-conscious resumption in modernity. Rather, the legacy is displaced in the very act of repeating it, its own eyeless sockets re-echoed and thus reinscribed in another version, just as the unintelligibility of Sophocles' *Antigone* will have been duplicated and displaced in Kierkegaard's uncanny rehearsal of it in this section-fragment of the first volume of *Either/Or*. Kierkegaard's text therefore rewrites Antigone for modernity so that Antigone can finally begin to see that she has indeed inherited her father's blind ignorance as a secret that she must herself continue to keep. For the one thing that this Antigone can never know for certain is whether and to what extent her father Oedipus was himself aware of this secret that he has from now on bequeathed to her.

In Kierkegaard's version, then, no one, including perhaps Oedipus himself, knows a thing about this secret; his crime of stubborn blindness has somehow gone virtually unnoticed in its "modern" re-edition. "That he has slain the sphinx and liberated Thebes is known to everyone, and Oedipus lives honored and admired, happy in his marriage to Jocasta."[13] Only the daughter, Antigone, knows the truth of all that remains concealed from the others, in other words, the radical inexplicability of their own nonknowledge or blindness. Antigone thus comes to self-awareness simultaneously as both daughter and fiancée, in other words in the impossible conjuncture of an inherited past and a promised future, and she does so at precisely the moment she "experiences" this secret blindness that has from time immemorial defined the existence of her father. The radical alterity of this experience tears Antigone asunder, and along with her the concept of history as self-presence and understanding. Because she is in a singular sense already "wed" to the past as a secret, Antigone cannot by the same token give herself to Haemon. Deprived of her projected marriage to Haemon, Antigone will thus also be deprived of the promise of a future that could somehow surpass the past that she now bears concealed within her. All that Antigone can carry forward is therefore the echo of a secret; or, rather, she will herself be carried by this secret, and in wholly unknowable directions. Kierkegaard's modernity, as repetition, thus requires a rethinking of history as an occurrence of radical interruption, discontinuity, and continual displacement—motifs that can in no way be reassimilated to organic models of history as a temporal and teleological process of development for both individual and collective subjectivities.

As Agacinski notes, however, such a model of history does serve to place Kierkegaard within a particularly noteworthy constellation of "modern" thinkers whose impact on twentieth-century thought has been equally decisive, though it has not always been registered in the same way or to the same degree of effectiveness. Agacinski mentions, for instance, Friedrich Hölderlin in this context, and the way he developed a model of history as break, or *caesura*, and precisely in relation to his own translations of Sophocles' Antigone. She could easily have also mentioned Walter Benjamin and his reading of the way "modernity" has to be understood in the writings of the exemplary French poet Charles Baudelaire on the basis of an experience of surprise and even *shock*. Much more work thus needs to be done in the reception of Kierkegaard, not only in terms of those cases where his texts have actually been read and may have had some direct or occult influence, but also, and perhaps especially, in those even more curious cases where it can be demonstrated that no contact whatsoever has taken place. The historical accident that Hölderlin in Germany, Kierkegaard in Denmark, and Baudelaire in France just happened at more or less the same moment to feel compelled in their writings to reconceive of history as the occurrence of caesura, repetition, and shock is too coincidental not to remain, like pure chance, forever beyond the reach of our attempts to control and understand them with the help of such familiar logical categories as chance and determination—never mind such historical categories as modern, premodern, and postmodern. It allows, at any rate, for a reconsideration of the way that Kierkegaard's peculiar conception of repetition as constitutive of existence in both its subjective and historical determinations necessarily dovetails with a modernity whose limits have not yet been reached, let alone surpassed, by our own obsessive reflections on it.

Of all of Kierkegaard's texts, it is no doubt *Fear and Trembling* that most vertiginously restages the problems of repetition, subjective existence, and the peculiar historicity that characterizes the modernity in which alone they might occur. And so it is no surprise that Agacinski will return to this text when she extends the question of Antigone's "legacy" to a level of generality that can no longer be qualified as being merely idiosyncratic or contingent. The fact that Oedipus himself is blind, and that he bestows this blindness as a secret heritage upon Antigone, could always be explained away by reference to the polytheism of Greek myth and thought or to the psychological effect Kierkegaard's father, Michael Pederson Kierkegaard, actually exerted on his own son Søren—in other words, by reference to secondary determinations that in the final analysis serve only to illustrate the particular kind of finitude they already presuppose as given. But with *Fear and Trembling* the law of the secret and the price to be exacted for it become *absolute*. Now it is God—as a principle of generality that by definition stands beyond all finitude whatsoever—who speaks, and what God says can have meaning only on the basis of the promises and demands that God makes—to Abraham, on Abraham, in the first place, and then behind Abraham, after Abraham, within history and for the rest of us. *Fear and Trembling* will therefore always have been the crucial text in this regard, not just because, like all of Kierkegaard's texts, it insists on the experience of existence as finitude. Rather, it is an inescapable text because it attempts to account for the peculiar way that each and every experience of finitude ultimately depends for its own possibility on an absolute law that is also infinite in scope. As such, all finitude, all existence remains conditioned by a law with which it has nothing in common and that therefore must remain an absolute secret for it. If we can be said to *be*, if therefore we *are*, and if we *exist* in finitude, it is merely as a result of the law of this secret. But to know this much is also to know that we ourselves remain radically separated from any true knowledge of this law to which we remain nonetheless and impossibly indebted. We are in our finitude only insofar as we experience an infinite distance from the absolute law of our own existence.

At least that is what, in the context of all her earlier writings, the title of Agacinski's last sustained encounter with Kierkegaard, originally published in 1989, will first of all suggest: "Nous ne sommes pas sublimes" ("We Are Not Sublime").[14] For Abraham, presumably, is sublime, and the possibility that Abraham alone can be sublime would therefore present us with an inescapable dilemma. If, to go further, we recall that the sublime, according to Kant, is that by comparison to which all else is small, then we begin to sense the proportions of the dilemma to which Agacinski seems to refer us here. How could Abraham, in his very sublimity, which is by definition his incommensurability, become an example, a rule, a measure in any way appropriate to the rest of us? We are not sublime; that is, we may not ever be sublime, like the one and only Abraham, but we had better nonetheless come to terms with the way this unbreachable distance that separates us once and for all from Abraham and his sublimity intimately concerns us, addresses us, leaves its mark on us in all that we do in history as sons and daughters of Abraham and his faith. We are not sublime, but whatever it is that we in fact are as historical beings, we are only as a result of what we thus call Abraham and his sublimity. This, however—and surprisingly enough—is not at all the direction that Agacinski pursues in her last essay, her adieu, as it were, to Kierkegaard. For this very reason, then, the difference between "We Are Not Sublime" and her other work on Kierkegaard becomes all the more compelling for us to document and explore.

Agacinski begins her essay by calling attention to the way that her reading of Kierkegaard's Abraham has undergone an important shift since she began rereading *Fear and Trembling* a few years after the publication of *Aparté* in 1977. Now—in 1988, that is—returning to the text after having put it aside for a considerable length of time, she is no longer inclined to view Abraham's willingness to sacrifice his son for God as the definitive example of faith, as the absolute risk of religious passion, or as a mysterious heroism that impinges on us while still lying beyond our reach. Rather, she is now inclined to view this exaltation of the great, the absolute, the incommensurable "with suspicion" ("We Are Not Sublime," 107). What could possibly have happened between the two lectures Agacinski delivered in Copenhagen in 1981 and "We Are Not Sublime," a paper she presented seven years later in Paris, at the Collège International de Philosophie, in October 1988? Is there a secret here that, if we could only know it, would allow us to explain why exactly Agacinski was moved to change from what she calls her "fascination" with Abraham's faith to her "suspicion" of this same Abraham and the sublime sacrifice of his son?

Agacinski hints at the possibility of just such a secret meaning when, in the opening pages of her essay, she self-reflexively glosses the "we" that appears so prominently in its title. Perhaps, she says, this is the "we" of a certain historical age, such as Kierkegaard's or our own, an age that is no longer able, like Abraham, to sustain a relationship to the absolute. Or perhaps it is the Hegelian "we" that no longer even feels the need for the sublime, simply because it has already surmounted the opposition between the finite and infinite. But, she then adds with a kind of wink, perhaps the "we" in her title is meant in a more oblique and private manner, the way, for example, Søren secretly addressed himself to Regine in so many of his own texts. In this last case, of course, it would be Sylviane Agacinski herself who, whatever else she was doing, was also writing this text on Kierkegaard in order to say to someone or other in her present or past life: "if only we were sublime, then, even beyond the loss, we should still go on loving each other in all eternity" ("We Are Not Sublime,"130).[15] Or, Agacinski next suggests, perhaps the indirect address of her title goes in yet a different direction, and is meant more like this: "We know that eternity is precisely what we do not have, and by knowing that, we are relieved of having to miss it. What we have is time, though time is all we have. We are not sublime." That is Agacinski's final hypothesis with respect to how her title might be intended, though she then qualifies things just a little further by adding, "in this case, it would mean: above all let's not be sublime, for all that exists is *finite*" (131). As though, in the end, Abraham and his sublime faith could function only as a lure and a temptation, cheating us for the sake of the unattainable infinite out of the only genuine existence we actually have left in which to love: that of our own finitude.

As fascinating as it would always be to pursue the question of how Agacinski's lived experiences have left certain traces in her written works, we should by now have developed our own suspicions about the capacity of such traces to help us to understand in any way whether and to what extent the text called "We Are Not Sublime" represents a genuine advance in the reading of Kierkegaard and, more particularly, of the text called *Fear and Trembling*. For in this respect, the same general law that applies to Søren Kierkegaard himself applies to Sylviane Agacinski, and this law is clearly enunciated on more than one occasion in *Fear and Trembling* by none other than Johannes de Silentio, its pseudonymous author: "Either there is a paradox, that the single individual as the single individual stands in an absolute relation to the absolute, or Abraham is lost" (*FT* 120; *SKS* 4:159). In other words, if Søren's broken commitment to Regine, or Sylviane's cryptic reference to a "we" that was not one day and perhaps will not ever be sublime, can hold any truly philosophical—as opposed to merely empirical and therefore anecdotal— interest for "us" still today, it can be only by virtue of the paradox that such particular and individual instances always also stand in an absolute relation to the absolute. It could not be simply by reading "Abraham" in *Fear and Trembling* as an indirect figure for Søren's giving up of Regine that we would ever initiate a truly "existential" analysis of faith or understanding; just as it would not be by reading the "we" in Agacinski's text as an indirect image for an actual human couple that we could ever approach whatever "truth" is still legible in Kierkegaard's text—even, and especially if that truth has to do with the limits of all philosophical understanding. In order for there to be "image" in the first place—to take Abraham for "Søren," or to take Agacinski's text as an address to another human being—there first has to be the *separation*, secret turning, *aparté* or irony, that displaces once and forever the "originality" of all finitude, including the one we happen to call "human." When Agacinski titles the final section of her essay "Human Loves," she takes her leave not only from Abraham but from the *aparté* of irony as well, since the finitude by which she characterizes the human also ensures its closure, its capacity to re- fuse, in the name of the human, the *infinite* indirection and thus unstoppable slippage that irony always implies. For a text that in this manner promises, as every text in fact does, to possess human interest for whomever one day wrote it and for whomever one day reads it is *not* necessarily or not *yet* a text that actually confronts the philosophical obligation to think the category of the human in all its potentially disruptive conditions of possibility. To determine whether and how such a paradoxical trembling, shudder, or collision between the individual and the absolute does in fact ever or anywhere occur, it would therefore be necessary once again to turn to the exemplary proper name we have inherited for just such an unthinkable event, in other words, Abraham. The Akedah or *binding* of Isaac is thus also and by the same token the *irony* of Abraham: his interruption of, and untying from, all that otherwise would bind him to the finitude of this one son, his entering into an absolute relation with the absolute, or inhuman, other.

The most curious aspect of "We Are Not Sublime," then, is precisely the way that it does not dwell on Abraham and his binding of Isaac; or perhaps it would be more accurate to say, the way that it does not dwell on Abraham as he is portrayed by Kierkegaard in the text of *Fear and Trembling*. It is as though Agacinski were adding her own, fifth variation on Abraham in order to counter the four little fictions that Kierkegaard includes in the Exordium section that precedes the main body of *Fear and Trembling*. "I'd like to think," Agacinski writes, "that Abraham would never have gone through with the sacrifice" ("We Are Not Sublime," 133). In this respect, Agacinski's Abraham is already not exactly identical to Kierkegaard's, and her Abraham moves even further away when Agacinski imagines that he never really *believed* that God would ultimately require the sacrifice of his son, Isaac. By taking Isaac to

Mount Moriah, Agacinski suggests, Abraham was actually testing, even teasing God: "You're asking me for my son? Alright, but I don't *believe* you really want that from me. . . . Let's see if God is really going to ask me to sacrifice Isaac. I just don't *believe* it" (134; emphasis added). It should be difficult, to say the least, for anyone to believe that Abraham, the father of faith, could in this way become precisely the one who does not or cannot *believe*, and in this particular case goes so far as knowingly to withhold his belief from God. For what would remain of faith once belief, credence, and the bestowal of credibility upon the word of another have been subtracted from it? Agacinski, however, asks us to believe in an Abraham who has a sense of "humor," a kind of subjective ironist, then, who puts God to the test by seeing just how far he is willing to go, just how serious the absolute is about demanding Isaac's sacrifice. "It might be," Agacinski concludes her version of the story, that "Abraham's faith consists less in his blind obedience than in his *skepticism*," which would by the same token amount to his *not* believing: "You're asking me for my son? I just *don't* believe it" (134; emphasis added). That a father might go to any length to resist believing in a law that would require the sacrifice of his unique and beloved son is certainly believable from a purely human and empirical point of view.[16] But what assures us that the kind of belief that is above all implied in Abraham's faith is an exclusively *human* faculty in the first place?

For instance, how could faith as a constitutive mode of belief ever be simply equated with "blind obedience," a secondary determination that already presupposes human agency as a byproduct of the knowing subject, that is, the subject who by definition should be able to tell the difference between seeing and not seeing what exactly is being asked of it? But it is precisely such knowledge that, in faith, Abraham will always lack. Could one even be said to "obey" the law—either blindly or with eyes wide open—without a prior and more unconditional "belief" that the law as such exists and exists as a consequence in the mode of an enunciation, a call, a summons to which one must first of all be willing to listen? Finally, and most difficult of all, how could "faith" ever be manifested in *not* believing? Kierkegaard's text, at least, seems not to waver on this point. If Abraham does not believe and with his whole heart and soul acknowledge the "impossibility" of keeping Isaac that he hears pronounced in the law, the pseudonymous author Johannes de Silentio insists, then "he is deceiving himself and his testimony is neither here nor there, since he has not even attained infinite resignation" (*FT* 46–47; *SKS* 4:141). Obedience to or freedom from the law is not yet at issue for Abraham, since both can become intelligible for him only through a prior belief, as unconditional as it is unjustifiable, in God's inaugural promise, which also happens to include the demand that he give up Isaac. Abraham undergoes a spiritual trial precisely to the degree that he would be tempted to *understand* God's word, that he could without further ado *know* its meaning as anything other than this promise that simultaneously demands that he separate himself from all that is most dear and thus meaningful to him. Abraham hears God's word first of all as this summons that is addressed to him in an absolute way; as such it is also that in which Abraham can originally only believe, in other words, that to which he can at first respond only by saying yes, which is also to say, "here I am." Faith thus remains incommensurate to obedience and freedom, activity and passivity, as they are ordinarily conceived from the point of view of the knowing subject, and in that respect faith must, as de Silentio reminds us, also go beyond "all human calculation" (*FT* 35–36; *SKS* 4:131). Knowing only that one does not and cannot know what it will have eventually meant to respond to the inaugural call of the infinite, the finite self will have always already been carried far beyond its own limits: "how Abraham entered into the paradox is just as inexplicable as how he remains in it" (*FT* 66; *SKS* 4:159). What Kierkegaard calls *existence*, a finitude that is at every instant renewing the shudder of its collision with the infinite, is this secret that necessarily exceeds the faculties of every human subject at the very moment that it makes them possible.

Consequently, as de Silentio insists, Abraham, who may speak only on condition of guarding this secret, also and for the same reason "speaks no human tongue or language" (*FT* 114; *SKS* 4:202). The concept of the human, it would appear, cannot emerge unscathed by Abraham's faith, and so it, too, as a stable philosophical category, gives way to trembling here. If it is true, as de Silentio also says, that "every language calls [Abraham] to mind," then it is equally true that every language also recalls that aspect of Abraham's faith that can belong to no human tongue, in other words, that secret element that is not itself reducible to the human as such.

Of course, it is also at this point that the divergence between Kierkegaard's text and "We Are Not Sublime" comes into full view. As a text that was written partly when Agacinski was "still fascinated" by Abraham and his faith, partly after she had become "suspicious" of this exaltation of the incommensurable, "We Are Not Sublime" is itself fractured, its own sutures of these two wholly incompatible moments—of "knowing" skepticism and "sublime" faith—sometimes blurring the lines between them. However, the last section, titled "Human Loves," is clearly written on the far side of a fascination with Abraham and his sublimity, and as a consequence it leaves no doubt about its own ambition to offer an alternative to "a sacrificial operation" that characterizes the sublime law to which Kierkegaard, according to Agacinski, was always to remain attached. Leaving *Fear and Trembling* aside, Agacinski turns abruptly to *Works of Love*, where she finds that Kierkegaard, writing in his own name for once, underwrites a concept of ethical love that would be essentially Kantian, and as a consequence, "egocentric" in nature. Such a concept, Agacinski goes on to suggest, reintroduces a kind of universal imperative whose ultimate aim would be to preserve the loving subject by freeing it for eternity from the temporal constraints of finitude. Set free from the despair that always shadows the finite self in its precarious attachments to any finite other, Agacinski argues, the self would at the same time become detached from every single empirical other as such. This ideal version of "religious" love, which Agacinski does not hesitate to ascribe to Søren and his broken promise to Regine, is willing to humble itself before the law of the eternal but not before the finite individuality of the other. At long last, and after all these years, one begins to hear, as in a re-flex, the concrete particularity of Regine's own voice rise up in protest against Søren's sacrifice of her.

If fluency, measure, and finesse are attributes of true eloquence, then it is certainly the case that Sylviane Agacinski attains in these final pages on human love a degree of eloquence that Kierkegaard himself rarely if ever managed to achieve in his writings. What is missing here—though in the sense of its having been excised, rather than in the sense of its merely being absent—is the nervous shrillness that tends to become audible in Kierkegaard's own text at precisely those moments when a simple affirmation of human finitude appears over the horizon. For Kierkegaard, as Agacinski knows as well as anybody else, Abraham is and will always remain the figure in which the most profound love of human finitude goes hand in hand, though unthinkably, with an inhuman belief that he must give it all up. Abraham's love for Isaac as the single other closest to him therefore also goes hand in hand with his treatment of Isaac as the absolute and wholly separate other. Agacinski's writings on Kierkegaard bring us in the end to the edge of this impossible task: to know just what kind of love it is that Abraham gives to Isaac, and further to know if there might exist any legitimate alternatives to such love. She herself, most emphatically with "Human Loves," would like to propose a thinking of love based on the "pure address of one singularity to another, the predilection of one finite being for another," and thus a knowing how to love that could do without all reference to the sublime and as a result to the absolute ("We

Are Not Sublime,"146). Such a love would, in its very capacity to accept the lack of eternity and immortality characterizing all things human, also include the possibility "to think the gift, and to think love as the gift; for what more can I give than my time, which is to say neither my life nor my death, but rather the essence of my mortality?" (145). Still, the story of Abraham as it is silently recalled by Kierkegaard suggests that one does not in love simply give *one's* time and *one's* mortality to the other, above all and especially not in the name of one's own finitude, without risk of any pseudonymous or fictitious contamination and interference. As we have seen, over and over again, it is precisely in its uncanny relationship to the most intimate other that the self in Kierkegaard is led to experience its own existence only in the derived mode of an "image"—which is also an unimpeachable secret. For the same reason, too, whatever the "gift" that is inscribed for all time in Kierkegaard's writing, it lies forever beyond the powers of the finite self—either to receive or to give it all on its own. What we call a "self" could therefore never find itself at the origin of such a gift but would rather constitute a displaced name for the trace of its effects, one of which, as Kierkegaard reminds us, is an uninterrupted trembling. What remains intact and always ready to tremble again in the proper name *Abraham* is that enigma wherein he received on behlalf of us all the gift of time in the very instant that he offered the gift of Isaac's death, which is another way of saying that "he" is not even the one we recognize as Abraham until after he undergoes this incomprehensible ordeal of belief at the hands of the absolute other. The desire to know whether it is humanly possible to love in such a way that one could make the trembling stop, that one could ever succeed once and for all in separating the gift of time from the gift of death, is no doubt the most enduring legacy that Sylviane Agacinski has bequeathed to all future readings of Kierkegaard.

FIVE

Fear and Trembling: "Who Is Able to Understand Abraham?"

Just how serious was Socrates when he claimed to know nothing? "When Socrates said that he was without knowledge [uvidende]," Kierkegaard writes, summing up his treatment of Socratic irony near the end of his thesis, "he nevertheless did know something, for he knew about his ignorance [Uvidenhed]; on the other hand, however, this knowledge [Viden] was not a knowledge of something."[1] At stake, as always for Kierkegaard, is therefore the degree to which the negativity of irony—its own nothingness—is serious; is to be, or can be, taken in earnest. And wherever the knowledge in question is one that has to do with historical actuality, or *existence*, then the possibility of irony, or nothingness, has to be considered to be among the most serious questions for whatever subject is able, like Socrates, to ask about it in this way. Why is it, then, that Kierkegaard will follow his 1841 thesis with the publication of what he called his "aesthetic" works—works that in fact aim to treat the most serious questions, but do so in a seemingly nonserious manner, duplicitously, and under the false pretense of literary pseudonyms? There is something odd, something paradoxical about the way Kierkegaard deals in 1841 with the philosophical question of irony in accordance with "serious" conventions;

in other words, by respecting an institutional framework that requires him to follow clearly defined rules and to speak in his own name. Just a few years later, however, from 1843 to 1846, he will write about religious questions in the string of books for which, in addition to the thesis on irony, he is most justly remembered—*Either/Or, Repetition, Fear and Trembling, Philosophical Fragments, The Concept of Anxiety, Prefaces, Stages on Life's Way*, and *Concluding Unscientific Postscript*—in an aesthetic mode of pseudonymity that, at least in appearance, takes itself even less seriously than the less seriously religious mode of academic philosophy.

If, as Kierkegaard also claimed in *The Concept of Irony*, historical actuality, *den historiske Virkelighed*, always stands in a twofold relation to the subject— partly as a gift from the past and partly as a task for the future—then why, ex- actly, when Kierkegaard makes his own transition from his past (as a student of Hegel's philosophy) to his future (as a religious thinker) does he not un- dertake this task in his own name? The question of transition, moreover, can- not be restricted here to the empirical journey that the person named Søren Kierkegaard is in the process of making for himself between 1841 and 1843, and by which he would complete the passage from philosophical scholar to religious witness, since it constitutes at the same time the essential difference that the impersonal and pseudonymous authors standing in for Kierkegaard are elaborating in their writings between philosophy and religion as two re- lated but nonidentical modes of taking existence, *Tilværelsen*, seriously.

Transition (*Overgang*), or more properly speaking, mediation (*Mediation*), is the category by which modern philosophy—in other words, Hegelian phi- losophy—has understood, though in distorted manner, mistakenly and thus misleadingly, what Kierkegaard will designate in *Repetition* as "repetition."[2] According to *Repetition*'s dissimulated author, Constantin Constantius, the Hegelian concept of mediation, *Vermittelung*, covers over rather than brings to light (*ikke forklaret*) how mediation actually takes place (*fremkommer*). That is, Hegel's philosophy does not explain whether mediation is to be conceived as a motion (*Bevægelse*) wholly accounted for by two factors, the way, for in- stance, a cause is always implied and even contained in its effect and vice versa; or whether something entirely new has to be added, and if that is the case, how this might be understood to happen. Constantin Constantius, repeating something he had already suggested on the very first page of *Repetition*, sug- gests that the Hegelian concepts of mediation and transition should both be considered contemporary versions of what the Greeks attempted, more origi- nally than Hegel, to think under the rubric of κίνησις—kinesis as motion and movement, but also as change. Speaking through his pseudonym, or disguise, Kierkegaard is therefore saying that we must rethink the Greek concept of kinesis in order first of all to dislodge Hegel's distorted understanding of it as mediation, so that we can prepare the way for something "new" to happen; that is, so that we might in the future allow what the Greeks had already thought as "recollection" to come into being, or existence—*Tilværelsen*—in a different mode, as "repetition."

It appears that for Constantin Constantius, the only thing that matters would be change or motion, and the only kind of change that constantly concerns him is the one that would pass from *knowledge* into *existence*. But how can a change in knowledge occur in actuality? Like the question Johannes Climacus asks at the beginning of *Philosophical Fragments*—How can the truth be learned?—that is the question with which *Repetition* has to begin. When the Greeks said that all knowledge is recollection [al Erkjenden er Erindren]," Constantin pursues his argument, "they said that the whole of existence [hele Tilværelsen], which is, has already been" (*R* 149; *SKS* 4:34). To speak of the Greeks, which is always to speak of what has been given to us as our philosophical heritage or past, is to speak of existence as the potential to know again what has already been. And this knowledge, for the Greeks, could come into being only through a movement of recollection. Just as Kierkegaard had argued in the thesis on irony that historical actuality relates in a twofold manner to the subject, Constantin Constantius will insist that what we have inherited in this way as a gift from the Greeks must now be doubled by what remains for us to accomplish as a task for the future. "When one says that life is a repetition," Constantin stipulates, "one says that existence [Tilværelsen] now comes into being [bliver nu til]." That is why Constantin will also say in this same passage that "repetition is the new category that must be discovered [Gjentagelsen er den ny Kategori, som skal opdages]." For, to return once more to the beginning of *Repetition*, "Just as the Greeks taught that all knowledge is recollection, new philosophy will teach that the whole of life is a repetition. Repetition and recollection are the same movement [Bevægelse], except in opposite directions, for what is recollected has already been, is repeated backward, whereas genuine repetition is recollected forward" (*R* 131; *SKS* 4:3–4). The "transition" that Kierkegaard must make from his thesis to the pseudonymous works—as it is prefigured by *The Concept of Irony* and then confirmed by *Repetition*—will therefore have to move from what has been given as the Greek concept of recollection to the task of discovering the new concept of repetition. And that movement from gift to task will also always involve a transition that passes from knowledge—what the Greeks called *recollection*—to life—what Kierkegaard renames *repetition*.

But this task—of repeating the gift of Greek recollection forward rather than backward, of discovering a new and therefore different existence, rather than knowing again an existence that always has already been—is first of all complicated by the obligation to confront what has in the meantime made our path to the gift of Greek recollection all but impassable: Hegel and his systematic misunderstanding of kinesis as speculative "mediation" and "transition." If Kierkegaard has difficulty speaking in his own name after the thesis on irony, this may well be because Hegel's philosophy now stands between the past of Greek thought and the task of all future thinking. "Hegel the impostor," Maurice Blanchot writes; "this is what makes him invincible, mad with his seriousness, counterfeiter of Truth."[3] The pseudonymous works can be read as Kierkegaard's attempt to find new names for combating the way that Hegel's concept of mediation counterfeits truth, to find a new way for getting past the imposture of Hegelian transition into a genuine future. That future, as Kierkegaard in his own name will ultimately spell it out in "The Point of View for My Work as an Author," is the task toward which his entire authorship is oriented: "how to become a Christian."[4] But in order to arrive there, it will from now on be necessary to pass through the detour—the mad seriousness—of Hegel's philosophy and all its disfiguring effects on what we have been given to think by Greek philosophy.

To some extent, all of this is already legible in *The Concept of Irony*, and it is sketched out in the juxtaposition Kierkegaard establishes there between Socrates and Christ. "The similarity between Christ and Socrates," the first thesis of this work reads, "consists essentially in their dissimilarity" (*CI* 349). The task of uncovering the future is the way toward becoming a Christian; but this will be possible only after the gift of philosophy's past—the history of philosophical subjectivity as it originated in Socrates—has been recovered from the distortions imposed upon it by Hegel's imposture. Since neither Socrates nor Christ is now available to us first hand, not even in the sense of either of them having left behind a primary text under his own name, it will always be necessary to approach them indirectly by way of what can only be called a historical mediation. And for Kierkegaard this unavoidable mediation will always have been provided by the deceptively counterfeit concept that Hegel names *transition*, or *mediation*. To the degree that Hegel has misconstrued Greek philosophy, Kierkegaard has to write the academic thesis—though he does so in the direct mode of a consideration of Socratic indirection, or irony.

To the degree that Hegel has misconstrued Christianity, Kierkegaard has to write the religious works that follow it—though in the indirect and therefore potentially ironic mode of the pseudonyms.

∞

It is a commonplace that Hegel's presence in *The Concept of Irony* is pervasive but ambiguous. As a contemporary reviewer aptly remarked, "Hegelianism ends with Kierkegaard's dissertation on irony, but even here it is not clear that Hegel has been renounced entirely."[5] And this point of view is reinforced by Kierkegaard's own admission in the *Journals* that he had allowed himself in the thesis to be "influenced by Hegel and whatever was modern." Looking back in 1850 at the period of the thesis, Kierkegaard goes so far as to exclaim: "What a Hegelian fool I was!" Whether or not one accepts such suggestions at face value, it is true enough that in the thesis the contestation of Hegel appears to originate from within the precinct of philosophy rather than from beyond it—as least in terms of the ostensible statements of the text. According to the thesis, Hegelian philosophy may be compromised because it lays claim to an understanding—and a mastery—of Socratic irony to which it ultimately has no right. But this does not make Socrates and his irony any the less "philosophical" in their own right. One aspect of philosophy—infinite absolute negativity—contests another—absolute knowledge—and therefore prevents the dialectical system of Hegel from completing itself in the promised synthesis of reason with history.

As a result of this discrepancy, however, it is not just Hegel who is renounced in favor of Socrates and his irony. Rather, Kierkegaard will recognize in this dilemma the obligation to put philosophy itself into question as a discourse of knowledge that could ever be adequate to the task of historical actuality, of subjective existence. If the chapter in the thesis on "irony as a mastered moment" has always seemed a bit contrived and out of place, this is because there is literally no room in the thesis for it. As the interruption of philosophical discourse by a religious element that would remain foreign to it, this section, as well as all the references in *The Concept of Irony* to the Christian, already belong to another register. Irony is not mastered by philosophy and the kind of knowledge that would be proper to it. Rather, Socrates and the infinite absolute negativity of his irony lead by necessity to his total isolation from empirical actuality, and thus to his death. Socrates dies in order that something beyond the actuality of empirical existence may yet come into being—though in Socrates this remains, according to Kierkegaard, the vagueness of a knowledge concerning the soul's immortality, which is still too philosophical, since it merely "recollects" itself as what it had always been, rather than "discovering" itself as something different.[6] For Kierkegaard, the death of Socrates coincides with the new task of religion, which will not be limited either to a knowledge or a recollection of existence. Surely, we must recollect what is given to us to know by Socrates—the self-administered dying to the world that is effected through ironic negativity—but we must recollect only in order to repeat this philosophical "knowledge" about death—which will also have been the "death" of knowledge—in a religious, that is, life-giving and thus futural mode. The pseudonymous works Kierkegaard writes between 1843 and 1846 will therefore have to address themselves to thinking this task: how to give oneself a future by repeating the past—what Socrates gives us in his (merely) philosophical acceptance and knowledge of death—in a new and utterly different idiom.

Another way of putting this would be to say that Greek philosophy has to be translated into Christian terms, though this cannot happen until Hegelian mediation is itself retranslated back into Greek recollection and then taken again—forward—as Christian repetition. It is in this sense that Kierkegaard's insistence on the irreducible role played by the Danish language in his relation to Hegel's philosophy should be understood. "When I speak German," Constantin Constantius says in *Repetition* precisely at the moment he fails in his attempt to "repeat" anything, "I am the most accommodating man in the world" (*R* 152). It could therefore be only through a new displacement of Hegel's diversion of Greek thought into the speculative idiom of German that Kierkegaard could resist an accommodation, a settlement that would always be conducted on Hegel's own terms. "*Mediation*," Constantin had already remarked in this context, "is a foreign word; 'repetition' [Gjentagelse] is a good Danish word, and I congratulate the Danish language on a philosophical term" (*R* 149). *Gjentagelse* repeats, takes up again, and even takes over Hegel's term—all in an effort both to recall and alter Hegel's obfuscation of Greek recollection. It was in a similar vein that Kierkegaard had earlier poked fun at Hegel's philosophical vocabulary in a loose entry in his diary in 1838. Taking aim there at *Aufhebung*, Hegel's nearly untranslatable term for the way in which philosophical mediation promises to conserve in a superior mode that which it surpasses and leaves behind it, Kierkegaard playfully inserts its Danish equivalent, *Ophævelse*, into an idiomatic expression for making a big fuss over something that isn't truly worth it. "The Hegelians," Kierkegaard wrote, "come up with many sublations [foranstalte mange Ophævelser] of the concept which are just not worth taking the trouble to fuss about [at gjøre mange Ophævelser over]."[7] By taking Hegel's German back into his own language, Kierkegaard subverts the philosophical pretension to extend and even overcome the history of philosophical thought through a speculative dialectic.

Kierkegaard's Danish is therefore not only the particular language in which he just happened to write; it is also one means he has at his disposal to enact the necessary deflection through which alone the speculative machine of Hegelian philosophy can be resisted and thus oriented otherwise. Danish, as it is put to work by Kierkegaard's writing, is itself a kind of repetitive pseudonym for this operation. Such a "pseudonymous" use of his own language entails constantly diverting its words from their usual mission, providing them with a kind of supplementary mask that serves momentarily to conceal their own identity while bringing to light new and unexpected possibilities for whomever now reconsiders—that is, *reads*— them seriously. *Gjentagelse*, repetition, is just such a mask or pseudonym within Kierkegaard's Danish. By repeating Hegel's word *mediation* in a different idiom, *Gjentagelse* takes leave of its ordinary place within its own language and is set free to resonate between the philosophical legacies it receives from both German and Greek. It thus opens a new space for something yet again, in other words, for something new to take place: its own future as another name for what still remains to be discovered as historical futurity. When Kierkegaard says, "Repetition is the new category, which must be discovered," he is not only describing the religious category that the "Young Man" in *Repetition* never reaches and that remains the task for all future thinking; he is also renaming the Danish word *Gjentagelse* as one of the ways such a religious task is now given the power to speak to the future within his text. The task must therefore be not only to discover the new category that will have been able to come into existence only beyond the Socratic imperative to know the limits of one's own knowledge. The task must also be to discover the way that all-too-familiar words, like *repetition*, can be made to speak to us in new and unsuspected tongues.

At least, that would be one means of accounting for the peculiar relation between *Repetition* and another pseudonymous text Kierkegaard published on the same day, October 16, 1843, titled *Fear and Trembling*.[8] For *Abraham* is itself another way of saying that which, from the start, will have offered the most extraordinary example of *Gjentagelse*, or repetition in history, though Abraham is never named as such in the text titled *Repetition*. Abraham provides this singular example of repetition because, unlike Socrates, he actually does accede to the religious category that lies beyond all philosophical cognition, and he does this thanks to that incomprehensible miracle by which he "repeats," or rather "takes back"—in Danish, *tager igjen*—the son that he had in that very instant already offered up and thus given away to the Absolute.) Repetition, *Gjentagelse*, then, is not just the new translation Constantin Constantius offers for the philosophical concept of *mediation*; it is also one possible translation for the religious concept of *faith* that will be treated under that name by the "author" of *Fear and Trembling*, Johannes de Silentio. *Fear and Trembling*—or, more properly, *Frygt og Bæven*—is itself the translation into Danish, or *repetition* in Danish, of a small fragment taken from Paul's Epistle to the Philippians: "Wherefore, my beloved, as ye have always obeyed, not as in my presence only, but now much more in my absence, work out your own salvation with fear and trembling" (2:12). Beyond the presence of any authority, in the absence, therefore, of all secure knowledge, Paul's letter suggests, there remains a call to "obedience," and this call to obey is also associated here with a "task"—a working-out of a future that goes by the name of "salvation." Still, or rather, above all, what Kierkegaard has retained in the title of his book on Abraham's faith is neither the obedience that one gives nor the task that one takes on. By repeating in his own translation *only* the "fear and trembling" that in the original qualifies the task of faithful obedience demanded by the text of this letter, Kierkegaard's pseudonymous author, de Silentio, suggests that whatever might remain to happen on the far side of philosophical knowledge—in other words, whatever could still take place beyond the serenity shown by both Socrates and Hegel in the face of death—can be conceived exclusively in terms of an *ordeal*—all the more terrifying and unsettling for its remaining by definition inconclusive, that is, a test of ignorance without end.

This is precisely the situation that de Silentio reproduces on the edge of his text, as a kind of prolegomena to any future reading of Abraham and his faith. Following the book's title, a short but equivocal exergue in German from Hamann, and a preface by the pseudonymous author on the problematic status of faith in contemporary Denmark, one encounters a remarkable exordium, a laying-out of the web in which the rest of the book will develop its own meditation on Abraham (*FT* 9–14; *SKS* 4:105–11). This exordium establishes an atmosphere of timelessness, one in which, "once upon a time," an anonymous person, as a child, heard the story of Abraham. Later, as a grownup, the same person read the story again, admired it even more, but began to understand it less and less. The story of God's call to Abraham in Genesis 22:1–2 is then quoted in Danish, and there follow four different but not unrelated interpretations of this command to take Isaac to Moriah and offer him on a mountain there as a burnt offering—from Abraham to God. De Silentio closes the exordium by pointing out that these interpretations represent only four among the many similar ways the man in question had pondered the event, each time returning home from his mental journey to Mount Moriah with the same response to it: "No one was as great as Abraham. Who is able to understand him?" There is a quasi-obsessional aspect to this individual's meditation on Abraham; "the older he became, the more often his thoughts turned to that story. . . . [F]inally he forgot everything else because of it" (*FT* 9; *SKS* 4:105). To remember Abraham is to forget everything else, *glemte han alt Andet*. To turns one's thought more and more toward Abraham's story, *desto oftere vendte hans Tanke sig til hiin Fortælling*, is the act of someone who turns away from philosophical thinking, *hiin Mand var ikke Tænker*, of someone who does not practice scholarly exegesis, *hiin Mand var ikke lærd Exeget*, and of someone who doesn't feel compelled to go beyond faith, *han følte ingen Trang til at komme ud over Troen*. Rather, what occupies the one who constantly thinks of Abraham and nothing else is precisely that which interrupts thought by subjecting it to a shaking, shuddering, trembling. "For what occupied this man," so says de Silentio, "was thought's shudder [Tankens Gysen]."

The exordium makes it clear, moreover, that the trembling of thought is the consequence of nonunderstanding: "That man was not an exegetical scholar. He could not read Hebrew; if he had known Hebrew, he perhaps would have easily understood the story and Abraham" (*FT* 9; *SKS* 4:106). The text leaves it undecided, and therefore forever undecidable, whether or not this particular reader, who was neither a philosophical thinker nor a Biblical scholar, would have in fact been able to "understand" Abraham and his story even if he had been able to read Hebrew: "havde han kunnet Hebraisk, da havde han *maaskee* let forstaaet Fortællingen og Abraham" (my emphasis)— even if he had known Hebrew the reader would only *perhaps* have been able to understand Abraham. Endlessly, outside of all determinable time, "once upon a time," a reader who cannot read this story of Abraham except by way of making a detour, by following a repetition of Abraham's story along the diverted path of a translated text, returns more and more to the same story with less and less understanding. The digression around philosophical and theological understanding is made necessary here by a certain oblique awareness of language and its foreignness. The shuddering of thought caused by nonunderstanding does not occur without this reference to language: the man could not read Hebrew, he could not follow Abraham directly, in the original; rather, in his approach to Abraham he is compelled to take the derivative and therefore indirect character of the story's language into account. Perhaps, even if he had known Hebrew—perhaps, therefore, even if he had been present on Mount Moriah as an eyewitness to that event, *at have været Vidne til hiin Begivenhed*—perhaps even, or perhaps especially if he had been there as a witness, then he would not have understood. No matter how that *perhaps* is turned, there remains even then the possibility of a foreign element to block access to an understanding of what was said in the Hebrew Bible, or perhaps even more originally, what was said directly between God and Abraham himself.

Why is it, then, that this one reader's journey to Mount Moriah and the event that occurred there between God and Abraham has to pass through a detour that goes by way of this reference to language? Johannes de Silentio alludes indirectly to this curious intertwining of Abraham and language when, at the end of the exordium, he describes the "thought" that, beyond philosophical reflection and theological exegesis, follows Abraham out to Mount Moriah over and over again. He calls it a kind of expedition, hike, excursion—or *wandering*: "Hver Gang han da efter en *Vandring* til Morija-Bjerget vendte hjem" (my emphasis); "every time he turned back home after making the trek to Mount Moriah," the reader would ask himself once again who could understood Abraham. This thinker who is not one has to leave home in order to turn his thought toward Abraham—but we know that he does not in fact ever have to leave home to make this turn away; he needs only think again about the foreign language in which he has read this story, or think in his own language about Abraham's foreignness in this story, to have his thought begin to leave home by trembling yet again. Although de Silentio does not say this out loud, there seems to be a connection between the way this man reads Abraham's story in a foreign language—his own language, but into which the foreignness to understanding that is Abraham's originality has been forever translated—and Abraham's own wandering away from home to Mount Moriah. Another way of putting this would be to ask: what exactly was the journey that Abraham made to Mount Moriah, and what happened there to his capacity to speak and understand his own language?

The tortuous road that must be followed—both by Abraham and Isaac, and by every reader after them, including both Hegel and Kierkegaard—to Mount Moriah always includes an injunction to leave one's home, which functions at the same time as this exposure to an unknown language; that is, to a language in which one's own understanding, one's domestic familiarity and sense of being at home, is exceeded and made to shudder or take leave of itself. But it is also and paradoxically the case that the road along which Abraham travels in this way will eventually lead to his receiving from God a new blessing, a progeny that God will describe in his blessing as being as numerous "as the stars of the heaven, and as the sand which is upon the sea" (Genesis 22:17). The blessing is in this way a promise, and the promise refers to the future existence of Abraham as it will be multiplied throughout history. Whatever is historical, whatever belongs to history and occurs within the limits of history, thus also results from this blessing that God bestows upon Abraham on Mount Moriah. When Isaac is returned to Abraham, when Abraham takes Isaac back, *tager igjen*, after God has tested Abraham by issuing the injunction to leave home and journey to Moriah to give Isaac away as a burnt offering to God, he becomes the new source of Abraham's future existence in time and in history. Abraham leaves home to make the trip to Moriah, but when he returns home afterwards, he does not come back to the same home; rather, he brings with him a new home, the futural space of God's promise in which Abraham and his progeny are to endure throughout historical time. On the edge of the edge of *Fear and Trembling*, the exordium stares in incomprehension—recollects over and over again how Abraham was able to enter history through the repetition of his having received Isaac a second time.

The *Promised* Land is therefore not just—and perhaps not even—a geographically circumscribable territory with determinable empirical limits. It is more originally, and importantly, the spoken blessing or gift of an indeterminate measure of time that passes through Abraham and attaches him to Isaac and their numberless future progeny in time. What constitutes a stumbling block for this straightforward interpretation of Abraham's seminal place in history—a stumbling block which lies at the source of *Fear and Trembling*—is the way that the blessing God speaks to Abraham in Genesis 22:16–18 is itself a repetition of the promise he had already given to Abraham in Genesis 12, 15, and 17. God had already commanded Abraham to leave his home in 12:1 and had given his promise to bless Abraham's seed in 12:7, and he reminds Abraham of the promise to give him both land and seed in chapters 15 and 17. Why then in chapter 22, after the birth of Isaac that in chapter 21 begins the actual fulfillment of God's promise, does God then tempt Abraham, putting him to the test of asking Abraham to give Isaac back to him again as a burnt offering?

The slight equivocation between the two verbs often used in the Bible to translate what God does to Abraham in chapter 22—God "tempted" Abraham; God "tested" Abraham—suggests the difficulty here. God might have tested Abraham by asking him to give up this one son, Isaac, for whom Sarah and Abraham had waited so long, if that is all Isaac was: this one son. But could one still call it a *test*, as opposed to a *temptation*, if Abraham were asked, in giving up Isaac, to renounce once and for all the entire covenant he had already concluded with God, and which was based on securing a historical future for him and all his descendents through Isaac? Not knowing for sure whether he is being *tested* or *tempted* is in fact the ultimate ordeal that Abraham must undergo when he hears God speak to him in Genesis 22:2. It is an equivocation between meanings that will also have always served to turn God's command into a foreign language even for Abraham. Johannes de Silentio is attentive to this equivocation in God's call to Abraham, for in his eulogy of Abraham he is careful first to say that "once again, Abraham was to be tried [forsøges]," but then he immediately appends to this a citation from the Biblical text, "And God tempted [fristede] Abraham" (*FT* 19).[9] It is in the space opened up by these two readings of how Abraham was subjected to God's voice—as a trial and/or as a temptation—that de Silentio will begin to articulate his conception of Abraham's faith, in response to the way it had already been understood by Hegel's philosophical interpretation.

Decisive for de Silentio is therefore the fact that Abraham will have manifested his faith not just once, but *twice*: first, when God asked him to leave home for an alien land and promised him, despite all appearances to the contrary, that Sarah would bear him a son; and then a second time when God commanded him to leave home for Moriah with his son Isaac, and to offer him there as a burnt offering. By the first example of faith, Abraham endures a rather straightforward test of dialectical *negation*: by leaving home behind and believing in something different, something that unlike home is not already there to understand before his very eyes, he turns the loss of nature into a gain for spirit. In the second case, which can only be God's way of tempting him, Abraham's faith would consist in his taking the fruit of God's promise, the spiritual unfolding of history through his son Isaac, and immolating it alive on Mount Moriah. For de Silentio, the crucial difference consists in the way these two modes of faith have to be considered in their relation to a history of meaning. Abraham undergoes a first trial of faith that determines whether the life he is living in the present will one day acquire historical significance by virtue of the gift of future time to be granted by his leaving home and receiving Isaac. But then Abraham's faith is once again tested, though this time in the mode of a "temptation": it is not simply a question of his not yet possessing a meaningful history, but more radically still, he is now asked to annihilate the one meaning history could ever have had for him: Isaac as the sign of God's promise fulfilled. It is as though, de Silentio adds, Abraham were not just being tempted, but indeed being "mocked" by God:

> So everything was lost, even more appallingly than if it had never happened! So the Lord was only mocking Abraham! [Saa drev Herren da kun sin Spot med Abraham!] He wondrously made the preposterous come true; now he wanted to see it annihilated [tilintetgjort]. . . . Now everything would be lost! All the glorious remembrance of his posterity, the promise in Abraham's seed—it was nothing but a whim, a fleeting thought the Lord had had [det var kun et Indfald, en flygtig Tanke, som Herren havde havt], and that Abraham was now supposed to obliterate [nu skulde udslette]. . . . That glorious treasure . . . the fruit of Abraham's life . . . — this fruit was now to be torn off prematurely and rendered meaningless [uden Betydning], for what meaning would it have if Isaac should be sacrificed! [og blive uden Betydning; thi hvad Betydning havde den, naar Isaak skulde offres!] (*FT* 19; *SKS* 4:115–16)[10]

By destroying Isaac, Abraham would not simply be deprived of all meaning, the way he would have been, for instance, "if it had never happened." Rather, de Silentio suggests, the meaning that had been promised and already delivered to Abraham by God is now *interrupted* in order to be taken up again, but this time the repetition would be a sham, a fiction, a mockery. The test, which seems to come first, is a test to determine whether meaning is possible at all. The temptation, which would repeat the preceding test, though in an even more serious fashion, is the possibility that meaning might itself be travestied beyond all recognition: the promise of history as pure and simple—that is, *mad*—imposture.

That Hegel, in his commentary on Abraham and his faith, never took seriously enough the threat to meaning and understanding that is posed by this second possibility is the complaint lodged against the Hegelian system of philosophical thought by Johannes de Silentio. "Hegel is wrong," de Silentio claims, "in speaking about faith; he is wrong in not protesting loudly and clearly against Abraham's enjoying honor and glory as a father of faith when he ought to be sent back to a lower court and shown up as a murderer" (*FT* 54–55). According to a stance that Kierkegaard will always adopt in regard to Hegel's dialectical mediations, de Silentio focuses on the difference between the result (Abraham receives Isaac a second time and returns home) and the beginning (Abraham sets out to slit his son's throat on Mount Moriah). This is the difference that, for Kierkegaard, also conditions the irreducible asymmetry between a formal logic of cause and effect (where the result is always already contained in the beginning) and the actuality of historical existence (where no outcome whatsoever can ever be given in advance). History is the space where decisive action is taken, and such action also always entails taking responsibility for that which cannot be known, calculated, or even imagined in advance: "the outcome," de Silentio insists, "cannot help a person either in the instant of action or with respect to responsibility" (*FT* 111). Only by taking the result for granted, in a purely formal manner, is Hegel able to economize on what de Silentio calls the "horror"— anxiety, distress, paradox—that afflicts all philosophical thought in the instant of undergoing Abraham's ordeal.

Taking the beginning with the utmost seriousness, on the other hand, de Silentio will identify faith with a radical suspension of any knowledge regarding future outcomes, and thus with the "new" category of historical actuality called "repetition." "If Abraham actually had sacrificed Isaac," de Silentio asks, "would he therefore have been less justified?" (*FT* 63). In fact, de Silentio dares to go even further still, and says, "We let Isaac actually be sacrificed. Abraham had faith" (*FT* 36). To think Abraham is therefore to expose one's thought to the monstrosity of the unthinkable: the possible destruction, or murder, of all meaning in history, period. And to make his own meaning clear here, de Silentio takes another jibe at Hegel:

autoimmunity

> I for my part have applied considerable time to understanding Hegelian philosophy and believe I have understood it fairly well; I am sufficiently brash to think that when I cannot understand particular passages despite all my pains, he himself may not have been entirely clear. All this I do easily, naturally, without any mental strain. Thinking about Abraham is another matter, however; then I am shattered [tilintetgjort]. I am constantly aware of the prodigious paradox that is the content of Abraham's life, I am constantly repelled . . . my thought cannot penetrate it. (*FT* 33; *SKS* 4:128)

Because thinking of Isaac as destroyed, *tilintetgjort*, would entail the loss of all meaning—"for what meaning would it have if Isaac should be sacrificed?]" (*FT* 19)—every genuine thought of Abraham's faith must risk being shattered or annihilated, *tilintetgjort*, in its turn. For, as de Silentio concludes, "faith begins precisely where thought stops" (*FT* 53). Is it any wonder, then, that Hegel's own thought "may not have been entirely clear," *ganske klar*, in precisely those passages where it is a question of Abraham and the threat to thought that is posed by his faith?

According to Hegel, the only product of thought—which is also the only form in which knowledge can appear—is the *universal*, the particular that is mediated through the general. The activity of speculative thought, as well as its sequential unfolding through history, is necessarily opposed to all that is particular, contingent, and individual.[11] The task, therefore, of each individual, of every particular "I," consists in constantly losing its particularity in order to express itself in the universal generality of thought. And it is at this point that language surfaces in Hegel's philosophical system, since it is language that provides the ordering principles through which the singularity of all that is particular can mediate itself in the generality that is always required of it by thought. If, as Hegel argues in his early writings on Christianity, Abraham represents the passage, transition, or mediation through which a natural and particular bond is broken in order to be subsumed within a more spiritual and universal relationship to the absolute, then there should be a place where this mediating function can be identified and understood in linguistic terms.[12] But, according to the argument Kierkegaard places in the mouth of Johannes de Silentio, this moment of linguistic mediation in the universal is precisely what is lacking in Abraham's story. When Abraham responds to God's call to take Isaac again, though this time in order to destroy him on Mount Moriah, he takes leave of the ethical as such, which is the universal:

> Abraham's act is totally unrelated to the universal, is a purely private endeavor. . . . There is no higher expression for the ethical in Abraham's life than that the father shall love the son. . . . Insofar as the universal was present, it was cryptically in Isaac, hidden, so to speak, in Isaac's loins, and must cry out with Isaac's mouth: Do not do this, *you are destroying everything* [Du tilintetgjør Alt]. (*FT* 59; *SKS* 4:153)

Isaac, to the degree he already carries within him the promise of all future meaning, of historicity itself, can therefore cry out in a language that, however it is coded, will always be universally understandable: Do not do this.

Abraham, however, cannot, without ceasing to be Abraham, without turning away from God as the unified source of all meaning, express and therefore mediate his relationship to God in any human language: "Speak he cannot; he speaks no human language [Tale kan han ikke, han taler intet menneskeligt Sprog]" (*FT* 114; *SKS* 4:202). For Abraham's relationship to the absolute is the condition of possibility for the universal meaning that now lies hidden within Isaac, and it is in fact this fullness of meaning that Abraham loves more than anything in Isaac. But God's call to Abraham is also a demand that, for the sake of maintaining his relation to the absolute, Abraham cut himself off from Isaac as well as the rest of humanity by slitting this one throat. Abraham could never express how, for the sake of preserving his bond with the ground of all human knowledge and discourse, he is about to sever every tie with the meaning of his own future by applying the knife to his life-blood, Isaac. "Abraham," de Silentio concludes, "cannot be mediated; in other words, he cannot speak. As soon as I speak, I express the universal, and if I do not do so, no one can understand me" (*FT* 60). It is by responding directly to God's call—"Here I am"—without mediation, in other words, without a second thought, that Abraham is now deprived of being able to mediate himself, and therefore of making himself understood in the philosophical generality of any known language. Or—but this would just be another way of saying again the same thing—it is because Abraham's response, "Here I am," initiates the binding of Isaac, and at the same time the undoing of every determinable meaning for the future of human thought, that Abraham would not know how to say in any intelligible fashion what is happening to him alone at that instant: that he is undergoing a test and a temptation by God himself. The test is that Abraham respond to God's call—and without this first response there can be no ground for any meaningful future, and therefore no room for Isaac's own growth as the fruit of Abraham's love. But this test—which allows for history as meaning to occur in the first place—includes at the same moment the temptation that, by responding to God's call, Abraham will do away with precisely that which the test made possible: Isaac as the living embodiment of all meaning in history.

The price to be demanded of Abraham by this ordeal, de Silentio tirelessly reminds us, is a "pledge of silence" (*FT* 21). In this silence also resides Abraham's *solitude*—his being kept separate from Sarah and Isaac for the sake of his being bound absolutely to the call of the absolute. "The knight of faith," de Silentio says, "is alone in everything. . . . [T]he true knight of faith is always absolute isolation: he is the single individual without any connections" (*FT* 79). With no connections to anything, *uden alle Connexioner*, the silence that Abraham keeps for the sake of the absolute keeps him in absolute isolation, *den absolute Isolation*; he is not just sequestered from his family, but isolated as well from humanity in general. Abraham is therefore not simply *not* understandable; he is positively *mad*: "Humanly speaking, Abraham is mad [afsindig], and cannot make himself understandable to anyone" (*FT* 76). This one thing that Abraham could never make humanly understandable is the fact of his not being in a position of mediation with the universal—for God's sake. To the rest of us, de Silentio insists, and precisely insofar—and as long as—we are seriously committed to articulating reason with historical action, Abraham must appear mad; he must appear in his words and his deeds as an utterly senseless murderer of sense itself.

If this were all that de Silentio were to say in *Fear and Trembling*, the book would still constitute a significant contribution to the future of philosophical thought, especially as it relates to questions of ethical and social comportment. For it would at the very least invite us to undertake a salutary demystification of the aberrant place still occupied in our philosophical and theological heritage by Abraham and the violent aberrancy of his faith.[13] But de Silentio goes further than this commitment to reason that remains nonetheless a prerequisite for all his considerations on Abraham. In addition to or beyond his disclosure of the way our philosophical and theological tradition has carefully kept concealed what one could now call Abraham's "secret"—the absolute madness of his readiness to respond "Here I am" to the absolute, at whatever cost to the faculty of reason and the ethical imperatives that have to be articulated with it—de Silentio still credits Abraham with providing us all with a genuine historical origin. "Venerable Father Abraham! Second Father of the race!" is how de Silentio addresses himself to Abraham before embarking on the properly philosophical examination of the challenge Abraham's faith offers to philosophy (*FT* 23). For Abraham, as we all know, did not come home empty-handed from Mount Moriah; he took back again what he was prepared to give up and kept Isaac, thereby opening a new space for the future of a meaningful history after all. Isaac would thus have also provided existential proof of how Abraham broke through to the "new category" of repetition, through which alone, Constantin Constantius insisted, every new historical actuality must at first pass. According to de Silentio, moreover, Abraham would never have been able to keep Isaac without such a repetition. ("You had to draw the knife, before you kept Isaac [at Du maatte drage Kniven, før Du beholdt Isaak]" (*FT* 23; *SKS* 4:121). But what exactly does it mean in this context "to keep" Isaac?

One thing that it does not seem to mean is that the test and temptation of Abraham will ever have been once-and-for-all accomplished or completed. If this one moment of Abraham's wandering from the path of the universal, of his turning away from any ethically understandable behavior toward his son, could have guaranteed for the future a smooth unfolding of reason in history, then that single violation of all meaning might at some later point have become susceptible to explanation, understanding, and thus a reconciliation with reason. But de Silentio makes it clear that this is not the case. Abraham will never have finished drawing his knife on Isaac, since the repetition through which historical actuality is originally acquired can only happen ever again, over and over, and without interruption. "The knight of faith," de Silentio claims, "is *constantly* kept in tension [holdes *bestandig* i Spænding] . . . kept in a state of sleeplessness [holdes søvnløs], for he is *constantly* being tested [thi han prøves *bestandig*]" (*FT* 79, 78). Abraham can "keep" Isaac only by being himself "kept" ceaselessly separated from the meaning of his future by the ordeal to which he is absolutely subjected by the absolute. At every moment, *i ethvert Øieblik*, Abraham is liable to return to the universal in which he would find repose, but such rest would be possible only on condition of "sneaking out of life" instead of "giving himself time to live"—precisely through giving Isaac up yet again, over and over, in repetition (*FT* 78; *R* 131).[14] Historical time, according to de Silentio, is therefore not reducible to a universal science of logic; it is not a continuum of mediated articulations, but rather begins tempestuously only on the recurring occasion of God's unique call to break with every other connection.

God's call to Abraham is thus a temptation in more than one sense. On the one hand, the call from God to Abraham is a temptation to the degree that to listen and respond to this call—"Here I am"—tempts Abraham to do away with the one thing he loves most: his son Isaac and all that this beloved son means, which is the future of historical meaning itself. On the other hand (and de Silentio will point this out on more than one occasion[15]), the call from God to Abraham is also a temptation in the sense that *not* to listen and *not* to respond to this call—choosing to "keep" Isaac and ignore God's call to give up Isaac and all that he means—would be to turn away from what, in the name of God, offers the absolute condition for the "universal" and all that binds Abraham, or anyone else, to it. The most dangerous temptation, to which Abraham at least does not appear to succumb, would be the naïve belief that his love for Isaac does not itself depend on the absolute in this way, the belief that Isaac's meaning for Abraham could therefore ever be kept without a constant reference to the absolute from which alone Abraham's human relationship to Isaac could ever issue. Abraham knows that he cannot choose Isaac in preference to the call from the absolute and still keep his love for Isaac—as well as the "universal" and the "ethical" that lie buried together in the loins of Isaac—without at the same time undoing the absolute as the only basis for love's own meaning. For without this reference to the absolute, called God, what could Abraham's love for Isaac in fact mean from a *human* point of view?

What exactly would Abraham be loving in Isaac if it were not in the first place the absolute as the *arche* and *telos* of all meaning—and therefore, as this absolute love of meaning, something that lies already beyond whatever else either Isaac or Abraham could be said to name without it? It is for this reason that the binding of Isaac will always have constituted a most curious double bind for Abraham, one to which Kierkegaard above all will have been attentive in sustained and uncompromising fashion.

Abraham is therefore bound to respond to God the instant he is called by him precisely because he, Abraham, loves Isaac in absolutely meaningful fashion. De Silentio seems to know that Abraham cannot keep his love for Isaac without constantly, and for the sake of keeping the meaning of this love absolute, drawing his knife on it. For the same reason, one could say that because Abraham loves Isaac above all else, God, as the name that is given here for the absolute, is forever bound to call Abraham away from Isaac before Abraham can, in every instant, take Isaac back again as this absolute love. Repetition, as the new category that must be discovered, is the historical "motion" through which Abraham engenders a history of meaning by constantly, uninterruptedly, interrupting its coming into existence in the human form of Isaac and the universal meaning that he always brings along with him. No sooner will the "universal" have begun to speak meaningfully through Isaac's loins than Abraham will be once again called upon by the absolute to draw his knife on it—in order to keep it once again. As long as history, as the space in which meaning can unfold, lasts—according to the singular model that emerges from *Repetition* and *Fear and Trembling*—there will have to be this mutual interference personified by the way Isaac, Abraham, and God come together and endlessly collide with one another. The power to promise the future is absolute here, though it becomes effective only by ceaselessly demanding from Abraham a radical suspension of its own fulfilment in Isaac. The convergence of Abraham, God, and Isaac necessarily occasions a shattering of the mutually dependent but profoundly irreconcilable conditions through which alone such an inaugural "moment" for history's unfolding could ever be constituted. Inextricably bound by God's inexplicable requirement that he give up Isaac in order to keep him, Abraham finds himself at each instant cut off from everything else. The temptation—this time not just for Abraham—would be to believe that it might one day be possible to cling exclusively to the potential for meaning that lies concealed within Isaac, without letting go at the same time of an absolute claim that must always underwrite and thus overtake it. Equally disastrous would be the belief that the absolute—be it called God, or love, or history—could ever be severed from its own implication in the cognitive and ethical systems of universality that it will have always set into movement along with Isaac's future. Faith, de Silentio is finally led to suspect, is therefore just as much a "temptation" for God as it is for Abraham. "In the same instant my soul is gripped by monstrous anxiety," de Silentio writes, "for what is it to tempt God [thi hvad er da det at friste Gud]? And yet this is the movement of faith, and it continues to be that" (*FT* 48; *SKS* 4:142). At every instant, then, faith also puts the absolute at absolute risk of doing away with the sole grounds for its own meaning.

In this respect, the version of Abraham, Isaac, and the absolute that Kierkegaard retells through the pseudonymous voice of Johannes de Silentio is remarkable for the way it passes over in near silence one of the Biblical story's most salient features. Kierkegaard's reading of Genesis 22 seems to freeze the narrative at the precise moment of verse 10: "And Abraham stretched forth his hand, and took the knife to slay his son." Or, rather, it would be more precise to say that Kierkegaard mobilizes the endlessly alternating juxtaposition of verse 10 with verses 11 and 12: "And the angel of the Lord called him out of heaven, and said, Abraham, Abraham: and he said, Here *am* I. And he said, Lay not thine hand upon the lad, neither do thou any thing unto him: for now I know that thou fearest God, seeing thou hast not withheld thy son, thine only *son* from me." Kierkegaard himself—or at least another pseudonym for whom Kierkegaard will take responsibility in *Concluding Unscientific Postscript*, Johannes Climacus—glosses the reading of Genesis provided in *Fear and Trembling* by Johannes de Silentio in the following manner:

> In temptation (when *God* tempts a person, as is said of Abraham in Genesis), Abraham was not heterogeneous with the ethical. He was well able to fulfill it but was prevented from doing so by something higher, which by *absolutely* accentuating itself transformed the voice of duty into an ordeal. As soon as that something higher sets the tempted one free, all is in order again, even though the terror, that this could happen even for one-tenth of a second, remains forever. How long the suspension lasts is of minor importance; that it is [at den er], that is the crucial thing.[16]

This Johannes stipulates that the temptation in question has to originate in the absolute—in the name of whatever guarantees the intelligibility of any act of understanding or cognition. This is so because only by relation to such an absolute could the constraints of the ethical—which function here as an equivalent for Hegel's universal, the unifying principles of a general science of logic—be legitimately considered a "temptation" for the thinking subject, in this case, Abraham. The paradox is that the absolute's promise to engender meaning in history (Isaac) interrupts itself, and that within the space of this unthinkable interruption for thought—the instant of its repetition of thought into existence—the universal laws of reason can be construed only as a temptation, since to follow them without interruption would entail a loss of the absolute condition of their own intelligibility as existing thought. As soon as, *Saasnart*, the absolute is reestablished in its absolute priority, in the instant that the subject responds to the call of the absolute—when Abraham says "Here I am," for instance—then whichever thinking subject might be tempted to turn its back on the absolute for the sake of the universal—in Abraham's case, for the sake of the history of meaning enclosed within his own son Isaac—is set free again by that higher power, *hiint Høiereiin giver den Fristede fri*, to follow the laws of reason and understanding.

But Johannes Climacus appends a crucial qualification to his reading in *Concluding Unscientific Postscript* that also confirms the originality of Johannes de Silentio's text on Abraham. By responding to the voice of the absolute, the one who is tempted not to listen to it is set free, and all order is restored, including and especially the universal order of reason that was interrupted by the temptation. However, that is not the end of the story here. Order is restored, Isaac is returned to Abraham, history resumes the course of its meaning, *even though* the interruption itself does not end: "the terror, that this could happen even for one-tenth of a second, remains forever." The subject who responds to the call of the absolute—the call to disconnect itself from every other relationship except this one that is called absolute—will be forever marked by the instant of terror, *den Forfærdelse*, through which its freedom to exist historically will have been given to thought. The drawing of the knife—no matter how long it will have lasted as measured in empirical time—remains forever behind, *bliver i al Evighed tilbage*, and thus repeats itself for thought at every new instant of its historical actuality as thought. Why is it that Kierkegaard's reading of Abraham's faith does not furnish a conclusion, a stop, and thus a satisfactory means for moving beyond the unsettling terror to which reason is subjected by the absolute? Why does Kierkegaard seem to leave Abraham's drawing of the knife suspended, allowing it in this way to return to haunt Abraham's relationship to both Isaac and God, that is, to the whole world and its history?

Rather than offering a positive answer to such questions, Johannes de Silentio's treatment of Abraham in *Fear and Trembling* hints obliquely at a possible response precisely by virtue of what it goes out of its way not to speak about. The turning point in the narrative of Genesis 22 occurs, of course, immediately after the angel transforms God's command to do away with Isaac into the interdiction not to lay a hand on him. For it is at that moment that Abraham turns away from the terrifying affliction to which he has just been subjected by being torn between his love for Isaac and his response to God's call. Abraham turns away from this ordeal, then, by lifting up his eyes, and what he sees by averting his gaze from what is happening down below is also what enables the experience of terror to appear subsequently in an uplifted, or *aufgehobene*, form. "And Abraham lifted up his eyes, and looked," the Bible reads, "and behold behind *him* a ram caught in a thicket by his horns: and Abraham went and took the ram, and offered him up for a burnt offering in the stead of his son" (Genesis 22:13). It is this moment of dramatic resolution and reconciliation, this substitution of the ram that is destroyed by Abraham in the place of Isaac, that provides the dialectical mediation, or *Aufhebung*, by means of which both Abraham and Isaac can finally overcome and leave behind them the ordeal of sheer terror they have just endured together on Mount Moriah. In the Bible narrative, the sacrifice of the ram leads directly to the new blessing Abraham will receive, in which the promise of a universal meaning for history that is enveloped within Isaac is affirmed by God for a second and final time. In the original text, the one to which the anonymous reader in *Fear and Trembling* does not have direct access, Abraham and Isaac can then go about their business, the meaningful business of propelling history toward its unfolding in philosophical universality. What remains most conspicuously as the climax in the original version is not therefore the shudder of that one unending moment that is left hanging—*bliver i al Evighed tilbage*—in Kierkegaard's Danish translation of it. Rather, what remains forever behind in the Biblical text to commemorate, in Isaac's stead, the end of Abraham's ordeal is that one burnt ram.

How could Kierkegaard, or Johannes de Silentio, or Johannes Climacus, have forgotten about the ram, since it is only by remaining behind on Mount Moriah that the ram marks this place as the sacred origin of the whole story? "[A]nd Abraham went and took the ram, and offered him up for a burnt offering in the stead of his son. And Abraham called the name of that place Jehovah-jireh: as it is said *to* this day, In the mount of the Lord it shall be seen" (Genesis 22: 13–14). Jehovah-jireh, which means something like "In the mount of the Lord it shall be seen," or perhaps "the Lord shall provide," or perhaps "the Lord will see to it," therefore commemorates the way that

Isaac's place was eventually taken by the ram. In the Bible, Abraham gives a name to the place where he was called upon by God to destroy his beloved son Isaac, and along with him any chance for a future of historical meaning. The name for the place where meaning itself was for one brief moment almost immolated continues, to this day, right here and now, to bear its own meaning, "God shall provide." This meaning, at least in the original Biblical version, also serves to commemorate the ram that—inexplicably caught by its horns in a thicket at that very instant—Abraham took in his hands and then gave in sacrifice to the absolute instead of giving up Isaac and along with him all of his meaning.

How strange it is that *Fear and Trembling* has nothing, or almost nothing, to say about this ram that by tradition intervenes in such a decisive manner in the story of Abraham, Isaac, and God![17] It is only by leaving aside the ram and the ultimate recovery of the story's own intelligibility that will always have been marked by its sacrifice, moreover, that de Silentio—along with all of Kierkegaard's other pseudonyms—manages to leave Abraham's knife hanging above Isaac at every instant. This is because, without the ram, there appears to be nothing left behind that Abraham could have simply destroyed in Isaac's stead in order to give determinate meaning to the name, "God will provide." And yet, it could not finally be claimed that de Silentio forgets the ram without remainder, since *Fear and Trembling* conveys in its turn a most peculiar trace of the ram through the ram's very absence from this text. After insisting over and over that Abraham must, for the sake of the absolute, keep silent before every solicitation to speak any language that would be humanly understandable, de Silentio also insists that Abraham cannot all the same draw the knife on Isaac without leaving behind "a word to say" (*FT* 115–17). In fact, the originary event that will have occurred in history through Abraham's faith could not constitute itself as an "event" in the first place without such a testamentary word. In Kierkegaard's text, the historical event of faith is necessarily verbal: "If this word was not there," de Silentio concludes, "the whole event [den hele Begivenhed] would lack something" (*FT* 116; *SKS* 4:203). It is not without significance that, at least in Kierkegaard's version of the story, the mark that Abraham's faith has to leave upon the world no longer includes the burnt ram that, in Genesis, eventually comes to signify, in Isaac's place, Abraham's faithful obedience to God. In *Fear and Trembling*, Abraham leaves behind a word that, instead of everything else he could have said on that occasion, according to de Silentio—and also instead of the ram whose burning flames illuminate the celebratory denouement of Genesis 22—says what it has to say by remaining utterly *blank*, by *saying nothing*, and thus by leaving an open space in the text. "But a final word by Abraham has been preserved [Imidlertid er der dog opbevaret et sidste Ord af Abraham]," says de Silentio, "and insofar as I can understand the paradox, I can also understand Abraham's total presence in that word. First and foremost, *he does not say anything*, and in that form he says what he has to say" (*FT* 118; *SKS* 4:206). The nothing that Abraham says here, he says in response to Isaac's request for explanation and understanding. Isaac, as the representative of meaning's future, naturally enough asks his father to speak in such a way as to make intelligible and explain their having left home one day in order to make a burnt offering on Mount Moriah.

In terms of philosophical discourse there is a surprising twist on Moriah, since Isaac comes after the fact to personify Hegel's commitment to a dialectical process of mediation that is always achieved through a language of question and disclosure, while de Silentio's Abraham functions like Kierkegaard's critical analysis of and resistance to such a language. "Isaac asks Abraham where the lamb is for the burnt offering," de Silentio writes, and then he provides Abraham's famous response to Isaac, citing from the Bible text: "'And Abraham said: God himself will provide the lamb for the burnt offering'" (*FT* 115–16). In this way, de Silentio focuses on precisely those words that— once the ram has been found and destroyed by Abraham in Isaac's stead— will have been able to commemorate the episode as the founding event of the meaningful history proceeding from it. After Abraham has seen the ram and then offered it in place of his beloved son, Isaac, the test will have been over, and the words, "God will provide," can begin to fulfill the promise that is threatened with extinction at the moment they are first spoken by Abraham in response to Isaac's anxious question. But by restricting his own attention to the *first* instance in which Abraham speaks these words, de Silentio deprives them of the recuperative value they will acquire only by virtue of being endowed with retrospective significance, that is, only *after* Isaac has been returned to Abraham. The subtle but all-important displacement that is operated in the Biblical text when Abraham realigns his response to Isaac with the commemorative site of his completed ordeal remains oddly missing from Kierkegaard's text: "And Abraham called the name of that place Jehovah-jireh, 'The Lord will provide': as it is said to this day, 'On the mount of the Lord it shall be provided.'" If de Silentio insists that, in response to Isaac's request to preserve meaning, Abraham's saying "God will provide" preserves only what he has to say, in other words, it preserves only a blank or *nothing*, then that is because at the instant in which de Silentio freezes the narrative to analyze its philosophical and religious significance, every determination of the meaning of Abraham's words has been radically interrupted—for him as well as for us. What exactly the Lord will provide on that mount—a lamb, a beloved son, a ram?—remains for that single instant, which will have lasted for an eternity, *bliver i al Evighed*, strictly unknowable as either meaning or the obliteration of meaning. On the point of Abraham's raised knife thus remains suspended the instant of terror in which Abraham can exist only by not knowing whether or not the absolute itself is demanding the absolute elimination of meaning as it has been determined in the form of Isaac and his future.

By "forgetting" the ram in this way, Kierkegaard's text has de Silentio constantly recall the shudder that Abraham's thought will have undergone for all eternity when it was subjected to the absolute requirement to abandon all knowledge and all understanding. Kierkegaard's version thus repeats—*tager igjen*—the ram that appears to put an end to Abraham's unthinkable ordeal, though it repeats this ram only by reinscribing it within the unheard-of possibility of something wholly new happening with it: the possibility of Abraham's *not* looking up from what is happening here and now, of his letting the ram go, letting it get away, and therefore giving it up as a fitting conclusion for this trial. For de Silentio's main point is that by remembering the ram—or by remembering whatever name we use to dispel and thus evade the terror of Isaac's sacrifice, by exchanging the ram for Isaac in such a way that the original trembling can be mediated through Isaac's return to Abraham and the meaningful history they together engender, in other words, through *our* history—one always forgets Abraham and the interruption of meaning that he had to endure in that place that, still today, means: the Absolute will provide—the source of all meaning.[18] *Fear and Trembling* repeats the story of the ram in such a way that the ram now remains caught in a thicket of another order. In the wake of Kierkegaard's text, the ram hovers for eternity in those words of Abraham, in the verbal space that lies between the first "God will provide," which remains incessantly suspended in the terror of suspended meaning, and the second "God will provide," which pretends to recover from that instant of interrupted meaning by always finding a new sacrificial victim to leave behind in its place. Is it any wonder, then, that in characterizing Abraham's legacy as it has been "preserved" (*ophevaret*) in that final word— "God will provide"—Johannes de Silentio will be compelled to acknowledge that this language of faith is ultimately indistinguishable from the language of *irony*? Abraham's response to Isaac's desperate request for knowledge and understanding, and thus to ours as well, so de Silentio concludes, "is in the form of irony, for it is always irony when I say something and still do not say anything" (*FT* 118; *SKS* 4:206). By preserving the shadow of Abraham's sacrificial ram in his words but without saying anything about what might now become of it, de Silentio's ironic repetition of religious faith offers yet another occasion for taking seriously whatever it is we still do not know or understand about its power to inaugurate our own historical existence.

PART TWO

Postromantic Irony

SIX

Signs of the Times: Nietzsche, Deconstruction, and the Truth of History

When it comes to the state of the university, the current situation seems fraught with uncertainties for the future. Today, perhaps more than ever, there is a sense of crisis in and around the academy, especially concerning the humanities. Most recently, of course, the crisis has been cast in predominantly financial terms, but the financial component of the issue goes hand-in-hand with a crisis of values that has been with us for at least the past quarter century if not more. The "value" of a degree in the humanities will of course be subject to particularly acute questioning whenever the cost of an education becomes increasingly disproportionate to the actual social, professional, and political "capital" against which it can eventually be measured and exchanged. But the unsettling discussions and decisions about the future of the humanities taking place these days, both inside and beyond the university walls, echo in their own way, though in a minor key, the ideological shrillness with which, during the 1980s and 90s, the same questions were debated in terms of the desirability of core curricula, the inviolability of a canonical approach to cultural artifacts, and the centrality of the principles and history of Western civilization for any undergraduate program in the humanities.[1] At such moments of real or perceived crisis, the university and especially the humanities tend to become a battleground on which defenders of longstanding cultural values and the familiar modes of evaluation that go along with them are pitted against a confusing array of enemies whose sole point of convergence seems to be the individual and collective aim of undermining all established values and institutions, including the values of meaning, knowledge, and understanding on which the university itself is founded and can be maintained.

Of course, whenever the debate is set up in such a lopsided and theatrical fashion, it becomes all too easy to denounce and deride the so-called attackers for any number of sound reasons, including their alleged confusionism, self-indulgence, immoralism, and, especially, the logical contradiction that seems to lie at the heart of any such a project. For what could be more self-contradictory than trying to establish as a (supreme) value in its own right the aim of undermining all values?

Before allowing oneself to be drawn into the whirlpool of conflicting interpretations and judgments in which the humanities appear caught today, it might be helpful to step back for just a moment to consider what happens when the issue is placed within a slightly different context. For, in truth, there is little hope for a genuine discussion when there is nearly always the over-whelming temptation to decide—quickly, effortlessly, unambiguously—in favor of those whose educational values can be easily measured by reference to social, professional, and political equivalents, and against those whose intellectual principles and methods cannot be so measured. Friedrich Nietzsche, who in one guise or another is likely to be called upon to testify in any struggle over traditional values, also tirelessly pointed out that the question of values is first and foremost precisely that, a genuine *question*. Any given system of values—its origins and effects, in particular—has to be critically examined and interrogated before it can reasonably be accepted, maintained, or altered. For values, unlike flowers or trees, rocks or birds, are never simply given; they must be constructed, or at the very least revealed, and as such they are always open to the rigor of philosophical debate and critique. As Nietzsche says in the preface to his study of the genealogy of moral values: "The *value* of these 'values' was accepted as given, as fact, as beyond all question. . . . Let us articulate this *new demand*: we stand in need of a *critique* of moral values, *the value of these values itself should first of all be called into question*."[2] While it would be naïve or foolish to question the legitimacy of the existence of a rock or a tree, this same question becomes a philosophical necessity for all values, and in fact it would be difficult to conceive of the operation of the university apart from its mission to ensure that such questioning be initiated and maintained—even in the face of an opposite tendency toward complacency and inertia.

What Nietzsche calls for, then, is *not* the annihilation of all values—which would ultimately be just as arbitrary and senseless as their blind acceptance and propagation—but rather their transvaluation or revaluation. This, according to Nietzsche, is the necessary task of putting into question, of weighing and assaying, the composition and status of values as values, since otherwise there can be no valid check against their potential to dissipate into empty slogans or even coercive programs. This is not an easy task, though, especially given the internal resistances such questioning is bound to meet. "Eine Umwertung aller Werte," a transvaluation of all values, Nietzsche says metaphorically in the foreword to *Twilight of the Idols*, is a "question-mark so black, so huge it casts a shadow over him who sets it up."[3] True to this prediction, moreover, such a huge, black shadow has not failed to attach itself to Nietzsche's own mode of questioning, threatening in the process to blot it out or keep it safely hidden from view. Among all the philosophical inquiries of the West, Nietzsche's examination of the fundamental principles and values of Western metaphysics is perhaps alone in the magnitude of its capacity to generate misrepresentations, scoffing, debunking, and out-of-hand condemnations that bypass the effort of serious analysis, or even direct acquaintance with the text. The Nietzschean themes of the healthy, the strong, the *Übermensch*, the will to power, nihilism, and the eternal return of the same, rather than becoming a true source of critical reflection and education, are still treated most often as straightforward values to be adopted or discarded without further ado. If only on account of such a regularly deficient understanding of Nietzsche's texts, it would be difficult to conceive how any true study of Western culture, or at least of its canonical texts of philosophy and literature, could simply dispense with the obligation, called for by Nietzsche from *within* its very own precincts, of posing once again the question of the value of all its values.

Paradoxically enough, however, whoever dares, like Nietzsche, to put the values of Western metaphysics seriously into question runs the risk of being accused and convicted, often without a hearing, of cultural and intellectual if not political and religious heresy. Why this should be so is suggested by Paul de Man in an essay entitled "Nietzsche and the Rhetoric of Persuasion."[4] Nietzsche's questioning of the main concepts of Western metaphysics, de Man argues, is difficult to take seriously; it is therefore difficult not to resist or to ignore, to the precise extent that it intervenes in and tampers with the most volatile of all relationships: the relationship and possible equilibrium between knowledge and power. Starting out from an interrogation of the value of values, Nietzsche's work ends up by questioning the legitimacy of the actual structures of power in whose shadow the philosopher of knowledge is always obliged to carry out such interrogations. It is at this point, where Nietzsche's philosophical critique of the values of knowledge and power threatens to call into question the continued exercise of these powers by their appointed representatives, de Man suggests, that it is liable to produce reactions of extreme defensiveness. Such reactions may in fact have less to do with the values considered in themselves than with the understandable investment those who at any given moment benefit the most from them have in protecting their own position from questioning.

Now what is relevant in the present context—epistemological as well as institutional—is that de Man himself refers to Nietzsche's mode of interrogating values and the ensuing complications introduced by this kind of questioning of the relations between knowledge and power as a kind of *deconstruction*. Analyzing a posthumous fragment that has as its subject the principle of noncontradiction and identity, which de Man also calls "the most fundamental 'value' of all," he locates an initial polarity and valorization in Nietzsche's text between the active performance of a deed and the passive truth of a cognition. Since, de Man argues, an extended reading of Nietzsche's text eventually discloses the instability of even this fundamental polarity, we must be willing to consider Nietzsche's writing as the place where "the possibility of 'doing' is as manifestly being *deconstructed* as the identity principle, the ground of knowledge, is being *put into question*" (*AR* 126; emphasis added). If we follow this brief hint by de Man that *deconstruction* can be another name for the Nietzschean operation of putting values into question—especially the distinction and valorization of "doing" and "knowing"—we do so not just because it offers a key for understanding this overused and underexamined term. No; we follow this hint for the much more paradoxical reason that the texts of "deconstruction"—that is, those signed by Jacques Derrida, Paul de Man, and others as well—now function regularly and systematically as the target of the same kind of "black shadow" that has befallen the question marks they are attempting to bring to light and read in Nietzsche's own text. For there is no more common response to the questioning posed by deconstruction than the attempt to silence it by assigning it the value of an antivalue whose alleged "nihilism," "irrationalism," or "meaninglessness" would relieve us of any further obligation to take it seriously, except perhaps to defend ourselves against it with all due diligence. But what would happen if, for once, we did not immediately allow the philosophical necessity of asking questions to be engulfed in the shadows of unquestioned assumptions and values, if we actually made an effort to bring the questions of Nietzsche and of deconstruction out into the light of a truly open debate?

Deconstruction, then, following up on de Man's reference to Nietzsche, is one name among others for a certain mode of questioning, and this mode of questioning puts to the test and rearticulates our most familiar values as well as the expectations that necessarily go along with them. Not just any old expectations, of course—and this, perhaps, is the first source of possible misunderstanding. Say that on a certain occasion someone has accepted an invitation to contribute an essay on Nietzsche and does not write one, or writes one in only the most occasional and superficial of ways; that may test a certain kind of expectation, but it would have little or nothing to do with deconstruction as it is understood here. For that kind of affront to one's expectations would simply be gratuitous, or perverse, or even dishonest. Rather than putting something to the test, this kind of surprise would in fact close down the possibility of truly testing anything whatsoever—except perhaps the patience of whomever would be willing to continue reading such an exercise in frustration. No, we are talking about a mode of questioning that tests our expectations and values by subjecting the knowledge from which they have been derived to critical analysis. For we only expect certain effects to follow from our systems of value and evaluation because we think we have, or can eventually have, sound knowledge about them. There can be no system of values, much less a transvaluation of values, that does not imply at the very least a necessary process of cognition, no matter how provisional or problematical.

The kind of questioning we are talking about therefore tests our expectations by carefully following or retracing the steps of an actual process of knowing, understanding, and evaluating the values that have been established and continue to be operable in any given context. Very often it happens, with de Man or Derrida, that the context in which the questioning of these values takes place has already been determined to be "philosophical" or "literary," but this is not always the case. Nor is it always the case that our very expectations about what constitutes, or limits, the philosophical or literary context in contradistinction to others—such as the psychological, economic, social, juridical, and political—would be left unchallenged by such questioning.

At any rate, here is the main stumbling block for anyone who would write about Nietzsche or the various deconstructions that can be related to his writings through analysis: because deconstruction names this mode of questioning, because it designates only this operation of actually putting to the test and rearticulating what we understand (or think we understand) about a particular text or context and the values associated with and derived from it, it is very difficult, if not strictly impossible, to *describe* deconstruction itself as if it were simply this or that identity or essence—a body of beliefs or values, a method, a system, what have you, that we could then understand *outside* the specific activity of just such testing. The problem is, how to provide a description that could adequately comprehend what names only the necessary work of testing and renewing the limits of all understanding—how describe such work, that is, without at the same time immediately and irremediably betraying that work? And, contrary to another common misunderstanding, the difficulty of these questions is by no means an invitation to endow the name with any meaning (or nonmeaning) that one chooses. As a question about and determined by the specific limits of knowledge, deconstruction resists simple affirmations in a way that is itself not simply describable, since such descriptions themselves always function according to unquestioned principles of knowledge and understanding. This problem, and the efficacy with which it is confronted, become in turn the measure of any text's relation to the questioning of cognitive expectations and values that is named by the term *deconstruction*. No description, account, or critique that economizes on this stumbling block can be said to have any genuine contact with deconstruction or with Nietzsche, or with a good many other texts for that matter, since such a description can always be shown to have replaced the actual operation of such questioning with an ideal value—no matter how negative or positive such evaluations tend to be—that would itself have to be challenged by this very questioning.

Deconstruction, it could be argued, ceases to be deconstruction the moment it ceases "working" on a particular understanding and starts "describing"—or being described as—what its work has accomplished or understood, or, more often than not, what it has thus far failed to understand and accomplish. In other words, there is no Sabbath, no day of rest, for this kind of questioning: "On the seventh day, God completed all the work he was doing and rested" (Genesis 2:1–2). That is an interesting textual example in its own right and, indeed, the beginning of a very Nietzschean question: What happens to the certitude we have with regard to all our values and knowledge at the precise instant that God himself takes a rest? Can God still be said to be God when he is just resting on that seventh day? It cannot be verifiably certain, of course, that there is a transcendental principle, such as God, at the origin of the world and all its activities, but it is guaranteed, and not only by the Bible, that if there was once a transcendental principle it did rest, and that this one day of rest was substantial enough to prolong its effects right up to the present day. That is why, according to Nietzsche, certain kinds of questions cannot themselves be put to rest once and for all. Kierkegaard, who at least in this respect is rather close to Nietzsche, says pretty much the same thing when he insists that "in the world of spirit"—by which he means only that world of (Hegelian) understanding and its limits that we have been talking about— "in the world of spirit . . . only the one who *works* gets bread."[5] No bread, no deconstruction, then, no Nietzsche or Kierkegaard, without working for it, and that means getting involved with it, doing it, giving examples of its work rather than just rehashing mere descriptions of it from afar. Such descriptions always bypass the actual work by keeping it at a safe distance and by refusing to test the limits of the description's own presuppositions and understanding about the difference between knowing-doing and describing. Deconstruction, like Kierkegaard, who in this respect is also a lot like Marx, insists on the necessity of *labor*, of work. Whenever deconstruction stops working and starts to rest by simply describing what its work consists of or results in, then it is no longer deconstruction, much less Kierkegaard, Nietzsche, or Marx. It is what Kierkegaard called *speculation* and what Marx called *ideology*; that is, it becomes the necessary object of critical analysis as well as its constant temptation.

Mere description, no matter what the level of its analytic precision or pretensions, is not deconstruction. But, one might now ask, where is the originality in that description? Is this peculiarity not a characteristic of any genuine occurrence—empirical as well as intellectual? Is a description of baseball an actual game of baseball, for instance? Or is a description of a grape-growing the same as the fruit of a grape? Would a description of mathematical computation constitute a genuine computation? And isn't it helpful or even necessary sometimes to describe how baseball takes place—especially if you're wondering whether you may one day want to play baseball or not? The trouble is, however, that *deconstruction*, as has just been noted, names a mode of testing whose very object of interrogation turns out to be, or at least to include, the cognitive mode of "description" itself—and this complication is no longer simply true of baseball or of any other empirical or intellectual event as such, especially those that occur in the mathematical and physical sciences. Deconstruction always asks what kind of knowledge mere description is capable of providing us with. "Description," as a certain mode of affirmation (or negation), as a certain assurance about knowing or understanding certain things, is itself always implicated—and implicated as a question or a problem, and not as a certainty—whenever anything like the questioning of "deconstruction" is at issue. Unlike the example of baseball or mathematics, then, a description of "deconstruction" is not simply *not* deconstruction, it is an outright resistance to and a refusal of deconstruction, and from the very beginning. Which is not to say that such a resistance and refusal is itself once and for all avoidable— since what have I been doing here if not *describing* the predicament to which all descriptions of Nietzsche and other deconstructions necessarily fall prey? But then that does not mean that *all* we can do is resist and refuse the necessary questioning of our own assumptions and values, that *all* we can do is describe, either.

Any text or context that has a relation to deconstruction—and no text or context, no matter what its overt or implicit content, is excluded in principle from having such a relation—will at some point have to confront the problem of cognitive description as well as the challenge of somehow moving beyond it. What is of interest here, as always, is not which texts happen to display the rather contingent banner—or, rather, stigma—of "deconstruction," but rather, how specific texts actually manage to put our expectations and their related values to a genuine test. In the case of those texts now going by the name *deconstruction*, of course, this means putting to the test whatever values and expectations have themselves come to be associated with this term in the various contexts in which it today continues to operate and produce effects. There can be no contact whatsoever with deconstruction, much less a refutation, neutralization, or deconstruction of deconstruction, without taking the trouble—which is also a risk—of giving an actual *example* of its activity as well. In order to assess the "value" of Nietzsche's transvaluation of all values or of other deconstructions, then, it is first necessary to show them "at work" or "in action," and this is not exactly the same thing as simply understanding them, explaining them, or evaluating them To put Nietzsche or related deconstructions in question is first of all to read the specificity of the question marks that are actually inscribed in those texts. This also means that on this particular occasion it is possible to put the relation between Nietzsche and other deconstructions to the test only by means of the following: describing *and* putting deconstruction to work as this enigmatic relation between describing—which seems inevitable if you ever want to "know" anything— and a gesture that would no longer be simply describing—which seems necessary if you ever want to "do" something. Deconstruction names an operation that—because it always takes place between those typically Nietzschean poles of "knowing" and "doing"—always has to do, fundamentally and inescapably, with the categories of "truth" and "history."

In definitional terms, such a description may already come as something of a surprise to whatever expectations we bring to the name of deconstruction: deconstruction inaugurates a critical analysis of the enigmatic relation between truth and history. Or rather, since it tests the limits of knowledge and power, we could say that this kind of questioning has as its object the truth of history, the truth that actually does happen as distinct from the "truth" that is merely believed, or described, or promised.[6] Deconstruction, it could be argued, is not just philosophy, or literature, or theology, political science, psychoanalysis, history, or any other cognitive field of inquiry, but is rather the critical analysis of what truly happens in all of them. This, it must be pointed out immediately, is by no means to privilege deconstruction as a particular name, to say that it and it alone possesses truth and occurs historically and that all else somehow misses the point or is inferior to it. No; it is merely to give one possible name to this operation of putting to the test—an operation that is made philosophically necessary whenever such values as "truth" and "history," or "knowledge" and "power" are at issue, as they always are. What would miss the point, on the contrary, would be to believe that deconstruction somehow tries to privilege itself in naming the truth of history—for in that case it might just as well call itself *ideology* from the start. There can be many names for the truth of history, provided only, of course, that one knows how to put each one of them to the test as well.

But what about language, after all? Isn't that important for deconstruction, too? Yes. Is language not so important, in fact, that deconstruction can be identified with the claim that absolutely everything, including the truth of history, can simply be reduced to what is often derisively referred to as a "free play of language"? Not so fast, and then also, not quite. If deconstruction pays a considerable amount of attention to language, this is not because it subscribes to the mindless or self-interested view that the truth of history is a mere fiction or myth that can be produced and manipulated at will. It is because *language*—and this term, as we now know, can be understood in very extensive ways—because *language*, of all the "things" that can be said to exist in the world, is the one in which it is always possible to remark—in which it is very difficult to ignore or not to remark—the strange relationship and potential gap that always holds between describing and doing, between modes of knowledge and action, between truth and history. A text—Hegel's *Phe-*

nomenology or Rousseau's *Confessions*, Marx's *Capital* or Proust's *Recherche*, our own Declaration of Independence or Baudelaire's poem "Correspondances," to name some examples—is made up of a language of description that can be analyzed for its logical or formal consistency *and* a language of action that can have historical effects by leaving material traces on the world. The "play" of language referred to by Jacques Derrida and others is a play of articulation between these two types of language, and is therefore a kind of play that can in no way be identified with mere frivolity. It is rather a term for the serious recognition that the space available for movement between a text's formal coherence and its referential force, or between its truth and history, always outstrips the possibility of a definitive calculation; in this way, every text can acquire a dimension of historical and cognitive openness that always remains to be determined anew. And it is this play of language, aptly characterized by Jacques Derrida as a play between force and signification, that makes it necessary to *read* texts in the fullest sense of the term—any text, no matter how dated and forgettable, such as, for example, David Lehman's *Signs of the Times: Deconstruction and the Fall of Paul de Man.*

This twenty-year-old book by David Lehman is not a text that could itself easily be called an example of deconstruction in any legitimate sense. And there is very little or perhaps even nothing at all to be learned about deconstruction by reading it, though that is certainly not a reason for recommending that it not be read. On the contrary, only by reading such a book with care would it be possible to learn firsthand, as it were, about a certain kind of anti-intellectual gesture and the actual historical effects it aims for, and that it always risks having at any time and in any place. Reading such a book as Lehman's never becomes entirely unimportant or anachronistic, because: 1) as a book that responds to and nourishes certain ideas that at a certain determinate moment were very much "in the air," it can be considered "historical" in the most topical of senses; 2) as a book that promises to inform readers about something called deconstruction it should contain a certain dimension of purely descriptive "truth" that can be measured in more or less precise ways; and 3) as a good example of just what deconstruction is *not*—that is, as a book that is calculated to be serious about both truth and history in only the most shortsighted and self-serving, that is, the most tendentious and least reliable manner conceivable—*Signs of the Times* can itself always be considered a necessary object of critical analysis and interrogation—no matter how short its actual "shelf-life."[7]

First, let us ask about the descriptive truth of the book. At an early point in *Signs of the Times*, after rehearsing a broad sampling of the ways the word *deconstruction* is now more or less casually used within the American vernacular, Lehman stops short to ask a necessary question: "What *is* deconstruction?" (*ST* 21). Naturally, this should be a key moment in any attempt to describe with precision an operation, like that of deconstruction, that is exceedingly complex both in its relation to existing modes of thought and analysis and to any claim to its own originality. One of the obstacles to describing just what deconstruction is, then, consists in the prudence such descriptions ought to display with respect to employing the definitional logic assumed or provided by other cognitive disciplines. One cannot therefore simply ask "What *is* deconstruction?" without taking the time to reflect, even if just a little bit, on the formal and logical presuppositions implied by this very question, "What is?" However, when David Lehman responds to the definitional question of deconstruction in his book, he does so not by quoting or even referring to Jacques Derrida, who coined, or re-coined, the term, or to Paul de Man, whose "fall" Lehman is supposed to be charting in his book, but by quoting someone named Michael O'Brien, author of an article in the *Chronicle of Higher Education*. Lehman quotes O'Brien: "For deconstructionists the world is made up of empty rooms, with impenetrable walls and no doors, in which individual minds are bent upon reading texts with a slight smile" (*ST* 21). The only thing worthy of note here, I'm afraid, is the dangling participle that makes it unclear whether it is the texts themselves or the so-called deconstructionists that would be doing the "smiling."

At this point it should already be asked, with or without a slight smile of one's own, whether that description is a serious attempt to define an operation of critical analysis that is purported to have baneful institutional and political repercussions. How could one even begin to measure the "truth" of such a descriptive definition? Do other examples of Lehman's descriptions—of the work of de Man, of Derrida, of Saussure, and of others—do anything to offset in any substantial way the derisive frivolity of this first definition of deconstruction?

These are some of the questions that any thorough study of Lehman's book should examine and attempt to answer with care. The overall tendency of the book, in any case, is to describe its object of study—the alleged "doctrine" of deconstruction and the allegedly mindless "dogmatists" who adhere to it—in such a way as to motivate the following summation, which is both angry and flamboyant: "The impulse of deconstruction is profoundly inimical to art (which it subordinates to theory), to biography and history (whose relevance it denies), to conventional methods of critical analysis (which it considers retrograde), and to any philosophy of action (since existential choices are always transmuted into irresolvable linguistic predicaments)" (*ST* 132). If, as any scrupulous reading of the texts of de Man, Derrida, and others would easily suggest, every one of these claims is either completely wrongheaded or at the very least massively reductive, then it becomes necessary to wonder about the motivations for such misleading and hyperbolic descriptions of deconstruction and of those who sign its texts. This, of course, is where the question of history arises. For if the purely descriptive affirmations of Lehman can be shown to be untrue by putting them side by side with the texts they are purportedly about, then there is reason to consider these affirmations less for the logical truth of what they "say" than for the performative force of what they "do," or would have us "do" after reading them. In other words, all of Lehman's descriptions of deconstruction, whatever their truth (or rather, lack of truth), are apparently calculated to produce a very specific effect, to make us act, to make us participate in history by acting upon it. What historical role would such a book have us play?

In what is undoubtedly one of the most decisive—and questionable—moments of his exposition, Lehman affirms, "[W]hatever else it is, deconstruction is a movement, a network of like-minded professors who fiercely promote one another's works and use their institutional power to further the cause. . . . Initiates are rewarded with teaching appointments" (*ST* 70). The "cause" that deconstruction is said to further, which is always interpreted by Lehman as a "doctrine" or "cult" propagated by what is here called a network of like-minded individuals, is ultimately linked to a "conspiratorial view of the world" that "is pernicious to the precise extent that it acquiesces in the curtailment of human freedom" (*ST* 267, 268). "Deconstruction," Lehman assures us beyond the necessity of any further questioning, "is a program that promotes a reckless disregard of the truth," and one of the effects of such a "programmatic skepticism" would be to "paralyze the will to act upon our destiny" (*ST* 267; 77; 110; 111). The appeal to the will to act—an appeal that comes as a response to an external threat that would paralyze the will and deprive us of our destiny—is unmistakable in this book. This appeal to a given community's will to act, and in response to the threat posed to its inner coherence and destiny by an invading network of outsiders—by what in this case Lehman himself calls deconstruction's "persistent assault on our fundamental cultural assumptions" (*ST* 26)—is not new. Its many versions have their own logical constraints and their own histories—and in the spirit of a mode of questioning that, unlike Lehman's own, takes the intersection of logical and historical truth seriously, the true logic and history of this particular appeal to the will should be analyzed patiently and as fully as possible.

This appeal to the will leads, when all is said and done, directly to the conclusion Lehman provides to his book, a conclusion that consists in a re-markable sentence—and this word is to be understood in both its senses, in its descriptive and performative usages, in its grammatical and its juridical connotations—a remarkable *sentence*, then, pronounced by Lehman on that "universe of fierce cabalistic disputation" in which the network of deconstruc-tionists "shrouds itself in cabalistic mysteries and rituals" in order to keep us in "a state of permanent mystification" that, ultimately, "would paralyze the will to act upon our destiny" (*ST* 25; 55; 111). The intellectual and historical ominousness of such a sentence should be carefully registered and interpreted, before we allow ourselves simply to carry out its program: "The signs are all around us. . . . It would be a mistake to think that we cannot by conscious action do anything about them" (*ST* 268). David Lehman—who especially in this respect is wholly unlike Nietzsche, or Derrida, or de Man—has said something else quite extraordinary in the penultimate sentence of his book, in the sentence that comes just before he urges us on to take conscious action by doing something about those signs that are all around us. He tells us in this book on "deconstruction and the fall of Paul de Man," a book that is also titled *The Signs of the Times*, that these signs about which he would have us do something, and do something consciously, by an act of the will—these signs of the times "can be all interpreted correctly": "Many of [these signs] are am-biguous, some are confusing, but they can all be interpreted, and interpreted correctly" (*ST* 268).

This is a truly amazing affirmation, coming as it does just before the incite-ment to action, presumably to save our destiny from those who would para-lyze our will for the sake of their own pernicious cabal. For if we put to use even the most elementary of those "conventional methods of critical analy-sis" to which Lehman claims "deconstruction is profoundly inimical"—which methods, I hasten to add, neither de Man nor Derrida has ever suggested it would be possible or even desirable simply to dispense with—we cannot help but read the subtitle of this book as an apposition to the main title. Decon-struction and the fall of Paul de Man *are* the signs of the times, then, and this means that the signs of the times referred to in the last sentence of the book, the signs that are all around us, soliciting our conscious action, can also be neatly summed up as whatever traces of deconstruction have somehow survived the actual "fall of Paul de Man." And if it is further true—despite any nuances, ambiguities, or even potential confusions and misunderstandings on our part—that all these signs can be interpreted correctly in preparation for doing something about them, then what choice of conscious action are we finally invited to take by David Lehman? Once we are persuaded that Lehman himself may be correct in interpreting and characterizing these signs of "deconstruction" as signifying a cabalistic network of like-minded individuals whose conspiratorial view of the world would ultimately paralyze our will to act upon our own destiny, what exactly are we supposed to *do* about them? Just what sort of book is it that proposes we not mistake our potential to do something about those omnipresent "deconstructionists" and their enigmatic will to paralyze our will to act? This question, which one should not too quickly or lightly answer for David Lehman or for oneself, contains the following question as well: Do we act consciously about whatever is signified by the name *deconstruction* by reading, analyzing, annotating, and perhaps even contesting in as scrupulous a way as possible the texts associated with it, or by doing something else with its texts and the individuals who write, sign, or even disseminate them?

It is time once again to turn to Nietzsche. In the book of fragments called *The Gay Science*, there is a fragment written under the heading "On the problem of the actor": "The problem of the actor has troubled me for the longest time. I felt unsure (and sometimes still do) whether it is not only from this angle that one can get at the dangerous concept of the 'artist.'"[8] Now this "concept" of the actor, or artist, also engages philosophical categories of considerable importance, for the questions of truth and history cannot fail to surface whenever the essential character trait of the actor, and the "dissimulation" (*Verstellung*) proper to him, is at issue in any serious way. This is because dissimulation, for Nietzsche, is defined by its problematic relation to the disclosure or unveiling of truth, and this process of truth's disclosure, or *aletheia* as Heidegger reminds us, and as it has most often been interpreted and understood on the basis of the canonical texts of Western philosophy, is governed both by a logic of adequation and by a temporality of historical development.[9]

But what is perhaps most noteworthy in this fragment on the problem of the actor is not this respectable and important inquiry into the philosophical relation between truth as the historical process of *aletheia* and a counter-power that deflects or dissimulates this truth, in what Nietzsche refers to here as the falsity of appearances. Rather, it is what is at first sight the fragment's most crudely topical, questionable, and even offensive feature. At the end of the fragment, after discussing several of the philosophical aspects of artistic dissimulation, Nietzsche quite simply comes out and names "Jews" and "women" as two particularly remarkable contemporary examples of accomplished "actors." Because of the seriousness of the issues involved here, the concluding passage of the fragment deserves citation in full:

> As for the *Jews*, the people who possess the art of adaptability par excellence, this train of thought suggests immediately that one might see them virtually as a world-historical arrangement for the production of actors. And it really is high time to ask: What good actor today is *not*—a Jew? The Jew as a born "man of letters," as the true master of the European press, also exercises his power by virtue of his histrionic gifts; for the man of letters is essentially an actor—he plays the "expert," the "specialist."—Finally, *women*. Reflect on the whole history of women: do they not *have* to be first and above all actresses? Listen to the physicians who have hypnotized women; finally, love them—let yourself be "hypnotized by them"! What is always the end result? That they "give themselves out" as something else even when they—give themselves up [Daß sie "sich geben," selbst noch, wenn sie—sich geben].
>
> Woman is so artistic. (*GS* §361)

The fact is, though—beyond or independently of the justified sense of distress and outrage one feels in registering the impact of these lines—a closer look at the *formal* organization of the fragment reveals a problem of a different, though not entirely unrelated, order. For the initial problem of the actor—the problematic deflection of truth into falsehood that is necessarily introduced into the discussion by the conceptual potential to dissimulate—has itself somehow been displaced or deflected midway through the philosophical analysis in order to become a none-too-rigorous social history of what Nietzsche calls *adaptability*. This new deflection reifies the conceptual terms of a philosophical argument by translating them into highly charged anthropological examples of self-preservation in the face of threatening circumstances. The place in Nietzsche's text where this occurs can be quite precisely located, since it happens when the purely aesthetic and nonutilitarian capacity to dissimulate "truth" is illustrated with a reference to the overdeveloped ability of actual Jews and women. Jews and women are therefore personified examples of the philosophical question regarding how truth has as its own essence a particularly disturbing property: the capacity to be dissimulated, to dissimulate itself as truth.

The "problem of the actor," which is in a certain sense the fragment's own title, can now be taken to refer not only to the theoretical problem of truth's dissimulation that Nietzsche is himself describing, but also to the additional problem this particular fragment occasions for any reading and understanding of such a problematic description. For how can we as readers explain the fact that an epistemological examination of the problem of the actor swerves, without any apparent reason or justification, away from its original philosophical object of inquiry and turns into a rather shabby historical description, or even indictment, of Jews and women? Moreover, it could not be argued that a system of simple parallels and equivalences is at work between the two parts of the fragment, since the logical problem of truth and falsehood that is exemplified conceptually by the art of acting is in no way adequate to explain the kinds of historical adaptability required of given individuals for their survival in society. Much less could the philosophical concept of dissimulation, by itself, help us understand why these specific character traits—posing, deceiving, manipulating—are allotted in an insinuating and derogatory fashion to all Jews and women. Of course, we know today, as if by instinct, that we will not have read Nietzsche adequately until we can account for the overdetermined place occupied in his writings—in their analytical descriptions as well as in their historical effects—by Jews and women. But this issue is brought home to us in a much more immediate fashion by this particular fragment. We will not even begin reading the text until we try to account for the way this tension is in fact played out in the perplexing relation articulated here between the beginning of the fragment, which is about the epistemological problem of the actor, and the end, which inexplicably deflects this problem by referring it to the historical existence of actual Jews and women.

It is not entirely by accident that the question of Nietzsche's relation to deconstruction finds itself embroiled in this way with the question of Jews and women. One reason for this, though perhaps not the only or even most important one, is that the question of deconstruction, as long as it is linked to the name of Paul de Man, will necessarily be marked in some way by de Man's involvement as a cultural correspondent for almost two years with a Belgian newspaper, *Le Soir*, that continued to function under and lend aid to the anti-Semitic, but also misogynistic, authority of the Nazi occupation forces.[10] It is true that this knowledge, which came to light only in 1987, about three years after de Man's death, can have the explosive effect of a bomb on the work of Paul de Man and deconstruction. That is, such knowledge can easily turn into the conscious action of reducing all of the texts associated with these names to nothingness—either by closing them up for good, or, what would amount to almost the same thing, by turning them into indirect but correctly interpretable stand-ins, or signs, for this one, true, historical fact. For if we now know all we need to know about the truth and history of Paul de Man and deconstruction by knowing about this particular link between them and both Nazism and the nihilistic ideology tributary to it, then what possible need have we to continue bothering ourselves about de Man and other deconstructionists by reading and discussing them? But can the kind of knowledge that would act, as in this case, consciously or not, like a bomb of pure destruction and annihilation still be said to be either true or historical in any sense worthy of those terms?

In this unlikeliest of places, where actual historical knowledge threatens to explode with the self-destructive violence of a bomb, the French poet and theoretician Stéphane Mallarmé may have something to teach us. In *La musique et les lettres*, the famous lecture on contemporary aesthetic developments in France that Mallarmé delivered at Oxford and Cambridge in 1894, the poet suddenly interrupts his reflections on music and poetry to ask about the very different kinds of relations that both link and separate literature and politics.[11] At issue for Mallarmé are two symmetrically related phenomena that had been occurring recently in the popular press, and he sees them together posing a threat to the integrity of both literature and politics. On the one hand, Mallarmé singles out for attention the publication and reception of Max Nordau's *Entartung* (*Degeneration*).[12] This book—a vulgar diatribe denouncing *fin-de-siècle* art, especially in France, as the "graphomaniacal" symptom of a general pattern of social and cultural degeneration—is of concern to Mallarmé only because of the potential danger inherent in the considerable popularity it enjoyed for a time in both Germany and France. Books like this are politically explosive, according to Mallarmé, not because of what they say, but because whatever they say—including, in the case of *Entartung*, the most far-fetched, libelous, and misinformed provocations—can always be passed off and begin to function aberrantly as the objective and irrefutable truth of scientific knowledge. The real problem with such "legends" and "melodramas," Mallarmé suggests, is not that they are fictions with no claim to scientific standards of truth, but rather that they do not know, or have somehow allowed themselves to forget, that they are such fictions (*ML* 71–72).

On the other hand, Mallarmé refers to the accusatory suspicion, current in Paris newspapers of the early 1890s, that a direct link could be made between the radical aesthetic theories of certain avant-garde literary movements and the revolutionary acts of political violence committed by contemporary anarchists (*ML* 72). Taking advantage of the occasion provided by the explosion of a bomb in the Chambre des Députés on December 9, 1893 by an anarchist named Auguste Vaillant, Mallarmé makes several key points about his own, subtly differentiated, thinking about the relation between writing, violence, history, and truth. First of all, Mallarmé says in no uncertain terms, the light that emanates from an empirical bomb is by no means the same kind of light that emanates from the pages of a book, and any insinuation to the contrary is an insult to both social realities and literary activity. For the kind of light created by a bomb of pure destruction, which also always has the disadvantage of injuring innocent bystanders, is all too brief to teach us anything, and therefore this kind of self-obliterating light can result only in a display of what Mallarmé calls a "definitive incomprehension" on the part of political legislators. In other words, we can never responsibly understand what we simply destroy and thereby forever erase from history and from the kind of critical light that alone can help to reflect and extend all its truths. In the second place, according to Mallarmé, and as a direct consequence of this constant risk of relapsing into incomprehension, the only truly effective way to participate in history and politics is by means of what he calls a book whose light (*éblouissements*), or truth, does not consume itself in one single flash. Such a written light, Mallarmé suggests, can occur only with the highly diffuse and constantly renewed illumination, or textual explosion, of all the so-called facts of history, the journalistic *faits divers* that name and describe the disparate events of everyday sociopolitical life. Journalistic publications always put such *faits divers* into circulation, though without subjecting them to genuine critical analysis. What interests Mallarmé in this context is the existence of "writers who remain off on the side. . . . Whether near or far, they maintain their distance, as though waiting for an occasion . . ." In the meantime, says Mallarmé in his own language, "ils offensent le fait divers," a peculiar affirmation suggesting that such writers take the raw facts offered by whichever stories monopolize the attention of the day, in order to put them into question, to deprive them, though otherwise than by throwing bombs, of the unexamined "credit" they enjoy in constructing the ever-changing news cycles in which society seeks its apotheosis (*ML* 72).[13] Whatever particular aims or issues Mallarmé sees as comprising the critical horizon of the writer in society, this much should be clear: authentically critical writing cannot, like a literal bomb, simply wipe out its object of analysis once and for all; nor can it—like the straightforward reporting of quotidien *faits divers* it must constantly interrogate and deconstruct—merely announce and describe it.

What this task of critical vigilance, called for more than a century ago by Mallarmé, would ultimately consist in with respect to the *fait divers* of Paul de Man's wartime journalism for *Le Soir* is not itself easy to describe once and for all. It would most certainly *not* consist, however, in a simple reduction of all of de Man's other writings, as well as other deconstructive writings, including the texts of Nietzsche referred to earlier, to the same dubious status as this one certifiably true, historical fact of de Man's having written for that paper. Mallarmé warns us that the truth of any given historical *fait divers*, as event and as mere description or report of events, must always be handled carefully, must in fact become the object of critical questioning in its own right, for such truth itself always has the potential to explode as a bomb of mere destruction, forever blotting out in incomprehension precisely what it was meant to reveal and thus to preserve through a historical act of understanding.

Martin Heidegger, who, as the saying goes, may have had his reasons, said something remarkably similar to Mallarmé's remarks in a reflection on the truth of history that dates from 1935: "Every report or description [Bericht] about the past, in other words, about the steps leading up to the question . . . is concerned with what lies at rest; this kind of historical report [diese Art des historischen Berichts] is an explicit laying to rest of history [eine ausdrückliche Stillegung der Geschichte]—whereas history is on the contrary a happening [ein Geschehen]. We ask historically when we ask what is still happening, even when, to all appearances, something belongs to the past."[14] Heidegger tinkers here, as elsewhere, with the crucial distinction that is disclosed in German between the words *Historia* and *Geschichte*—history as a report or description of what has happened, and history as the actual event that must happen in its own right. The truth of history, then, is itself put into movement, *Bewegung*, when we interrogate such words and concepts, for history, Heidegger reminds us, can always be determined in at least two very different and perhaps incompatible ways—as descriptive knowledge and as actual occurrence. Heidegger goes on to call this particular movement he is talking about, which is always waiting to take place between the two modes of history, "uncanny." In fact, Heidegger says that such a movement of history, arrested for the time being between the words and concepts of *Historia* and *Geschichte*, is "uncannier," *unheimlicher*, than what we ordinarily call movement itself (*WT* 44; *FD* 34). Heidegger seems here, then, though in a very enigmatic way, to be asking about a kind of history that would consist in somehow moving the truth that is merely at rest in description toward happening as a truly historical occurrence.

Before dismissing this "uncanny" idea of Heidegger's as merely a self-interested attempt to lay certain aspects of his own past to rest, let us also note that he does suggest here that simple reports about the past are not only inevitable, they are also indispensable insofar as they provide the preliminaries, *Vorstufen*, for true historical questioning. There is, therefore, no question of hiding or laying to rest, much less condoning or excusing, the simple fact of Heidegger's affiliation with the Nazi Party, or of de Man's writing for a collaborationist newspaper. These are condemnable acts each in its own way, and one should have no difficulty in condemning them, while keeping in mind what distinguishes them from each other. But the risk, according to Heidegger as well as Mallarmé, is that a mere report or description—or condemnation, or condonation, for that matter—stops short because it can serve ultimately to remove us from another kind of necessary historical operation by remaining stuck in the affirmations of mere commonplace. "If we do not want simply to parrot opinions," Heidegger warns us in his essay, "but would rather grasp what we ourselves are saying and usually mean, then we are immediately caught in a veritable maelstrom of questions" (*WT* 47; *FD* 36). Only by carefully asking about the kind of truth that could *still* be happening in every historical event, including in all of the texts now signed by Mallarmé, Heidegger, and de Man, would it be possible to avoid falsifying the truth of their historical occurrence by replacing them with empty formulae. Each of these texts, of course, each of these signatures, has its own specificity, and only a detailed description and analysis of individual texts would be able to participate historically in the truth that may still be happening in any one of them. Mallarmé, Heidegger, and de Man provide some shorthand names for this participation in a historical truth that can occur only beyond the preliminaries of mere description—names that are, moreover, as potentially misleading as they are economical. In Mallarmé's text this participation is called *writing*; in Heidegger's it is called *questioning*; and in de Man's, *reading*. These names are not all the same for all three writers—and this could make an enormous difference in many different and important respects—nor are they the same in every one of each writer's own texts. In ways specific to each writer and to any given text, though, they all begin to name that enigmatic relation between truth as description and truth as occurrence, between description and event, or between truth and history, that is at issue for all of us.

Sooner or later, then, it becomes necessary to ask about how all that has just been said can be related back to those names that are so prominently inscribed and displayed in Nietzsche's text on the actor: the Jews and women with which fragment 361 of *The Gay Science* seems to come to a grinding halt. But is it really still necessary to ask about what is resting, like a bomb, in the descriptions Nietzsche gives of these particular names? Do we not already know full well, and with all the historical precision of its disastrous consequences, just how such descriptions must finally end up? But isn't it precisely because this knowledge and this history is still itself always in danger of disappearing in a mere catalogue of platitudes that can be thoughtlessly repeated and trotted out to justify the most aberrant intellectual and political behavior, that we remain obligated to ask once again, patiently, seriously, how much we actually do know, once and for all, about the truth of our own history?

This question about repetition and history, about knowledge and thoughtlessness, about the necessity to continue asking questions even in the face of what we think we must already know, in order, finally, to produce a future for history itself, is treated by Nietzsche under the universally recognized and barely understood terms of the *eternal recurrence*. The eternal return, according to Nietzsche, not only names the riddle of understanding how any truly historical moment must always confront the simultaneous challenge of overcoming an infinite past and opening up an infinite future; it names in addition the threat posed to true knowledge by the recurrent possibility of its relapse into empty chatter.[15] In the thought of the eternal return, Nietzsche writes in another fragment of *The Gay Science*, lies the "greatest weight." But this greatest of weights, Nietzsche goes on to suggest, can be brought to bear on every single thing—every thought about truth and every historical action— only by putting it in the form of a question that also contains the potential to transform whatever it touches: "If this thought were to acquire power over you, it would transform you as you are and perhaps even crush you; the question, for each and every thing, 'do you want this again and again countless times,' would lie as the greatest weight on all your conduct!" (*GS* §421). The weight of this thought, which Nietzsche also calls a "riddle," is itself liable to become an enormous burden for every understanding of history: for how could it be that by unremittingly returning to this question of the eternal return it would become possible to exert enough pressure on the usual patterns of our thought and conduct to crush and transform the cycle of what otherwise always threatens to remain an even-more-vicious recurrence of the same beliefs and behavior?

We must return, then, to the bomb, or the stick of dynamite, lying in wait for us in Nietzsche's text. For it is only through tirelessly coming back to interrogate the complexity of its explosive device that we might for once register what may still be happening there historically, or may be waiting to happen there—and perhaps this time as a less familiar truth than the bomb of pure obliteration, or nihilism, that is so easy to take for granted in all of Nietzsche's texts. What is happening, for instance, not in the straightforward description of Jews and women easily readable at the end of the fragment, but rather, in the relation Nietzsche's text articulates—and not just in this particular fragment—between the actor, or the artist, and Jews and women? How, exactly, does the writing of the fragment prepare for and produce the naming of Jews and women as actual historical examples of the more general epistemological problem raised by the dissimulation of truth? Asking the question in this way doesn't necessarily change anything at all, of course. In fact, the descriptions we have before us remain exactly the same, and they can still be read—descriptively and historically—to mean the same things we are mostly already familiar with. But on the other hand, this is not necessarily the way things have to turn out. It is true, on occasion, that things happen in ways we do not necessarily expect or control. And when it is a question of reading a text—like this one, for example—this means that we may not yet know all that is already truly happening in it.

If, for instance, we take Nietzsche at his word, we will perhaps not so easily forget that the philosophical concept initially interrogated in this fragment is not simply a neutral or inert entity, but is itself inherently *dangerous*: "The problem of the actor has troubled me for the longest time; I felt uncertain (and sometimes still do) whether it was not only from this angle that one could get at the *dangerous* concept of the 'artist'" (*GS* §361; emphasis added). The concept of the "artist," then, which first becomes accessible only by way of the art of acting, and which is later to be illustrated in a social context by the Jew—"What good actor is today *not* a Jew?"—is "troubling," Nietzsche warns us. And this troubling aspect of the question is also aggravated by the presence of an as-yet-unspecified "danger." Not the least unsettling thing about this dangerous concept, moreover, is the historical tendency of those who examine it not to take it and its uncertainties seriously enough. The un-named danger in the concept is thus liable to become all the more serious and threatening to the extent that it is most often not even recognized *as* a danger: "I felt uncertain (and sometimes still do) whether it was not only in this way that one could get at the dangerous concept of the 'artist'—a concept that has so far been treated with unpardonable good-naturedness [mit unverzeihlicher Gutmütigkeit]" (*GS* §361).[16] Just what is so dangerous about this concept of dissimulation that every relaxation of critical judgment toward it represents for Nietzsche an inexcusable lapse?

The answer, at least the one Nietzsche gives in this particular fragment, is that this concept involves a power so explosive that it is capable of wiping out the essence of a person's character: "the delight in dissimulation exploding as a power that pushes aside one's so-called 'character,' flooding it and at times *extinguishing* it "(emphasis added).[17] Whenever we deal with the concept of the artist, then, we are dealing with a *power* that threatens to break out, *als Macht herausbrechend*. What this power breaks out of, of course, would be whatever limits have been assigned to it, and this breaking of the limits will always have to occur at the risk and peril of whomever seems originally to exist by virtue of them. Because every lapse of attention with respect to this power can therefore turn out to be fatal for the very one who sets it loose, no such lapse could ever be justified and therefore excused. The dissimulating power of the artist is dangerous, Nietzsche tells us, because it is in this way *excessively* "adaptable" or "flexible." As "an excess [ein Überschuss] of the capacity for all kinds of adaptations," it "can no longer be satisfied in the service of the most immediate and narrowest utility," and thus it always threatens to eradicate the very "character" of the one it was supposed merely to manifest and preserve.

So far, Nietzsche seems merely to describe, from the outside as it were, the essential traits of this excessive power to dissimulate that is the hallmark as well as the most dangerous risk of the actor. And to the extent that a clear distinction can still be made between the "dissimulator" being described and the philosophical "I" doing the describing, then no lapse of attention on the part of the text about dissimulation and its concomitant danger—loss of self and its determinable needs and aims—need be considered or suspected. The claim to truth held out by the philosophical critique of the loss of essence or truth entailed in the aesthetic power to dissimulate is not, therefore, at least at first, in question in this text by Nietzsche. But Nietzsche does not stop there, of course, for he goes on to add one more question to the inquiry, and this is decisive for any genuine reading and understanding of what will happen in the rest of the fragment: "perhaps all this describes not *only* the actor's essence? [Alles das ist vielleicht nicht *nur* der Schauspieler an sich?]" Is there a place, we must now ask in our turn as readers, where Nietzsche's own philosophical inquiry into the problem of the actor runs the risk of dissimulating itself, the risk of a dissimulation so powerful and far-reaching, in fact, that it would threaten with extinction its own claim to truth by exploding beyond the reach of any properly philosophical understanding?

Such a question takes us back to the excess of "adaptability" Nietzsche associates with the artistic power of dissimulation. It is possible to dissimulate an essence only where we suppose there is first of all an essence that could eventually be disclosed, just as the concept of adaptability ordinarily presupposes a content or essence that can then be adapted *to* whatever lies around or beyond it. But Nietzsche's text also exceeds this traditional philosophical model of essence and accident, interior and exterior, or cause and effect, by introducing the possibility of an *original* power to dissimulate and adapt. What is most excessive in this regard is not simply that the power to adapt can eventually break free of the power exerted on it by what are called here needs and desires, but rather that the power to dissimulate is itself conditioned only by a form of adaptability that from the beginning escapes all other powers, no matter what they are called. And this would still be the case even and especially when this power manages to reintroduce the concept of a lost essence, whose own needs and desires it thus serves to dissimulate always and again. This particular excess is what Nietzsche refers to in this fragment as an *inner* craving for a role or a mask, for an irreducible *Schein* or appearance that has itself no essence, "das innere Verlangen in eine Rolle und Maske in einen *Schein* hinein." This strangely "inner" appearance, or *Schein*, so excessive that it can no longer be related back to an essence that would in any way be separable from it, either as its origin or its end, is also described in more detail by Nietzsche in an earlier fragment of *The Gay Science*:

> *The consciousness of appearance.*— . . . I suddenly woke up in the midst of this dream, but only to the consciousness that I am dreaming and that I *must* go on dreaming lest I perish—as a somnambulist must go on dreaming lest he fall. What is "appearance" for me now! Certainly not the opposite of some essence: what could I say about any essence except to name the attributes of its appearance! Certainly not a dead mask that one could place on an unknown *x* or remove from it! (*GS* §54)

To wake up suddenly, then, but only to the consciousness that one is dreaming and must go on dreaming—this is how Nietzsche describes the necessary outcome of the philosophical critique of appearance, or *Schein*. What could this mean with respect to the strange economy enacted within the fragment on the actor, which leads from the artistic power of dissimulation to the referential identification of this attribute with Jews and women? First of all, it alerts us to the fact that the "adaptability" at issue in this fragment has very real, if problematic, limits. It may be possible, Nietzsche is warning us, to adapt ourselves to the state of epistemological sleepwalking into which we are plunged by our inability to know for sure anything about the essence of things. But that sudden recognition can in itself do nothing to change the fact that, at least philosophically speaking, we do indeed continue to dream.

And the reason for this, Nietzsche points out, is that the radical falsity of appearance, or *Schein*—which, because it has been deprived of an essential and thus necessary origin and end, is as a consequence absolutely adaptable or flexible, *geschmeidig*, in its first position—tends also to become absolutely resistant or intractable once it assumes any given shape or form. The originary potential for infinite adaptability, Nietzsche's own writing describes and demonstrates, thus eventually hardens into an attribute that "becomes domineering, unreasonable, and intractable [herrish, unvernünftig, unbändig]" in the long run (*GS* §361). We are now prepared to note that two of the names Nietzsche's own writing gives to this thoroughly unstable structure of appearance, at least in this particular fragment, are *Jews* and *women*. That is, the names *Jews* and *women* occupy the place in this fragment where the conceptual categories of radical flexibility and radical intractability come together in an impossible way, and thus necessarily threaten the philosophical coherency of Nietzsche's own argument about dissimulation. For if, on the one hand, the words *Jews* and *women* are used in this fragment to name a generalized power of philosophical dissimulation that, as the fragment itself argues, can never legitimately be identified by reference to any given concrete empirical examples—since in that case, dissimulation would acquire its own essence and no longer function *as* dissimulation—it is also true that, on the other hand, *Jews* and *women* are themselves proper names that ultimately cannot help but indicate, as well as isolate and target, specific groups of living beings. The philosophical argument about the possibility of dissimulating the truth cannot prevent itself from turning into the rhetorical example, and therefore the potential error, of attempting to identify with historical and cognitive precision the locus of this truth of dissimulation.[18] Why this should be so is also exemplified in an economical way within this fragment on philosophical and historical dissimulation.

At the key moment in the demonstration, when the turn is being made from philosophical abstraction to historical actuality, Nietzsche makes use for the first time in the fragment of a very particular device, a rhetorical figure that in this case is a metaphor: "Such an instinct for excessive adaptability will have developed most easily in the families of the lower class, who had to survive under changing pressures and coercions, in deep dependency, who had to cut their coat according to the cloth [welche sich geschmeidig nach ihrer Decke zu strecken hatten]" (*GS* §361). The expression "to cut one's coat according to the cloth," a mere rhetorical device, then, is easy enough to read and understand, as properly meaning "to make the best of things" or "to adapt oneself to the situation at hand," cognitively or practically speaking. All such figures—at all times available to the writer of philosophical abstraction and argumentation—are themselves "adaptations" that have in essence no determinate value. For who would be sufficiently naïve to believe, for instance, that Nietzsche is writing in this fragment about literal coats? The word *coat* here, like the dissimulation of *Schein* of which it is itself an example, is a mere covering, an envelope that in itself is absolutely empty and, therefore, absolutely adaptable to any circumstances whatsoever. But this mere appearance, this empty envelope of a purely adaptable rhetorical "coat," because it too, and by definition, is always capable of exceeding the "deep dependency" in which it originally seemed to function, can always come to lord it over all the other anthropological "instincts" it eventually finds itself surrounded by, whether they be speculative and philosophical, or normative and historical in nature. The rhetorical example, Nietzsche thus warns us—which, like the *Schein* of appearance it illustrates and necessarily dissimulates, is at first neither philosophically reliable nor historically precise—can always, though mistakenly, be taken to command the ultimate meaning of both history and philosophy.

What is excessive and intractable in this kind of adaptability, Nietzsche goes on to write, in what is undoubtedly the fragment's most remarkable sentence, enables those who possess it to learn "gradually to turn their coat to *every* wind and virtually to *become* a coat [befähigt almahlich, den Mantel nach jedem Winde zu hängen und dadurch fast zum Mantel werdend]" (*GS* §361).[19] How is it possible to read and understand, with any degree of philosophical or historical precision, the proper meaning of *this* coat, *Mantel*, that now serves to cover the meaning of Nietzsche's text? The sentence that uses the coat as a mere figure, or as an infinitely adaptable *Schein* with no intrinsic essence, value, or referent of its own, also asserts—simultaneously and thus abusively or impossibly—that this radically dissimulated coat is nonetheless in the process of becoming—a literal *coat*. But a coat that in essence is nothing but mere appearance and that, in spite of this, begins to acquire the value of an actual coat is, in addition and equally necessarily, a cloak of pure deception for whomever would try to put it on or take it off—that is, for the mind that would understand it simply and definitively as either a literal or a figural coat. Nietzsche's own sentence therefore describes and enacts how an originally ungrounded tropic power, or *Schein*, in philosophical language has no reliable means to stop itself from coming to rest in the equally ungrounded literality of a referential name, or concept. The truth of dissimulation becomes absolutely false the minute it dares to name itself with philosophical rigor, as it cannot fail to do if it is not to remain at the wholly preconscious level of utter confusion and chaos.

This particular inconsistency, so glaring in the case of the "rhetorical" coat of adaptability, is exactly parallel to the inconsistency that governs the general economy of the entire fragment as it moves from the original philosophical category of dissimulation, or *Schein*, to the social and historical discrimination of actual Jews and women.[20] For, although the logic of the fragment would require it, it is simply not possible for the names *Jews* and *women* in Nietzsche's text to function simultaneously as philosophical examples for the radical dissimulation of a *Schein* devoid of essence, *and* as straightforward descriptions of socially and historically identifiable subjects. Once we become aware in this way that the first part of the fragment not only describes the dangerous economy or disfiguring power, *die Verstellung als Macht*, of the "mask," or *Schein*, of artistic—that is, *rhetorical*—adaptability, but also gives an example of this economy in the excessive "coat" that functions simultaneously though defectively as figure and as the literal meaning of this figure, it is no longer possible to understand the naming of Jews and women at the end as a simple description. Or, rather, at this point in the reading, these names must themselves begin to exceed the strict limits of description and cognition that might otherwise manage to circumscribe and contain whatever activities and effects they come at any given moment to designate and stand for.

The excessive adaptability such names require of their eventual identification and meaning now occasions a gap, a hole, or a far-reaching interruption, between the first part of the fragment—which describes what Nietzsche knows to be true philosophically—and the last part—that truly names, in spite of what he should already know about the deceptive and unreasonable character of all such naming. The fragment is itself fragmented, or exploded, then, and in such a way that its own meaning is no longer possible to contain or control in a coherent manner, "good-natured" or not. This explosion—which Nietzsche also characterizes as something monstrous that has to occur in the mode of a crisis—itself has a name, and Nietzsche tells us what it is: "Ich bin kein Mensch, ich bin Dynamit"; "I am no man, I am dynamite."[21] Because it occasions a textual rather than a merely empirical explosion, however, the dynamite in Nietzsche's text, like the bomb in Mallarmé's or de Man's, moreover, requires a patient labor of reading its fragments prior to deriving any values or actions from them. What would now be inexcusable, *unverzeihlich*, Nietzsche ultimately suggests, is not the written explosion that prevents description and naming, or truth as knowledge and truth as occurrence, from coming together once and for all without a hitch, for such an explosion has in fact happened textually, and therefore belongs irreversibly to history. We have no control whatsoever over the truth of that explosive occurrence, which we call *irony*. For the same reason, the question of making excuses for or accusations against such ironic explosions is no longer fully pertinent or adequate to them. What would always be textually as well as historically inexcusable, then, would be to pretend we could go about our business, the strict business of naming, describing, understanding, evaluating, and thus taking conscious action on things and others, as though nothing had taken place to upset—"*beunruhigt*," Nietzsche says in the first line of his explosive fragment; that is, to disturb and disrupt—our day of rest or sleep.

SEVEN

Death in Venice: Irony, Detachment, and the Aesthetic State

Mit der Ironie ist durchaus nicht zu scherzen.

— FRIEDRICH SCHLEGEL, "Über die Unverständlichkeit"

It would certainly be ironic, as they say, if it turned out that one of the most celebrated theorists and practitioners of irony in the twentieth century had actually misconstrued what makes irony into such an unruly and troublesome factor within the discourses of literature and philosophy alike. Such may indeed be the case for Thomas Mann, whose critical essays and literary fictions are regularly cited whenever romantic and postromantic irony becomes a topic for serious consideration. For if, in the case of Socrates, Kierkegaard wondered just how serious the Greek thinker could be about irony, since while rightfully maintaining his ignorance, Socrates still exhibited a certain degree of knowledge about that ignorance, then, in the case of Thomas Mann, one might well wonder how serious he was about irony precisely to the extent that for Mann, irony appears to have become a highly refined, self-assured, and comprehensive mode of knowledge—though not so much a knowledge, like that of Socrates, about his ignorance, and therefore about what he could not know, as a knowledge about what little difference all that one knows might actually make in the world. In this respect, at least, Mann might legitimately be taken as one of the more significant exemplars of the way a certain understanding of irony in the European romantic tradition leads from Schlegel, Hegel, and Kierkegaard directly to Nietzsche—and then attempts to move beyond all of them. "When Nietzsche," Mann once wrote, "questions the value of truth for life, there again I see the whole ironic ethos."[1] But as we have just seen, whatever Nietzsche may have thought about the value of truth for life, his texts go a considerable way toward suggesting just how dangerous it becomes for all kinds of lives when one dispenses with a sustained critical examination of the way that true values are not just formulated, but are always also applied as forces of constraint and coercion on social and political realities.

The question of irony as it is posed by Thomas Mann concerns the relation between art and life, and in particular, between literature and society. If the construction of philosophical truths can be shown to lie, like fiction, at an infinite remove from social and historical actualities, then the "value" of literature, as the exposure of the error and deceit implicit in every claim made about any truth providing a basis for anything beyond its own elaboration, becomes at the same time a rather dubious contribution to real life. Irony, or the ironic ethos, as Mann refers to this attitude that he associates perhaps all-too-quickly and casually with Nietzsche here, would be the infinitely self-aware disclosure—in philosophy or in literature—of its own futility. The freedom to indulge in an intellectual activity that in the end will have little impact on the referential contexts in which it is always situated is paid for by a gnawing suspicion about the writer's ultimate impotence. But that impotence can in its turn find ample compensation in the brilliance and perfection of the diverse forms in which it is able, over and over, to display its powerlessness and therefore innocence. Such would be one of the most familiar and widespread reappropriations of romantic irony in the age of modernity, or even of postmodernity. A historical and thematic scheme of this type also provides a convenient bridge from German romanticism to at least part of its continuation in French letters and thought of the twentieth century, since it is precisely with regard to their shared understanding of a figure such as Nietzsche and his "ironic ethos" that Thomas Mann and someone like André Gide can be fruitfully set side-by-side. Art as a sophisticated construction of deception that gradually reveals it own deceptiveness is a philosophical premise that underwrites the themes as well as the style of Gide's *Counterfeiters* and of Mann's *Confessions of Felix Krull, Confidence Man.*

Relieved of both the naïveté of Schlegel—who took seriously the philosophical and political consequences that necessarily result from the successful creation of every new mythology—and the anxiety of Kierkegaard—who took seriously the religious and existential trials bequeathed to us still today by Abraham—an infinitely nimble and alert ironic consciousness like that of Thomas Mann can devote itself to creating literary works of great ingenuity, works in which some of the most unresolved philosophical issues raised by romantic theorists of irony can themselves be subjected to ironic treatment by means of postromantic rhetorical techniques. Thus, in *Joseph and His Brothers*, Mann returns to Kierkegaard's treatment of Abraham and Isaac in *Fear and Trembling*, though he does so with such a light touch that the terror by which Abraham is constantly gripped when he hears the voice of the Absolute demand his son Isaac in sacrifice is replaced, in Mann's version, by a good-natured bantering between father and son. Jacob and Joseph provide a suitably updated model for the vexed relationship between Abraham and Isaac, and in doing so they also encourage us to consider ourselves from a privileged standpoint that would be at least several generations removed from the impasses of romantic irony.

In the short section called *Die Prüfung*, "The Test," Mann restages Kierkegaard's text by interiorizing to the second degree all those features that for Abraham and Isaac constituted the terror of actual "history." Jacob is not depicted in the present time of his distress as was Abraham, when obligated by God to leave his home and travel to Mount Moriah; rather, he is shown recounting to Joseph the grief he felt when he, too, was called upon to sacrifice his beloved son. But that is not exactly how it was, either, since the "call" Jacob received did not issue directly from the Absolute; instead, it occurred just now, inside Jacob's own consciousness, and as a result of Joseph's having told his father a story in which he mentioned the house of Abraham. For Jacob, the very name of Abraham also brings to mind Abraham's legacy, which Jacob then translates into a vision of himself enduring Abraham's ordeal. For the same reason, the distress that this testing causes to Jacob cannot be tied to any referential occasion or effects, for it occurs exclusively in the displaced form of a purely mental fiction. Jacob tells Joseph that he was able to experience Abraham's ordeal simply by representing it to himself in a metaphorical mode, by *imagining* what he *might* have done if he had actually been called by God to give Joseph up. The instant upon which Kierkegaard has his pseudonymous stand-in de Silentio linger, the point at which Abraham raises the knife above Isaac's head, is replaced in Mann's novel by a retrospective dialogue in which Jacob tells Joseph about his imaginary testing, and Joseph offers Jacob a reassuring interpretation to soothe the merely hypothetical distress his father has just endured from the thought of having to give up his own son. "I thought of God, and it was terrible," Jacob explains to Joseph; "It was *as if* my hand were the hand of Abraham lying upon Yitzchak's head."[2] The ironic twist that Mann provides to the story is that Jacob's dread, in his fictional rehearsal of Abraham's ordeal, is caused not by his having imagined that he would sacrifice Joseph, but on the contrary that he would refuse to carry out God's command:

> And when I drew out the knife and put the knife blade to your throat, I faltered before the Lord, and my arm fell from above my shoulder, and the knife fell, and I tumbled to the ground, falling on my face and biting the earth and the grass of the earth and striking it with my feet and my fists, and I cried: "Slay him, You slay him, O Lord and Destroyer, for he is my one, my all, and I am not Abraham." (*Joseph*, 80; *GW* 4: 105)

The back and forth between Jacob and Joseph that follows Jacob's narration reproduces the self-reflexive movements of an interpreting consciousness that gradually realizes that the very fact of already knowing about the story of Abraham and Isaac implies that one also possesses the power to know the outcome: "Yet in the next instant," Joseph reminds his father, "in the very next, the voice would have sounded and called out to you, 'Do not lay your hand upon the boy and do him no harm!' and you would have seen the ram in the thicket" (*Joseph*, 80; *GW* 4:106).

Jacob at first resists Joseph's suggestion that knowing about Abraham's faith also means knowing that the ram would in the next instant have been provided as an adequate substitute for the son's sacrifice. Joseph's interpretation, Jacob replies, is the ironic product of wit, *Witz*, and thus it misses the point of Abraham's ordeal, which was precisely that of the radical unknowability of history's future. However, Joseph turns the tables one last time on his father and argues that by imagining a new ending for the story—one in which the father refuses to follow any command to annihilate the son—Jacob is in fact creating a new concept for the Absolute. Jacob, Joseph now proposes, should not think of himself as having defied God, but rather he should congratulate himself for having invented on his own a better version of the story. In fact, Joseph suggests, by altering the ending of the old story, Jacob actually takes the place of God and provides an example of truly divine wisdom, *die Weisheit des Herrn*: Jacob shows eminent good sense when he declines to follow the outmoded and barbaric pattern established by Abraham's cruel God and chooses "love" over "faith."[3] "Spoken like an angel," Jacob shakes his head in wonder at his son's capacity to re-configure the meaning of Jacob's imaginary ordeal, amazed that Joseph can put everything in such a reassuringly witty manner, *daß seine Rede gewitz ist durch und durch*. Nonetheless, Jacob concludes, despite its having been told "with the holy oil of wit [mit dem Salböl des Witzes]," Joseph's version of Jacob's story still reaches only "half the truth," and the other half remains untouched by it.

In the gap left between these two competing truths, personified in the conversation between Joseph and Jacob as the imaginative power of intellect and the historical forces that remain recalcitrant to it, Thomas Mann created a world of fiction in which the intellect and actuality were variously portrayed in relationship to each other, colliding at times destructively, sometimes running parallel without touching directly, and even, at times, colluding in hidden and unpredictable ways. But what seems to have maintained itself intact through each and every literary representation of this uneasy relationship between historical and philosophical truth could be called the ironic detachment of the writing consciousness that observes them both from a safe distance of authorial self-control. There can be no clearer theoretical statement of this attitude than the last chapter of Mann's *Reflections of an Unpolitical Man*, entitled "Irony and Radicalism." Starting from what appears to be a simple opposition between intellect and life, *Geist* and *Leben*, Mann then puts the two "worlds," the two "voices" of intellect and life into a relationship that he calls "a perpetual tension without resolution" ("Irony," *RUM* 420; *GW* 12:569). The mission of art, *ihre Sendung*, Mann goes on to argue, is also what determines its true source as *irony*: "its mission lies in maintaining equally good relations with both life and pure intellect. . . . [I]t lies in its central and mediating position between intellect and life. . . . Irony is always irony toward both sides; it directs itself against life as well as against intellect" ("Irony," *RUM* 421, 422; *GW* 12:571, 573). Distant, aloof, disinterested, neutral—such are the constitutive attributes of the ironic consciousness with respect to both history and intelligence.[4]

We know of course that the political views that accompanied Mann's theoretical reflections on irony in 1918 changed a great deal in subsequent years, resulting in particular in his stark reconsideration of German history and its politics during the twentieth century. However, that in itself does not mean that Mann's earlier understanding of irony as a principle of aesthetic detachment to be adopted in literary writing with respect to both political and intellectual truths underwent the same kind of transformation as his personal political beliefs and allegiances. If anything, Mann may have become even more adamant about preserving the dimension of ironic distance through which alone all art, and especially literature, could maintain its special freedom from everyday cares and concerns. "In its equanimity [in seiner Gelassenheit]," Mann wrote for a lecture he delivered at Princeton in 1939, "irony acquires an almost monstrous sense: the sense of *art* itself, a universal affirmation, which, as such, is also a universal negation; an all-embracing crystal clear and serene glance which is the very glance of art itself [ein sonnenhaft klar und heiter das Ganze umfassender Blick], that is to say: a glance of the utmost freedom and calm, a glance of an objectivity untroubled by any moralism."[5] A decade later, in 1952, Mann would return yet again to the question, this time in a radio program commissioned for the BBC and entitled, appropriately enough, "The Artist and Society." At this late stage of his life he is careful to affirm "the tie that irrevocably exists between art and politics, intellect and politics."[6] Yet when it comes to saying anything more specific either about the way that tie, *die Verbindung*, functions or the way it might best be examined and understood, Mann resorts to evasive clichés or vague pronouncements, such as, for instance, "Art is not a power, it is only a consolation" ("Artist," *CV* 105; *GW* 10:399). Behind that willingness to offer a consoling vision of art's relation to society stands another, more familiar, insistence on Mann's part that the artist maintain a critical distance from everything else in the existing world.

Although the term *irony* does not appear in this particular passage, it is clear that what Mann in "The Artist and Society" calls the critical perspective inherent in the use of literary language would also be equivalent to an ironic consciousness of it. "It will not surprise anyone," he writes, "if in pursuing the question of the artist's relationship to society, I think first of all of the artist of the word [den Künstler des Wortes]" ("Artist," *CV* 99; *GW* 10:391). And he goes on immediately afterward to describe how such an artistic relation to the word, another word for which would be *irony*, will always relate itself to the world beyond it: "[I]t can be established here that a certain opposition to reality, life, society, is inseparable from the existence of the writing artist, for the very reason that he is in league with the word [eben weil er dem Worte verschworen ist]. Actually, he develops from an early stage a feeling, composed of formal and intellectual elements, of superiority over the existing world, over bourgeois society."[7] The artist, no doubt, lives in the world and does what he or she can to make it, more or less, a better or worse place on a day-to-day basis. But when the artist is writing, then the words that he or she uses in a critical and therefore ironic fashion lift the artist up above the world. In fact, in this short radio piece Mann goes so far as to suggest that it is precisely by offering to the rest of the world a formal and intellectual vision that is "superior" to the worldliness of the day-to-day world that the artist might make his or her most valuable contribution to its betterment through words. "Art," Mann concludes, "no matter how bitter an accusation it may lodge, no matter how deeply it may bemoan the corruption of creation, regardless of how far it may go in its ironic treatment of reality and even of itself," will never go so far as to shake its fist at life: "It is allied with the good, and its foundation is goodness. . . . If it likes to make us laugh, it is not by bringing scornful laughter [Hohngelächter], but rather a cheerful serenity [eine Heiterkeit], in which hate and stupidity are dissolved" ("Artist," *CV* 105; *GW* 10:398–99). Thomas Mann shows here his willingness to expose himself to a common enough, though perhaps for all that nonetheless deadly, trap: the belief that if only the rest of us could for once see the world with all the objectivity and lucidity of the true ironist, then we, too, might be granted access, if only for one "consoling" moment, to the serene cheerfulness, *die Heiterkeit*, of its airy vision. Friedrich Schlegel, at least, came to quite a divergent understanding of irony when he analyzed the way it functions within literary language. He said that thanks to the ironic element that can be found living in even the smallest fragments of words, what ultimately shines through all genuinely poetic constructions is an original power "of error and madness, or of foolishness and stupidity."[8] The difference is too striking not to occasion a more deliberate examination of how irony actually functions within Thomas Mann's own fiction.

In "The Artist and Society," Mann grapples with a question that serves as a leitmotif throughout his literary production. Do the arts have their foundation in goodness, and can they therefore reliably promise a serene clarity of vision in which hatred and stupidity might ultimately be dissolved? Do they serve more to divide or unite, and do they end in solitude or lead to community? Another way to put the same question would be to ask: If we want to preserve—or, alternatively, perhaps *change*—this or that society in particular, what kind of role could the arts play in achieving—or thwarting—such an objective? If there is one text by Thomas Mann in which these questions appear by necessity in their most crystallized and therefore overdetermined form it would be *Death in Venice*, his famous short novel from 1912.[9] For only in Venice is one actually confronted with a social structure that has taken on the fixed shape of an aesthetic object—and confronted for the same reason with an aesthetic object that functions simultaneously as a social organism. In Venice alone is it possible to find—or rather, only in Venice is it impossible to avoid—a stunning confrontation with the shared "foundations" of society and the arts. Set like a jewel in its watery band, Venice appears as the concrete embodiment of a social space that is nothing but aesthetic, and as the embodiment of a thoroughly artistic model for all social relations. Like everything else in Venice, moreover, the lines of demarcation between art and society appear to shimmer and glide according to the alternating tides of the sea and the circular movement of the sun.

It should come as no surprise, then, that when the decorated author Gustav von Aschenbach experiences difficulty advancing the text on which he was working just before the story begins, he will little by little be drawn toward Venice. To some extent, Venice represents for Aschenbach a simple continuation of the artistic effort he felt constrained to interrupt at home in Munich. In Munich, where art and society are clearly divided from each other, Aschenbach works by writing inside and living—when he lives—outside his house. But in Venice, the social exterior of the city is no longer segregated from the internal space of aesthetic productivity and appreciation; Aschenbach will for once feel free to pursue his artistic interests along the shore of the Lido, where all the dividing lines of inside and outside, up and down, far and near seem to intersect in a blur of light and shape. The main thematic tension of the text is in fact generated by the way the synthesis that Venice should offer to Aschenbach, the "solution" it ought in principle to provide for the difficult and delicate problem he had encountered before the text opens, does not in fact materialize as expected. On the contrary, rather than leading to the hoped-for remedy for his aesthetic ills, the visit to Venice instead reveals a profound split between the poles of art and reality that lie personified within Aschenbach's character. It is at this point as well that one can begin to speak of irony as the principal stylistic component of the novella. As Mann remarks in "The Artist and Society," it may be true that the aesthetic, the moral, and the sociopolitical are indivisible spheres precisely because they always meet in what he calls "the problem of humanity"; but that certainly doesn't mean that their indivisibility results in their compatibility. "Through their very unity," Mann observes there, "we become aware of a dismaying disunity: the disunited and self-contradictory quality of the intellectual spirit and of its relationship to the problem of humanity" ("Artist," *CV* 101). *Death in Venice* is an ironic text not because Aschenbach's short vacation from writing in Munich turns out to be an antidote more deadly than the symptom it was meant to cure; it is ironic to the extent that it gradually allows for an awareness of the disunity that results from the competing but nonetheless indivisible components of humanity itself.

For if it is true that the separation of art from society, of the intellect from life, can lead to a sterile and ultimately untenable vision of both art and life, then it is equally true that an attempt to bring them together in the same space can produce a collision of surprisingly destructive force. The aesthetic distance from life that, at least before his arrival in Venice, Aschenbach always seems to have observed for the sake of his art, his capacity for keeping himself balled up like a fist instead of letting himself open out like a freely hanging hand, has at least preserved him from making an out-and-out fool of himself. The aesthetic impulse in Munich may have been overly closeted, as it were, but that very compartmentalization seems to have succeeded in keeping Aschenbach out of real trouble before his arrival in Venice.[10] Once the artist recognizes the option, or even the obligation, to allow social issues to impinge upon the domain of art, it then becomes inevitable, by virtue of an inverse but symmetrical corollary, that aesthetic judgments will be applied to the sociopolitical context in which they always function. And whenever this happens, we may be certain that it won't take long for the thoughtful artist to begin considering in his work a number of unsettling possibilities for his life. If in Venice everything, including a mere taxi-cab, is susceptible to appearing in a purely aesthetic light, then sooner or later the artistic sensibility will set itself up for a dangerous fall.

And this is exactly what happens when Aschenbach encounters Tadzio shortly after being taxied to the Lido by gondola:

> With astonishment Aschenbach noticed that the boy was entirely beautiful. His countenance, pale and gracefully reserved, was surrounded by ringlets of honey-colored hair, and along with the straight nose, the enchanting mouth, the expression of sweet and divine gravity, it recalled Greek sculpture of the noblest period; yet despite the purest formal perfection, it had such unique personal charm that the beholder felt he had never encountered, either in nature or in art, anything so consummately successful. (*DV* 44; *GW* 8:469)

By concentrating the boy's whole essence in this one attribute, his countenance, and by connecting its various qualities—nose, mouth, expression—back to the whole by means of definite articles rather than possessive adjectives, the text emphasizes how Aschenbach's very first perception of Tadzio freezes him into the aesthetic mold of a Greek statue. In this passage, the ironic effect reaches its maximum when the most human aspect of Tadzio's appearance, his "unique personal charm," is allowed to emerge only in apposition to his countenance, *Sein Antlitz*, a visible shape referred to here by a German noun that is neuter in gender and that thus calls for the impersonal pronoun *it* when replaced later on in the same sentence: "it had such unique personal charm that the beholder felt he had never encountered anything so consummately successful." This thing, *etwas*, that Tadzio becomes for Aschenbach from the moment he lays eyes on it turns out to possess a very recognizable model: the famous Greco-Roman sculpture called Il Fedele or Spinario. Viewing Tadzio through Aschenbach's eyes, the initial description of the boy lingers over one particularly significant feature: "no one had ever dared to cut short his beautiful hair; like that of the 'Boy Extracting a Thorn' [*der Dornauszieher*], it fell in curls over the forehead, over the ears, and still lower over the neck." In a text replete with religious and mythological allusions, this one seems to have generated scant interest. And yet precisely to the extent that this reference to a classical artwork is not in the first place either religious or mythological, but rather exclusively aesthetic in nature, it becomes deserving of a second look.

Much has been made, for example, of the way *Death in Venice* can be read as a dramatization of the Dionysus and Apollo figures that, already in Nietzsche's *Birth of Tragedy*, were themselves a dramatization of two different but inseparable aesthetic principles that can be shown to be operative in any art form. But once one focuses on the Dionysus/Apollo pair, it becomes easy to forget the actual theoretical ground from which the two figures arise in Nietzsche's text and to consider them instead as simple existential possibilities, independently of any philosophical examination of the aesthetic category as such. If all that *Death in Venice* is about can be related back to questions of personal behavior—uptight people tend at some point to "lose it"; the repression of unacknowledged sexual urges will often enough lead to their taking revenge on us in an unwholesome fashion—then the fact that Gustav von Aschenbach is a nationally acclaimed writer of fiction and criticism would remain of only secondary and derivative importance. To note that Tadzio appears to Aschenbach first of all as a human embodiment of a Greco-Roman statue is to be cautioned at the same time about taking for granted the existential status of any of the innumerable "personifications" of abstract ideas that appear throughout the text. It may just be that what the text is actually about is not accessible *except* by way of a detour through its theoretical treatment of art. And in that case, its most profound and problematic subject could turn out to be the rhetorical power of personification that is as liable to manifest itself in art as in society.

At any rate, it is only by considering Nietzsche's *Birth of Tragedy* as a critical reflection on the philosophical category of the aesthetic—prior to taking it as a key for understanding Aschenbach's personal struggle to maintain intellectual control while being beset by the dark and unruly forces of unreason—that one might also restore to Nietzsche's text the crucial place occupied there by Socrates. For Socrates, it will be remembered, is the one who replaced the aesthetics of tragedy with the epistemology of aesthetics, thus setting the stage for the development of aesthetic theory as it will be carried out in German romanticism in the wake of Kant, leading all the way up to Nietzsche's critique of aesthetic theory in *The Birth of Tragedy*. And Socrates, moreover, unlike Dionysus, Apollo, or Nietzsche, actually does appear in his own name in *Death in Venice*. It is in chapter 4 of the novella—after Aschenbach takes advantage of the fortuitous pretext he is offered for remaining in Venice when his luggage is sent by mistake to Como instead of being sent on to another resort on the Adriatic—that Socrates appears in the text.

Looking out at Tadzio as he plays along the Lido's coastline, Aschenbach imagines that he is gazing upon "Beauty itself, on Form as a thought of God, on the one and pure perfection which dwells in the spirit and from which a human image and likeness [ein menschliches Abbild und Gleichnis] had here been lightly and graciously set up for him to worship" (*DV* 60; *GW* 8:490). From this analogical image of beauty represented in human form by Tadzio, Aschenbach's thought produces a stream of cultural recollections, *seine Bildung geriet ins Wallen*, until it eventually arrives at a vision of Socrates. Socrates, for once, has been led outside the walls of Athens, where he is reclining on the grass near a cool spring of crystal-clear water accompanied by a handsome young boy. The Venetian scene on the beach thus reproduces for Aschenbach the backdrop of sun and water against which Plato's *Phaedrus* unfolds, a dialogue in which Socrates will instruct Phaedrus on the unique power of aesthetic images as a spur to both desire and virtue:

> For Beauty, dear Phaedrus, only Beauty is at one and the same time truly lovable and visible: it is, mark well, the only Form of the spiritual that we can receive with our senses and endure with our senses. For what would become of us if other divine things, if Reason and Virtue and Truth were to appear to us sensuously? Should we not perish in a conflagration of love, as once upon a time Semele did

before Zeus? Thus Beauty, for the sensuous being, is the path to spirit [So ist die
Schönheit der Weg des Fühlenden zum Geiste]—only the path, only a means,
little Phaedrus. (*DV* 63–64; *GW* 8:491–92)

But the speech that Socrates makes in Plato's text, it should be recalled, and
which Aschenbach is paraphrasing in this passage, is addressed directly to the
boy, Phaedrus, and furthermore it is offered as a palinode, a retraction and a
correction of two earlier speeches made to Phaedrus, by Socrates and, before
him, by Lysias.

The point Socrates is trying to make with Phaedrus has to do with education, and more precisely, with the role of authority that the teacher necessarily occupies within the educational framework—a framework which, as we
know, always allows for a considerable degree of volatility within the intellectual relationship that brings teacher and student together in the first place. In
Plato's dialogue, then, the exposition of abstract philosophical concepts—like
the soul, love, beauty, memory, desire, virtue, and knowledge—are doubled
by a didactic performance in which Socrates demonstrates for Phaedrus the
motives and results associated with two very different kinds of teaching. What
makes the *Phaedrus* so richly complex is therefore the way that it intertwines
its own philosophical discourse on aesthetic education with a dramatization of
the possible pitfalls attendant on actual pedagogical practice. Socrates would
like to teach Phaedrus the truth about beauty, but that strictly philosophical
lesson is itself inscribed within a very practical warning about the way both
mind and body are exposed to powerful forces of seduction from the minute
a knowledge of beauty (possessed by the teacher) encounters a concrete example of beauty (personified in the student). In fact, the *Phaedrus* opens with
several different but interrelated scenes of seduction: not just the one that
unfolds when Phaedrus lures Socrates outside the walls of Athens by promising him a beautiful speech, but also, and especially, the speeches that both
Lysias and Socrates make to Phaedrus on the highly seductive topic of "how
to seduce a beautiful boy."[11]

In Aschenbach's case, on the other hand, the pedagogical dimension that is
so strongly, though problematically, in evidence in Plato's text is attenuated to
the point of extinction. Aschenbach's relation to Tadzio remains exclusively
imaginary since it never advances beyond an aesthetic attitude of pure contemplation; *his* address is not directed to Tadzio but is rather a rhetorical fiction,
a simulated apostrophe that ultimately has no other object beyond its self-

enclosed execution. As soon as Aschenbach is finished rehearsing for himself the didactic scene of aesthetic theory that is played out in Plato's dialogue between teacher and student, he turns the actual physical presence of Tadzio into a mere occasion for his own productivity: "He suddenly desired to write. . . . from Tadzio's beauty [nach Tadzio's Schönheit], he gave form to his brief essay—that page and a half of exquisite prose which with its limpid nobility and vibrant controlled passion was soon to win the admiration of many" (*DV* 62; *GW* 8:492–93). The activity in which Aschenbach is engaged in Venice is therefore not educational—it is not a process of *Bildung*, and it does not even include Tadzio directly or personally. Rather, as the text emphasizes with its own words, Aschenbach relates only formally to the form of Tadzio's beauty: from the boy's beautiful form, *nach Tadzio's Schönheit*, Aschenbach gives form, *er formte*, only to his own essay, *seine kleine Abhandlung*. From this point on, the dehumanizing effects of Aschenbach's aestheticization of Tadzio gradually become more marked, and more pernicious for both the artist and the *objet d'art* the boy has become for him. At the end of chapter 4, although—or, rather, perhaps because—Aschenbach has still not managed actually to speak with Tadzio even when he is given the opportunity, he will whisper, out of earshot of the intended object of his words, "I love you." Finally, in chapter 5, once Aschenbach has learned for sure that Venice is rife with cholera, he imagines performing "a decent action which would cleanse his conscience," namely, disclosing the truth to Tadzio's mother so she would be able to remove her family from harm's way by leaving the infected island immediately (*DV* 80; *GW* 8:514–15). But this fictional scenario ends the same way as Aschenbach's earlier dreams of having genuine contact with Tadzio: in a discreet silence that is anything but "Platonic." The last pages of the tale—which recount Aschenbach's visit to the hotel barber for a cosmetic makeover, his stalking of Tadzio through Venice until he sinks abjectly onto the steps of a cistern in a deserted campo, his collapse, sideways, as he dies hallucinating in a beach chair set out on the Lido—are curiously overdone in their effort to suggest just how far Aschenbach has lost touch with aesthetic as well as social reality.

By providing a stark contrast to the feverish delirium into which Aschenbach finally disappears, the brusque staccato of three sentences that suddenly punctuate the end of the text suggest that Aschenbach's individual fate should be understood principally in light of its relation to the larger social context in which it has been carefully situated from the start. In the very last sentence of the text, the subject is no longer Aschenbach or even his death; rather, it is the entirety of "a world" that is now left behind, "respectful and shaken," to deal with this news.

It may just be that *Death in Venice* is about the individual Gustav von Aschenbach—in his deeply conflicted relationship to both aesthetics and sexuality—only insofar as the drama of his life reveals a tension at the heart of all sociopolitical reality. And that tension—which is certainly not absent from Plato's text—has to do with the crucial but volatile role of aesthetic theory in the constitution and maintenance of the state. If the first sentence of the novella mentions the dangerous threat that hangs over the continent in the years just before World War I, and the last sentence returns the focus from Aschenbach to the "world" that is left to negotiate that threat without him, then there is good reason for suspecting that the real subject of the tale is not its main protagonist who, after all, is not even named in the title of the text. If Venice is one of the more apt personifications of aesthetic theory from Plato to Aschenbach, then the "death" that matters most for a reading of the novella could involve the value that has until now been assigned to art within the traditions of philosophical and political thought alike. In this case, Aschenbach would merely incarnate the type of aesthetic model that functions as a principle of social and political organization at a particular time and place, that is, early twentieth-century Europe. "In order for a significant intellectual product to have a broad and deep effect," we are told in chapter 2, "there must exist a hidden affinity, indeed a congruence, between the personal destiny of the author and the universal destiny of his generation" (*DV* 30; *GW* 8:452). And it doesn't take much effort to discover in what the "secret" correspondence between Aschenbach's art and the surrounding world consists. It is the unquestioned belief in the convergence between the aesthetic and the sociopolitical that the European continent has inherited from a long and complex history of classical and romantic thought. Whatever doubts about art remain in Plato's text seem to have vanished in Aschenbach's world, a world that is most clearly shaped by the particular thrust given to post-Kantian aesthetic theory by Friedrich Schiller.

Aschenbach may not be much of a teacher for Tadzio when they are both on vacation in Venice, but selected pages from his works have been singled out by the German Ministry of Education, *die Unterrichtsbehörde*, for inclusion in their required textbooks, *die vorgeschriebenen Schul-Leserbücher*, whenever school is actually in session (*DV* 33; *GW* 8:456). Chapter 2 of the novella, which interrupts the narrative present of the story in order to fill in the historical background of Aschenbach's rise to national prominence as an author, suggests that Aschenbach's artistic theory and practice are in conformity with their age precisely to the degree that they coincide with Schiller's ideal of the aesthetic state. For Schiller, the aesthetic state is not just concerned with art; it also functions as a political ideal that ultimately relies on the mediating role of beautiful forms to provide the necessary articulation between mind and body, intellect and life, by means of which all modern democratic states have to organize their social space. In this regard, it is not without significance that Aschenbach's writings come more and more to display the official air of an educator's stance, *etwas Amtlich-Erzieherisches*. Certain critics, chapter 2 observes early on, had already recognized how closely Aschenbach's essay "Intellect and Art" resembled Schiller's 1795 *Raisonnement*, "On Naïve and Sentimental Poetry," an essay that has been called the single most decisive turning point in the history of romanticism. With the later reference to the way that something of the educator's attitude, *etwas Erzieherisches*, can be increasingly found to characterize the demonstrations of Aschenbach's mature period, it becomes possible to note the echo of Schiller's *On the Aesthetic Education of Man* (*Über die Ästhetische* Erziehung *des Menschen*). And, of course, there are the repeated references to Aschenbach's "dignity" (and Tadzio's natural grace) that recall Schiller's essay "Über Anmut und Würde" (On Grace and Dignity). Finally, an oblique intertextual reference that *Death in Venice* makes to a short story Mann had written to celebrate the centennial of Schiller's death in 1905 clinches the filiation between these two like-minded thinkers of aesthetic theory: the two candles Aschenbach places at the head of his manuscript in order to write recall the pair of candlesticks that function the very same way in "Schwere Stunde" ("A Weary Hour," or "Harsh Hour").[12] But by far the most telling juxtaposition of Schiller and Aschenbach emerges only indirectly from the narrator's striking description of Aschenbach's physical appearance. What is important in this description of Aschenbach is not any particular feature of his outer aspect—the way the particle "von" is attached to Aschenbach's name to single him out as an official representative of state culture—it is rather the aesthetic interpretation that is given to Aschenbach's physical appearance, an interpretation that is quintessentially Schillerian in terms of both its method and content. The passage in question is the one that concludes chapter 2 after the long digression about Aschenbach's career by suddenly bringing the text back into the present of Aschenbach's preparations for his departure to Venice:

Significant destinies [Bedeutende Schicksale] seemed to have passed over this head, which usually inclined to one side with an air of suffering [dies meist leidend seitwärts geneigte Haupt]. And yet it was art that had here taken over that fashioning of the physiognomy [und doch war die Kunst es gewesen, die hier jene physiognomische Durchbildung übernommen hatte] which is usually the work of a life full of action and difficulty [welche sonst das Werk eines schweren, bewegten Lebens ist]. . . . Even from a personal point of view, art is a higher form of life [Auch persönlich genommen ist ja die Kunst ein erhöhtes Leben]. It delights more profoundly, it consumes more rapidly. It engraves on the countenance [das Antlitz] of its servant the traces of imaginary and intellectual adventures [die Spuren imaginärer und geistiger Abenteuer], and in the long run it creates, even in an existence that outwardly has been one of cloistral tranquility, a fastidiousness, hyper-refinement, fatigue, and nervous strain, such as a life full of excessive passions and pleasures can seldom bring about. (*DV* 34; *GW* 8:457)

As Schiller's English translators point out, the paradigmatic figure that dominates his entire aesthetic theory is *chiasmus*, the crossing over of opposing attributes by means of a third term through which antithetical properties can ultimately be brought into a relationship of symmetry and harmony.[13] Art, for Schiller, names that intermediate space of imaginative play thanks to which sharp antinomies such as ideal and actual, mind and matter, freedom and necessity can be made to pass into and unite with each other. Aschenbach, it turns out, is the ideal contemporary embodiment of Schiller's aesthetics not just because of what he writes, but also because in his case his physical looks seem to mirror perfectly the aesthetic activity of his mind. By dint of the free play on which it is ultimately founded, Aschenbach's artistic creativity has permitted him to reach a "higher life," one in which he has been able to form, *durchbilden*, his outer appearance (*Antlitz*) entirely by means of his inner faculties (*imaginäre und geistige Abenteuer*), achieving thereby a unique convergence of destiny with meaning (*bedeutende Schicksale*), and of passive suffering (*Leiden*) with active movement (*Bewegung*).

But from whose point of view is the singular accomplishment of this aesthetic education—*jene künstliche Durchbildung*—that has left its visible traces on Aschenbach's external features being noticed and remarked upon? The question takes us back to the narrative voice in which *Death in Venice* in its entirety is recounted, an impersonal voice that shifts without warning from objective third-person observation to a kind of *style indirect libre* that frequently enough adopts a point of view that intersects if it does not coincide exactly with Aschenbach's own perspective.[14] In the case of the passage just cited, however, which deals with Aschenbach's physical appearance and begins with a series of strictly observable objective details—"Gustav von Aschenbach was of rather less than average height, dark and clean-shaven"—it would be difficult to maintain that it is constructed wholly from either Aschenbach's personal point of view, or that of the anonymous narrator. Nearer in perspective to the last sentence of the tale, where the news of Aschenbach's disappearance is received by "a respectful, shaken world," the passage claiming that Aschenbach's outer features entertain a strict correspondence with the imaginary adventures he has "lived" in an exclusively artistic fashion also recalls the earlier affirmation about the necessary existence of "a hidden affinity, indeed a congruence between the personal destiny of an author [like Aschenbach] and the universal destiny of his generation" (*DV* 30; *GW* 8:452). In all three cases it is a question of what Roland Barthes might call the point of view of doxa or ideology—though in this particular instance, as we have seen, the ideology in question is in no way anonymous or diffuse. The promise of executing a chiasmic crossing between sensuous appearance and hidden meaning, between action and thought, between life and art, and, ultimately, artist and society is readily identifiable in Mann's novella as the aesthetic ideology that is associated by the text itself with the theoretical writings of Friedrich Schiller. By subtly bringing into view the Schillerian concept of the aesthetic that underlies both Aschenbach's artistic development and the ideological assumptions of his time, the narrator of *Death in Venice* also exposes them both to critical analysis.

It can therefore be no mere accident that at the precise moment Gustav von Aschenbach prepares to leave for Venice in chapter 3—the perfect site in which to test the mediating power of "beauty" to effectuate every imaginable chiasmic crossing between form and matter, thought and feeling—"life" is itself shown to be utterly superfluous. For, according to the aesthetic principles articulated in chapter 2, not even the most excessive referential passion or pleasure could ever match the kind of enhanced experience that is offered by artistically produced imitations of them: "ist ja die Kunst ein erhörtes Leben." Moreover, as soon as the aesthetic phenomenon is taken as a legitimate substitute for lived experience—and that gesture must remain art's most profound source and intention whether or not this is actually acknowledged—the symmetrical crossing of life and art will always be decided, asymmetrically, in favor of art. Considered from this standpoint, one would have to admit that Aschenbach is in some sense "dead" before he ever steps off the boat in Venice since, by recognizing the necessary idealization through which art yields a higher and more intense form of lived experience, he has already definitively cut himself off from the possibility of undergoing there anything but "imaginary and intellectual adventures." If the inner tranquility of the intellect can take on the external attributes of action and passion more intensely than any lived life, then life in the outer world of sociopolitical reality can itself be lived as though it were a purely aesthetic phenomenon—a refinement of empirical experience that is always and necessarily "a hyper-refinement [eine Über-feinerung]." To the wearing down in Munich of the physical body through an art of the imagination will therefore have to correspond the aesthetic mummification of thought that is carried out by a thoroughly imaginary life in Venice.

When Aschenbach initially notices Tadzio and inspects him as though he were just one more reproduction of a famous Greco-Roman statue, he is merely confirming the basic principle of disinterested contemplation that underwrites the philosophical category of the aesthetic as such, and which has had to inform his life and work as an artist from the start.[15] What makes Venice different is simply the way that it no longer prevents the aesthetic construction of reality—equally operative though hidden safely out of view at home in Munich—from rising to the surface. That Aschenbach is unwilling or unable, for reasons of his own, to acknowledge and come to terms with this revelation before it is too late is his problem, and not that of the literary fiction that invents his sorry case in order to expose and demystify it from a superior position of knowledge. This standpoint is of course that of irony, the subtle but constant distance the narrative voice establishes for itself with respect to Aschenbach as well as to everything else that occurs in *Death in Venice*. What the ironic perspective allows to emerge in each case and cumulatively in them all is the romantic and Schillerian belief that the aesthetic model could ever provide a firm basis for anything other than deception and self-deception. A reality that is constructed on a principle of "play" can only result in a play-reality, as is evidenced on the Lido when Tadzio and his friends work together to build an international sand castle whose fate will be determined by the inevitable erosion brought on by the rhythmical tides of the Adriatic (*DV* 47–50; *GW* 8:474–77). From the very first lines, moreover, the narrator hints at how the novella's treatment of Aschenbach is to be related to the equally fragile political state of Europe in its entirety, since the appearance of the main character in the story is made to coincide with precisely that moment in which "our continent manifested such a threatened bearing" (*DV* 23; *GW* 8:444). The artificial construction of the national identities and international relations in which Gustav von Aschenbach plays his appointed role as aesthetic and cultural representative is about as sturdy as those sand castles he watches Tadzio and his friends building on the Lido. And soon enough the tides of history will exert their own destructive forces on the sociopolitical shape of the continent as a whole.

If, at the very end of the text, the world is said to be shaken—*eine respektvoll erschütterte Welt*—by the news of Aschenbach's demise, this is also because the narrator's irony has gradually exposed just how shaky and unreliable the concept of an aesthetic state—for Aschenbach, for Venice, for Europe—remains as a foundation for personal and historical actuality. Whereas Schiller envisions *beauty* as the middle term of a chiasmic crossing that brings together form and matter, freedom and necessity, intellect and life in a seamless whole, the narrative voice of *Death in Venice* drives them apart by laying bare the ironic nature of every possible mediation between them. Thomas Mann said as much himself when he looked back on the novella in 1918:

> To the extent that it is ironic, art is melancholy and modest [Melancholisch und bescheiden ist auch die Kunst, insofern sie ironisch ist]. . . . Whether anyone for whom the path to the intellect leads through the senses can reach wisdom and true human dignity [Weisheit und wahre Manneswürde] is a question I once asked about in a story, in which I allowed an artist who had "become dignified" to realize [machte ich fraglich in einer Erzählung, worin ich einen "würdig ge-wordenen" Künstler begreifen ließ] that people like him must necessarily remain dissolute and therefore mere adventurers of feeling [notwendig liederlich und Abenteurer des Gefühles]; that the magisterial posture of his style has been lies and foolishness [Lüge und Narrentum], his noble attitude a trick [eine Posse], the confidence the masses had in him quite ridiculous [höchst lächerlich], and that educating a nation and its youth through art is a risky undertaking to be forbidden [Volks- und Jugenderziehung durch die Kunst ein gewagtes, zu verbietendes Unternehmen sei]. ("Irony," *RUM* 422–23; *GW* 12:573)

According to Mann's own testimony, if we can still take it at face value here, irony is a conscious technique of understatement, of modesty or *Bescheiden-heit*, rather than of hyperbole, and so it eschews the grand gesture or *die große Gebärde*. The ironic consciousness is melancholic rather than grandil-oquent, but it travels resolutely along this negative path until it arrives at understanding—Mann uses the term *begreifen lassen* to describe the conscious grasp of his own plight that Aschenbach is finally permitted to acquire once he has paid for such understanding with a loss of dignity and even life. In this respect, a hermeneutic relationship between author, narrator, and character is produced by the fictional construction that also brings all three figures into alignment with one another. What the ironic narrator knows at the beginning of the tale, the main character can learn only at the end, arriving at this knowledge through the negativity of his own death, but by the same token leaving that knowledge as a legacy to the self-aware author, narrator, and, now, the attentive reader.[16] The author, whose ironic perspective provides both narrator and character with their source as well as their end, also achieves in his writing a level of self-understanding that transcends them both: "Insofar as I allowed the artist in the story to grasp this in a melancholy-ironic mode," Mann concludes, "I remained true to myself—which is the point that matters to me [Indem ich es ihn melancholisch-ironisch begreifen ließ, blieb ich mir selber treu,—was der Punkt ist, auf den es mir ankommt]" ("Irony," *RUM* 423; *GW* 12573). Staying true, faithful, loyal to the self and what it knows about itself—*blieb ich mir selber treu*—is how Thomas Mann understands the ironic consciousness that is able to mediate constantly between mind and matter, *Geist und Sinnlichkeit*, without itself ever falling prey to a belief in their ultimate unity. Mann's irony, it turns out, relates to Schiller's beauty in a strictly antithetical way—where Schiller theorizes beauty as the formative power to unite disparate elements, Mann theorizes and utilizes irony as a tool to reveal the fissures and break such constructions apart. And this simple reversal between aesthetic construction and ironic dispersal is therefore itself susceptible to precisely the kind of chiasmic crossings that determine Schiller's own concept of beauty as free play in the first place. Whether the artist, like Schiller, is a builder of unity, or, like Mann, a demolition expert who undermines such beautiful constructions makes little difference in the end, since both activities are the result of a highly self-conscious intention and mastery of form.

Hidden in the antithesis can actually be found the promise of a partial synthesis. By holding Aschenbach, as opposed to Schiller, up to ridicule, the narrator and the author of *Death in Venice* imply that Schiller's own understanding of the aesthetic state was already less *naïvely* anachronistic and more *sentimentally* prudent than the contemporary ideologies that have ensued from it. To the extent that Schiller insisted that the aesthetic state was and could only be an ideal, it already emphasized a measure of negativity in its own theorization and understanding of beauty. Thomas Mann's aesthetic of irony is therefore different from Schiller's aesthetic of the beautiful only in degree, and not in kind. Mann's irony encompasses an attitude of aesthetic detachment that has become more self-aware and cautious as a result of a fuller consciousness of precisely those historical developments that Schiller could not himself anticipate. The shared belief in the aesthetic remains nonetheless unshaken in both cases. The demolition of unity, the ironization of aesthetic and political unity by means of which Mann's own aesthetic constructions are built is not itself subject to questioning. This negative aesthetic, or aesthetic of negativity, always promises at the level of hermeneutic understanding the same kind of aesthetic unity between form and meaning that it denies on the level of lived experience. As any number of readers have noted, moreover, the unparalleled achievement of *Death in Venice* as a masterpiece in its own right consists in the virtuosity with which it exposes the pose of aesthetic virtuosity as a mere hoax, *Lüge und Narrentum*. It is a literary fiction that teaches, with a negative effectiveness that only irony seems able to guarantee at this point in history, just how risky it always is to grant the aesthetic a role in the educational mission of any given sociopolitical state. And it claims to know all this with a self-professed combination of "melancholy and modesty" (*Melancholie und Bescheidenheit*) that provides the best protection against relapsing into the kinds of ridiculous and foolish aesthetic errors it diagnoses and then discards for us.

While there is no indication that Thomas Mann is being the least bit ironic when he makes these rather immodest claims for his own irony, there is at least one place in *Death in Venice* where such an understanding of irony's relation to the self and its capacity for knowledge and understanding reaches its limits. In the fifth and final chapter, there is a scene in which another allegorical figure for the author suddenly appears in the text. This figure is strangely unlike either Aschenbach or the narrator, although he also shares attributes belonging to both of them. He too is an artist, a street singer to be precise, and like Aschenbach and the narrator he has achieved a level of accomplishment that entitles him to be called a "virtuoso" at his chosen art form. The distinguished group with which he is affiliated, however, lacks both the nobility bestowed upon Aschenbach by the state and the cool detachment the author grants to the narrator. The street singers who are performing in the text at this point belong to the confraternity of *Bettelvirtuosen*, beggar-virtuosi, though the compound noun leaves open the question of whether they are virtuosi artists who just happen also to be beggars; or virtuosi at begging; or even, perhaps, whether they are trashy virtuosi—virtuosi who are poor excuses for virtuosi, and therefore thinly disguised virtuosi who are only pretending to be very good indeed at what in fact they are not. The real talent, the leader of the beggar-virtuosi, plays the guitar, but he also plays another role, for he plays his instrument only while performing "in the character of a kind of baritone-buffo" (*DV* 72–73; *GW* 8:505–06). Oddly enough, the baritone-buffo is not really a singer either, since he hardly has a voice, but he displays a remarkable gift for mimicry and is bursting with comic energy. On several occasions, the buffo stands detached—*stand er abgetrennt*—from his group, but only in order to step menacingly close to the audience for which he is supposed to be performing. He seems detached as well from his own status as pure buffo, since at one point we are told that he is in fact only "half actor," the other half of his occupation consisting in that of a pimp, or *Zuhälter*. As such, he is not only "entertaining," he is also "brutal, audacious, and dangerous"—"brutal und verwegen, gefährlich und unterhaltend." In short, the buffo is "a suspect figure," "eine verdächtige Figur," and he brings along with him "his own suspect atmosphere," "ihre eigene verdächtige Atmosphäre" (*DV* 74; *GW* 8:507–08).

The figure of the buffo, as we know from Friedrich Schlegel, moreover, is the figure *par excellence* of irony, though of an irony that can no longer be considered in terms of a "modest" sense of one's own limits and therefore of one's own understanding.[17] Everything about the figure of this irony is excessive, and therefore suspect: not only what it is, but what it knows, as well as whatever could possibly be taught or learned by breathing the suspect atmosphere it always brings along with it. Unlike the author and the narrator of this text, who eventually conspire to "allow the artist to grasp" the strict limits of his aesthetic competence, the buffo is described as "the alien being," *das fremdartige Wesen*, who greedily collects everybody's money while telling them whatever they want to hear, no matter what its relation to actual truth or reality might or might not be. Or, more exactly, the buffo reassures everybody with respect to what they think they want to know, but he does so only up to a certain point. For in the end, the buffo can no longer be said even to be communicating with his audience; that is, he no longer tells or teaches anybody anything that could be clearly circumscribed and thus comprehended. The buffo takes his leave from *Death in Venice* by speaking in an unintelligible dialect, *in unverständlichem Dialekt*, that trails off in a series of explosions, not just of laughter, but of laughter, scornful laughter, and simulated laughter, *Lachen, Hohngelächter, Kunstlachen* (*DV* 76; *GW* 8:509–10). Surprisingly enough, though, this suspect and meaningless laughter is just as infectious, *ansteckend*, as the deadly cholera that it seems to make everyone present at the show momentarily, and at their peril, forget. Far from signifying the kind of detached tranquility, or *Gelassenheit*, the elevated and serene distance, or *Heiterkeit*, offered by art—and by means of which, Mann said in his 1952 radio program "The Artist and Society," he still hoped to dissolve the hate and stupidity that he felt characterized the uncultured masses of humanity—the laughter that is contracted by exposure to the buffo in *Death in Venice* points to a far more problematic possibility.

The buffo is detached all right, for the text specifies that his laughter comes only when he is able to restore aesthetic distance, *bei wiederhergestelltem künstlerischen Abstand*, between himself and all polite society. But this time the status of such detachment is anything but clear, or *heiter*. In the context of the buffo's performance, moreover, the term *Heiterkeit* can no longer be translated according to a classical or romantic conception of "serenity," "gladness," or "bright cheerfulness," since in this suspect atmosphere it has become a self-propagating and thus mindless hilarity, having no other object but its own uncontrollable contagion:

> The buffo sobbed, his voice wavered, he pressed his hands against his mouth and hunched his shoulders, until at the right moment an insuperable laughter burst, howled, and exploded out of him with such authenticity that it became infectious and communicated itself to the audience, so that an objectless and exclusively self-propagating hilarity swept over the terrace as well [mit solcher Wahrheit, daß auch auf der Terasse eine gegenstandlose und nur von sich selbst lebende Heiterkeit um sich griff]. (*DV* 76; *GW* 8: 510)

Because it has no object whatsoever, the "serenity" of this *Heiterkeit* could be said to constitute the most radically detached, disinterested, and purposeless attitude imaginable. Devoid of any purpose other than keeping its own purposelessness alive—"eine gegenstandlose und nur von sich selbst lebendige Heiterkeit"—this mode of detachment, or irony, which has no relation to any object, can also have little to do with knowledge or understanding. Its hilarity is so pure, so clear, so *heiter*, that it doesn't even claim to know about its own lack of knowledge, which is also to say, its stupidity. And before assuming that we can simply reattach the buffo to a chain of leitmotifs or metaphorical figures, all of which taken together signify the Dionysian impulse to abandon oneself to sensuous pleasure and intoxication, we should be willing to acknowledge that the text itself points in another direction.

For the *Heiterkeit*, the mad or wild "serenity" with which the buffo infects the audience at the Hôtel des Bains on the Lido, occurs at another crucial moment in the novella as well, and at that point every connection to the surrounding themes, metaphors, and figures is severed. In chapter 3, once Aschenbach has made up his mind he must leave Venice for good, after he travels with all due melancholy down the Grand Canal on the vaporetto that takes him to the station, he is told that his baggage has been sent off in the wrong direction. The episode could be considered the turning point for the entire plot, since without this accident Aschenbach would have been deprived of any pretext for changing his mind. At that precise moment, Aschenbach is gripped by "an unbelievable hilarity," "eine unglaubliche Heiterkeit erschütterte seine Brust" (*DV* 55; *GW* 8:484). This time, of course, the hilarity, or *Heiterkeit*, that shakes him *does* have an object: the errant baggage offers Aschenbach a perfect occasion for declaring his unwillingness to travel without baggage, and therefore for deciding to return to the Lido—and to Tadzio. But if the scene with the buffo establishes the buffo as the *cause* of a hilarity that has no *object* or telos, then the scene with the luggage is remarkable for the way in which the *object* of Aschenbach's "unbelievable hilarity"—Venice, and along with it the personification of the aesthetic that is embodied by Tadzio—has no determinate *cause*. Or, rather, it has a cause, but this cause is itself occasioned by a sheer accident: why *was* the luggage sent to Como instead of where it was supposed to go?

The question returns us in its own roundabout way to the buffo. For it is evident that for the sake of the story—as theme, as figure, and as meaning—the narrator, or the author, has need of this accident by which Aschenbach can be given the occasion to remain in Venice instead of following his declared plan to head for "a little coastal resort not far from Trieste" (*DV* 52; *GW* 8:480). To the extent that the accident of luggage sent astray belongs to the ordinary repertoire of aesthetic devices upon which every artist must rely, it in no way threatens the coherence of the tale; nor, more importantly, does it threaten the conscious control the artist can always claim to have over it. But why Como? For the "accident" with the baggage to be truly effective, it ought to be devoid of any other significance within the narrative economy of the text—aesthetically speaking, it ought to be without object or interest, a purely disinterested device at the service of art and the artist's meaningful intention or his intention to construct meaning aesthetically. And on the narrative level—of theme, figure, and meaning—this is obviously the case, since no mention of Como or anything related to that city plays a role in the text. Should one look at the language of the German at this point in the text, however, one is liable to notice something uncanny, even though this particular feature of the text seems until now to have eluded the attention of its readers.

Just as Aschenbach enters the station and prepares to take his ticket, an anonymous hotel employee appears and informs him that his trunk has already left. "Already sent off?" Aschenbach asks, and the employee responds, "Of course—to Como!" Aschenbach echos: "To Como?" The German version, written in a *style indirect libre* that is difficult to translate, reads: "Der Mensch zeigt sich und meldet, der große Koffer sei aufgegeben. Schon aufgegeben? Ja, bestens,—nach Como. Nach Como?" (*GW* 8:484). Considered from the inside, from the standpoint of its meaning, there is nothing at all suspect here—as Schlegel had suggested, on the inside of the ironic text there reigns a serene mood of ever-rising consciousness, or *Heiterkeit*. But on the exterior—where Schlegel claimed to find the style of an ordinary good Italian buffo—the words uttered by the hotel employee and then repeated in echo by Aschenbach are as audaciously suspect and dangerous as the performance given by the actual buffo in chapter 5. For "nach Como" is a nearly perfect anagram for the one place in the whole world Aschenbach wants least to find himself traveling again: Munich. Not in English, of course, nor even in German, for München has as little to do with Como as Munich, at least on *their* outside. But to the ear—or the eye—of "an ordinary good *Italian* buffo," Munich would be—*Monaco*, the Italian name for the capital city of Bavaria. The very crudeness of such a gratuitous, even asinine suggestion—*nach Como* in German, it just so happens, can function as a scrambled translation of *Monaco* in Italian—is proof positive of its relation to the buffo and the kind of irony by which Schlegel characterizes the "transcendental buffoonery" of poetry. The "detachment" at work—or at play—in the little skit performed on the edge of Venice when the author writes "nach Como," and Aschenbach—for an instant unable to believe his ears and then trying desperately to regain his bearings in this swamp of language into which he has just fallen—mindlessly repeats "nach Como?" is a foreign bit of nonsense, a genuinely buffo-like effect that brutally interrupts the text's highly dignified and graceful German prose. As such, it also threatens to pull Thomas Mann's writing off course and send it in a completely wrong direction, and thus to give it a totally foreign sense: "Aschenbach's trunk had been put with some wholly different baggage [mit andere, fremder Bagage], and taken off in a completely erroneous direction [in völlig falsche Richtung geleitet wurde]." Paradoxically enough, however, it is only by lapsing for this one instant, by momentarily going wholly awry, that the text provides its author with the means of reaching any destination at all. That the direction that the novella means to take from here on out would depend so massively on the false route the baggage accidentally takes "nach Como" constitutes too significant a coincidence not to affect the meaning of the entire text.

The direction the novella is made to take at the train station linking Venice to the rest of the world, to *terraferma* as one says, is therefore entirely false, fake, bogus, and deceitful because, like the buffo in chapter 5, it can no longer be brought back under the sway of any conscious intention or self-control. Its law is the strange, foreign, bandit law of the letter prior to its domestication in the word, prior to its realignment with any particular "object"—such as Aschenbach's desire, or the narrator's aim, or the author's understanding of what he is or is not doing with and in his own language. The irony of such *Heiterkeit*—the *Heiterkeit* that grips Aschenbach on this occasion as well as the *Heiterkeit* the buffo then spreads out over the entire beach resort in chapter 5—is so detached that it can claim no knowledge, either about where exactly it has come from or where it might one day end up. It is all the more suspect and dangerous to the degree that one never even knows that one is being carried along, or rather, carried away with it. "Detached from everything," Maurice Blanchot writes about such a serenely neutral irony, "including one's detachment."[18] The detachment of which Blanchot speaks also speaks through the "dialect" of the buffo—the one spoken by the character in the text as well as the one spoken by the language of the text—and it remains unintelligible not only to Aschenbach, but ultimately to the narrator, author, and reader of *Death in Venice* alike. The stupidest thing of all would be to pretend that we could one day learn how to shake free of it once and for all.

EIGHT

Terrible Flowers: Jean Paulhan and the Irony of Rhetoric

> What Tarquin the Superb said in the garden with the poppy heads was
> understood by the son, but not the messenger.
>
> —J. G. HAMANN

How is literature possible? The question is actually the title of an essay written by Maurice Blanchot, which is itself a response to a most enigmatic book
by the French editor, critic, writer, and literary theoretician Jean Paulhan,
called *Les Fleurs de Tarbes, ou, La Terreur dans les lettres* (*The Flowers of Tarbes,
or, The Terror in Literature*).[1] In what way, exactly, does Paulhan's *The Flowers
of Tarbes* ask about the possibility of literature? Can the question of rhetorical flowers, that is, the question of whether and how literature is possible, be
asked without its having immediate and far-reaching consequences that are
not just literary in nature, but also of considerable interest for their potential
impact on philosophy and even politics? Here is what Blanchot writes at one
point in his essay on the text by Paulhan published in 1941: "The book we
have just considered, is that really the work that must be read? Isn't it rather
just the appearance? Would it not be there merely in order to conceal *ironically* another essay, more *difficult* and more *dangerous*, whose shadowy ambition one can only divine?" Whatever lies behind Blanchot's own questions
about Paulhan's *Flowers of Tarbes*, those questions also serve to trace out the
elements of another suggestion here. The possibility of an author's shadowy

intention, concealed behind an appearance that calls for divination beyond it, is connected to a mode of writing characterized as both difficult and dangerous, and the further possibility of reading this difficult and dangerous essay hidden in the book is itself framed by reference to a certain maneuver: irony. Does the question—how is literature possible?—lead inevitably to the question that eventually shadows all reading and writing: how is irony possible?

Blanchot's question about the relationship between literature and irony—which he is careful not to answer—serves to connect his writing with the interrogation of irony that occurred in its most sustained and intense manner in and around German romanticism, and in particular in the writings and reception of Friedrich Schlegel.[2] Could it be that untangling the complex history of philosophy and literature leading from Schlegel to Blanchot, Paulhan, and beyond would afford a reliable means of addressing these questions? Can a genuine understanding of the specifically postromantic French context of Paulhan's *Flowers of Tarbes* become accessible only by means of a critical narrative reconstructing this text's relation to romantic theories of irony, literature, and philosophy? No doubt the answer would be yes.[3] But it is an affirmative answer that would at some point also have to take into account what Blanchot called in his response to Paulhan's ironical writing the difficulty and even the danger of divining the true essay concealed behind *The Flowers of Tarbes*.

Another of the most astute contemporary readers of Friedrich Schlegel's writings on irony and its relation to philosophy and history, Paul de Man, cautions against precisely such recourse to historical narratives for understanding irony's relation to the possibility of literature. The danger, it turns out for de Man, is the danger ultimately posed to all philosophical understanding by irony. In conclusion to *Allegories of Reading*, whose subtitle, *Figural Language in Rousseau, Nietzsche, Rilke, and Proust*, reminds us that this book, too, like Paulhan's essay on allegorical flowers, is actually about the possibility of literature, de Man refers to Schlegel and then writes laconically, "[I]rony is the systematic undoing of understanding." Extending that rather terse formulation slightly in a 1977 lecture on irony and Schlegel, de Man also states that "any theory of irony is the undoing, the necessary undoing, of any theory of narrative. . . . As a result, it also makes it very difficult to conceive of a historiography, a system of history, that would be sheltered from irony." And in another similar formulation that he uses in a personal letter of 1982, de Man writes: "Irony is a dangerous term, because people think they know what the word means and this forecloses all understanding. 'Reading' is much better."[4] Reading, irony, incomprehension, danger: what do they have to do with the possibility of literature, and how, beyond any simple narrative history, do they relate the German romanticism of Friedrich Schlegel to more recent writers such as Jean Paulhan, Maurice Blanchot, and Paul de Man?[5]

In order to make some headway on these questions, it would be helpful to turn to Jean Paulhan's text on literature and the *terror* particular to it. For we should begin by recalling that Paulhan's book on rhetorical flowers is not just about the possibility of literature; it is about the "terror" that he names in the sub-title as the constant corollary to the question of literature. What Blanchot points to as the danger inherent in writing and reading ironically, and what is specified by de Man as the undoing of the understanding, is qualified by Paulhan, understandably enough, as a kind of terror before all letters, or literature. But what could be so terrible about a little book on the rhetorical flowers that make literature possible, and how could such seemingly harmless considerations lead to anything like the "foreclosure," much less the "undoing," of understanding? And, finally and most terrifyingly of all, if there is something—call it *irony*—in the very possibility of literature that threatens us and our understanding, what, then, would constitute a legitimate response to such a threat on the part of the literary, philosophical, or even political critic?

"If it's true," Jean Paulhan writes near the beginning of *The Flowers of Tarbes*, "that criticism should act as a complement to the arts, as their conscience as it were, then we might as well admit that the literature of today doesn't have a very good conscience."[6] With these words that rather handily tie together the activities of literature and criticism from the start, Paulhan suggests in his typically understated manner that something is wrong with the dominant economy regulating the contemporary response of criticism to literature. The French word *conscience* that Paulhan uses here to characterize the relationship between literature and criticism means both "conscience" and "consciousness," and so the passage also suggests the possibility that nothing but a bad conscience about literature is available today because there has so far not been any genuinely critical consciousness of it. The problem, Paulhan is suggesting, has to do with the way we critics tend to consider literary texts these days—in a manner that is insufficiently conscientious. Or, rather, the problem is even more serious still.

It's not just the case, Paulhan goes on to add, "that serious critics have long ago given up evaluating novels or poems; it may well be that they don't *consider* them at all" (*Fleurs*, 34; *Flowers*, 5). What could it possibly mean to suggest that those whose very job is supposed to be literary criticism do not even consider their proper object of study, poems and novels, for instance? Should that indeed be the case, then it's no wonder Paulhan would associate such a lack of consideration for literature on the part of literary critics themselves with a corresponding bad conscience. But it would be even less of a wonder, of course, that such a suggestion on Paulhan's part in 1941 would not receive an abundance of attention from precisely those literary critics he accuses both of failing to do their job and then of suffering from a bad conscience on top of this failure. For who wants to hear that they are out of touch with their own *métier*, not to mention their own conscience or consciousness? And to be honest, who in fact *has* heard of *The Flowers of Tarbes*, much less studied the text with any real attention?[7] To the extent that Paulhan's writing on literary language is inaugurated through this very critique of criticism— which is not just theoretical but also practical and even political in its outright challenge to prevailing practices within given institutions—it remains difficult to consider the most provocative elements of the book's own reading practice without somehow finding a way to relegate them to a distance far enough removed from our customary business to leave us all in peace.

All the confusion, which eventually makes it difficult to gain either a clear conscience or a clear consciousness, Paulhan notes, stems from the "mystery" that is commonly attributed to poetry in particular, and to letters in general. "It's easy to talk about the mystery in poetry," Paulhan writes in the first line of *The Flowers of Tarbes*, "and so we end up talking about it ad nauseam . . . though without really saying anything " (*Fleurs*, 23; *Flowers*, xxvii). Rather than trying to confront the mystery seriously and patiently, as should be its appointed task, literary criticism has lost its way by merely taking it for granted, and then spreading it. The mystery, according to Paulhan, is therefore not that literary language is mysterious; everybody and his (or her) brother knows that. What is truly mysterious is that literary critics seem always and everywhere in a great hurry to neglect the analysis of that mystery in favor of just about anything else, including politics, or what is referred to at the end of Paulhan's prefatory note as "today's thousand more urgent questions: misery, solitude, violence" (24; xxvii). Paulhan's work is exemplary, and exemplary as well is the resistance that has characterized its reception, including a pragmatic resistance even to translating it into other languages, to the precise extent that it remains committed to examining the actual mystery of literature long enough to disclose its true terrors.

For the problem, Paulhan reminds us at the beginning of another one of his texts, "La Demoiselle aux miroirs," turns out to be much less paradoxical than the *solution* to this problem, which merely serves to displace and therefore aggravate the original paradox.[8] The true problem is not really the problem of the mystery in literature after all; it is the problem of the *solution* to this problem, which does indeed turn out to be the *terror* produced in response to literature's originary mystery. To suggest that there is mystery in literature is one thing, even if along with suggesting that literature is mysterious one adds the rather provocative barb that literary critics don't seem to know what to do about it, in other words, how to read it. Of course, that isn't just the gesture of Jean Paulhan, it's the gesture Paulhan inherits directly and takes over in large measure from the French prince of poetic irony, Stéphane Mallarmé. It was Mallarmé, it will be recalled, who said in the 1896 text "The Mystery in Literature," "Faced with aggression, I prefer to reply that the contemporaries do not know how to read."[9] The aggression in question, of course, did not fail to be repeated on this mysterious pronouncement, stereotypically as it were; and so critics have forever afterwards echoed, not that they did not know how to read, but, rather, that Mallarmé did not know how to write! At least, so the saying goes, Mallarmé did not know how to write intelligibly enough to warrant our reading his texts the way in which they ask to be read.

What remains of significance in reading Jean Paulhan and his irony is that in displacing, ever so slightly, Mallarmé's title, "the *mystery* in literature," into "the *terror* in literature," Paulhan draws our attention by the same token to a strange complicity in literary language between mystery and terror, as well as to a movement that takes us irresistibly from mystery to terror. How exactly does the terror in literary language emerge from its mystery? And perhaps it is also time to begin translating, or displacing, the French term used by both Mallarmé and Paulhan here—*les lettres*—a little more *à la lettre*, or literally: how does the original mystery *in letters* eventually emerge in and as a mode of genuine terror?

Paulhan begins his examination of the mystery of literature, and the terror particular to it, in the most straightforward fashion conceivable, with what he calls a "childish" question: "Qu'est-ce que la littérature?" or, "What is literature?" This is a childish question, he admits, but also one that is avoided or evaded throughout one's entire life.[10] And it is avoided precisely in order to prolong this childish life—a certain kind of life, that is, that refuses at all cost to stop in order to consider the terror before the possibility of its own death. Because, it just so happens, it *is* death, and a certain kind of sickness unto death, that according to Paulhan inhabits the mystery of letters and infuses them with terror. "I was talking about literature," he says in the first chapter of *The Flowers of Tarbes*, "but I could be talking just as easily about language. . . . The malady of letters after all would be of little consequence, if it did not reveal a chronic malady of expression" (*Fleurs*, 35; *Flowers*, 6). And, one could add at this point, the chronic malady of expression would itself be of little enough consequence if it did not reveal not just a malady, but death itself. "Who wouldn't be ready to abandon literature to its fate?" Paulhan asks at the end of this chapter; "But thinking itself is compromised along with it. We only wanted to put to death the artist, but now it's all of mankind that ends up with its head chopped off" (37; 8). This reference to having one's head cut off, of course, reminds us that Paulhan's text on "terror" necessarily functions within a double register, and that one meaning of the terror, the one Blanchot called more difficult and more dangerous, may thus be concealed behind the other, which is merely its innocuous and superficial appearance.

On the one hand, the referent in question for *The Flowers of Tarbes* appears to be patently and clearly linguistic—the terror is a purely rhetorical one; it is the terror proper to letters. Or rather, according to the metaphorical register that is most often taken as the one governing Paulhan's text, just as in society, in literature too there exists a "terroristic" impulse. Those self-appointed guardians of literary propriety, the critics, respond to the mystery in literature by refusing to consider it because they cannot simply, once and for all, do away with it. Instead of dealing with the mystery in literature, then, they displace it by demanding of the writer, whom they now hold responsible for it, a clarity and authenticity that would be anything but mysterious. Such a demand is terroristic to the precise extent that it bypasses entirely the literary object it might be competent to judge, and passes judgment instead on an object over which it has no competence whatsoever, the person of the author.[11] On the other hand, and already implicit in the first understanding of the terror in literature, the referent of Paulhan's book on terror can always exceed its merely figural dimensions and become literalized in specifically historical and political ways.

For, once the question of a death sentence enters the text—"we only wanted to put to death the artist"—and no matter how metaphorically it is at first handled with respect to the empirical person of the author, the actual referent can no longer be prevented from recalling the literal Terror of 1793, where having one's head chopped off would indeed mean undergoing a beheading very much *à la lettre*. And the duplicity of the word *terror* as it is inscribed within Paulhan's text from the start becomes all the more mysteriously significant to the extent that, beyond the linguistic and historical references it by turns mobilizes, there now flickers yet another possibility: the historical reference to 1793 can be taken up once again, rhetorically *and* literally this time, to refer to the immediate political context in which Paulhan actually published *The Flowers of Tarbes*. After publishing a shorter version in serial form in 1936 in *La Nouvelle Revue Française*, Paulhan published *Les Fleurs de Tarbes* for the first time as a volume in 1941, and that means it appeared in the historicopolitical context of Nazi-occupied Paris.[12] To the extent that even the metaphorical terror, that is, the one that is proper to literature and letters, always includes the critical displacement away from the mystery in the literary work and onto the personal identification and condemnation of the author taken to be responsible for it, it also already includes, at the very least, a prefiguration of referential versions of literal terror, those of 1941 as well as those of 1793.

No doubt, all this potential slippage from literal to figural meaning—especially when it is a question of chopping off heads that can belong either to flowers or to people—is why Paulhan is so interested in that little sign he claims to have found posted at the entrance of the public garden in Tarbes, a sign that occasions the title of his book. In the second chapter of *The Flowers of Tarbes*, titled "La Misère et la faim" ("Poverty and Hunger"), Paulhan relates the following anecdote: 'At the entrance to the public garden in Tarbes, one sees the following sign: 'It is forbidden to enter the garden with flowers in hand'" (*Fleurs*, 39; *Flowers*, 9). Then Paulhan turns the sign ever so slightly in a different direction: "The same sign can also be found, in our time, at the entrance to Literature" (40; 9). Tarbes is a city in southwestern France—known more for its white beans, *haricots tarbais*, than for its public garden—and Paulhan is obviously using the anecdote allegorically to illustrate his argument about the terror in literature. The reference to the natural flowers in the public garden of Tarbes thus functions as a rhetorical flower in its own right, and it signifies in this case that the proper meaning of these flowers, the referent with which Paulhan's text is most concerned, is not the literal flowers of Tarbes but rather figural language in general. It is because cut flowers from the outside can always get mixed up with and mistaken for flowers from the inside—and vice versa—that the public guardians of Tarbes have prohibited entering the garden with any flowers. The point Paulhan seems to be making could be summed up as follows: to the degree that confusion is always possible between literal and figural uses of language—the outside and the inside of literary language, as it were—the self-appointed guardians of literature have prohibited anyone from entering its precinct with literal language and anyone from coming out of it with figural language. The "entrance" being referred to in this way would mark the difference between serious and non-serious uses of language, or, closer to home, between ironic and nonironic uses of language. But by telling the story this way, Paulhan ends up illustrating the impossibility of obeying the law at the very moment one proclaims it, since, at least in Paulhan's version, only an example that turns literal language (the flowers of Tarbes) *figural* and that turns figural language (the rhetorical flowers of literature) *literal* can grant access to the literal meaning of the sign that is erected in order to banish the illicit circulation of metaphor from its own precinct. And this, finally, explains why Paulhan, at the end of *The Flowers of Tarbes*, rewrites the original prohibition, "It is forbidden to enter the public garden *with* flowers in hand," in this new form: "It is forbidden to enter the public garden *without* flowers in hand" (166; 93). The upshot of all this rhetorical (and nonrhetorical) slippage is that the text that is ostensibly about literature uses and thereby displaces a historical and political referent, the Terror of 1793, to help make its point about the functioning of all language. But once one notices this first figural displacement of history and politics that is effected by means of literary language, it becomes hard to stop there. Perhaps, at least in 1941, the use of the historical Terror to figure the rhetorical terror in letters is itself a mere rhetorical ploy to conceal an even more immediate political reference to the actual terror of the Nazi occupation, which did indeed threaten to compromise thinking itself in quite literal ways, and for many different types of people.

But even if that particular concealed and therefore secret meaning is relevant to Paulhan's text—and it could never be simply or entirely ruled out—his use of *terror* as a rhetorical flower in the first place will always include at least the possibility that any reference to the ultimate seriousness of historical and political realities will be completely obscured and thus lost in the process. By what right, finally, can Paulhan make use of a genuine political terror to serve his polemical point about a merely rhetorical terror, even if the figural power of displacement so designated can always reemerge once again in the *public* garden of referential discourse, albeit clandestinely? Thus, there results a profound uneasiness that any conscientious reader is bound to register in confronting and attempting to understand the word *terror* in Paulhan's text, as it now begins to lurch indiscriminately between a vocabulary of life and death that would be sometimes proper to linguistic realities, and sometimes proper to political realities. One has to wonder why any author would risk this confusion between reality and verbalism by having recourse for both contexts to the very same term, *terror*, that can always and everywhere spell the literal brutality of empirical suffering and death as well as the "metaphorical" malaise one might feel before certain metaphors. Would the literary gesture that exploits tropes of terror not always and in principle also be a grievous error, the potential degradation and even perversion of a deadly serious history into gratuitous wordplay? Is the recourse to such subtle "ironies" not also the sign of diminished earnestness and responsibility on the part of criticism, indeed on the part of the critic as political as well as literary agent and authority? No wonder Paulhan begins his book by referring to a bad conscience, since he may be offering his own critical consciousness as the first and best example.

It could be, however, that the real error is not the one commonly associated with an interest in wordplay that is considered inordinate and therefore unhealthy, but rather the terroristic insistence, against all evidence to the contrary, that referential versions of terror could ever be adequately accounted for and dealt with independently of their implication within language and the terrors particular to it. Implicit in Paulhan's argument is the suggestion that actual terror—the irreducibly political as well as the rhetorical types—is always and everywhere possible only to the extent that it already inhabits all consciousness at its very foundation, which is itself a foundation composed of language and the mysterious play of its letters. What strikes terror, and subsequently produces terrorists of all kinds, including literary theorists, is the possible disjunction between language and cognition; in other words, what Paulhan's text characterizes as the potential dissociation of the act of thought and the linguistic means that makes such thoughtful acts possible in the first place.

The two traits that Paulhan consistently associates with terrorists in *The Flowers of Tarbes*, then, are first, a recognition of the original terror inscribed within letters; and second, the frivolousness of their own terroristic response in the face of this terror. "The first trait consists in the gravity of the question they raise," Paulhan states, "which is, whether literature promotes or ruins the one event that matters: the mind and its free play" (*Fleurs*, 79; *Flowers*, 36). What is most terrifying for criticism, and what it refuses to consider without dodging it by means of various terrorisms, according to Paulhan, is therefore the irreducible mystery of free play in letters that makes it forever impossible to know for sure whether one really knows anything at all, including the true identity of one's own self. "For," Paulhan goes on to say, "it is not only the problem of letters and their fidelity that is raised (and resolved in its fashion) by the Terror, but also the communication of each subject with itself: self-reflexivity" (135; 74). Paulhan's book on the possibility of literature, *The Flowers of Tarbes*, was bound to catch Blanchot's attention to the precise extent that, in its own secretive manner, it raises the question of whether and to what degree literary language functions simultaneously as the means for grounding, as well as for interrupting, the self-reflexivity of the self-conscious subject.

Now the mystery of language and the subjective self-reflexivity it serves both to condition and disrupt, or the difficult and dangerous essay that Blanchot suggests is concealed, perhaps even unintentionally, behind *The Flowers of Tarbes*, and which he invites us to read beyond it, is not just any old question. The terror that attends upon the possibility that the self-reflexivity of the thinking subject cannot itself be determined with absolute purity or certainty is itself a crux of considerable philosophical importance for the entire tradition of German romanticism and its aftermath. One of Paulhan's obvious antecedents here, perhaps the most powerfully insistent theorist of this particular terror associated with the mind and its free play, in other words, with freedom and spirit, and therefore one of the grandest terrorists of them all, was Hegel himself. The moment of philosophical Terror, as distinct from rhetorical terror—though perhaps they go hand in hand—is identified by Hegel with an extreme form of abstract universality, one in which the self-conscious freedom of the individual subject is reduced to a point so empty that it no longer is even aware of its own nullity. Without a reliable middle term to connect what it actually is and what it mistakenly takes itself for, Hegel argues, the subject falls prey to an operation of pure negation, a negativity so thoroughgoing that it produces only "death." Hegel goes on to qualify the kind of death that is at issue here as "the coldest and meanest of all deaths, where there is no more meaning involved than that of cutting off a head of cabbage."[13] The rhetorical figure of the severed cabbage head that Hegel happens upon as an apt illustration for what it is like when subjectivity and its self-consciousness are reduced to the status of a mechanical tic is a curious one, and only the apparently irresistible momentum of the Hegelian system could manage to conceal the terror of meaningless disfiguration that is inscribed within it.[14] Such a figure reminds us that there could be no such thing as empirical terror if there were not, already and further back than could ever be immediately observable, the terrifying possibility that one's own thought can always become empty and mechanical through and through. And the historical reign of terror to which Hegel alludes without naming it outright helps to suggest that it is indeed at those moments when one succeeds most in spreading terror that one is most likely to reveal the emptiness of one's own thought and the unacknowledged terror that goes along with it. Paulhan's persistent interest in the linguistic phenomenon of the potentially mindless cliché, *lieu commun* or commonplace, which is indeed the underlying theme of *The Flowers of Tarbes* as well as of many of his other texts on poetry, proverbs, and everyday language, should be understood as his way of confronting the philosophical problem posed by the ultimate precariousness of all self-reflexivity and understanding that is achieved through the mediation of language and thought.

The radical threat that is always posed to consciousness by the unthinking and automatic cabbage head—in other words, the thoughtless stereotypes, commonplaces, *lieux communs* or clichés whose formulaic devices litter all language—*that* is what is ultimately meant, by Hegel as well as Paulhan, by genuine terror. To respond to the terror of this threat by demanding a purity of thought and a guaranteed freedom for thought from all manner of contamination—that is, to demand and set out to produce at any cost absolute innocence for thought—would be to respond to the original problem by adding Terror to terror.

Which, of course, is exactly what Paulhan, as opposed to Hegel in this context, says that all terrorists actually do: "We call *Terrors* those passages in the history of nations . . . when it suddenly appears that what is necessary to the conduct of the State . . . is an extreme purity of soul, and the freshness of a communal innocence" (*Fleurs*, 61; *Flowers*, 24). To require, for the sake of establishing or preserving any given political institution, at any given historical moment, only innocence and purity of thought where there is always also irreducible mystery and secretiveness—clearly that is in some sense frivolous, as Paulhan claims in his text. But it is a frivolousness that doesn't come without its own modes of political violence and, of course, its own brutal efficacy. As one possible "solution" to *le mystère dans les lettres*, though, the multiplication of Terror upon terror is a most strange displacement of the original problem, and so it could hardly be considered definitive. But are there other alternatives? In other words, is there any one solution to the mystery that could ever be considered final?

Paulhan's own response to the dilemma seems to have been to pay as much attention as possible to the actual impurities of self-reflexive thought, rather than to lay claim to some prior or subsequent innocence, purity, or unity for it. The obstacle to any innocence, Paulhan finally has to admit, is provided by the object of study itself, the particular language in which we are always obligated to think as well as express, that is, speak, ourselves and our minds.

Every attempt to theorize fully the linguistic devices that allow thought to occur in the first place is implicated in the very functioning of those devices, and thus is caught in a deflected image of its own theoretical reflection upon them. There can therefore be no reliable metalanguage capable of observing and mastering the devices of language—literary or critical—from a safe distance, Paulhan says in the "Dossier" he adds to *Les Fleurs*, "because the particles, rather than being real *elements* of our object, turn out to be specific *deformations* that we impose upon it in order to think it " ("Dossier," *Fleurs*, 251).[15] Hence Paulhan's abiding interest in the stereotype or *lieu commun* that incessantly interrupts all thought. What makes the linguistic stereotype interesting, says Paulhan, is its *unmistakably* linguistic character. The obviously linguistic nature of the cliché reminds us that we always think through language; but because it is so easily identifiable *as* language, it also makes itself into an easy target for terrorists who are eager to police and enforce the purity and superiority of all thought over mere expression (*Fleurs*, 102–03, 131; *Flowers*, 50–51, 72). But the *lieu commun* cannot simply be approached by the thought police without producing upon the policing effort itself a reciprocal effect of disorder and contamination: "and so our thought cannot prevent itself from deteriorating and falling into disorder as soon as it attempts to seize the commonplace" ("Dossier," *Fleurs*, 252). The commonplace is thus always identifiable as language rather than thought, but then it also always resists being taken hold of by thought without thereby also infecting it with its own mechanical characteristics.

The problem, Paulhan explains, is that depending on one's point of view, the cliché is precisely that element of rhetorical conventionality that always allows *simultaneously* for the erasure of linguistic expression in the completed thought *and* for the erasure of thought in the snares of its expression. As a set phrase that in itself is *nothing but* a recognizable form of language, the cliché can always be repeated thoughtlessly and mechanically for its own sake; or, on the contrary, and for the very same reasons, the commonplace can be repeated otherwise, taken up anew in an act of thought that would be entirely original with respect to it. "The *lieux communs*," Paulhan says, "can be intelligent or stupid, I can't say which, and see no means ever to know with rigor." To this particular cliché of undecidability Paulhan gives another name; he calls it, "a *monster* of language and reflection" (*Fleurs*, 142–43; *Flowers*, 78). What is monstrous here is not just the duplicitousness of the *lieu commun*, it is also the irreducible split that such a monstrous figure introduces within the speaking subject that it also serves to reflect and thus express. One can easily enough admit, along with Paulhan here, that the *cliché* is intelligent or stupid, depending on one's particular point of view. But who could ever say that one is *oneself*, depending on the circumstances, either a thinking subject or an unthinking machine, and from *whose*, or rather, from *what* point of view could such a possibility be enunciated, much less examined critically? The mystery in literary letters thus becomes a terror of radical alienation when it is reflected toward the inside of the speaking subject, as it always must be. Hence, and for the same reason, the "ironic" admission by Paulhan at this point of the text—that he himself will never know with rigor—should be taken in a dead-serious sense.

Nonetheless, Paulhan's ironic nonknowledge, unlike the blind demand for total knowledge made by the terrorists, opens onto a mode of thinking that is able to acknowledge, and therefore contend with and perhaps even occasionally divert, some of the more perilous modes of displacement, deformation, and contamination to which all thought is subject. What each of Paulhan's texts tirelessly reminds us—always seeming to start out again from a different source of mystery, always seeming to end up pointing to the same possibility of terror—is that all thought, to the extent that it is always a thinking of the subject through the language of its own *lieux communs*, is itself susceptible to a degradation into unthinking clichés that it always only borrows from others in the first place. And this potential degradation of thought is one mystery that lies beyond the power of any subject to know and control all by itself.

Every understanding of self-reflexive thought brings us back to another *language*; but every consideration of this language involves the self in another act of *thought*. The ensuing situation, at least as it is inscribed in Paulhan's texts, is neither a simple paralysis nor a formal symmetry, but is rather a fully armed *battle* in which language and thought are pitted against each other. Whether one begins with thought or language, one will always end up coming back to language. But such a return to language will never be acknowledged as such by the rhetorician through whom the return is executed. When thought examines itself, it must always acknowledge the place that the rhetorician's language occupies within it, whereas the language of the rhetorician—which is fundamentally thoughtless in this regard—will always *claim* a power of thought to which it is in no way entitled. The language of rhetoric therefore turns out to be just as terroristic as the language of terror, since the one illusion of which it can never rid itself definitively is that it, too, thinks. "The responses of both Terror and Rhetoric," Paulhan writes, "derive from the same principle, which, roughly speaking, is that thought is more valuable than language: that in the final analysis language *must* yield to thought. . . . This bias is not without analogy, in its obvious *authority*, with that other, purely moral, bias, that attends upon *battles* between the mind and body and that finally *imposes* the submission of the body. So it is with language, that body of thought."[16]

Now, what thought wins in this perennial struggle with language is the only prize finally worth fighting over: the referential function of language, the claim of one's own thought to rule over the world it articulates and thus dwells in. "Whoever stops at my language," says Paulhan, by now merely quoting, that is, repeating, Montaigne's words, "I would prefer that he be quiet. 'I am not a writer,' says the writer. And with these words we are joyfully returned [renvoyés] to love, to might and fear, to the things of the world" ("La Rhetorique,"*OC* 2:157; "Rhetoric," *PP* 45). The submission by rhetorical flowers to the ultimate force of thought is also and simultaneously a joyous return of language and thought to the real "forces" of the world, including the sometimes less-than-joyful referents "love" and "fear," joined as they are here by the dubious mediation of "might" (*la force*). The very formulation of this force, though, should alert us to a potential complication within it: "nous voici *renvoyés* aux choses du monde"—where the return to the world can itself only be accomplished by another turn or reference to a *language* of force, of *renvois* or "relays," in which the command to banish language always has to be declared anew. What if the force of thought itself came from elsewhere, from a ruse of rhetoric that could never be wholly proper, and thus present, to the subject through which it has to be enunciated? In other words, what if the very decision to suspend rhetoric in favor of thought and reference were itself contaminated by a rhetoric that always managed somehow to conceal its rhetorical status?

Paulhan himself, of course, suspects as much: "It is always *other words* that are used to establish that one has escaped from words" (*Fleurs*, 139; *Flowers*, 77). And so the conclusion is also built into the argument: "Such is the illusion to which every Terror obligates the writer. Language occupies no less a place. But it cheats, and doesn't admit that it is language" (160; 89). But if thought can win out over language only by a new deception or illusion about language—and Paulhan's own writings are nothing if not a constant tracking down of various linguistic illusions of this type—then how can we categorize such a "victory" from the point of view of the thinking subject that always lays claim to it?

One of the terms Paulhan uses to characterize this inevitable if unwanted return to rhetoric in the pragmatic victory of thought and reference over language is *tragic*: "One could say that poetry is something much more tragic and profound than has ever been imagined" ("La Rhetorique," *OC* 2:166; "Rhetoric," *PP* 55). What is tragic here is the referential function of language, torn apart between a terror that demands the singularity of its due in pure thought, and the stereotypical rhetoric that alone can allow such a demand to be made intelligible. The pure and simple victory of the forces of reference is always tragic to the extent that it is, at least in part, and unbeknownst to it, beholden to a ruse and illusion produced by its inveterate enemy. Referential modes of Terror always believe they are combating the treachery of someone else's rhetoric, when in fact they are merely working to accomplish it in ever-more-treacherous ways.[17] The most profound tragedies of all result in this way from the Terrors that are always *duped* by the unacknowledged powers of rhetoric upon which they, too, must ultimately rely for their own effectiveness. For such Terrors always claim entirely for themselves, for the purity and innocence of their own thought, the power to return "to the things of the world" that has in fact been lent to them from elsewhere. Victims of a mistaken belief in the possibility of their own purity, terrorists stop at nothing in their rage to eliminate whatever resistance they find in others, including the other as stereotype, *lieu commun*, or cliché eventually devoid of all meaning for the terrorist.

Paulhan's other, apparently less tragic, response to this self-perpetuating Terror is itself well enough known to have become something of a cliché in its own right. "Clichés can regain their right to citizenship in literature," he says rather disingenuously near the end of his text, "from the moment they would finally be relieved of their ambiguity and confusion" (*Fleurs*, 143; *Flowers*, 79). And then he concludes: "Now, it ought to suffice, since the confusion comes from a doubt about their nature, simply to agree, once and for all, that they will be considered as clichés. In short, it suffices to make common the commonplaces. . . . To that end would be required, at most, some lists and a little commentary." What is Paulhan saying here when he says, let's agree to make commonplaces truly common? The conventionality of language that makes dupes out of all those who are afraid of being duped—that is, that makes terrorists out of the terror glimpsed in the mysteries of language—can be overcome if we simply agree on a new convention, one that agrees once and for all *not* to look too closely at words. The dream here, of course, is that of a

universal grammar, a dream of pure and simple classification that would register and record all the clichés and provide a readable commentary for them.[18]
But the choice to which Paulhan points is too symmetrical not to raise some
new doubts. If the terrorists wreak tragedy in their rage to eliminate the stereotype, Paulhan's grammarians cannot avoid appearing rather ludicrous, and
even simple-minded, in their rush to embrace them. What would be the price
of such an all-inclusive grammatical solution to the problem of rhetoric and
its clichés? Where could we find the final point of view that would allow us to
see, and to see precisely by not looking too closely at them, the commonality
of all the commonplaces?

In the penultimate section of *The Flowers of Tarbes*, titled "Rhetoric, or the
Perfect Terror," Paulhan hints at the possibility of a solution so peculiar as to
risk upsetting any understanding that would be based on a simple alternative,
such as the one between terror and grammar, which, by merely reversing the
tragic and comic poles of one and the same impulse to overcome the cliché,
does not even offer a true alternative. "Irony," Paulhan finally writes out in all
its terrible letters, "irony, emphasis, a slight deformation, a subtle discrepancy
or *décalage*, a drop of the voice, by providing something like a zone of reflection around the cliché, suffices to warn us that 'we can go ahead,' that we are
no longer at risk of being dupes" (*Fleurs*, 145–46; *Flowers*, 79–80). No doubt
about it, the perfect grammar for overcoming rhetoric, the guardrail to end all
guardrails against the impurities of misunderstanding, would therefore have
to be a text composed of nothing but ironies, deformations, discrepancies,
accents, italics, quotation marks, parentheses, and so forth and so on. Paulhan's text indicates in this way that there can be no grammatical totalization
of rhetoric, no reading of *The Flowers of Tarbes* without a pinch of the irony
and rhetorical *décalage*, or discrepancy, between consciousness and language
that made it necessary to write it in the first place. There can be no protection
from the terrors of rhetorical dupery that is not also a deadly ironic trap as
well; no referential guardrail against the mysteries and confusions of letters
that is not also, and inevitably, a springboard right back into them.

"The railing that a far-sighted mayor places before an abyss," Paulhan says,
"might seem to inhibit the traveler's freedom. The traveler would be mistaken, of course, since it only requires a little effort to jump right in. . . . So
it is with rhetoric" (*Fleurs*, 154; *Flowers*, 85). As an operation that can never
economize on traveling in or near the abyss of thought, as a self-reflexive act
of understanding that must pass through language and its abyssal figures, every reading of Paulhan's text—and not just Paulhan's of course—is, as Blan-

chot suggests, a concealed and therefore secret practice of irony. But it is an ironic practice of reading in which the subject can never quite coincide with its own thought because of the commonplaces and clichés in which such thought must be written out in the first place; and so it is ultimately a reading that always takes place at a certain remove or distance from itself, as well as from its own understanding. Whenever it becomes necessary to read— that is, to understand—Paulhan's writing ironically, it also becomes, for the reasons specified by both Blanchot and Paulhan, practically impossible ever to accomplish such a reading, since in taking place as irony the reading will always leave a residue that is both figural and literal, both literary and referential, within its own aberrant understanding. Irony is the non-pure identity of the subject and its language, thought, and action. And this nonidentity will necessarily affect every attempt to regain control over it by narrating, and thus understanding, it retrospectively—for instance, as the historical unfolding of a theory and practice of irony as it is moves through and beyond German romanticism to twentieth-century French writing.

Such is the difficulty as well as the danger of Paulhan's writing on the possibility of literature that is hidden in *The Flowers of Tarbes*. But it is a difficulty and a danger that no amount of theory or terror—literary or political—can do away with, and so it continues to provide a shadowy occasion for all manner of political and literary readings to occur in its wake. Irony is in this way productive of history at the very moment it defies all historical formalization. If, as Mallarmé suggests in "The Mystery in Literature," the contemporaries do not know how to read, it is now possible to add that this is also, and in an even more profound sense, because, as Paulhan indicates in *The Terror in Literature*, no reading could ever be simply contemporary with itself and its own figures of understanding, no matter what their rhetorical or referential status. "Poorly informed," Mallarmé reminds us in another text on action and its rhetorical constraints, "is the one who would claim to be his own contemporary, deserting, usurping with equal impudence, when the past has ceased and a future delays its arrival or when both mix themselves perplexedly together in view of masking the gap between them."[19] Less poorly informed, and refusing to mask the gaps of actual history—which also name the mystery and terror in letters—would be texts like those of Mallarmé, Blanchot, and Paulhan. Like their noncontemporaries in German romanticism, moreover, such texts never cease to perplex, which is to say resist, every effort either to overcome or simply to abandon their unstoppable irony.

PART THREE

The Irony of Tomorrow

NINE

On Parole: Legacies of Saussure, Blanchot, and Paulhan

> Nous l'avons détruit, nous avons libéré l'étoile—sans rayon désormais; il roule obscur, l'astre du désastre, disparu, comme il le souhaitait, dans la tombe sans nom de son renom.
>
> —MAURICE BLANCHOT, *L'Écriture du désastre*

Nothing could be simpler, or so it might seem, than to know what it means to take someone at their word. But when that someone is a writer, and that writer is named Maurice Blanchot, then the question of his giving us his word, or of our taking him at his word, can become a source of genuine anguish, if not outright despair. "Reading is anguish," Blanchot wrote, "and this is because any text, however important, or amusing, or interesting it may be (and all the more so that it gives that impression), is empty—at bottom it does not exist; you have to cross an abyss, and if you do not jump, you do not comprehend."[1] Now among all the words Maurice Blanchot has given us, is there one from now on that is more likely to bring us face to face with the anguish and abyss of reading than that of *disaster*? Should we take him at his word, Blanchot gives us his word that writing is the disaster and that the disaster is writing. No wonder that reading would occasion anguish and despair at the instant we consider crossing the abyss that such a word gives us to take, grasp, or comprehend. Disappearing into the ruined space of disaster, catastrophe, calamity, the word that Blanchot gives us also marks the contours of a certain tomb, though a tomb whose proper name, either as origin or end, will always have been obscured by its being incessantly on the move, rolling unceasingly away from our anxious grasp.[2] By the light of what kind of star would it now be possible to track the word that has been given in this way only through its unstoppable errancy, through its fall into a sepulchral space of separation from its own rays? And what kind of authority would we need at our disposal in order to grant the existence of such a disastrous *parole* in the first place?

Nothing, or so it might seem, could be farther removed from the dark constellation of reflections enshrouding Blanchot's writing of the disaster than the sunny atmosphere of clarity in which Saussure's *Course in General Linguistics* makes its way from one didactic point to another in laying bare the hidden principles of language and the way that it functions. And yet, as is well known, it is precisely Saussure's most original founding gesture that threatens to turn the entire semiological enterprise into a sterile science of dead-end fragments and simplifications. For, it should always be recalled, Saussure's *Course*, like any text for that matter, is able to begin only by giving us its word, its own inimitable *parole*, though in such a way that it seems to be immediately and irremediably retracted from us. That luminous and now famous word that Saussure first gives us, of course, the one that will always have enabled his text to get underway as a systematic *Course*, is *la langue*. But have we ever adequately stopped to consider how *la langue* itself appears, only to withdraw from us in a mode of unthinkable obscurity? Before Saussure's own text brings about this tectonic shift within the French language between *la langue* and *la parole*, *la langue*—as a system of purely formal conventions, which can subsequently be defined and then known only in its strict opposition to *la parole*, as a particular execution of these conventions—does not and cannot exist as such. It can only be *la parole* of Saussure's own text, the active and idiosyncratic fact of the *Course* as a concrete instance of linguistic materiality, that releases *la langue* as a genuine force of semiological analysis and knowledge for the future.

La langue is therefore not just a formal system whose empirical existence Saussure was able merely to observe or deduce; it is also, as testified by the neologism that it will become only in the wake of Saussure's *Course*, a material event that his text has to inaugurate in its own right.[3] Louis Hjelmslev's essay "Langue et parole," an attempt to resolve what he called the fundamental "ambiguity" lying at the heart of Saussure's distinction between langue and parole, gives some indication of the radicality of this event. In Hjelmslev's stratified vocabulary, what Saussure actually does in the *Course* is to execute an individual "act"—of parole—that retrospectively necessitates an alteration of all "usage"—in this particular case, of *la langue*—which then and only then can be regarded as the norm for every possible "schema—of intelligibility."[4] For Hjelmslev, usage is everything, since "the norm" is a merely fictive law projected onto usage, and every individual act must conform to the existing limits fixed by its potential to signify. But in the case of Saussure's distinction, the use of the word *langue* to refer precisely to the systematic elements of language by their pure opposition to acts of *parole* constitutes a "change of definition" that, Hjelmslev notes, "would involve a change of language" and thus the appearance of "another language from the one we know" ("Langue et parole," 82). Whenever the available range of usage is exceeded in this way, Hjelmslev adds, "the description of usage itself would itself have to be modified" (88). Saussure's improvisation therefore leaves an indelible mark on the entire French *langue*, and beyond it, on the description and knowledge of language as such. We can from now on understand what langue is, in contradistinction to parole, only because Saussure's *Course* implemented this particular parole of langue in the first place. And it did this when it made the langue into the only possible object of linguistics by virtue of its difference from parole.

In the more familiar terms of the *Course* as it is ordinarily expounded, langue is a semiotic system that, like all social institutions, is based on certain determinate patterns. These abstract and formalized conventions, unlike the concrete and heterogeneous instances of parole, can be delimited and then studied in themselves to produce a mode of scientific knowledge. This is why Saussure places such insistence on a further characteristic of his distinction: langue will constitute only that which is absolutely essential in language's capacity to signify, whereas parole will comprise all those factors and functions of signification that remain in whole or part accidental and contingent. In other words, in order to learn anything epistemologically reliable about language—and since language is the "most important" of the innumerable semiotic systems that make up social life in general, therefore in order to learn anything worth knowing at all—it is necessary once and forever to separate language from itself, to sever the generality of langue from its intimate ties to the immanent particularity of parole. "There can only be," Saussure assures us in the firm tone of a practicing surgeon, "one solution to all these problems: it is necessary right from the start to place ourselves squarely in the domain of langue. . . . By separating langue from parole, we also separate what is social from what is individual, and what is essential from what is merely contingent."[5] In an ironic gesture that has not gone wholly unnoticed—even if it hasn't often been remarked as such—Saussure thus asks us to take his word for it—to believe him *sur parole*, as it were—that we can only learn what language is in its most systematic and knowable state once we have excised all instances of parole from our examination of langue! And, of course, this originary *acte de parole*—the one Saussure gives us in the very name of langue, moreover, though only in order to cut all others away from it—is at the source of the rich and inconclusive history of Saussure's own reception.

For of all the Saussurian legacies to future thought, none has been more subjected to investigation, judgment, and sentencing than this founding bifurcation between langue and parole. Between language as social system and language as individual practice, as we have just seen, Saussure seemed to find an absolute incompatibility, and in the face of this paralyzing alternative for any rigorous attempt to produce knowledge about language, he resolutely chose the systematic coherence of langue as the only proper object of study for linguistics. There can be no doubt, moreover, that the dominant reception of Saussure still considers such a priority given to langue over parole to characterize in its essence what goes by the name of *structuralism*, a wholly *dépassé*, if interesting, moment in the much larger scheme of linguistic, literary, and cultural history. This emphasis on langue—on language as a system, but language construed as such as well—is still widely regarded as Saussure's fundamental fault, or defect; indeed it is as though he had committed a kind of infraction against the larger and more encompassing laws of both language and history. For having introduced into the study of language a split between system and act, state and evolution, signification and intention, Saussure will therefore stand accused of methodological malfeasance—as punishment for this misdemeanor, he will have been sentenced to a cell of theoretical detention and rehabilitation.

Paul Ricoeur summarizes the situation with admirable clarity when he resituates certain insights taken from Emile Benveniste's linguistics of discourse within a more philosophically oriented argument about the constitution of subjective and historical truth. "The task," Ricoeur writes, "is to *reclaim* for the understanding of language what the structural model *excluded* and which is perhaps language itself as an act of speech [acte de parole]. . . . Our task today is the condition for an *integral* understanding of language; to think language should be to think the *unity* of that very reality which Saussure has *disjoined*, the unity of langue and parole" (emphasis added).[6] Saussure's text is thus routinely put under suspicion and confined to very specific limits for having committed an offense that, Ricoeur says, "does violence" to language itself. Saussure's violent crime would be precisely the one of having cut into the integrity of language by severing the historical and subjective reality of parole from a scientific consideration of langue, all for the sake of a "reliable" but merely hypothetical and thus highly dubious knowledge of its systemic principles. The ensuing judgment against Saussure for having wrongfully privileged langue in this way is not without appeal, though. Ricoeur finds Saussure guilty of having excluded certain fundamental elements of parole from his model, but does not condemn Saussure for that to simple exclusion. Rather, Ricoeur calls for an operation of "reclaiming" or "retrieval" (*récupération*)—to salvage Saussure's formalist model by bringing it back into contact with precisely those individual and historical elements of language it is accused of having wronged. The task, Ricoeur says, is not simply to banish langue from all consideration, but much rather to reintegrate it within the concrete reality of parole so that language itself can be understood from now on as a social space of historical integration and unity.

And so it is always in order to retrieve the usefulness of the *Course in General Linguistics* for our own thought that we agree to grant Saussure's langue what might be called a kind of parole, allowing it once again to circulate within today's theoretical discourses in the humanities and social sciences, though only on condition of remaining under strict supervision. The paradox, of course, is that such gestures repeat the very thing that Saussure's text is being censured for, since one can readmit langue to theoretical reflection only by enacting determinate strategies, discrete acts, and specific conditions of parole. If, as Saussure had suspected from the start, parole is precisely what infringes upon the systematic laws of langue, then every recuperation of Saussure's original transgression, rather than actually serving to reform it, will become complicitous with it. For, it can always be asked, by exactly what right and authority could any subsequent theoretical discourse ever grant parole to Saussure's langue, since Saussure's own text is itself nothing but this inaugural enactment of *la langue*—as an irreducible but heretofore unrecognizable *signe*, if not genuine signature—through its inaugural power of parole?

By pretending to consider Saussure's exclusion of parole from langue as a simple *délit* or offense that might and should have been avoided, and that can now be remedied and legitimated by a new *acte de parole* instantiated by their own texts, readings such as Ricoeur's not only mask far-reaching tensions between what can and cannot be known about language and all other social systems. They also, implicitly or explicitly, lay claim to a highly suspect authority of parole to know and to police the frontiers of just such knowledge. If Saussure insists upon the necessary separation of the systematic and formal nature of langue from the unruly but coercive power of parole, he does so precisely because he remains attentive to the original asymmetry between the powerless knowledge offered by langue and the unknowable power that is always unleashed in parole.[7] What has most often been lost in the reception of Saussure is thus an awareness of the precise ways in which his own text serves to resist underwriting just such claims to legitimacy and authority. Indeed, in the section of Saussure's *Course* that assigns to *la langue* the preeminent place it will have to assume from now on in any reliable science of language, the material facticity of *la parole* is also disclosed as the only truly historical means by which langue will ever have been given access to this position: "langue is necessary for parole to be intelligible and produce its effects; but parole is necessary for langue to occur at all [pour que la langue s'établisse]; historically, the fact of parole always comes first" (*Course*, 18–19). This "circle," as Jacques Derrida has referred to it, would not be hermeneutic in any classic sense, and therefore it would not lend itself to an operation of reattachment of beginning to end.[8] When Ricoeur speaks of restoring the unity to what Saussure has disjoined, he mistakenly takes Saussure's *parole* for exactly what it is not, the systematic closure and intelligibility of langue, and thus he fails to see that the disjunction at issue is irreducible to them both.

The fact is, parole, by *having* to speak first, and first of all by having to speak for and thus herald the intelligibility of langue, serves to disjoin langue from itself from the start; and that remains the case no matter how much, like Ricoeur's text, it would claim to do otherwise. Parole, just as we have seen in the writing of the *Course* itself, must come first in order for langue to happen historically. But in order for this parole to function effectively, that is, to achieve intelligibility as what it always will have been only subsequently, it must at the same time already be disguised as precisely what it is not yet, which is to say the systematic coherence of langue. The parole that announces and thus lays down the law of langue's future intelligibility also and by the same token transgresses it simply by virtue of preceding it. This gaping enigma, which one could perhaps now venture to call the *paroling* of langue, is originary with respect to all the subjective freedoms and responsibilities that can eventually be granted to langue by its parole. In Saussure, at least, such a parole is not and cannot be granted by any determinate authority, such as philosophy, theology, or linguistics, least of all by one claiming a specific privilege or legitimacy for its own discourse. It is rather the cleft authority upon which any and all intentionality can eventually come into limited and thus provisional possession of its own langue. By drawing attention to the way Saussure's text enacts from its very beginning this kind of paroling of langue, we uncover a historicity to language that is unconditional, though not at all simple in nature. It is always a discrete act of parole that grants material reality and thus gives genuine authority to a langue that would otherwise remain an empty and isolated possibility—but it is always langue that, through the power of its parole, then promises to be governed in its behavior by semantic laws that have not yet been formulated, much less tested for consistency or coherence of meaning. Langue is therefore poised equally, though in a most volatile and unpredictable position, between a prior act of parole that grants it the freedom to occur historically, and a future moment of critical reckoning in which it will have to account for its borrowed potential to become and remain a unified system of intelligibility.

But who is really going to take any of that seriously? The *paroling* of langue? Mere word play, *calembour*, paronomasis. What is little more, after all, than a rather sorry pun works by allowing Saussure's founding distinction for structural linguistics, *langue/parole*, to become contaminated by its purely accidental relation to idiomatic English expressions taken from the legal and penal systems, such as, for instance, "to be granted parole," "to parole," or "to be paroled," and so on. The possibility of such frivolousness, in its very frivolity, moreover, brings us back to our starting point, namely to Maurice Blanchot and his not-so frivolous text *The Writing of the Disaster*.[9] Asking, examining, and intervening in some of the most troubling and unresolved questions of our time, Blanchot's text returns over and over again to consider the way the French word *désastre* can, if it is treated with sufficient intellectual energy and perseverance, prompt us toward a richly suggestive but ultimately unwarranted understanding of the all-important philosophical distinction between concealment and disclosure, or truth and error. The French word for *disaster* hides, though it can also be seen to shelter within itself, a root that idiomatic usage can no longer or not yet see or hear clearly: *astre*, a word for celestial bodies of light capable of providing us with a source of "illumination." Blanchot's text outlines in this way a question about whether and how we could learn to read the writing of the disaster, *l'écriture du désastre*, as constituting a kind of writing granted to us *by* disaster. Can a questioning of the word *disaster*, that is, also teach us something about the way disaster as such could one day become a mode of disclosing the truth, helping us to rediscover an originary light or star whose path has up until now been lost or hidden within the innumerable disasters of history? The most frivolous—the play of the letter—can always turn into the most serious—and this in fact does happens here when the concealment and disclosure at play in the French word *désastre* are then turned by Blanchot's text toward an encounter with Heidegger's questioning of the (Greek) word for truth, *aletheia*.[10] From a mere pun—uncovering and thus revealing the light, *astre*, concealed within the word *désastre*—can eventually be derived a most compelling question for our own historical consciousness, if we only stop to listen to its call to us from within language. What is the truth of the disaster, and can this truth, no matter how dark and dangerous it has become in our history, be made to shine anew?

Blanchot's response is remarkable, even astonishing, for its tenacious resistance either to legitimate or to dismiss the philosophical relation of concealment and disclosure, of forgetting and remembering, that Heidegger finds at play in the word *aletheia*, and that Blanchot extends, within his own language, to the word *désastre*. Rather, Blanchot says at one point, a writer such as Heidegger, who returns to the root of certain words that are considered fundamental and is able from these words and their roots to develop variations of both thinking and language, "makes 'true' the idea that there is in the root a power that is at work and that also incites to work" (*WD* 107; *ED 166*). For Heidegger, as is well known, truth as *aletheia*, or as a mode of unconcealment, has been concealed through its translation into truth as *veritas*, or a mode of adequation and correspondence. This slight shift in meaning can actually be recovered, argues Heidegger, from within the heart of the Greek word *aletheia* by heeding its formation from the alpha privative *a-letheia*. Truth, now read as *a-letheia* or un-concealment, is to be understood as a wresting or even robbing what is true from a countermovement of concealment, *lethe*, that is there from the beginning.[11] But, suggests Blanchot's text, what is philosophically "true" in this demonstration is *not* what Heidegger says about the Greek word for truth, for that belongs to a mode of truth that could be demonstrated neither by philosophy nor by history with respect to the way *a-letheia* was in fact thought by the Greeks. What is *true* and beyond question here is rather that Heidegger puts this word for truth to work in new ways for his own thinking about truth. In doing so, according to Blanchot, he also eventually manages to make the idea that its root contains an effective power of philosophical explanation and understanding "work," or succeed—despite whether it is in any epistemological sense "true" or not. Indeed, this paraphrastic translation into English of Blanchot's text would itself offer an example of the way such new possibilities for thought are always at work in words, and not only at their root, but in their cross-pollination between languages as well. Blanchot begins by saying that in this context believers and nonbelievers alike get things at once wrong and right ("non-croyants et croyants: tous deux ayant tort et raison"). If a writer, Blanchot goes on, receives from words and their roots an impetus—that is, if certain words give a writer an *occasion*—for transforming both language and thought, then we ought to acknowledge that there is in such words "une puissance au travail et qui fait travailler [a power that is at work and that also incites to work]." Of course, the French word *travailler*, which should be translated by the English word *work*, does not include at its own root the sense of "working" as succeeding. *Ça ne marche pas.* But, on the other hand, and always according to the logic of Blanchot's remarks, such a possibility does take root as soon as *travailler* is carried over and grafted onto the English stem *work*. It is "true" that what does not quite work in the French word *travailler* works nonetheless in its English equivalent. If writing the French word *travailler* into English can expand thinking in either or both languages, then such a translation from language to thought might be made "true" after all—no matter how it relates to words and their roots. It will therefore not suffice either simply to take Heidegger at his word here, Blanchot suggests, or merely to dismiss out of hand what he has to say about the truth as it is hidden and disclosed by the word *aletheia*. Rather, philosophically and historically speaking, one has to begin to account for the very precise way that Heidegger's writing of the truth in this word now aquires the power to *travailler*, or "work"—by changing for the future the way we think about truth as well as language.

Now that particular understanding of the power at work in words whose play is put to work in this way is not something that Blanchot could have read, as such, in Heidegger's own text. Rather, it is an understanding of the mysterious relation between language and truth, work and play, that he owes in large part to Jean Paulhan, in particular to a little and little-known text titled *Alain, ou la preuve par l'étymologie* (Alain, or Proof by Etymology).[12] For it is in this text that Paulhan goes about the delicate task of exploring the "nature and play," that is, the laws according to which etymology works (*Alain, OC* 3:280). Etymology concerns the semiotic relation between words and their meanings, though it does so by privileging the way any given word can be traced back to a form and a meaning that precede the ones it has today or might acquire tomorrow. As Paulhan is quick to point out, moreover, the word *etymology* doubles as its own best advertisement, since *its* roots can be traced back to the Greek phrase *etumos logos*, or *true* meaning (3:265). The "proof" by etymology to which Paulhan refers in his title, then, is to be understood as an epistemological one: etymology undertakes, and then claims to demonstrate, the true meaning of words by reconstituting a knowledge of their origins. The "proof by etymology" is thus always the proof *of* etymology, where the root of "true meaning," the *etumon*, is both the means and the end, the vehicle as well as the destination of knowledge. The problem is, however, that the status of this "truth," or of the proof of authentic meaning that is reached by recovering the word's *etumon*, is not itself epistemologically univocal or sound. Paulhan's text thus reaches back behind etymology to ask how the authenticity of a word's ultimate "truth" can itself be authenticated. In what kind of ground do the roots of words actually grow?

On the one hand, Paulhan reminds us, the demonstration of true meaning derived from etymology is mere play, like an ordinary play on words (*jeu de mots*), since the only genuine "science" of etymology, made possible by the developments in modern linguistics over the last century or so, leaves no doubt that etymological explanations are at best either redundant or inconclusive, and at worst, downright misleading (*Alain, OC* 3:275–77). On the other hand, it remains a *fact*, however contrary it may run to the clear evidence of linguistics, that writers and philosophers alike, indeed all ordinary language speakers, continuously rely on learned as well as folk or literary etymologies as an authoritative means of establishing and justifying the truth of their own discourses (3:267–68, 278). The enigma on which Paulhan thus focuses our attention turns out to be a subtle but most provocative one. For Paulhan's text on etymological proof is not just a demystification of its epistemological pretensions, and this is what sets it apart from so many other critical texts on the subject. The real interest of this text, and one that Blanchot's reading of Heidegger will pursue and even extend further, is the way in which it underscores that proof by etymology—the search for and validation of the "true" meaning of words by means of nonscientific procedures of knowledge production—continues everywhere unabated *despite* the demonstrated inadequacy of its premises as well as its conclusions.[13] How and why, Paulhan's little text dares to ask, does proof by etymology retain a special kind of efficacity in determining "true meaning," a practical efficacity that serves to resist the most rigorous linguistic and epistemological critique?

Paulhan's answer is surprising only for its simplicity and obviousness. *How* the search for "true" meaning by etymological procedures is able to bypass the findings of linguistic and epistemological analysis stares us in the face, it is so blindingly obvious: it belongs to an entire series of devices that have little or nothing to do with the kind of truth reached by scientific methods, including those of both modern linguistics and classical logic (*Alain, OC* 3:280, 300). Rather than obeying the laws of a science of linguistics or a logic of philosophy, etymological "proof," says Paulhan, is always *literary*, no matter how learned it may appear.[14] In fact, in order for etymological proof to work at all, Paulhan argues, it *must* be literary through and through, for only then could it exceed the merely verifiable history of a word's signification—which may be epistemologically sound, but which remains of limited explanatory value with respect to the purely accidental changes that have altered the word's true meaning throughout its history (3:275–77). Etymological proof, on the other hand, is a "rhetorical ploy" (*tour de rhétorique*), and as such it always goes beyond the truth of the observable laws of linguistic evolution in order to *explain* and therefore *motivate* in its every detail the ultimate meaning of any given word, as well as the entire edifice of corollary arguments that can also be built with it (3:280–82). Etymology, then, like "poetry" for Mallarmé, is a fiction, but it is a "supreme" fiction in that it serves to repair the original defect of all language, which defect is to permit an indefinite diversity of meaning without being able to offer a philosophically coherent explanation and thus justification for its own arbitrary capacity to make any one of them be true.[15] Etymology dispenses with the methodological constraints of both linguistics and philosophy, and thus it allows even the most random features and functions of language to appear fully motivated and meaningful within the context of their own fictive constructions. It is decidedly not a form of verifiable knowledge, "une science" or "une connaissance," says Paulhan, but rather the fulfillment of a mere desire to know, "un souhait," which could never be otherwise satisfied by language.

Why such "etymological" fictions—which by this point in Paulhan's text have been extended to include effects of paronomasia, ellipsis, antithesis, allusion, and all the other devices and wiles of a generalized rhetoric—manage to resist the laws of scientific observation and classical logic that always and everywhere challenge their epistemological legitimacy is simple: they possess an undeniable *force* that both linguistics and philosophy, far from effectively contesting, actually require for carrying out their own programs.[16] Paulhan says this force is itself something of a fiction, since it consists in an etymological "projection," the sudden and unexpected "discovery" of a meaningful design, or explanation, underlying the structures of language. It is the projection that allows for and makes the discovery in language, but it is the discovery that then serves retrospectively to "prove" that indeterminate or even arbitrary connections between words, parts of words, and the philosophical systems they eventually allow to be constructed upon them can all be traced back to the single and overarching purpose that has now been projected upon them.[17]

For example—though this example doesn't come from Paulhan's text—it is precisely such an operation that underwrites Heidegger's sustained attempts to recover what so far has been concealed from us in the Greek word for truth, *aletheia*, as the un-concealed or *a-lethe* whose event is also vouchsafed to us as a destiny for our own thought.[18] Such a "projection," Paulhan adds, which appears all the more "violent and irrevocable" for its requiring more time and more work to discover and then refine, ends up in an irresistible convergence, an apparent synthesis in which "the inevitability of a natural phenomenon" joins forces with "an intellectual voluptuousness composed simultaneously of pleasure and power" (*Alain, OC* 3:284–85).

That such a fiction of true meaning tends eventually to "impose itself" with the "stability, permanence, and self-certainty" of proof, concludes Paulhan, does nothing to change the fact that it results from "fallacious intentions" and "chimerical origins." The entire process is itself a "trap," Paulhan had already warned, but a necessary one that always works by offering itself to our continued reflection (*Alain, OC* 3:282–83). By reinforcing the intellectual pleasure we cannot help but feel at our own sense of cognitive power, the etymological projection, and even "rhetoric in general," thus "dupes" us into bestowing upon its random discoveries an unfounded legitimacy that could be only provisional and partial at best, since we always lend it without any firm basis in knowledge—the actual source of the intellectual pleasure and power we take from language remaining a "secret" necessarily kept from us (3:285–86). Should the structure of this formulation, if not the very terms, bear an uncanny resemblance to the asymmetrical and dysfunctional relation in Saussure between the virtual coherence of *la langue* and the coercively discontinuous acts of *la parole*, this would not be purely by accident. It may be that etymology, like Saussure's langue, always has pretensions to forming an impersonal system that obeys verifiable laws; but in its own reliance on happenstance, contingency, and individual as well as collective desire, it behaves in fact like parole. Indeed, Paulhan's etymology does not merely resemble Saussure's parole, it is nothing but an instance of parole through and through. That is to say, for both Saussure and Paulhan, the "true meaning," or etymology, of any given parole always entails the usurped authority to speak power to truth. In Paulhan's text, this becomes clear when *la parole* is examined as a specific case of etymological proof in its own right. For, as Paulhan suggests, *la parole* is never just one example of etymology among others. *La parole* constitutes the most privileged example of etymology conceivable, since it doesn't just provide an illustration of etymology at work. Rather, thanks to the example provided by its own etymology, *la parole* finally serves to reinforce the circular proof of all etymology and certifies it, as it were, as an effective ploy for establishing "true meaning" in general (3:265). "What happens if we consider *parole*?" Paulhan asks. "The term comes from the Greek, *parabole*, which designates Christ's word, or truth par excellence" (3:266). What could be further removed, at first glance, from Saussure's understanding of *la parole* as always being too individual, momentary, and willful in its operation to provide reliable access to true knowledge, than this retracing of *la parole* back to a divine origin in the word of God, or truth incarnate?

Etymology, or the true meaning of a word, seems to find its perfect complement and justification in this etymology of *la parole*, which then uncovers the *word* as the ultimate foundation for truth. The true meaning of the word *parole* would teach us in this way that words are themselves the best way to reach truth. In the beginning was the Word, and etymology is the path that allows us to retrieve its true meaning. But Paulhan's entire argument is aimed against taking at face value the status of just such an etymological "proof" of the "divine origin" of all words. And so, when he returns to the example of the particular proof occasioned by *la parole*, he shows how the privileging of *la parole* as an instance of authority that can be traced directly back to the word of God, and thus to the ultimate ground for true meaning, is itself predicated on a rhetorical sleight of hand.

The etymology of *la parole* is not really a proof at all, but rather the construction of a "myth"—"le mythe du mot original," Paulhan calls it—and whatever authority such a myth eventually claims to ground the truth is entirely arbitrary and therefore unwarranted. As Paulhan had argued in a 1938 text on the power of words, the myth of this authority is based on an illusion, but the regularity of our belief in the illusion ends up by endowing the myth with the power of "natural law."[19] When it comes to retracing the true meaning of *la parole*, there is no reliable means of justifying any one meaning over all the other possibilities at hand: "C'est au choix," Paulhan says at last, in mock frustration—"take your pick" (*Alain, OC* 3:278–79). And if *la parole* eventually gains the power to impose a single truth on us as though it were the word of God, this is not, Paulhan says, because it has been granted to us by divine authority. On the contrary, it is we who learn to bestow upon all its discrete relations of proximity and mere contingency a unified network of meanings that can eventually point to a much more serious, and even sacred, design at work.[20] "And so it is with *parole*," Paulhan then sums up: "Yes, our word comes from *parabole*, Christ's teaching. But before *parabole*? Well it just so happens that the Greek word *parabolè* means only *confrontation, comparison*; it's a simple term of rhetoric, like *metaphor* or *antithesis*. And before the rhetorical sense? *Parabolè* meant only *proximity, contiguity*: two events produced at the same time, two things that find themselves placed next to each other. And at that point there's not much that is very serious or sacred about it" (*Alain OC* 3: 279). Like all etymology, moreover, *parole* is a figure for the way language in general functions as a projection of epistemological authority that works, not because it is based on true knowledge, but rather because it lends us back the power we constantly but without justification attribute to it: the power to speak, and thus to know, the ultimate truth. Paulhan's etymology brings us back to the "circle" Saussure's course had already struggled to identify and then escape: in order for speaking subjects to have a meaningful parole, they must obey the formal laws of *la langue*; but in order for *la langue* to come into being, it must first be given parole by the entire community it can then be said to govern. *Parole*, then, *is* etymology and nothing but etymology insofar as it always serves to motivate, and ultimately to legitimate—though only in the mode of a rhetorical fiction—an entire series of permutations between language and meaning that in themselves are devoid of explanatory value with respect to the origin and end of their own true meaning.

Whereas Saussure, once he was compelled to notice this unpredictable and intractable element in the power of parole, had sought to control its disruptiveness by cordoning it off from the systematic study of the "constitution and laws" governing all signs (semiology), Paulhan takes a somewhat different tack.[21] Indeed, as we have just seen, the etymology of the word *parole*—and the parole of etymology for that matter—entails an infraction against the epistemological laws of both linguistics and philosophy by claiming to possess a form of "true" knowledge that cannot be justified by either linguistic or philosophical methods alone. However, to the extent that neither the discourse of linguistics nor that of philosophy, nor any meaningful discourse as such, could ever simply do without recourse to the very same words (paroles) and true meanings (etymologies) that they also serve to call into question, the ensuing "trap" offered by paroles and their etymologies becomes itself inevitable, and therefore constitutes a new kind of "law" in its own right.

This strange "conclusion" to Paulhan's argument becomes readable in the two rambling chapters he appends to the body of *Alain*. The chapters themselves are called "Notes et Observations," and each takes the form of a letter responding to critical reactions to an earlier text by Paulhan, titled *Petite Préface à toute critique* (A Short Preface to All Criticism).[22] What links both responses together is the unexpected though recurrent claim by Paulhan that his own work remains governed by the possibility of attaining a critical point of view on the rhetorical operations of language that would itself be epistemologically legitimate, despite those very disruptions of philosophical and linguistic laws that seem always to be enacted by the literary object, or any object partaking of literary elements, which is to say all language. "My whole point," Paulhan writes in the first response, "is in fact to use literature as the basis for sketching out a system of knowledge that would be precise and rigorous, in short, scientific" (*Alain, OC* 3:289). But is such knowledge possible whenever language is involved, which is to say always? If, as Paulhan argues in the rest of this text as well as in his others, the "critical methods" available to us for the study of language are themselves always the result of an "illusion of language"—such as those afflicting and disqualifying both terrorist and rhetorical methods of analysis—then, Paulhan imagines himself being asked by someone else, "wouldn't such an enterprise have to be merely chimerical?"

Paulhan's answer to this question offers what is perhaps the most surprising twist of the entire essay. For, says Paulhan, the possibility that every critical method taking language as its object of study—whether it be literary, political, or philosophical in nature—proceeds at bottom from an "illusion of language" in no way counters the need to continue the undertaking of "critical reflection" with ever more precision and rigor.[23] "That would be just one more reason," says Paulhan, "for pushing the inquiry even further" (*Alain, OC* 3:290). Far from leading to a dead end, or to a relativistic approach where no discrimination whatsoever is possible among the competing "critical values" that necessarily emanate from different "critical methods," Paulhan's dogged pursuit of the traps, confusions, and illusions hampering the formation of any truly reliable system of knowledge about language only reveals the problem to be one that is that much more imperative to address (3:302). In a chapter interrogatively entitled "S'il existe des lois de l'expression" (Whether there are laws of expression), Paulhan returns yet again to a question that is ever-present in his texts, which he doesn't hesitate in this context to qualify as "a simple case of the most important problem concerning mankind" (3:297). The specific challenge addressed here is the formation of a critical method appropriate to the study of literature, but Paulhan also says this is merely one instance of the much larger question of whether there are "laws" governing the exact way that words are related to meaning, or language is related to thought, and finally, that mind is related to body, and spirit to flesh.

This question, in all its universal generality, from the functioning of language to that of literature, and on to the extralinguistic domains of philosophy and politics, remains an insurmountable stumbling block for metaphysicians, critics, poets, and linguists alike, Paulhan says, to the precise degree that such regional discourses all fail to discern the "laws" governing how thought can be directed by language, or inversely, how language can be directed by thought. But if the only dependable law governing our knowledge of the way language works is one that consists in the regularity with which critical method falls prey to illusions, traps, and errors in attempting to respond to this question, then where exactly does that leave us with respect to the kind of knowledge that Paulhan's own text, in the name of truth, both demands and proposes? When the law becomes itself a rule of error, then how can the critical enterprise of discovering truth lead to anything but radical failure? As early as 1936, in the first version of *The Flowers of Tarbes*, Paulhan had spoken of just such a "law of failure" to describe the regularity of error that upsets critical method from within.[24] And yet this law of failure, even in the 1936 text, was not the final word on the matter, but rather a fresh opportunity to find a way out, a way to hope for a "solution," that, by subjecting its own critical reflection to methodical scrutiny, would not simply repeat the same errors of "Rhetoricians" and "Terrorists" alike. What has become, we may now ask, of this law of failure and the paradoxical hope of finding a methodological solution by the time Paulhan writes *Alain, ou la preuve par l'étymologie*?

Etymological discoveries, as Paulhan amply demonstrates, belong indeed to all those "illusions of language" that serve as proof, alas, not for the establishment of "true meaning," but only for the necessary failure of every rhetorical device to provide a firm ground for securing knowledge. However, as is typical of Paulhan's texts, especially of their endings, it is precisely at the moment when all seems lost that a new way of considering the problem is introduced into the argument. Blanchot, in the first text he devotes to Paulhan, "Comment la littérature est-elle possible?" draws attention to this signature move by Paulhan, and also points out that it can occur only when the "writer . . . accepts the law by means of which he enters into an obscure zone where there is neither pathway nor marking." Approaching Paulhan's conclusion about language's trap of "permanent illusion," and describing the ensuing space of methodological uncertainty that is opened up by it, Blanchot says at this point that "we need to take one more step, though without believing it will take us very far."[25] This last step, or *pas*, to which Blanchot refers with respect to *The Flowers of Tarbes*, is also taken at the far end of *Alain*, after Paulhan has tried every resource of critical method, only to find them all wanting. Still, he says, "there remains one hope" (*Alain, OC* 3:296). What is this one remaining hope—*espoir*—according to Paulhan? As Blanchot suggests, it will have to be a step beyond hope, which will actually obscure hope by stripping it of every recognizable feature. In other words, this last hope can be no mere hope; in fact, as it turns out, the obscure hope Paulhan holds out to us is only the shadowy hope of despair, *l'espoir du désespoir*, and therefore only another step back into language and all its problems and obscurities.

In a gesture that anticipates Blanchot's reinscription of Heidegger's *a-letheia* in *The Writing of the Disaster*, though with his own off-hand and understated manner, Paulhan, at the end of the text on etymology, thus gives us a new word and a new etymology for "hope"; he does so by turning the word "despair" into the only hope we will ever have to reach a true knowledge of our own language and all its predicaments. "There remains one hope," Paulhan writes with respect to discovering the semantic laws that govern language (and that language governs), "or, rather, perhaps it could be said—a desperate solution [Il reste un espoir. Ou plutôt—dira-t-on peut-être—une solution de désespoir]" (*Alain, OC* 3:298–99). The tinniness of the translation here is, as always, highly overdetermined. It also may help to reveal something more complex and far-reaching at work here than a merely aesthetc effect of assonance in the pair of words *espoir/désespoir*. In French, Paulhan is able quite artfully to make *espoir* resonate with and be swallowed by its antithesis, *désespoir*. Our one hope (*espoir*), Paulhan seems to be saying, is to give up hope (*désespoir*). But Paulhan does not say just that either. Between hope and despair, Paulhan inserts another word, and that changes the assonantal play between *espoir* and *désespoir*. Once one is deprived of hope, one can begin, perhaps, to learn what it means not to hope, that is, to retain hope only in the mode of its deprivation: *dés-espoir*. But that operation could hardly be called, as it is here, a *solution*. How could "despair"—as a concept as distinct from a word—ever be meant as a solution for anything, much less for this all-important problem of determining the laws that govern language and its capacity to convey meaning? Despair, properly speaking, is not and could never be a "true" solution, since by itself genuine despair would merely aggravate the original problem, whatever it was.[26] But isn't that the point of the whole argument, after all? "A desperate solution," like everything else in language, moreover, is already and forever a pat phrase whose "true meaning"—neither quite total despair, for one continues in such cases to act as though one were pursuing a goal, nor yet wholly a solution, since a genuinely desperate solution cannot but include a certain necessary degree of failure—could never be traced back to, or derived from, its roots in any dependable fashion. And yet, tracing despair (*désespoir*) back to its etymological root in a hope that has been ruled out (*dés-espoir*) is exactly what Paulhan does in order to explain and remotivate the "desperate solution" he manages in fact to offer at the end of this text. To some degree, it must even be granted that Paulhan's wager succeeds since a solution for which "hope" has been all but lost in "despair," a "solution" that can from now on function only by hoping against hope, as we say, would actually offer a decent translation for the current signification of "desperate solution," whose own meaning with respect to the relative success or failure its undertaking will have for the future always remains open and thus to be decided.[27] Despairing of discovering a positive law that would ever permit direct access to a "true knowledge" of language by somehow avoiding all of its traps or illusions, Paulhan therefore proposes instead a methodological solution that would be ruled first and foremost by the recurrent *fact* of language's potential to deprive us of anything but illusory truths.

"Yes," Paulhan acknowledges with respect to the arguments and proofs advanced by any given critical method, "they are based on illusory assumptions—but the illusions that serve to establish such assumptions are themselves facts that are perfectly real" (*Alain, OC* 3:298). What is *true*, as Blanchot, following directly in the steps of Paulhan, had pointed out with respect to Heidegger's "truth" (*aletheia*), is therefore not the philosophical knowledge that a study of the relation between language and meaning, or between language, meaning, and world would disclose and then allow us to reach. What is true and perfectly real is the way that words necessarily produce an illusion of knowledge as soon as we examine with methodological rigor the way that they actually work. And since, by not stopping to make such an examination, we merely allow the play of such illusions to function all the more coercively on our thought, we have no choice but to ask these questions about truth and reality with obsessive regularity if we are to think at all.[28] There can be no hope of ever escaping illusory judgments about thought and language, for the reality is, we always make them willy-nilly inside language, and thus without ultimate rhyme or reason—whence the despair. But since the absence of rhyme and the nullity of reason are themselves perfectly constant and regular in our judgments, we could at least begin to examine critically the laws of their functioning, and thus our own willingness to conform blindly to their play—hence the hope.

Such, at least, would be one, no doubt desperate, attempt at rendering, and thus translating, Paulhan's next step into the unknown: "Et, certes, Rhétoriqueurs et Terroristes jugent à tort et à travers—mais c'est suivant des torts si constants, et des travers si réguliers qu'à défaut d'être savants, ils se changent eux-mêmes en lois" (*Alain, OC* 3:298). While he clearly despairs of making any critical judgment that would not itself somehow be "à tort et à travers"—yet another commonplace within the French language, and one that means perpetually in error and therefore ultimately "groundless"—Paulhan emphatically does not despair of the one hope remaining to all users of language, Rhetoricians and Terrorists alike, which is to subject the inevitability of that very law of error to renewed critical analysis.[29] And so, in the same sentence that has to use a mere tic of language, "à tort et à travers," to qualify all cognitive judgments about language and thought as being ultimately groundless—à tort et à travers—he also breaks that very cliché apart into its discrete elements, "des *torts* si constants" and "des *travers* si réguliers," and begins in this way to subject the rule governing the conventionality of its own language to a new force of reflection and dispersal. For, Paulhan goes on to suggest, it would be precisely for want of performing such an epistemological analysis of rhetorical devices—"à défaut d'être savants"—that the users of any given language always risk becoming merely used by it. When that happens, he concludes, Rhetoricians and Terrorists alike turn themselves into the groundless and mechanical laws they should be subjecting to ceaseless interrogation: "but it is by conforming to such constant errors, and such regular confusions that, for want of a critical method, for want of knowing what they are talking about, they themselves turn into laws [qu'à défaut d'être savants, ils se changent eux-mêmes en lois]." Of course, nothing can ever guarantee that Paulhan's own "desperate solution," uncovering over and over again the way that language always works ironically to dissimulate and thus deprive us of every definitive truth or security, will not itself turn into a merely repetitive tic, error, or confusion.[30] Like any true parole, moreover, this one last glimmer of hope has to be given or received according to a law that could never prevent it from falling back into simple despair or disaster. But, at least in the case of Paulhan and Blanchot—and thanks to the writing of the disaster and the etymology of despair—the hope and light held out by such paroles would, in addition to conforming to the letter of their law, also serve to warn us against taking its authority for granted.

TEN

"What Is Happening Today in Deconstruction"

> Tout langage, sans doute, se rapporte à autre chose qu'à lui-même ou au
> langage comme à autre chose. Il ne faut pas ruser avec cette difficulté.
>
> —JACQUES DERRIDA, "Cette étrange institution qu'on appelle
> la littérature"

In all likelihood, bibliographies will one day reveal that none of the proper
names, movements, currents, or themes comprising the many strands of
French thought in the twentieth century solicited more or more varied attempts at description and definition than *deconstruction*. No doubt, it also produced the most frustration, since it is increasingly clear that in every case
such attempts at description and definition fail to achieve their goal in satisfactory fashion. The failure is built in to the extent that, even in French,
the very word *déconstruction* already belongs to more than just one language,
thus making any effort at adequately delimiting a clear and univocal meaning
impossible from the start. Ceaselessly translating, back and forth, between a
rigorous language of metaphysical and ontological concepts forged from the
philosophical demand to state the truth of all that is, and a literary language
whose unruly power to say with assurance whatever it wants to say—to say,
therefore, in its own way and without limitation whatever happens, whatever
almost happens, and whatever fails to happen—offers a radical challenge to
all philosophical formalization, *deconstruction* is a name for what can always
disrupt our understanding of every concept, every name, and every happen-

ing, including those that serve to delimit and then relate philosophy and literature, theory and practice, concepts and events, truth and illusion, history and imagination.

Although neither the German philosopher Martin Heidegger nor the French poet Stéphane Mallarmé ever wrote the word *deconstruction* as such in his own language, it would not be overly abusive to suggest that the possibility of deconstruction is more or less and in some measure the possibility of reading together the traces their writing has left in and beyond the twentieth century. A helpful, if complex, starting point in pursuing such a possibility is provided by someone who did write the word *deconstruction,* Jacques Derrida, and whose own writings have been hyperbolically attentive to the existence and survival of both Heidegger and Mallarmé. What interests Derrida in the cases of Heidegger and Mallarmé—though these are only two among a potentially endless series of other proper names joined to them in all kinds of different ways—is not that they simply did exist, but just as much and more, the unique way that, taken together, their writings provoke a reconsideration of what we call existence; a reconsideration that must be undertaken at one and the same time according to the constraints of philosophical cognition and the possibilities of literary inventiveness. Whatever else it is or is not, and no matter how contrary to our expectations, inclinations, or received ideas, deconstruction is also one of any number of names for this inherited interference of philosophy and literature in the only way that existence can actually be said to occur.

Derrida himself came close to stating this explicitly on a number of different occasions, including at a conference in California in 1987, when he made the following hypothetical assertion, delivered in English: "For instance, one assertion, one 'statement,' a true one, would be, and I would subscribe to it: 'Deconstruction is neither a theory nor a philosophy. It is neither a school nor a method. It is not even a discourse, nor an act, nor a practice. It is "what happens," what is happening today. . . . Deconstruction is the case.' . . ."[1] It is noteworthy that the "statement" or the "assertion" concerning what deconstruction "is" (and as a result, what it "is not") is qualified, even affirmed by Derrida here as "true"—though there is an ever-so-slight ambiguity that Derrida's words preserve between a true "statement" and a statement that is "true." In this sense, by virtue of its reference to what is (and as a result, what is not) true, deconstruction necessarily depends on an affirmative relationship to classical modes of philosophical thought and writing. On the other hand, it is equally clear—if not at first glance, then by remarking the quotation marks

I have just put around certain key philosophical terms used by Derrida—
statement, assertion, is, is not, true—that Derrida has been careful to inscribe
philosophy's capacity to make statements about deconstruction within a kind
of "as if" clause—he speaks here only *as if* deconstruction could be determined solely on the basis of the philosophical imperative to seek insight into
"that which is," and then state unequivocally all that is "true"—in theory, in
philosophy, for schools, according to methods, as a discourse, an act, or a
practice, on the one hand; and, on the other, that which truly "happens" and
is happening today. The entirety of the philosophical statement about what is
true is therefore conditioned by its appearance in a language that is bounded
in the first place by what "would be," a highly restrictive condition that, as
Mallarmé might say, insists on the statement's own "virtuality": "For instance,
one assertion, one 'statement' . . . a true one, *would be*: 'Deconstruction is neither a theory nor a philosophy. . . . It is "what happens," what is happening today.'" The conceptual assertion about deconstruction that *would be* true philosophically has been translated here by Derrida into the grammatical mood of
the conditional, that is, into the rhetorical mode par excellence of a literary
or poetic text. This is so because the "truth" of which the assertion only pretends to speak definitionally can, in order to remain legitimate, be simply
and in a straightforward manner neither that of philosophy nor of literature,
but rather would be the truth of what actually "happens" by displacing, and
thus exceeding at every point, the preestablished limits of the metaphysics,
ontology, and rhetoric without which neither literature nor philosophy could
be articulated in their very difference from each other. Nonetheless, while it
can be reduced neither to the idiom of philosophical thought nor to that of
literary fictions, such truth as manages in fact to happen in deconstruction
must somehow learn to speak in both languages at once if it is not to disappear
within its own muteness, which is also to say, without a trace.

  Such a curious intervention on the part of Jacques Derrida about deconstruction's enigmatic possibility, then—and in addition to his translating
Heidegger's writing of the *Ereignis* into the problematic *avoir lieu* of Mallarmé's text, and moving them both closer to the American idiom of *what's
happening*—should also give us pause for thought. For it is in fact a pseudo-
statement that threatens to strike occasions like this with a certain kind of
paralysis before they even have a chance to get off the ground. Faced with the
task of trying to say what deconstruction is or means, one is immediately beset
by an acute dilemma that appears impossible to resolve to anyone's satisfaction.
Either, for the sake of explanation or convenience, one turns deconstruction

into precisely what it is not—a univocal theory, philosophy, method, school, discourse, act or practice—and thereby misses the point of deconstruction, no matter how extensively one appears to discuss it or how brilliantly one puts it into play; or, writing in more than one language at once, one runs the risk of frustrating the legitimate demand for understanding to such a degree that nothing is given a chance of taking place—unable or unwilling to read what is not written in the customary mode of simple descriptive assertions or recognizable practices, the potential reader merely gives up at the start.

But the stark alternative here between misunderstanding and nonunderstanding is actually quite promising, insofar as it stands only at the beginning, not at the end of the story. Deconstruction, as Derrida also points out, can and does happen, and that means it can always happen on the many and diverse occasions of considering how and why deconstruction could never be adequately described and defined as a theory, philosophy, school, method, discourse, act, or practice. To the extent, though, that whatever happens can obviously do so only with respect to a great many other things that cannot really be said to happen, deconstruction, like all else that truly happens, could take place only on the far side of the trying aporias, the nonhappenings of misunderstanding, and the simple refusals to understand—in short, on the far side of all the dead ends beyond which everything worth the trouble has to begin. It is not only possible, then, but even necessary on an occasion like this one to begin in patient bewilderment: *deconstruction*, what *is* that, and what could that *mean*?

If we are to think at all seriously about deconstruction, Derrida seems to suggest by first attempting to set it apart from what it is not and what it does not mean, then we will have to become attentive to how exactly it would have to occur in ways that *differ* from all those things that seem already recognizable and thus familiar to our thought. This would be true even, and especially, if we were not thinking anything at all. Because whatever deconstruction names can happen neither as a theory nor a philosophy, neither as a school nor a method, not as a discourse, an act, or a practice, it follows that deconstruction will also not be easy for us to think or talk about, to define and therefore translate and recognize, in those very same terms that have for so long served to organize our thinking about almost everything we are and all that we think we know and do. It will therefore have to pledge to *defer*, or postpone for an indeterminate period of time and space, simple recourse to such familiar patterns of thought, speech, knowledge, and action. But what terms do we possibly have at our disposal to speak of an "event" that would differ from in this way, and therefore suspend indefinitely, all the accustomed terms for what we usually think is happening all around us?

Deconstruction, then, is not just an attentiveness to what, beyond the ontological and metaphysical concepts of philosophy and the rhetoric of literature, can actually happen today; it is as well an attentiveness to the way such occurrences, beginning right here and now, can and must also be translated into *other* idioms. The aporetic structure of the alternative encountered at the outset always seems to repeat itself anew at another stage. In order to consider deconstruction seriously, we obviously cannot have recourse to terms that would, immediately and without further ado, be absolutely different from those we already have at our disposal, for then they would not even be recognizable as terms. But we must simultaneously admit that those terms we already do recognize as familiar could never be adequate, as such, to address the difference that an event like deconstruction would actually make to them and all else. How can the terms we now have somehow become something else, something different? How can the languages in which we now think, know, and act be translated, or repeated, in such a way that they would no longer be the same languages? Just as with Kierkegaard's writing about existence, finitude, and faith and irony, so too with their *repetition* in deconstruction: either they happen in each unique instance with the suddenness of what is genuinely unheard of and therefore strictly incalculable—and then we must come to terms with all the challenges and alterations that this would necessarily entail for our customary modes of thinking, understanding, and acting—or else, there simply are no such things, and every attempt at understanding what they name is all the more pointless to the extent that it succeeds only too well in explaining what it in fact prevents from taking place.[2]

As simply one rather modest example among others, let us take the very word *deconstruction* itself. In what sense can it be given as an example of what happens, to what extent can the *name* "deconstruction" be considered an instance of what the text of Derrida suggests is happening in deconstruction today? Insofar as deconstruction repeats some part of Heidegger or of Mallarmé, inasmuch as it also translates something from Kierkegaard, Nietzsche, Freud, Husserl, Joyce, Blanchot and a good many other signatures as well, it does not remain absolutely unrecognizable in the uniqueness of a "pure" originality. And yet deconstruction—even if its occurrence could not be said to belong exclusively to Derrida, as though it were in some sense his "property" or "progeny" alone—is as a term specific enough to the idiom of his signature to make the drawing of comparisons as well as differences pertinent, if also problematic, for an encounter with it.

For once we grant deconstruction the power to occur, the term for this happening is immediately engulfed in a swarm of questions that could neither be taken for granted, as though we already possessed adequate answers for them, nor dismissed out of hand, as though they simply did not matter. For instance, to what extent does the inscription of deconstruction within Derrida's writing differentiate his signature from crucial antecedents like those of Kierkegaard, Mallarmé, Nietzsche, Freud, Husserl, Heidegger, Lévinas, and Blanchot? How is the inscription of "deconstruction" itself altered when it is repeated within Derrida's own corpus at different moments and in different contexts? Or, what becomes of deconstruction when it is taken up anew and transformed in the writings of Sylviane Agacinski, Jean-Luc Nancy, or Philippe Lacoue-Labarthe, as well as others in French; or when it is translated in certain writings by Paul de Man into an American idiom? What happens with, or to, deconstruction when it is linked with the work of an architect such as Peter Eisenman or Bernard Tschumi, or with the work of a clothing designer such as Jean-Paul Gaultier or Christian Lacroix? What can be pertinently said or understood about a film entitled "Deconstructing Harry," or even a *New York Times* recipe for "deconstructed rabbit"?

In other words, if deconstruction is not the sole property of Jacques Derrida, then to whom and how exactly can it be said to belong, more or less freely and legitimately, on each occasion of its use or its occurrence? Because it necessarily involves a change each time that it is repeated, each time that it is translated from one context, from one language, and from one signature to another, the possibility of tracing with the requisite patience and detail the complex itinerary of this repetition and its meaning, not to say its operation, over the past forty years becomes immediately problematic, even suspect. With the limited time and ink available to pursue such a project of retracing, it will always be necessary to make certain choices, to take certain risks, and to impose certain strategic limits to the contours drawn around or by the word *deconstruction* and all that it has by now touched and sustained in return from what has touched it. To the degree that simple descriptions of the disciplinary, personal, institutional, or geographical activities and developments now associated with *deconstruction* will only reduce it to those very same codes or classifications that deconstruction aims to put into question, they can and should be avoided in a context like this.

While it therefore may be of anecdotal interest to retrace the manner in which deconstruction in France seems to have evolved within certain disciplinary parameters—it was at one point a questioning of structural linguistics and anthropology from a philosophical perspective and idiom—and within certain institutional constraints—it also involved a negotiation of and with the way the teaching and learning of philosophy is conducted within the French educational system—such tracings would in fact result in avoiding the most relevant and pressing issues. So too, the way the word *deconstruction* was at one time or another associated with a comparative literature or French department here or there, with a department of religious studies or philosophy somewhere else, would also be to some extent interesting and informative. No doubt an entire genealogy of deconstruction could be imagined, capable of charting an intriguing series of personal and institutional affiliations that, at one point or another, included, in the U.S. alone, Johns Hopkins, Yale, Cornell, SUNY Buffalo, the University of Minnesota, and the University of California at Irvine, to name just a few. But in the end, each time deconstruction is understood as something that occurs as an individual personality or group dynamic, a disciplinary discourse, or an institutionalized structure at a specific moment and place, it is just as surely misunderstood according to traditional models and methods for narrating biographical, interpersonal, intellectual, institutional, and geopolitical histories.

On the contrary, however, and whatever deconstruction names, it could only come into being as a radical interruption and displacement of precisely those models for understanding historical occurrences. Moreover, to the degree that deconstruction always takes as its target the presumed closure—or close-ability—of metaphysical and ontological concepts, it also always involves a probing to the limits of precisely those rights and responsibilities that have governed the constitution and reach of the person, the institution, the state, and the regional discourses and effects in which they operate and attempt to reproduce themselves as such. In the present context, this means we should become attentive to some of the following unresolved and potentially irresolvable tensions: according to which specific criteria, in fact, can responsibility for deconstruction either be assigned or claimed? By what right, where and when, can it be said that one is speaking, thinking, or acting in the name of or on behalf of deconstruction? Conversely, where and when can it be said that deconstruction is being trivialized, exploited, betrayed, or adulterated beyond recognition? All of these questions assume a kind of uneasy inevitability for us today. For they comprise at one and the same time the most equivocal and essential challenges addressed by and to what is happening in deconstruction. The possibility of responding to them in innovative ways, moreover, impinges not just on cognitive or aesthetic considerations, but on all the sociopolitical, juridical, and ethical categories that are currently in place or in question as well.

In order to make some headway simply in gauging the magnitude of these challenges, it may be helpful to ask for once exactly how the French word *déconstruction* might have come to be written in the first place. On the one hand, it is always worth remarking that Derrida did not himself invent this word from scratch; it existed in French long before what we now usually call *"la déconstruction."* In a sense that remains to be determined, this also means that Derrida could only be said to have inherited it from somewhere else, even as he consciously took it as his own and repeated it in different ways. On the other hand, the frequency, extension, and force with which the name—and not only in French, of course—has been put into circulation subsequent to Derrida's writing of it in his texts have all but effaced the earliest traces of whatever this word served at first to repeat and thus displace within Derrida's texts. In his "Letter to a Japanese Friend," written in 1983, Derrida attempts to reconstitute, some twenty years after the fact, the way the French word imposed itself upon him, more or less as a free choice, in the course of writing *Of Grammatology.*[3] This scene of recollection, in a mode at once factual, speculative, and allegorical, recounts the way "deconstruction" was from the beginning written in an idiom more than just double. The opportunity to read what Jacques Derrida says he knew and did not know, what he meant and did not mean when he first wrote the word *déconstruction* constitutes too important a resource to be left out of any genuine engagement with it.

La déconstruction, it turns out, was first of all the consequence of a conscious attempt by Derrida to translate and readapt into French several words that had already been circulating in another language, namely German. Most notably, this attempt by Derrida was aimed at the words *Abbau* and *Destruktion* as they occur in writings by Martin Heidegger around 1927, and as they mark in Heidegger's texts a force of difference with respect to the structure of classical ontology, the entire history and architecture of Western metaphysics in its attempt to determine being as presence.[4] But secondly, Derrida recalls having found the translation for Heidegger's terms only after discarding one obvious possibility in French, *la destruction,* because that word seemed to him too negative in its implications, too close to a mere demolition or annihilation to serve the affirmative purpose he had in mind for himself. Derrida says that

he then looked in the dictionary in order to check on another potential translation that had at first occurred to him rather spontaneously—and therefore
without his full awareness, much less his full control: *la déconstruction*. In an
effort to translate according to his own intentions a very particular undoing
of Western ontology and metaphysics with which he was acquainted only in
someone else's language, Derrida thus happened, by accident as it were, upon
a term offered by his own language and which was until then unfamiliar to
him, but which could subsequently be put back to work anew as a translation
for both Heidegger's words and for Derrida's own rewriting of something he
had read in Heidegger's text. Such would be deconstruction.

In the *Littré* and *Bescherelle* dictionaries, Derrida goes on to recall, and by
what seemed to him even then a stroke of luck, he discovered in the 1960s that
the word *déconstruction*, which had indeed already signified in French a coming undone or coming apart of the linguistic structure governing the grammar or rhetoric of a given text or even of a whole language, could also be
associated with a "mechanical" connotation as well, one in which buildings
or machines could be disassembled, sometimes in order to transport them
and put them to work somewhere else. At the same time that Derrida was attempting to rewrite the originality of Heidegger's philosophical gesture into
French, he began reading a specifically linguistic and mechanical potential
of deconstruction that was already sedimented and therefore silently at work
within his own language. To the deconstruction of philosophy that Derrida
was trying to translate was thus associated, in a wholly contingent and therefore unintentional manner, supplementary connotations arising from displacements within grammar as well as from mechanics in general. Out of
the past of Derrida's own language, but unbeknown to him as such, came
anonymous possibilities for reconstructing Heidegger's idiom into a future
signature for deconstruction's undoing of not just metaphysical and ontological structures, but of the linguistics and spatiotemporal mechanics that have
always been their implicit corollaries.

At the "origin" of the *déconstruction* in Jacques Derrida's own text, then,
lay this chance encounter between Heidegger's philosophical dismantling of
Western ontology and metaphysics and another chain of lexical associations
that, in French at least, already included the potential to disseminate its contextual reach far beyond any given region, discourse, or model of structura-
tion. By joining, or more precisely, by allowing a joining of the two different
languages from which came the *Abbau* of Heidegger and the *déconstruction* of
his own French, Derrida's text thus marks the source of a double inheritance,

and a debt that traverses more than one kind of temporality at the same time that it traverses more than one language. There is no doubt a singular originality to Derrida's very first use of the word *dé-construction*, as it now appears on page 21 of *De la Grammatologie*.[5] The writing of the word, *dé-construction*, emphasizing in the first instance the separation of the prefix "dé" from its semantic stem, occurs in part 1 of the book, titled "L'Écriture avant la lettre" ("Writing before the Letter)," in a subsection of the first chapter called "Le signifiant et la vérité" (The Signifier and Truth). "The 'rationality'" Derrida writes, "—but it might be necessary to abandon this word for the very reason that will appear at the end of this sentence—that governs such extended and radicalized writing [la 'rationalité' . . . qui commande l'écriture; the "rationality" of such writing] no longer comes from a logos and it inaugurates the destruction, not the demolition but the de-sedimentation [la dé-sédimentation], the de-construction [la dé-construction] of every signification having its source in logos." De-construction begins in this sentence by attaching itself to the way a de-sedimentation in writing of all those meanings that remain tributary to logos and its principle of reason sets itself off from a concept of destruction as mere demolition. Heidegger, as an example of putting into question all metaphysical determinations of truth, is referred to immediately after this, though Derrida also suggests that Heidegger's own determination of truth may not escape metaphysical determinations either. De-construction is therefore a kind of writing—though a writing so extended and radicalized that it can no longer be limited to any semantically determined concept of "writing"—that from the beginning re-inscribes disparate elements found in more than just one language: Greek (*logos*), Latin (*ratio*), German (*Destruktion*), and French (*déconstruction*) at the very least. It is a re-writing that simultaneously re-constructs in today's French both Heidegger's philosophical gesture with respect to Western metaphysics and certain legacies it has received from the French lexicon.

In this, the word *dé-construction*, as a special instance of the generalized occurrence it names without delimiting, now engages as well as exceeds such classically determined oppositions as being/naming, originality/secondarity, activity/passivity, writing/reading, intention/accident, self/other, and a good many others to boot, including those of building up and tearing down. But should anything else be said on this particular occasion about the inaugural juxtaposition in Derrida's text of *la dé-construction* with *la dé-sédimentation*? What are the chances that in this juxtaposition there lies another potential for signification that—beyond every semantic determination having its source in the logos, in particular, according to this section of *Grammatology*, beyond every metaphysical determination of truth as logos—might now be read or written there? If, as Derrida's own writing suggests, the kind of "rationality" that governs writing is not itself governed by reason and its logos, then it becomes eminently possible that written into the words *dé-sédimentation* and *dé-construction* is a shared element of volatility susceptible of extending and even escaping their semantic determination as philosophical concepts.

Falling together at precisely this point in Derrida's text, the two words invite us to read the way that each of them begins with the separable prefix "dé," and these two "dés" can at that instant begin to acquire a wholly new force of signification that not only is not governed by reason or logos but that, in addition, no longer resonates with Heidegger's philosophical thought. Rather, the two *dés* in question begin to recall (and replay) the poetic writing of Mallarmé, namely, the text that for convenience sake is often called *Un coup de dés jamais n'abolira le hasard*. Once again, what are the chances that this first use of the word *dé-construction* alongside *la dé-sédimentation* was meant by Derrida to rewrite the German idiom of Heidegger's philosophical thought into the poetic idiom of Mallarmé's French? Without in this particular case ever being able to possess the kind of knowledge or assurance offered by metaphysical determinations of truth, reason, and signification, one might nonetheless consider such a possibility, if only in order to recall, momentarily and economically, that Derrida himself would in his later writings go on to say (or write) a great deal about *chance* and the way that in deconstruction it always unsettles, or *dé-sédimente*, the grounds of metaphysics.[6] Without metaphysical grounds to support a determination of their meaning, moreover, these *dés* in Derrida's text can now begin to fall in ways that are extremely difficult to circumscribe, explain, or understand philosophically. They can recall but also deflect in new directions whatever Heidegger wrote about falling, *Verfallen*, and about thrownness, *Geworfenheit*, for instance. The way the *dés* in Derrida's text fall or are thrown can therefore also occasion a kind of *dé-tour*, *dé-viation*, or *dé-clinaison* by which Heidegger's text is made to turn away from itself and move into closer proximity with the French writing of Maurice Blanchot as well as that of Mallarmé. "Beyond the serious," Blanchot writes, "there is play, but beyond play, to seek that which out-plays [*déjoue*]: the gratuitous, from which one cannot escape [*auquel on ne peut se dérober*], the occasional under which I fall [le casuel sous lequel je tombe], always already fallen [toujours déjà tombé]."[7] The seriousness of the gratuitous mentioned here by Blanchot is implicated in crucial ways with what he also calls the writing of the *dés-astre*, a de-constructive writing in which Heidegger's philosophical constructions of earth and sky can be made to tremble and fall like dice in their turn. *Déconstruction*, then, the word and the happening, should always be read alongside an operation of *dé-sédimentation* that unsettles the ground of metaphysical concepts and their meaning, and that unsettles in particular the metaphysical determination of truth as originary logos. For only once this ground of metaphysics begins to fall away can the *dés* of chance—that is, perhaps, the *dés* of change—be thrown again by *dé-construction* and *dé-sédimentation*.

Now, very little of the full range of these lexical resources and intentional and nonintentional structures of the term was easily legible in the overdetermined wager of the first published instances of the word *déconstruction*, which themselves were in fact rather casual and discreet. For, obviously, it could only be as a peculiar sort of subsidiary accident, in addition to the one that prompted Derrida to write "dé-construction" in the first place, that this particular term, more so than many another, would come in time to be isolated, scrutinized, and reappropriated incessantly by innumerable discourses, making Derrida's own repeated attempts in other texts to determine with ever more precision the limits of the word he had put into play in *Of Grammatology* just one particular constellation among many such examples henceforth to be read and interrogated with more or less consciousness, more or less scrupulousness.

By this point, in fact, the word has attained such wide currency, especially here in the United States, that it is regularly used not only to characterize all of Derrida's own writing, but also to delineate an entire genealogy of intellectual, institutional, and sociohistorical happenings whose precise relation to "deconstruction" necessarily becomes increasingly diffuse and problematic in direct proportion to their uncontrolled and uncontrollable proliferation. After all, the word *deconstruction*, Derrida reminds us, was not meant originally in his text to have any particular privilege or centrality in referring to a potentially endless series of other interventions in the way Western philosophy has sought to determine a host of concepts and practices—always articulated with those of writing, reference, and intentionality—throughout its social, economic, and politico-juridical history. Derrida did not therefore simply intend for the word *deconstruction* to become identified as the first or last word on the matter, or as a kind of shorthand, in a word, a coded signature that would somehow befall his own work, his own language, or his own historical situation. And certainly he could not himself ever have intended for the word to become a stereotype, frequently enough used to ignore, exploit, or undermine the deconstructive event, the always unique occurrences that are in fact happening in deconstruction today.

As the spectral site of all of this, as both the affirmation of its doubly derived and disseminating potential as well as its negative deflection, parody, and ossification in endless clichés and mindless formulae, deconstruction itself can therefore be nothing simple, nothing univocal, nothing constructible in the sense of an architectural whole, mechanical procedure, or cognitive synthesis. As an indefinite series of knots composed of numberless different strands, each of which has already been folded back upon itself in ways that make it more than just double, the term *deconstruction* from now on exceeds the limits of any proper name, including that of Jacques Derrida, the one whose own signature has become nearly synonymous with it. If deconstruction, the event, names what happens as a force of difference, then surely the term's own destiny also offers us a most singular example and testimony of the enigmatic ways that such differences must always happen.

A straightforward inventory of the ways the word *deconstruction* has become exorbitant with respect to itself would therefore have to mention, if only in passing, the unforeseeable, often invigorating, though always heterogeneous destinies of deconstruction as it has been reiterated within a growing number of nonunified contexts that it will also have served to alter and ultimately transform. What of deconstruction today in literary theory and criticism, philosophy, theology, legal studies, political theory, cultural, postcolonial, and transnational studies, gender, queer and ethnic studies, architecture along with the visual arts and fashion, to name only some of the most obvious and ongoing examples of its errant translation and dissemination? Paradoxically enough, the innumerable ways the word *deconstruction*—in addition to naming meticulous interventions made under countless different circumstances and signatures—can also appear today in all kinds of contexts to mean as well as to occasion radically incompatible, often enough empty, incoherent, suspect, or irresponsible effects—that in itself attests to the way that the most scrupulous, vigilant, and prudent determinations of the intentions, words, concepts, and gestures with which we think and act can never guarantee the kind of purity and integrity that we might wish or even claim for them. Always set loose among chains of indefinitely transformable forces whose play lies forever beyond our own power to control once and for all, nothing we say, do, or think can ever be kept wholly free of an incalculable enmeshment with them: "il n'y a pas de hors-texte."[8]

But if the occurrence of deconstruction teaches in this way that the purity and integrity of thoughts, words, and deeds, in other words, of ourselves as well as the particular world we inhabit alongside all others, is not simply possible, is in fact strictly and principially impossible for quite demonstrable reasons, this is not in order to repudiate them or exonerate us. On the contrary. The responsibilities—ethical and political as well as epistemological—engaged by virtue of the words and deeds one puts, or puts back, into circulation among others are not thereby attenuated, but rather hyperbolically exacerbated by their structural lack of purity. The impossibility of absolute integrity could never make every specific breach of unity and identity the same; rather, it makes the responsibility of negotiating as carefully and patiently as possible among all the singular examples of imperfection, deformation, and adulteration all the more binding and consequential on each and every different occasion of their actual occurrence. The syncopated, dislocated, or, better, dis-adjusted temporality occasioned by such a hyperbolic responsibility—which reaches into a past without origin at the same time that it opens into a future of endlessly altered horizons, including those alterations that will have had the power from then on to reconfigure even the contours of the past—is what we also call *today* in deconstruction, in other words, *history*.

It is here, by means of naming and thereby transforming history, that one can begin to glimpse the critical power of deconstruction, as well as some of the reasons for the innumerable and tenacious modes of resisting it. For the mistaken belief that one can achieve purity—of individual, community, or state identity—can become by the same token a most coercive device of oppression and expropriation of others. Confronted by actual elements of heterogeneity, the tendency to reappropriate an illusory purity that never was present to itself as such passes most economically by way of compensatory ruses that also possess genuinely repressive force. The phantasmatic purity that can never be rationally demonstrated as having been a simple natural (or ontological) fact in the first place continues nonetheless to be implied, promised, simulated, claimed, or imposed by virtue of a fiction in the second. Such fictions are, more or less, and always under specific circumstances and conditions, constructed by dint of unintentional complicity, mutual agreement, formalized instruction, or paramilitary and even military force. The conventional nature of the ensuing "unity" does not make it any more of a fact; but the facticity of such a fiction can itself become highly resistant with respect to any contestation it is liable to encounter in its drive to consolidate and perpetuate itself as an unquestioned power of mastery. To the extent that deconstruction is inaugurated by and reinaugurates gestures of actual difference, it also serves to *interrupt* both claims to purity and procedures of appropriation, which are always based ultimately on an indissociable but fictitious unity of source or purpose. It follows, as Paul de Man has pointed out, that deconstructive gestures, whatever and all other names they go by, can become invaluable tools in unmasking, and possibly even resisting, the ideologies of appropriation and mastery they also help to account for and on occasion engender.[9]

One very understandable, if still suspect, consequence of this is that deconstruction tends to be summarily dismissed by those institutions and their representatives that would be most threatened and have the most to lose by having their own unexamined claims to mastery and purity exposed, in whole or in part, as illusory. If, as was stated at the outset, deconstruction were to differ from all our familiar terms, if it were to resist underwriting without further ado sanctioned ways of considering all the things we think, say, and do, then we should not be overly surprised if deconstruction were itself to become an object of particular resistance for our investment in keeping things the same, in maintaining things the way they are, or the way we think they are, despite our frequent willingness and ability to make all kinds of superficial adjustments among them.

Thus, rather than taking the indeterminate amount of time and trouble that would be necessary to learn in what specific ways deconstruction must differ from what we ordinarily think we know about the purity, or unity and cohesion, of metaphysical, phenomenological, ontological, and linguistic identities, it will always be easier to denounce deconstruction for wanting to do away with the very notion of the subject, and for having nothing to teach us about real people and the real decisions they must make in the real world of here and now. Or, when the deconstructive gesture is accompanied by a painstaking labor over the innumerable heterogeneous elements that are constitutive of any determination of intention, meaning, truth, and justice—which are all part and parcel of the problem of the subject and its identity as well as its every calculation and decision within a given context—it will always be more convenient to deflect the impact such elements would perforce have on our customary terms by dismissing deconstruction as an instance of nihilistic tendencies. An economical, if entirely wrong-headed, caricature of deconstruction therefore pretends that, since we can never know the ultimate truth or meaning of anything, we might as well just give up on addressing essential questions of right and wrong in a serious way. More aggressively still, one can imply or claim that deconstruction, whatever it may once have been or wanted to be, in France, or in the twentieth century, is simply *passé*, and is therefore no longer something to be reckoned with at all, happening here and now, for today and tomorrow.

But such forms of resistance to deconstruction, while they are widespread, ignorant, and often enough pernicious, are themselves gross oversimplifications of the real problem. To speak as though there could in this way be friends or foes, theorists, practitioners, proponents, opponents, apologists and finally memorialists of deconstruction is to reintroduce yet again the most unquestioned authority of the human subject in the surreptitious rhetoric of proper names, places, and dates. *Who*, it seems we always want to know in the final analysis, can be identified as being, speaking, or acting for and against deconstruction? Who are, and are not, more or less, now and then, here and there, the so-called deconstructionists? While it is most definitely true that what we call deconstruction could neither simply desire nor actually accomplish the outright elimination of singular subjects, proper names, and signatures in particular places and at specific moments—nor the kinds of genuine responsibility to read, analyze, argue, and decide scrupulously that accrue to them in the treatment of any given topic, such as deconstruction, if it actually is one—the most radical aspects of its occurrence still elude us when they masquerade in these guises.

If deconstruction were to occur, it would have to inaugurate a difference, and therefore a difference within the current concept of the proper name—including all that such a concept helps to delimit and govern, the nonconceptual and nondiscursive fields with which it is also, always and everywhere, articulated and implicated. For this reason as well, we should now be willing to recognize how aberrant it is to continue using the term *deconstruction* as though it, too, could ever name some absolutely proper and identifiable unity of being, intention, signification, procedure, or act. Whether in the guise of a subject, object, or project, deconstruction could in fact happen only as an open susceptibility shared with every other unique occasion of difference. Each such happening would go by a name more or less appropriate, more or less hospitable with respect to a given context or occasion. Deconstruction is difference itself, which is just another way of saying that difference always has to occur as self-difference, or the radical inability of any identity ever to coincide in an absolute way with itself in any given time, place, or tongue, as origin or end, as pure necessity or sheer chance.

It can therefore be no mere accident that the specific element in which identity finds itself most singularly at home, that is, the dwelling place we refer to idiomatically as one's "own" language, is of particular interest and importance to every instance of deconstruction. But can we still assume that we know what we are talking about when we refer in this way to our own "language"? To the extent that no identity—personal, communal, cultural, religious, political, and so forth—can be described, implied, promised, simulated, claimed, or imposed without first passing through the medium of a given language, it necessarily follows that examples of deconstruction can never economize on the inaugural differences that reside in and proliferate beyond all languages. The difference a given language makes is always disseminated across its own idiom as well as the diverse identities on whose behalf it has to be proffered, spoken, or written. Nothing like an identity—on the order of subject, object, or predicate, and whatever their degree of complexity— could ever be affirmed, and *a fortiori* attested, validated, or verified outside a particular act of language. But no one language can be absolutely proper or equivalent to whichever identity it eventually allows to be endowed upon thought, word, or deed. Between the circumscribed identity and the language it uses to mark its own borders must intervene the slightest cleft, interval, or beat—a point or a measure of contact as it were—since otherwise neither one would be susceptible to communicating with, affecting, touching, or being affected or touched by the other. Without this intervening space of yet another language—of the language of the other—the language of the self—the selfsame language—would remain hermetically sealed, and therefore impossibly out of touch with everything else, including an experience of the peculiar separateness pertaining to its own untouchable identity. Every identity— and precisely to the extent that it is absolutely unique and therefore wholly other—requires a uniquely proper language in which to announce itself, if it is not to disappear without a trace. But it is also through the residue of this obligation to pronounce its own identity—the means of its self-constitution as well as its self-preservation—that the language most proper to the one is by the same token entrusted to and made dependent upon an incalculable number of others. In this way, that which is unique—and from the moment it is called upon to affirm itself as such—is already embarked upon becoming a universal property, placed forever at the disposition of anyone else at all.

Deconstruction is this remarkable situation of what, as different from all else, must as a consequence be thoroughly unique, though it is also a situation of unique necessity and impossibility at the same time. A unique experience—that it would have to be, if such were purely and simply possible—which is also to say it can be neither purely and simply necessary, nor purely and simply impossible. Deconstruction is thus both necessary up to the point of its impure impossibility, and impossible only to the extent of its finite and therefore limited necessity. Compelling deconstruction to speak in the name of definitional language, in the name of a unique identity defined once and for all as itself alone and nothing else, one could always try to say: "more than just one language." But this would also be another way of saying: less than one *whole* language. The one and only language that would be absolutely proper also has to be more than just the one if it is to be confirmable, or attested to as language at all. Therefore, and in addition to being the only proper one, such a language would always be less than purely proper as well. As the one language that is also more than one language, it is more and less than language itself. And so it cannot any longer be said to be just language; in its own self-difference would also reside other traces—retrospective reminders and proleptic announcements—of extralinguistic effects—juridical, political, economic, technological, ethical—traces, therefore, that would not be reducible to what we customarily call language. Every single identity, including deconstruction for that matter, desperately needs its own language to come into being, but it is precisely this singularity that the nonpure identity of language with itself always differs from and thus serves to interrupt. It is the very language of identity that compels it from the start to defer and disseminate itself to countless others, always elsewhere. The necessity of forging a proper language for an irreplaceable singularity is therefore also necessarily impossible, since the only language that could effectively affirm the identity of a given instance would also have to suspend it in deference to a wholly anonymous other, without whose own future possibility such hypothetical affirmations would by definition remain not just blank but forever unremarked as such.

No matter how much affirmations like these actually differ from and therefore threaten to disrupt our familiar concepts of thinking, speaking, and acting, there can be no question of using them as a pretext to evade the very real challenges of every stamp they always and again serve to recall, however obliquely or imprecisely. It is not because the necessity of expressing each and every unique example in its own proper language is strictly impossible that we are left free either to give up on the task or pretend that it has already been or surely one day will be accomplished. We can do nothing but keep working at a language finally proper to all that we are trying to think, say, and do, no matter how badly we are bound always and again to fail at it. For in this we are not confronted by a choice to be for or against what is nonetheless happening here and there today; but rather, we are confronted by the only way that we, as well as those choices that might still be left to us, can even be said to occur in the first and last place.

ELEVEN

Bewildering: Paul de Man, Poetry, Politics

> As you know, Paul was irony itself and, among all the vivid thoughts he
> leaves with us and leaves alive in us, there is as well an enigmatic reflection
> on irony and even, in the words of Schlegel which he had occasion to cite,
> an "irony of irony."
>
> —JACQUES DERRIDA, *Mémoires for Paul de Man*

It is no easy task to determine the proper place of the "political" within the
writings of Paul de Man. The difficulties inherent in the question stem not so
much from the absence of references to history and politics in his writing—on
the contrary; it is a rare text by de Man that does not mention law, politics,
economics, social unrest, war, or revolution. The problem arises instead from
the way such references can become intelligible only in the context of analyses
that are themselves not in the first place either historical or political. What
one does not find in de Man's archive—at least not among works composed
after World War Two—is a consideration of the political that would not first
have to address complications that are specifically textual, and that have to
do with literary concerns on the one hand and philosophical concerns on
the other; or in somewhat more restricted terminology, that have to do with
rhetoric and epistemology. "One should . . . not forget," de Man warns char-
acteristically about proceeding too quickly from literary-critical analysis to
critique of ideology, "that we are dealing with textual models, not with the
historical and political systems that are their correlate."[1] As a "correlate" of
the textual models from which it necessarily derives, whatever is properly

political is therefore not accessible to thought in any direct or immediate fashion. Rather, genuinely historical, political, and ideological questions— and it would be worth asking whether and to what extent de Man conceives of the possibility of separating any one of these from its necessary intertwining with the others—can be effectively and legitimately addressed only on the far side of a critical-linguistic analysis of concepts. And these concepts will always be conditioned by textual features that are both rhetorical and epistemological in nature.

A case in point is provided by the opening of the essay "Hegel on the Sublime," in which de Man economically spells out both the imperative of treating literary, philosophical, and political issues together and the unwarranted tendency to introduce into the mix principles of exclusion that would somehow isolate the literary from either contaminating, or being contaminated by, the all-important coordination between the other two. The conclusion de Man draws here, and which he inscribes within a "tradition" of thinkers stretching from Kant to Hegel, Marx, Adorno, Benjamin, Althusser, and Derrida, is that the trajectory that joins intellectual discourse to political action must inevitably pass by way of the aesthetic category in which the confrontation with literature is impossible to avoid. Therefore, and despite the near-mechanical regularity of such reductive gestures, no valorization of aesthetic experience at the expense of either epistemological or political considerations, nor any dismissal of the category of the aesthetic as an autonomous and thus self-reflexive totality having no impact on the others, could ever succeed in achieving its stated aims. A given philosophical thinker, de Man observes laconically, "is politically effective because of, and not in spite of his concentration on literary texts."[2] If you want to think productively about genuine political activity, that is, if you want to bring thought together with action, he seems to be saying, you should go read some more fiction! Can such a suggestion be taken seriously? This is the kind of baffling statement that is upsetting for our most familiar understanding of both literature and politics. Upsetting enough, de Man argues, that rather than face up to its challenge, we will resort to numberless strategies in order to dismiss it outright, ignore it politely, or domesticate it into the kind of reassuring schemas that pretend to restore us to a sense of philosophical and ideological equilibrium.

As luck would have it, one means of escape from this dilemma is obligingly offered by a remark de Man himself makes in connection with the very argument which, in "Hegel on the Sublime," alerts us to the danger of falling prey to the philosophical and political seductiveness of such schemes. For "Hegel on the Sublime," as is well known, was part of a series of six lectures that de Man delivered at Cornell University in February and March of 1983. When he was finished delivering the last lecture, on Walter Benjamin, he granted to Stefano Rosso an interview commissioned by RAI (Italian Public Service Broadcasts). And in the very last of his responses, de Man addresses the "book" he is at that moment in the process of writing, and to which the essay "Hegel on the Sublime" would have properly belonged, had this book ever been completed. De Man died in December of that same year, and the six Messenger Lectures, along with the interview that sealed them, were almost immediately detached from their original context and disseminated among several different published volumes. Two lectures, on Baudelaire and Kleist, were published in *The Rhetoric of Romanticism* (1984); three lectures, on Kant, Schiller, and Hegel, became part of *Aesthetic Ideology* (1996); and the last lecture, on Benjamin, can be found, along with the interview, in *The Resistance to Theory* (1986). Given the circumstances, it is tempting to hear de Man's voice in that final response to Rosso as constituting something like his last word on the subject. And since the subject involves the place of the political in the projected volume, it is all the more understandable that we would look to this remark as a key to de Man's own perception of what he had been able to accomplish as a critic and a theorist. "I have the feeling," he says there, "[that] I have achieved some *control* over technical problems of language, specifically problems of rhetoric. . . . I feel now some *control* of a vocabulary and of a conceptual apparatus that can handle that. It was in working on Rousseau that I felt I was able to *progress* from purely linguistic analysis to questions which are already of a political and ideological nature."[3] This moment can easily acquire paradigmatic significance, for it appears to correspond to an act of self-reflexive assessment in which de Man turns back to survey his career, summing it up with the full authority that seems to come only from the privileged vantage point of hindsight. The relation between language—conceived extensively enough to include the rhetoric of literature as well as the epistemology of philosophy—and politics would be fundamentally "historical" in nature. It would mark a *passage*, in the strict sense of the term: a sequential movement that crosses from one moment or point to another in order to join them together. In this case specifically, the move by de Man from language-oriented studies to an overt concern with the political also appears as a progression that passes from the purely linguistic analyses in which it must begin to questions that can later on be considered in the ideological and political terms that had always been part of them.

Nonetheless, there is something odd, something disconcerting in this affirmation by Paul de Man about finally gaining "control" over rhetoric, about ultimately having made "progress" from purely linguistic analysis to political and ideological questions. It is not just the irony—perhaps unintentional, though with de Man one will never know for sure—in the claim to have gained control over the technical problems of language at precisely the moment when he would be compelled to stop writing once and for all, as though he were providing one last, spectacular, example of the way a claim to mastery over rhetoric could coincide only with the death of all writing. Rather, it is the more profound disruption that occurs as soon as one notices, as one must simply by reading de Man attentively, the way that these very words *control* and *progress* are themselves decisive components of "a vocabulary" de Man has just employed in the Messenger Lectures, components that serve to activate "a conceptual apparatus" that from now on will permit him to "handle . . . the technical problems of language, specifically problems of rhetoric." And once one considers the way this vocabulary of "control" and "progress" functions within de Man's own readings—for instance, to take but one example, in the second of the Messenger Lectures, devoted to Kleist's *Über das Marionetten-theater*—then it becomes strictly impossible to take them at face value.

For what would it mean, in the interview, to gain "control" over the problems of rhetoric that, in Kleist's text, are themselves what always and again account for as well as determine the repetitive "loss of control" that is disclosed by the reading carried out by the lecture? To put the interview back together with the lecture on Kleist to which it was originally attached serves only to bring out the way the interview begins to resemble the dialogic frame that encloses Kleist's text without in any way managing to gain control over its meaning. As a scene of instruction, moreover, the dialogic interview with de Man is highly satisfying—if not nearly as entertaining as the lecture—in its capacity to formulate its intended meaning with the kind of economy and clarity that is only too distressingly missing from the lecture.[4] But since the lecture on Kleist—despite all its vertiginous twists and turns—finally reveals just how dubious is the authority on which such staged scenes of teaching ultimately rest, one would in fact have to be, like the character named K in Kleist's fiction, rather absent-minded or "distracted"—*zerstreut*—not to suspect at this point a discrepancy between what the interview says about de Man's authority and what his readings actually do with it. De Man's recourse to a vocabulary of control and progress at the conclusion of his lectures therefore resembles nothing so much as the teleological conclusion that seems to be reached at the end of Kleist's text, and about which de Man himself says: "[W]ithin the bewildering and mystifying context, it provides an enclave of familiarity, an anchor of the commonplace in the midst of an uncanny scene of extravagance and paradox. It [is] very easy to forget how little this pseudo-conclusion has to do with the rest . . . and how derisively ungermane it is to the implications of what comes before" ("Kleist," *RR* 268). In the case of Paul de Man, of course, "what comes before" the teleological pseudo-conclusion of the interview is the set of six readings that are enacted by the lectures. And the story they tell about the relation between language and politics is anything but a simple narrative of gaining control and making progress—especially over the technical problems of language. If it remains nevertheless true and inevitable that the mutually determining relation between rhetoric, epistemology, and politics can become accessible only in the mode of a *passage*, then it will be precisely the "vocabulary" and the "conceptual apparatus"—in other words, the rhetoric and the epistemology—of the passage that will constitute the main burden of situating the political in de Man's writings.

If there is a thread that weaves its way through each of the six Messenger Lectures and then stitches them all together, it would indeed appear in the generalized principle of *articulation*. Articulation is what binds the various members of the puppet's body together in Kleist's *Marionettentheater*, as is evident in the compound noun *Gliedermann* used to name him, and it serves as an overarching figure for joining the entire set of de Man's lectures into something of an "unpublished manuscript" in their own right. Scattered like the fragments of a broken jug or amphora, the six lectures and interview still bear the marks of a virtual volume from which they will have been detached, testifying by the same token to the future possibility of gluing them all back together again. Such a potential for articulation indeed becomes crucial for an understanding of the final lecture on Benjamin's "Task of the Translator," where de Man deliberately introduces that potential to convey the sense Benjamin is seeking to attach to—what else could it possibly be—the metaphor of a broken vessel (*RT* 90)! It accounts, moreover, for de Man's recurrent interest in Kant's *Critique of Judgment* as the point of articulation between theoretical and practical reason, or between cognition and free will. It is as well what determines de Man's analysis of Hegel's *Aesthetics*, and within the *Aesthetics* the problematic place of the sublime, as "the passage" from objective to absolute spirit, or the articulation between politics, art, and philosophy. Finally, it is the question of articulation that constitutes the inaugural gesture of the opening lecture on Baudelaire, which specifies this question as "the link" between epistemology and rhetoric, a question that is persistently carried out in philosophical texts from Kant to Nietzsche, and that manifests itself in Baudelaire's famous sonnet "Correspondances" as the implied project to achieve a "seamless *articulation*, by ways of language, of sensory and aesthetic experience with . . . intellectual assurance" (*RR* 244). If the passage from language to history and politics always ends up in de Man's writing as the critical analysis of *articulation*, this should come as no great shock, for language *is* articulation and nothing else. But in that case, what actually occurs—in Kant or in Kleist, in Hegel, Baudelaire, or Benjamin—when the articulation that is language makes its obligatory passage from its own specifically linguistic devices to understanding and history, that is, the passage from rhetoric to epistemology, politics, and ideology?

A possible response to this question takes a hint from the fourth of the Messenger Lectures, on the sublime in Kant's third *Critique*.[5] From the beginning, the lecture is concerned with the necessarily interdependent relations between substance and structure, or between bodies and their architectonics, as well as with their mutually determined motions. The question can be taken as yet another version of what we have been calling the *passage*, or *articulation* between language, philosophy, and politics considered in themselves as articulated structures or "bodies" that move among and transform one another. Kant's analytic of aesthetic judgment, and within this general division, the section on the sublime, will provide de Man with the means of suggesting that Kant has to have recourse to linguistic models in order to resolve the paradoxical relationship between transcendental and metaphysical principles that is always involved here ("Kant," *AI* 72–74). On the one hand, within the section on the mathematical sublime, Kant will try to demonstrate how reason demands that an infinitely large quantity become a sensory intuition in the imagination, or how the formal infinity of number must be articulated with the totality of space in its extension and magnitude ("Kant," *AI* 77). According to de Man, this demonstration, which Kant attempts to accomplish in several different ways, cannot become intelligible for thought without first introducing a tropological model in which the rhetorical figure of synecdoche serves as a substitute for the properly philosophical syntheses of apprehension and comprehension which remain as a result beyond the power of the mind to accomplish on its own. In like manner, de Man will take advantage of Kant's consideration of the sublime from both a mathematical and a dynamic point of view to ask whether another linguistic model, alongside the tropological one needed to explain the system of number-extension, will become evident in the case of the system of number-motion. Tropes that take parts for the wholes they cannot in fact ever reach provide a rhetorical passage from the infinity of number to the totality of extension; but what puts the world that is then composed of all these partial bodies into motion?

The answer, de Man suggests, can be read in the section on the dynamic sublime, where the exposition introduces at once the notion of might in a quasi-empirical sense of fright, pitting man against nature in a scene of armed combat in which the combined forces of soldiers, diplomats, and generals can then be enlisted in order to declare victory over the power of the natural world. Generals, Kant assures us, are more admirable in the battle to illustrate the dynamic sublime than diplomats—presumably because generals' power depends less on the back-and-forth of cognitive argumentation than on their unimpeachable authority to issue commands. The enigma posed here becomes legible in a certain ambiguity displayed by Kant's own terminology but not addressed as such at this point by him: does man have within his power a special force (*Kraft*) equal to or even greater than the raw power (*Macht*) of nature; and how could the capacity for aesthetic judgment (*Urteils-kraft*) be employed to answer such a question? Thus, rather than develop a straightforward philosophical argument from a kinetics of gravitational motion, Kant's treatment of the dynamic sublime, according to de Man, can be fully explained only by expanding the cognitive dimensions of language to include elements of force, violence, and imposition ("Kant," *AI* 78–79). The analysis of the mathematical and dynamic sublime leads de Man to uncover in each case a function of language that is implied but unacknowledged within the structure and motion of Kant's own text. The knowledge of all bodies, as de Man reads Kant, is not attainable by properly philosophical methods and can be achieved only by means of tropological devices such as synecdoche. Nor can the subsequent motions among themselves of such incomplete and therefore impaired bodies be fully accounted for, de Man argues, by purely physical concepts such as gravity, since they are also always subject to a world of other forces that, like the power of performative language, remain free to defy both natural and cognitive restraints.

We seem to have reached a provisional conclusion, for at this point in de Man's reading it becomes evident that the challenge of extending philosophical cognition to the totality of the phenomenal world, a challenge always involved in the experience of the sublime, moreover, cannot be met without employing synecdochal tropes that take parts for wholes that for the same reason always turn out to be essentially incomplete. And as a consequence of this epistemological limitation, the practical efficacy required in the world of ethical and political action cannot be achieved without supplementing these pseudo-cognitions with a force that is provided by performative models of language. The proper place of the political—of what happens as both history and ideology in the writing of Paul de Man—can therefore be located in the critical analysis of language, and more precisely, as we have just seen in the lecture on Kant, in the passage from a language of tropes as cognition to a language of performance as force. This is of course merely a paraphrase of what de Man himself says in his own attempt to clarify these developments when he returns to them at the beginning of the fifth Messenger Lecture, on Kant and Schiller: "The topic that has emerged . . . has been the question of reversibility . . . linked to the question of *historicity*. . . . The model for that . . . is the model of the *passage* from trope, which is a cognitive model, to the per-formative. . . . Not the performative in itself . . . but the *transition*, the *passage* from [one] conception of language . . . to another. . . . And this *passage* . . . occurs always, and can only occur, by ways of an epistemological critique of trope. . . . *History* is therefore . . . the *emergence* of a language of power out of a language of cognition."[6] This resonates somewhat with what de Man will say later on in the Stefano Rosso interview, where he speaks of a "critical linguis-tic analysis" able to treat questions having to do with "the relation between tropes and performatives, of [the] saturation of tropology as a field that in certain forms of language *goes beyond* that field" (*RT* 121). But this similarity, as we have also seen, is something of an illusion, since in the lecture de Man is very careful—as he is not in the interview—to insist that this passage, this movement, this occurrence that is historical, is "something which one could call a *progression*—though it shouldn't be. . . . History, the sense of the notion of history as the historicity a priori of this type of textual model which I have been suggesting here, there history is not thought of as a progression" ("Kant and Schiller," *AI* 132, 133). History, according to de Man, and as we should know by now, is the passage that moves beyond cognition to performance, from thought to actual and therefore political power. But this passage, which takes one irreversibly from acts of knowledge to something that actually oc-curs and does something to change the face of the world as such, is not to be thought of in any way as a progression. How, then, is it to be thought?

It is curious, though not without didactic potential in its own right, that in the interview that takes place immediately after the lectures, de Man will relapse into the very vocabulary of "progress" that each of the six Messenger

Lectures takes in its own way as the target of an epistemological critique of trope. It suggests that in some sense de Man is not able to read what he has just written into his own text—though it is certainly understandable that after doing all that reading in the lectures he would himself be a little tired or distracted in the conversation with the radio interviewer afterwards. At the very moment that de Man is making history in the lectures, he seems to confuse it ideologically with his own personal progress in the interview, since, as he has taught us, ideology is precisely that which prevents one from reading—whether one's own or anybody else's text, for that matter. On the other hand, what is truly perplexing is not the way that de Man himself falls into this trap, since by itself that would be of merely contingent interest, but rather the way the lectures themselves argue that this particular relapse into ideology is inevitable from the moment history actually occurs.

One rather compact instance of the argument can be found in the prologue to the first Messenger Lecture, "Anthropomorphism and Trope in Baudelaire."[7] Working from a truncated version of Nietzsche's well-known but less well-understood question/assertion, "What then is truth? A mobile army of metaphors, metonymies, anthropomorphisms . . . ," de Man neatly condenses the analysis he will work out in much more detail with regard to Kant's third *Critique*. First, he identifies metaphor and metonymy as rhetorical tropes, an identification that allows him to read Nietzsche's qualification of truth as "an army of metaphors and metonymies" to mean that truth is a coordinated collection, or system, of tropological displacements between any given subject, such as truth itself, and its potentially endless expansion into different but related predicates. Truth is in this way the straightforward possibility of definition by means of an infinitely varied set of propositional substitutions among its own terms. To read Nietzsche's sentence closely is therefore to conclude that truth *is* a trope, though there is at this point nothing inherently disruptive in the idea that truth, like any other trope, moreover, has to involve motions that avoid being merely tautological in nature. The passage in Nietzsche's sentence from trope to anthropomorphism, however, alters the formal definition of truth as trope to include a new determination of a specific kind of empirical entity. In distinction to trope, the term *anthropomorphism* implies the prior existence of humanlike beings whose potential to engage in substitutions and exchanges among themselves and others—both anthropomorphic and nonanthropomorphic others—can always be challenged, defended, or imposed on the basis of whatever has been taken to constitute the "human" in the first place. When truth moves beyond being tropological—as it must in order to know anything more than its own purely formal consistency—it generates values (ideologies) that are then subject to struggle among their competing claims and forces, only one of which is grounded in cognition. This, then, is the moment in de Man's miniature critical-linguistic analysis of Nietzsche's sentence fragment when history can be said to occur, when a language of cognition makes the passage to a language of power.

Hence, also at this point, the double reading that is required by the quali-fier and noun *mobile army*. The army of cognition is a rhetorical army of *tropes*; but the army of force can always become an actual army of anthropomorphic *troops*. The cognitive "mobility" of metaphorical figures is by no means equiv-alent to the tactical "movement" of personnel units. The single noun *army* thus relates to its objective correlatives—tropes and anthropomorphisms— in two entirely incompatible ways. The truth of history and politics emerges at the precise moment when, thanks to the reading, the army of troops is mobilized from out of the moving collection of tropes, that is, when strategies involving the deployment of actual force go beyond the synthesizing motions of cognition, and when the stage is then set for a battle between radically asymmetrical powers. What interests us in the present case is de Man's con-clusion: "How the two modes of power could exist side by side certainly baf-fles the mind, if not the grammar of Nietzsche's tale" ("Anthropomorphism," *RR* 243). We begin to suspect why reading de Man regularly turns out to be such a perplexing experience. The articulation, the putting side-by-side of cognition and performance that *is* the mind in action, is said here to *baffle* the same mind through which alone they can appear and be understood in their very difference from each other. The passage from epistemology to politics, from tropes to performance, a passage that passes through language, is said to *baffle* the grammatical articulations of the tale whose principal objective is to convey this necessity with all possible clarity.

Rather than providing us with a genuine conclusion, then, de Man's read-ing points in fact to the obligation of retracing a path to what could only be called another starting point. For the coming together in history of cogni-tive with performative language that eventually baffles both the mind and the grammar of all possible narratives must itself form a residue in which this very failure to understand and to narrate is in its turn marked or articulated, and obviously not just in the ideological mode of a new narrative about history. If history, and *a fortiori* the political, must be thought as occurrence, as de Man never tires of reminding us, then it will have to leave a material trace wherever and whenever it can be said to have actually happened. De Man himself tells us that this happens—it always happens and has to happen—only by way of an epistemological critique of trope; for instance when, as in the reading of Nietzsche, the notion of truth as trope is pushed to the breaking point, and when something other than tropes, such as the anthropomorphic figures in this example, suddenly emerge from the closed system of formal substitutions. Our question now becomes: how exactly in the writing of Paul de Man is this passage beyond trope itself marked out or articulated? Where is it in the writing of Paul de Man that the emergence of a language of power from a language of cognition can be said to occur as an actual event in its own right?

The answer leads back to a formulation that recurs variously throughout the Messenger Lectures as a kind of refrain. "The bottom line," de Man insists at the end of the fourth lecture, "in Kant as well as in Hegel"—but this "bottom line" is also written into the lectures on Baudelaire, Kleist, and Benjamin—"is the prosaic materiality of the letter" ("Kant," *AI* 90). The shift from a tropological to a different mode of language effected through epistemological critique must itself be articulated in such a way as to leave its mark on the world, though not simply in the mode of either tropological or performative structures of language. The name de Man gives to this marked articulation that he also calls history is curiously enough the *letter*, or more precisely, the prosaic *materiality* of the letter. History in de Man is *prosaic* because it should always be read according to the letter—*à la lettre* as it were and as they say in French. This implies, among other things, that *history* is itself a loaded term that can always be understood and/or performed in all kinds of mutually incompatible ways, many or even most of which are at the furthest remove from what Paul de Man calls *actual history*, much less its genuinely material and political dimensions. When practical action loses touch with cognitive analysis, history becomes pure ideology and power politics. But when cognition attempts to bypass the question of its own ideological potential, it collapses into an idealism that is all too easily reappropriated by precisely those ideologies it refuses to acknowledge and thus fails to engage historically. Only when history is maintained within the inextricable knot of its cognitive and performative dimensions does it become history *à la lettre* for de Man—that is, history as it necessarily occurs in the passage from knowledge to action, and that also leaves a material trace on the world it therefore changes. This trace is in the same way and for the same reasons what de Man calls the prosaic materiality of the letter that alone articulates and thus archives the passage into history as writing.

To ask about the political archive in de Man is therefore to ask how the political dimension of history can itself occur, or happen, only in such a para-doxical mode; that is, only as an event that is both singular in its coming to pass and infinitely repeatable in the written trace its passage will as a conse-quence have left on the world.[8] We are led, then, from our earlier question— how does the passage from trope to performance occur in the writing of Paul to de Man?—to a new question: in the materiality of *what* letter does this passage to history in its properly political and ideological dimension leave its mark on de Man's own text?

One possible response can again be found in the fourth Messenger Lec-ture, originally titled "Kant on the Sublime." According to the logic of de Man's reading, and as he spells it out in the following lecture on Kant and Schiller, it is in the shift from the mathematical to the dynamic sublime, in the passage from a tropological to a performative model of language, that the occurrence of history can be located in the third *Critique*. "One could say," de Man jokes in the lecture he delivers two days later on Schiller, referring to the singularity of this event in Kant's text, "that in the whole reception of Kant from then until now, nothing has happened, nothing at all" ("Kant and Schiller," *AI* 134). What is odd, however, and well worth remarking, is the way that de Man's reading of Kant does not come to a stop at that point; in other words, it in no way concludes with the identification of this truly his-torical occurrence in Kant's text on the sublime. Rather, it is precisely there that he goes on to ask, quite abruptly in fact, whether and where this passage to the event becomes "apparent" in Kant's text at *another* moment, though without its being openly stated as such ("Kant," *AI* 79).[9] This is the moment, moreover, when de Man's own text begins to make things happen. After in-serting a break or blank into his reading here, de Man undertakes to show that Kant's text is indeed marked in an indelible manner by the passage from trope to performance, in other words, by history as it has to emerge from the ar-ticulation of the section on the mathematical sublime with the section on the dynamic sublime. What follows is de Man's treatment of the General Remark that concludes the analytic of aesthetic judgment in the third *Critique*. In this ever-so-aptly named "re-mark," *An-merkung*, de Man finds what he is looking for: the passage from trope to performative effectuated by the epistemologi-cal critique of the sublime leaves its trace on the world when Kant goes on to consider how, within the sublime, the starry heavens that cover the earth's surface appear as the purely *architectural* construct of an all-encompassing vault (*ein weites Gewölbe*). More precisely, de Man adds, the world of natural space can at this point no longer be seen as nature but must henceforth be regarded as a function of art as *techné*, that is, as a building, in fact, as a certain kind of house.[10] But before rushing to take up abode there, we should examine with a bit more care the materials with which, always according to de Man, this particular house, temple, or crypt is necessarily traced out and erected.

For it is here that de Man focuses on Kant's reminder about how nature, in its sublimity—that is, its radically nonteleological aspect—is to be considered as pure architectonic construct. In the first place de Man notes how, at this moment of Kant's text, the capacity to find nature sublime is a distinctly *poetic* faculty. If we want to have access to the sublime by entering nature as if passing into the architectonic of a covered house, then we will have to learn to do it the way the poets do, "wie die Dichter es tun."[11] But how is the poetic to be understood here—and, especially, what role does it play in the key transition from pure to practical reason that remains the burden of Kant's entire investment in the aesthetic? Taking his cue from the way Kant links the sublime with the poetic faculty of constructing the heavens into a vast arch bounded at the horizon by the floor of the sea, de Man wonders if we should regard Kant as anticipating in this manner certain themes prevalent in romantic poetry as well as in the later Heidegger. Poetically we dwell upon the earth from the moment we inhabit natural space as though it were a house built to shelter being. The problem with this reading, according to de Man, is that the sublime in Kant's passage is *not* structured like that kind of house, since it is not a dwelling, and it can therefore neither offer nor deprive us of shelter. Beyond shelter, otherwise than shelter, then, the construct that Kant's poet builds into the sublime experience of nature has little to do with the aesthetic reception of poetry as it has developed from Kant's text all the way to Heidegger. In fact, the only example that de Man can finally offer for the way "nature" appears to poets as a building in Kant's text is itself a rather strange poetic device, and it serves only to underscore the divergence of the nonteleological sublime from any symbolic and therefore aesthetic elements. In a lesser-known passage from Kant's *Logic*, de Man finds a metaphorical comparison to illustrate his point about the way poets erect nature into a bounded space, as opposed to the way all other human beings—Hölderlin, Wordsworth, Heidegger, presumably—conceive of such covered buildings for the purpose of both dwelling and shelter. "A wild man," de Man translates, himself, from Kant's text, "sees a house of which he does not know the use. He certainly observes the same object as does another, who knows it to be definitely built and arranged to serve as a dwelling for human beings—*als eine für Menschen eingerichtete Wohnung*. Yet in formal terms this knowledge of the self-same object differs in both cases. For the first it is mere intuition, for the other both intuition and concept." And then de Man supplies the conclusion: "The poet who sees the heavens as a vault is clearly like the savage, and unlike Wordsworth" ("Kant," *AI* 81).[12] According to de Man, the poet, at least when he is acting poetically, "as a poet does it," is not really a man, is not exactly human; he's not a real *Mensch* as we like to say, the same as everybody else. The poet, insofar as he constructs nature in a thoroughly nonteleological manner as a house that is manifestly *not* a dwelling or a shelter, is therefore a wild man, *ein Wilder*.

Or, it would be better to say: the poet is a certain kind of wild man, since the poet is most definitely not simply or naturally wild in any sense of the word. What is wild, de Man will make clear, is the poet's *prosaic* capacity to find nature sublime, to consider the world in a thoroughly literal and therefore nonteleological manner, entirely devoid of both concept and perception, understanding and sensation, as well as all the tropological exchanges in which such pairs necessarily partake. For when Kant says that, in the sublime, the poet "sees" the sky as a vault, he cannot mean that in a figural manner, since in that case the poet would already be substituting an intellectual content, a cognition, for what is happening materially before his very eyes. Still less could we call what the poet "sees" in the sublime a mere perception, since in whatever form the starry skies appear to the naked eye, they in no way constitute an empirical vault, roof, arch, doorway, window or any other architectural element of an actual building. Neither as conceptual knowledge, then—for instance, the heavens as a metaphorical house and shelter—nor as pure sensation—for instance, the starry skies as nothing but starry skies—the only access the poet can have to the sublime passes therefore through what de Man has been calling the formal materiality of the letter, in this case, *ein weites Gewölbe*, the frame of a vault that freezes, burns, or better, *etches* the sky into an undeniable but utterly blank notation.

It is in this way, in the articulated space of a signifier, that history *à la lettre* leaves its mark on the world. The passage from trope to performance, accomplished by way of the epistemological critique of the mathematical and dynamic sublime, issues first of all, as it must, in this "re-marking" of the world as pure frame. It consists therefore in the erection of an archival vault for the inscribed signifiers that have to result from any genuinely historical event. De Man himself states this with all possible precision in the lecture on Kant and Schiller, when he indicates what also always happens in the wake of such events: "[T]he transition from the trope to the performative . . . will always be reinscribed within a cognitive system, it will always be recuperated . . . in a tropological system of cognition again. . . . [But] the regression from the event, *from the materiality of the inscribed signifier in Kant* . . . is no longer historical. . . . The event, the occurrence is resisted by reinscribing it in the cognition of tropes, and that is itself a tropological, cognitive, and not a historical move" ("Kant and Schiller," *AI* 133, 134; emphasis added). Where is it, we must now ask, that the materiality of this archival vault that is erected in Kant's text is then reinscribed within a tropological system of recuperation that is no longer historical in de Man's sense? And what, if anything, is de Man's own text able to do in the face of this unavoidable regression and relapse?

The architectonic of the letter, the *techné* by which alone the event is materially inscribed on the world, appears juxtaposed in Kant's text to a second architectonic, one in which de Man retraces the construction of a new tropological narrative of recovery and recuperation. But this narrative, which recounts the all-important sacrifice that imagination will have to make to align itself with the superior powers of transcendental reason, is not a simple repetition of the earlier version of tropological structures and their transformations played out in section 26 of Kant's text. For this time, concerning the interaction between the faculties of imagination and reason, de Man is careful to note that the tropes have expanded well beyond their merely formal operations of syntagmatic succession and paradigmatic substitution, in other words, far beyond the quasi-totalizing synecdoches of the earlier section. What could remain only implicit in the first shift between the mathematical and the dynamic sublime, that is, in the blank that signals the actual occurrence of history, will now have to become legible in the General Remark as the juxtaposition of *both* the materiality of the letter *and* the emergence of overtly political and ideological discourse.

Unlike the straightforwardly tropological relationship between apprehension and comprehension dealt with in sections 25–28, the relation between imagination and reason now manifests itself in the Remark as an actual conflict, or battle, between unequal but mutually dependent forces. Just as in the Nietzsche sentence from the first Messenger Lecture, de Man will identify the political dimension of Kant's text with the moment when tropes move beyond the confines of their closed circulation to name specific entities and agents, and do so independently of any philosophical justification for their constitution as such. Tropes have a tendency to generate norms or values, in other words, systems of interpretation whose authority, like that of ideologies, is empirical through and through, since it can no longer be restricted to purely formal structures of exchange and meaning. In the course of the Remark, the tropological transformations of metonymy and metaphor that were described in section 26 "are personified or anthropomorphized" into the properly named faculties of "Reason" and "Imagination," which then square off and challenge each other for supremacy. "Like the five squabbling faculties hilariously staged by Diderot in the *Lettre sur les sourds et muets*," de Man continues, "the relationship between [reason and imagination] is stated in delusively interpersonal terms" ("Kant," *AI* 86–87). In the third *Critique*, the "conflict of the faculties," whether we find it hilarious or not, is therefore no longer represented as a merely academic exercise. Its implications become thoroughly political from the moment it pits the empirical freedom asserted by one anthropomorphic figure against the unequal and transcendent claim to freedom of another anthropomorphic figure. The binding claim of reason as opposed to the free play of imagination, and which is upheld by means of recourse to a greater law and greater power, cannot be understood independently of the political and ideological ramifications that are inscribed within it. "The aesthetic," de Man has already emphasized in the lecture on Kleist (*RR* 264), "is primarily a social and political model, ethically grounded in an assumedly Kantian notion of Freedom," and this is one of the passages in Kant in which such a notion needs to be critically examined. Hence, at this point in de Man's reading, the sudden and otherwise inexplicable references to Antigone and Iphigenia, tragic figures whose sacrifice of free will remains forever inseparable from the legal, political, and interpersonal struggles to which their acts ceaselessly bear witness. Hegel, as de Man well knows, will say nothing essentially different when he discusses both Iphigenia and Antigone in his *Aesthetics*. Nor will Kierkegaard when he identifies Antigone as the key figure in the transition from the aesthetic to the ethical that is carried out in *Either/Or*. What will always have been in play in imagination's struggle to become adequate (*angemessen*) to reason, despite its irreducible difference (*Unangemessenheit*) from it, is not only the provisional agreement, or truce, that is negotiated by the third *Critique* between competing "states" of mind; what will have been in play is as well the irreducible historical and political differences between actual states that are the necessary correlate of such struggles.

The crucial shift that de Man thus traces, from the formal structures of tropes described in section 26 to the practical actions carried out by anthropomorphic figures in the General Remark, also demands to be accounted for in terms of Kant's own text. The justification is provided by Kant's insistence in section 29, immediately preceding the General Remark, that an aesthetic judgment about the sublime requires a predisposition to the feeling of practical ideas and not just concepts; in other words, the sublime must somehow be connected to a capacity for moral affect.[13] Moral affectivity, in short, is what in an aesthetic judgment of the sublime would refer imagination to the practical sphere of law and politics, just as taste is what in an aesthetic judgment of the beautiful refers imagination to the theoretical sphere of the understanding. We may find Kant's actual examples of affective judgment bland or silly, de Man had remarked with a smile in an earlier version of this lecture, but we need to develop a "taste" for them if we are to appreciate what is ultimately at stake in the sublime.[14] For according to the explicit logic of de Man's reading, the articulation of reason with practical action, the raison d'être of the third *Critique*, will pass by necessity through the affectivity of the sublime, whose appearance also happens to coincide with the problem of freedom as it unfolds in the conflict between imagination and reason. Now this conflict, as we have seen, is resolved, at least in appearance, through what de Man himself calls a "complicated and slightly devious scenario" of confrontation, negotiation, sacrifice, and exchange between opposing anthropomorphic powers. But this drama of personified faculties, which by its emphasis on the interplay of freedom, inequality, and submission already enacts the referential political sphere that it also serves to prefigure, is itself predicated on an even more fundamental transformation that has to take place at the level of affect, one which will ensure the link between a feeling for the sublime and moral feeling. In order for imagination to accomplish its appointed task, to ally itself eventually with reason by giving up its empirical freedom in exchange for the even greater freedom promised to it by the transcendental authority of reason, it must, according to de Man, recover from an initial shock.

It should come as no surprise, mild or otherwise, that de Man would be particularly responsive to this shock, since it is of course the one that lies at the very root of the sublime.[15] "Die Verwunderung," Kant writes; "shocked surprise, which borders on terror, seizes the onlooker before the spectacle of towering mountains, gushing cataracts, and wastelands plunged into darkness" (*Critique*, 129; *Kritik*, 195). This description recalls Kant's earlier and perhaps better-known characterization of the "feeling" produced by an encounter with the sublime, which occurs "through a momentary interruption of the vital forces [das Gefühl einer augenblicklichen Hemmung der Lebenskräfte]" (*Critique*, 99; *Kritik*, 165).[16] But we now know from de Man's reading of the poet's "material vision" in what this shock, this suspension and thus loss of every life force, effectively consists. The affect of the sublime is shock because it has to register the failure of representation, and along with it a sudden encounter with the formal materiality of language. It resides in that "moment" when every feeling is radically suspended, where there occurs an "experience" so devoid, so free of interest that it cannot be reappropriated under any organic category, be it of body or mind, or some combination of them both. The "blank" that de Man archives between the mathematical and dynamic sublime must therefore be understood, he will insist at the end of the lecture, as the architectonic space of this shock. Without the articulated blank, moreover, there would be no such thing as either cognition or performance, much less the passage from one to the other, that is, history as the space of the political and ideological. Into this vault de Man will reinscribe the materiality of Kant's signifier. He does so by reading the shock of the signifier *à la lettre*, as that which alone juxtaposes side-by-side in Kant's text the poet's vision of the sublime with the allegorical attempt to understand and thus recuperate from it. The drama of the faculties has no choice but to tell the self-serving story of how imagination, and then reason, will ultimately be able to overcome the historical shock of the sublime by rearticulating it with the illusion of tranquil admiration, the necessary precursor to the respect (*Achtung*) that is always required by moral law. But such ideological relapses, de Man warns, despite their inevitability, will always be marked by the original trauma, bordering on terror, to which they owe their own existence.

Only the poet who is wild or the wild man who is poetic can read the singularity of this blank archived in Kant's third *Critique*, which de Man locates in the inscribed signifier that occurs in Kant's own text at the precise instant it undergoes the onset of sublime shock: *die Verwunderung*. Such would be de Man's material vision of history as *wounding*, a critical art or techné that fractures—poetically, savagely—the political and ideological constructions of authority it remains powerless to prevent from taking place yet again in the wake of its own writing. The burden of the political thus becomes the ever-recurrent challenge of refashioning this wound of the signifier—

Wunde-rung—into a process of philosophical questioning—*Wunder-ung*—
that would one day prove adequate to heal it. De Man's text will go on to
retrace the way Kant's analysis of the sublime attempts to accomplish this by
turning the wounding shock—*die Verwunderung*—into a reflective power of
"admiration," a *Bewunderung*, Kant claims, "that results whenever harmony is
achieved between ideas and their concrete representation [*wenn Ideen in ihrer
Darstellung zusammenstimmen*]" (*Critique*, 133; *Kritik*, 199).[17] Such harmoni-
ous agreement, moreover, the ultimate goal of the entire argument, can be
effected only by replacing the shock and quasi-terror of the letter by a new-
found tranquility, one in which the mind would then exercise its freedom to
think and act with reason in the world ("Kant," *AI* 84–86). This coincides
with the most political moment of all in de Man's text, since it also directly
engages the question *par excellence* of the political. By extending slightly de
Man's own formulation, "There is history from the moment that words such
as 'power' and 'battle' and so on emerge on the scene" ("Kant," *AI* 133), one
could now say: history becomes political from the moment that words such
as "freedom" and "justice" and so on emerge on the scene. And this moment
occurs in the General Remark when it addresses the law by which freedom is
necessarily apportioned or measured out—*gemessen an*—among the conflicting claims forever put upon it by anthropomorphic figures at once imaginary
and reasonable. How can we then fail, no matter the price, to assent to the
passage from history's blank shocks to the wonders of transcendental reason?
De Man in no wise opposes the law of this passage, moreover; far from it, he
emphasizes over and over its ineluctable hold on us. However, the passage
occurs in his own writing in a critical mode that could no longer be called
simply ideological, much less tropological, since it repeatedly submits itself to
this law only in order to unsettle the foundations of its claim to authority.

   In the particular instance of reading Kant, this happens when de Man af-
fixes his signature to the imperative of grasping the proportionality of imagination's relation to reason—their *Angemessenheit*, then—the taking of a common *ratio* without which no law or politics would ever be thinkable ("Kant,"
AI 89–90). The paradoxical requirement of finding a standard for measurement, or *Maßstab*, which governs not only the analysis of the mathematical
sublime but the possibility of aesthetic reflective judgment as such, already
implies an analogous obligation in the practical sphere, and Kant himself does
not fail at this point to offer the exemplary case "in concreto": the actual
degree or magnitude of civil liberty and justice that is allotted by the state
to its subjects ("die Größe der öffentlichen Freiheit und Gerechtigkeit in

einem Lande"; section 25, *Kritik*, 170; *Critique*, 104). Having duly noted how the notion of the sublime ultimately hinges on imagination's elevation from the pure shock of *Verwunderung* to a respectful *Bewunderung* before reason's sovereignty, de Man concludes his reading by wondering how a genuine incommensurability between such powers—the original *Unangemessenheit* of the still phenomenally determined imagination to the extrasensory domain of reason—could ever be converted without remainder into their congruity, or *Angemessenheit*. The "bottom line"—which in de Man refers every bit as much to the political as to the economic and financial discourses from which it is in the first place borrowed—would also be the line that articulates the irreducible distinction, and thus *inequality*, between all true differences and the merely hypothetical adequacy or equation that can only ever be imagined to prevail among them.[18] Without such a bottom line, de Man now adds, the constant alternation, or passage, between terms like *adequacy* and *inadequacy* would proceed to the point where one can no longer tell them apart. At precisely this point, where the crucial articulation of theoretical with practical reason is supposed to be ensured by the sublime and self-sacrificing labor of imagination, the ineradicable difference between terms like *equality* and *inequality* threatens to disappear without a trace.

It is at this point as well that de Man will draw his own line between *Verwunderung* and *Bewunderung*, and by doing so disarticulate once and for all their presumed compatibility within the unifying principle of the sublime. De Man, who is often thought to have forgotten all about the reality principle in the name of literary fictions, is unsurpassed in his capacity to remember that the fiction of "comparative" or "proportionate" equality remains the most ideological of historical and political evasions. By supplying from his own language what we can now call an *ironic* equivalent for the radical incompatibility of *Verwunderung* and *Bewunderung* that is covered over in Kant's text by the figural reconciliation of the faculties, de Man's writing stubbornly resists the seductive idea that the actual occurrence of shock and terror could ever be subsequently harmonized or made congruent with admiration and respect.[19] At the point where one can no longer tell the terms *Unangemessenheit* and *Angemessenheit* apart, de Man's reading thus underlines, the actual economic and political inequalities to which such terms also always refer would be allowed to fade from view. Hence the eruption at this point of a new line that passes between and splits them apart in de Man's own writing.

The passage that transforms imagination's inadequacy to reason into adequacy, the promotion from empirical inequality to transcendental equivalence that remains the aim of all that *Verwundering* and *Bewundering* in Kant's analysis of the sublime—how could de Man have possibly resisted translating it at one stroke with *bewildering*? "And are we not made to assent," de Man asks in a kind of mock conclusion, "to the more than paradoxical but truly aporetic incompatibility . . . because of a constant, and finally bewildering alternation of the two terms, *Angemessen(heit)* and *Unangemessen(heit)*, to the point where one can no longer tell them apart?" ("Kant," *AI* 89–90). The constant shuttling by which we are always made to swallow this passage between wholly unequal terms, de Man says, is not just bewildering; it is *finally* bewildering, bewildering at last and in its finality, bewildering definitively and without end, never mind an ultimate purpose. In the materiality of *bewildering*, then, the ceaseless shudder of *Verwunderung* and *Bewunderung* is at last arrested, though manifestly not sublimated, sublated, *erhoben* or *aufgehoben* in any sense that could ever be conceived as adequate, or *angemessen*. Up to a point, it could even be said that *bewildering* is the most inappropriate, or *unangemessen*, signifier imaginable for the task assigned by reason to our obligatory passage from shock to admiration and respect, or from *Verwunderung* to *Bewunderung*. But that is also because such a signifier, taken prosaically and therefore *à la lettre*, actually succeeds in reopening the concealed wound that remains forever at the origin of Kant's thinking of the sublime. That wound, as we have seen, is the one that is suffered, for the sake of history, moreover, by the poet who is also a wild man. For only a poet, like de Man, can ever be wild enough to restore the wound to its proper place, in the endlessly inappropriate play of the signifier. No house or dwelling can be built to domesticate or recover the wildness of that wounding letter, whose errancy inhabits the architecture of all being—a be-wild-err-ing, then, that in Paul de Man's writing is finally and wildly historical as well as poetic and political.

Coda: Dark Freedom in J. M. Coetzee's *Disgrace*

What is the relationship between freedom and knowledge? Is it possible to be free without knowing it? Alternatively, is there something about knowledge and its conditions of possibility that imposes exacting limits upon the concept and experience of freedom? These are among the questions that emerge from reading J. M. Coetzee's strangely disturbing novel *Disgrace*.[1] They have to "emerge" from a reading because they are not there at the beginning. Or, rather, the questions are there from the start, but in the unacknowledged and displaced mode of answers, of presupposed "solutions" for problems that no longer seem of direct concern to the protagonist of the fiction, David Lurie. "For a man of his age," the novel begins, "he has, to his mind, *solved* the problem of sex rather well" (1). David Lurie's "age," moreover, is not simply his biological age of fifty-two years. It is also the "age," or epoch, of a certain kind of self-assured knowledge—the knowledge that this particular self, and he alone, can use his mind to solve rather well all the problems with which it is still confronted in what is described as "a post-religious age," an age that is "post-Christian, posthistorical, [and] postliterate" (4; 32). For a man of his age—in short, the postcolonial era of South Africa—David Lurie has pretty much figured things out, thanks to the vast body of knowledge he possesses, or believes he possesses, about all things.

This is David's profession, after all, for he is a professor of European romanticism who, in this postcolonial age that is as posthistorical as it is postliterate, can have only one real student—himself. "He continues to teach," the novel continues, "because . . . it teaches him humility, brings it home to him who he is in the world. The irony does not escape him: that the one who comes to teach learns the keenest of lessons, while those who come to learn learn nothing" (5). What is most ironic, perhaps, is the way in which "humility" is originally paired in David's own mind with an attitude of "irony." Even before anything in the novel is allowed to "happen," so to speak, David's own understanding of his "humility"—precisely *because* he considers it "ironically"—quickly reverses itself into the most compulsive form of subjective superiority. The irony that David possesses is one of the legacies he seems to have inherited from his study of European romanticism. Detached, refined, urbane, self-assured—Professor Lurie appears to hover at an infinite height—not only with respect to his unfortunate students, but in relation to everyone else as well. What kind of teacher is this? To teach others in order "to bring it home to him [who teaches] who he is in the world," could that not also be said to have characterized the kind of ironic teaching Socrates practiced? In Socrates, however, the appearance of subjective self-consciousness did not go without the potential for others to learn something as well—at least in the case of Plato, for starters. But while David thinks that through his own teaching he "learns the keenest of lessons," he also considers that "those who come to learn learn nothing." The teaching power of Socratic irony, according to Kierkegaard, whose thesis, *On the Concept of Irony*, remains among the most perspicuous and far-reaching analyses ever undertaken, was a result of Socrates' *ignorance*. Socrates could actually learn something, because in fact his ignorance was at least in part "serious," or genuine. The kind of "irony" David Lurie appears to possess, the irony that does not "escape" him, also has a relationship to ignorance: he derives his own sense of superior intelligence and understanding from comparing these qualities to everyone else's ignorance.

As a result, this heir of European romanticism, who shows no awareness of any limits to his capacity to exercise "keen" thought and self-understanding, "has long ceased to be surprised at the range of ignorance of his students" (32). As a teacher who has no serious interest in his students, David will therefore not compare himself to Socrates. If he has a model in mind for his own ironic attitude, it would more likely be taken from Byron than from Socrates. David Lurie therefore conceives of himself along the lines of a postcolonial Don Juan or Lara—a superbly self-conscious and alien being, full of "secret pride," and exiled to the lowest terrestrial reaches of Cape Town. "He stood a stranger in this breathing world," David reads aloud from "Lara" to his classroom full of ignoramuses, "An erring spirit from another hurled; /A thing of dark imaginings, that shaped/By choice the perils he by chance escaped" (32–33). As if "by chance," David finds himself from the beginning in a state of disgrace—fallen into a "middle" age, a postromantic and therefore degraded era where he has become a mere "adjunct," part of a new, "rationalized" African university system in which, "without warning, his powers fled" (3; 7). In this "transformed and . . . emasculated institution of learning," we are told, "[David] is more out of place than ever" (4). But within this unfamiliar world in which David now breathes so laboriously, he still imagines, however darkly, that he can "shape by choice" whatever paths and perils of erring might still remain open to him in this transformed space called South Africa.

One of these paths leads him to enter, uninvited, his student Melanie's apartment, where, by a specifically masculine-shaped choice, he will subject her to barely escapable peril: "At four o'clock the next afternoon he is at her flat. . . . He has given her no warning; she is too surprised to resist the intruder who thrusts himself upon her. . . . 'No, not now!' she says. . . . *Not* rape, not *quite* that, but undesired nonetheless, undesired to the core. As though she had decided to go slack, die within herself for the duration" (24–25). Another path, frayed from a spectacular reversal, will compel him, by chance, to encounter a similar peril from a radically different perspective: "Three men are coming toward them on the path" (91). These are the three intruders who will thrust themselves upon David's daughter, Lucy. This time, the rape that was "not quite that" in the earlier scene will be brutally repeated—not just as rape, but as a multiplication of rapes—and in the most literal fashion. At the heart of *Disgrace*, then, is the inverted path on which David travels, from being a perpetrator of an act that is "not quite" rape to being someone who is "not quite" a witness to a scene of multiple rape.

Why does "rape" become in this way the iterative figure around which the novel is constructed, and, more curiously still, why is David Lurie's relation to rape always qualified by a highly restrictive economy in which "acting" and "knowing" are always out of balance? In other words, when David is himself acting on Melanie, the text suggests that he is "not quite" raping her. And when Lucy is being brutally raped by the three intruders, David is not allowed to witness this directly, and therefore he cannot ever fully "know" exactly what happened to her. Just as in the passage from Byron's "Lara," the distinction between chance and choice is never allowed to crystallize into a simple alternative, so too the relation between the subject's freedom to act and to know becomes unsettled by a series of fundamental obscurities. David knows that he is acting on Melanie, but the act itself is neither one thing (rape) nor another (not rape). Lucy is most definitely raped by the three strangers, but David's knowledge of that rape is a form of nonknowledge, since he wasn't really free to be there to see it for himself—and even if he had been, we later learn, he could not ever have known it from the one point of view that really matters: hers. "*You weren't there. You don't* know *what happened*," insists a strangely disembodied voice, a voice that partly echoes what Bev Shaw has just said to David in the present, and partly repeats an earlier statement that Lucy had addressed to David when she resisted his attempts to regain a position of paternal authority over her after the attack. "Do they think," David wonders concerning all women, "that where rape is concerned, no man can be where the woman is?" (140–41).

Could it be that there is something about the very fact of "rape" that imperils the category of freedom in its relation to knowing and acting, at least as they have been conceived in the wake of European romanticism, and as they are exemplified in the point of view of David Lurie? For it is not only the case that when David can know for sure what he is doing to Melanie, it is not actually, not quite, called rape; and also not only the case that when the three strangers are actually raping Lucy, David cannot quite know, not for sure, what precisely that is. It is also true in this text that the act of rape—what one could, though only by a perverse twist, call the "freedom" to rape—exemplifies a very peculiar kind of free choice. On the one hand, at David's hearing, where he is asked to respond to the complaint lodged against him by Melanie, he deflects the question of his own agency in the act by means of a familiar and self-serving gesture: "Very well," he begins, "let me confess . . . I was not myself . . . I became a servant of Eros" (52). What is remarkable about David's defense by reason of not being himself is that he himself freely admits it is not really a defense: "It is *not* a defence," David replies to one of the committee members, "I give you a confession. As for the impulse," he continues, "it was far from ungovernable. I have denied similar impulses many times" (52). The oddity of the position will not go unnoticed by the committee.

For how can David claim *both* that his act was dictated by a force beyond himself—he was a servant of Eros—*and* that he nonetheless could have resisted such a force had he so chosen—he had been able to deny similar impulses many times? How, in sum, can David's act have been his and not his at the same time? "We are going round in circles," Farodia Rassool says at this point (53). This particular scene of circular errancy will end with no clear resolution. By maintaining what he later calls his *"freedom* of speech, [his] *freedom* to remain *silent"* (188), David ultimately frustrates the entire process of the hearing. No matter what he says, David still seems to be saying nothing, at least nothing that can be "heard" according to the conventions governing this investigation into what he might have known (and not known) about his own use (and abuse) of power over his student, Melanie. It seems clear, moreover, that David is merely prevaricating. If this is irony, it is of the self-conscious and self-serving type.[2] David is using the reference to Eros as a cover to conceal what he may indeed know about his own actions. Despite the loss of his job that this stance will entail, David appears at this point to preserve both his own knowledge and power to reveal or conceal this knowledge.

It was Eros, and not exactly, not quite David, who forced his way into Melanie's apartment, depriving her of her own body: "she is too surprised to resist the intruder. . . . But nothing will stop him . . . [it was] undesired to the core . . . as though she had decided to go slack, to die within herself" (24–25). By exploiting the literary allusion to Eros as an alibi, David refuses to go slack in his turn, and thus he protects his own autonomy from being violated by the questions and demands of the committee.[3] David's behavior appears consistently to be motivated by his desire to retain and manifest his own freedom: free in the first place to penetrate unbidden the secluded space of Melanie's apartment; free in the hearing to maintain his own privacy by refusing to speak, as demanded by the committee, "from his heart" (54). At the far limit of his powers, even in this posthistorical age, David clings to some of the familiar structures of colonial exploitation and appropriation. The power to conceal knowledge about past abuses becomes fully complicitous with the loss of power to perpetrate those abuses in the same exact acts today. In David's case, the pretension to know but not to speak thus perpetuates the abusive freedom to act that now finds itself curtailed in other respects.

However, once David undergoes the shock of experiencing these same forces of expropriation in reverse, as victim rather than perpetrator, his own relationship to both the power to act and the power to know begins to change. "What if," David wonders, "after an attack like that, one is never *oneself* again? What if an attack like that turns one into a *different* and *darker* person altogether?" (124). Called to account for his actions at the hearing, David had no difficulty deflecting responsibility by claiming that he fell, momentarily, under the sway of another, the god of Eros. Deprived of the power to choose his own actions freely during the assault, he now repeats that gesture in an uncanny mode by questioning whether one can ever continue "being" oneself after such a violation. David's earlier assurance about surrendering himself temporarily to Eros later becomes a more unsettling hypothesis. "What if one is never oneself again" constitutes the most threatening of questions when asked by the one whose very existence as a self depends on maintaining itself intact from such a disintegrating possibility. Of course, in this particular instance, David is not at first even aware that the question concerns him specifically. He believes he is asking this question only about Lucy, the daughter whose strange behavior after the attack, which consists in her becoming increasingly estranged from her father, is troubling to his understanding of the world and his own place within it. But further on, it is precisely this possibility of becoming "a different person altogether," and therefore one who, having turned "darker," is no longer recognizable even to himself, that ineluctably surfaces: "He does not understand what is happening to him" (143).

What does it mean in this novel to turn "darker"? It certainly does *not* mean that David can simply continue to identify with Byron's Lara: "He stood a stranger in this breathing world. . . . A thing of *dark* imaginings, that shaped by choice the perils he by chance escaped" (32). These dark imaginings of Lara, which David himself imagined sharing with the fictional fallen angel of romanticism, are associated with the pride and wantonness of unlimited freedom—a freedom of choice or caprice unchecked by any human limits. Rather, the turning darker that dawns on David after the assault on his imaginary freedom to stand apart in this breathing world recalls the way he had actively reinterpreted the name "Melanie" at the very moment he became truly interested in her. "Melanie—melody: a meretricious rhyme. Not a good name for her. Shift the accent. Meláni: the *dark* one" (18). What David appears to learn through *Disgrace* consists in an undoing of the lyric imagination he had always associated with European romanticism. Precisely that which he at first takes himself to be, a student of romantic poetry as song and as melody, turns out to be meretricious and therefore thoroughly misleading. David's transformation after the attack, the possibility of his changing into someone altogether different, also points to a process of becoming more like Meláni—more precisely and literally, a process of *melanization.*

If *melanization* refers to a darkening process that will bring David unexpectedly closer to Meláni, then it will necessarily involve a loss of his earlier ironic detachment, a loss of the insulated and autonomous self that he once was, or believed himself to be. But if Meláni is *"the* dark one," Dávid can never become exactly that, either, for he will never be the *same* as Meláni. He can never quite return to being wholly himself again, the white one, but neither will he simply become "the dark one," or even one of the *black* ones, like Petrus, or like the three intruders who rape Lucy, for instance. David is from now on merely "a darker person altogether" than he was before the turning point of the attack—a point that turns him away from who he was and turns him toward both Meláni and Lucy, as well as toward his new "neighbor" Petrus. Above all, this darkening turn will consist in the trying process of David's no longer being so certain of his own capacity to act and to know according to the purely subjective and presumably romantic criteria by which he conducted his life in the past. What David experiences in the first half of the novel as his *freely* keeping in the dark his own knowledge of his behavior, including what he did (or what he imagined he did not do) to Meláni, will therefore change into a disconcerting experience of darkness—one that will sorely try his freedom to know or act exclusively through his own understanding of what it means to choose and to act on such choices.

For example, in the second half of the novel, David is consumed both with trying to discover something about Lucy's attackers and with acting so that that he can have an effect on Lucy's own future after the attack. But, in both cases, David is repeatedly confronted with his impotence to penetrate the darkness: he is able to learn nothing for sure about the attackers, and his renewed attempts to regain paternal influence over Lucy end only in her increasing distance and independence from him.

"Does Petrus *know* who the strangers were," David wonders. "Was it because of some word Petrus let drop that they made Lucy their target. . . . Did Petrus *know* in advance what they were planning? In the old days one could have had it out with Petrus" (116). In this scene, David finds himself in the place of the committee members at the hearing: he is frustrated by Petrus's unwillingness to say what David assumes he must in fact know. Consequently, David is prevented from acquiring a kind of knowledge that, at least in his own eyes, would make the unforgivable event more accessible to an act of retributive "justice" by giving it a proper name and thus condemning it: "He does not care how he gets the words out of Petrus, he just wants to hear them. . . . *Violation*, that is the word he would like to *force out* of Petrus. *Yes, it was a violation*, he would like to hear Petrus say" (119). But in this scene, it is Petrus who, repeating David's earlier gesture, exercises his own freedom to remain silent about whatever it is he might know about that assault on Lucy's freedom, and so David ends up powerless, either "to force the words out of Petrus" or "to send him packing," as would have been possible "in the old days" (116).[4] If indeed Petrus knows anything specific about the "violation" endured by Lucy, he now shelters this knowledge from being violated in its turn by David's attempt to learn something more particular about it. Instead, in this melanized world where David and Petrus are unwilling neighbors, he and Petrus provide mirror images for each other, working side by side, in silence, to protect the privilege of not sharing with the other what each of them might think he knows only for himself.

In Lucy's case, David would like to pry out of her what he calls "[her] secret; his disgrace" (109). The exact relation between Lucy's secret and David's disgrace remains unclear here, the odd mark of punctuation, the semicolon, serving both to join and to separate them in the grammar of the phrase. It is precisely the fact of having "shared" the experience of the attack with Lucy—without however knowing what exactly that experience was for her—that troubles David the most. In the immediate wake of the assault, David is therefore anxious to reassume the paternal control the attack demonstrates that in fact he no longer possesses, if he ever did. He imagines that he now knows the path Lucy ought to take—namely, a return to Europe that would make her future into a symmetrical reflection of his past—but he must acknowledge at the same time that this imaginary knowledge is deficient precisely in regard to what in fact he did not see for himself in her past. Thus, and in order to recover as much of his lost privilege as possible over Lucy, David will need to know something more about her that only she could reveal—what actually happened when she was raped and why she refuses to speak about it with anyone, including David. "Why aren't you telling the whole story," David coaxes Lucy, "why don't you want to tell?" (110, 111).[5] Lucy's response to David, though originating from far different motives and resulting in far different consequences, is yet another version of the failure to know and to act that David must endure when he confronts Petrus. "This is my life," Lucy calmly tells David at last. "I am the one who has to live here. What happened to me is my business, mine alone, not yours, and if there is one *right* I have it is the *right* not to be put on trial like this, not to have to *justify* myself—not to you, not to anyone else" (133). Having had her freedom tried to the extreme by the actual rape, Lucy adamantly resists in its aftermath a new trial of her right to silence, to privacy, and thus to a special kind of secrecy—without justification.

It is a remarkable paradox that the novel goes out of its way to emphasize this one, highly restrictive, and thus "dark" freedom: the right *not* to speak, and thus to keep the truth darkly secret. David claims this right in the first half of the book, when he refuses to bring into the light what he is supposed to know but what he will not pronounce out loud. Petrus makes use of the same right in the second half of the book, when he will not reveal what David assumes he must know about his true relations with Lucy's attackers. And, finally, Lucy herself has recourse to this peculiar freedom to remain silent when she resists David's entreaties to make public the violation she has experienced at the hands of the three rapists. To formulate the pattern in this way, however, is also to expose the radical difference that separates Lucy on the one hand from Petrus, and on the other—and especially—from David.

For David, and to a lesser degree for Petrus, what one chooses to keep silent is what one knows to be a violation of someone else that one has either committed oneself or knows about without lifting a finger to prevent it or examine it critically. In Lucy's case, however, the asymmetry is glaringly obvious. The silence to which Lucy demands the right has nothing to do with anything she did or has any true knowledge about. All she *knows* is the unthinkable aggression that happened *to her*, and this was a violation that could in no way leave intact what it means to be a freely acting and knowing self. "I am not the person you *know*," Lucy finally writes to David, "I am a dead person and I do not *know yet* what will bring me back to life" (161). Thus, Lucy's silence is not a simple choice that would preserve a secret knowledge that she herself possesses and therefore could either freely keep for herself or share with another of her choosing. Rather, Lucy's silence, as she herself suggests, is the silence of the grave—the silence into which the violated self falls and "dies" at the hands of the violator, and which as a result no longer leaves the "same" self behind to speak in its "own" name, or for itself. The one that Lucy may have been before is now gone—and all she really "knows" for the time being is *that*: the radically expropriated space of a lost past and an indeterminate future. Lucy's silence, unlike the silence of David and Petrus, in no way protects a hidden knowledge that she keeps for herself; it marks a blank in the entire system of knowledge-production and its communication in the mode of accepted truth.

David comes closest to understanding this when he meditates on rape as the inverted figure of what he had earlier celebrated as eros: "Rape, god of chaos and mixture, violator of seclusions" (105). Lucy will not tell her story precisely because it is no longer "hers" to tell. Chaotically, her "own" experience has been taken from her and mixed with all manner of others in violation of her self. It does not therefore *belong* to her in any proper sense of the term, and she will keep silent rather than pretend, unjustifiably, to be its "owner." Lucy's secret must therefore be considered not as something she possesses and refuses to share with others. Rather, Lucy's secret, her violent dispossession at the hands of the rapists, her consequent darkening and turning into something altogether different from what David always imagined her to be as his daughter, is something just as inaccessible to her as to everyone else. The sole difference—but it is decisive—is that she does not claim to know in what secret she is from now on being held. This refusal to feign the authority of knowledge is what, in response to David's impatient demand to know what is happening to her, Lucy will call her indeterminate time of *waiting*: "Now I can only wait. . . . A month. Three months. Longer. Science has not yet put a limit on how long one has to wait. For ever, maybe" (125). This, of course, is also a reference to Lucy's other secret, a secret "child" to be fashioned from the difference the rape in her past will have made when it gives birth to Lucy's unknowable future. Whether Lucy decides to maintain the biological pregnancy—which she does—or to terminate it—a choice David advocates—there can be no "scientific" knowledge capable of putting a "term" to Lucy's waiting; that is, to the darkness she has now become for herself as well as for others. No science, no history, no story can legitimately claim to illuminate it.

Ownership, moreover, is the overdetermined concept to which David had had recourse in his earlier attempt to seduce Melanie: "a woman's beauty does not *belong* to her alone," he tells her, "she has a duty to share it. . . . She does not *own* herself" (16). At that stage, of course, the challenge that is put to ownership, to what is most essential, most proper to anybody's property, including the property of one's *own* body, is meant to be merely playful. These are, David admits to himself at the time, "smooth words, as old as seduction itself. Yet at this moment he believes in them." Later, in the inverted world of violent dispossession where David is forced to dwell, such words will not sound so smooth, nor will they have anything to do with seduction. "A risk to own anything," David ruefully opines immediately after the attack reveals the menace lurking beneath his playful banter with Melanie by stripping it of all rhetorical ornament (98). In both cases, however, what is at stake for David is self-preservation. Women, he believes at the start of the novel, should be willing to give themselves away—preferably to men, and above all men, to him. Others, he fears after the attack, especially black others, constitute a grave threat to the ability of men like him to own anything, including their daughters. It is for this reason, at least up to the point where David himself begins to darken and turn into a different person altogether, that David's thinking and behavior is always dictated by the need to protect himself, if not always by retaining what he "has" in the form of empirical property, at least by maintaining what he "is" in the most proper sense of his identity. For the same reason, David is intensely concerned with Lucy's secret—the story of her past (disgrace) as well as her future (recovery).

If the story of the rape spreads, David fears initially, then Lucy—and by extension David—will lose an important measure of control, or ownership, over this story, which is itself a story of the self's lost integrity. David's first impulse is therefore a gesture of damage control: recovery from the assault will have to include erasing the physical traces as well as reassuming the authority to speak in one's own name. By asserting her right *not* to speak, by refusing to put the story of her rape into her own voice, as though it still belonged properly to her, Lucy frustrates David's desire for a narrative explanation that could, even if only retrospectively, presume to describe, interpret, and therefore understand the unthinkable event that has befallen both of them. Of course, Lucy's right to remain silent, her repeated invocation of a freedom not to speak, remains itself powerless to prevent others from speaking in her place, from usurping in this way a freedom that does not properly belong to them either. "Like a stain," David worries, "the story is spreading across the district. Not her story to spread but theirs: they are its *owners*" (115). At this point, David persists in believing that whatever is not claimed and protected as one's own property—be it as a body, an action, a knowledge, or a story— can become available to someone else for ownership. This belief prolongs the error he made when he imagined that he was free to possess Melanie's body at the very moment she appeared, for reasons the novel will keep in the dark, to give it up: "She does not resist. All she does is avert herself: avert her lips, avert her eyes. . . . As though she had decided to go slack, die within herself" (25). Neither Melanie nor Lucy will ever reveal in her own words what it must have been like to "die" in this way at the hands of another. At the hands or in the voice of another, for the "stain" of which David speaks is yet another usurpation, yet another claim to possess the story to which one is not entitled, and about which one knows literally next to nothing.[6] Rape upon rape, and coercive story upon coercive story, such would be the increasingly violent gestures of appropriation and reappropriation that define all colonial (and postcolonial) attempts to regain control, in other words, *ownership*, over a postcolonial situation of chaotic admixture from which nothing can blot up the lack of proper conduct, knowledge, understanding, and discourse.

Servants of eros, or desire, or rape, or history, or science—servants of whatever "god" one chooses to call the impersonal impulse to drive forward, to mark territory and claim it for one's own—it is primarily the "men" in *Disgrace*, both black and white, who, again according to David, first act without knowing exactly why and then afterwards "tell themselves many things [because] it is in their *interest* to make up *stories* that *justify* them" (156–58). But if the excessively self-interested freedom to make up stories justifying their acts can never catch up to the lack of understanding that drove them to commit these same acts in the first place, then such stories will become in their turn only further blind and violent acts of defective knowledge or even of nonknowledge. It is no wonder, then, that the one right Lucy steadfastly claims is the right not to "justify" herself; that David will forever be deprived of Melanie's first-person testimony; and that the novel itself will fall oddly silent precisely on those occasions when one most wants, or even demands, to hear it speak with the voice of its own knowledge and authority.

What critical act of interpretation, for instance, could ever legitimately claim to understand and thus explain Lucy's "mad" decision to keep the child that will have been born only on the far side of this fiction, but, as David underscores, will necessarily emerge from "seed driven into the woman not in love but in hatred, mixed chaotically" (199)? And what still untold story could ever hope to bring to light, and thus justify, the peculiar darkness into which Melanie, in many ways the actual "source" of David's "own" story, disappears over the course of the novel? Let us not forget that Lucy comes more and more to blot out Melanie in the second half of the book. Melanie herself is relegated to the status of a mere stage prop; no longer present in David's life, she plays the role of an actress who merely recites her memorized lines in a darkened theater, neither acting nor speaking publicly in her own name. By the end of the novel, she has become a ghostly presence, represented, in her proper identity, only at a double remove: by her boyfriend, Ryan, at the theater where she is performing and, at the home where she no longer resides, in the displaced figures of her father, mother, and younger sister. Can we say that the increasing centrality of Lucy—whose very name means "light"—helps to restore at least a semblance of David's power to acknowledge, understand, and therefore begin to remove the stain that has for centuries been spreading across his race and has now reached within his own familial lineage? Or, rather, would it not be more accurate to consider Meláni, herself of mixed origin, as a kind of remote force that silently casts a shadow over the "dark" future that is from now on being carried in the hollow at Lucy's core?

Speaking of Lucy's madness and of Melanie's disappearance, where is the story that would justify—that is pin down, describe, explain, and eventually comprehend with any degree of authority—what David himself refers to as his increasingly "stupid, daft, wrongheaded service" to the dogs in *Disgrace?* Finally relieved, it would appear, of the need to establish every relationship on the demands of subjective desire and possession, that is, freedom and knowledge, David is described for once as "giving" another being something without asking for anything in return, though this giving outside of all exchange takes place only at the moment that the other disappears once and for all from every grasp. "He has *learned* by now," the text says—reserving for very near the end of the novel the suggestion that David was after all capable of "learning" something new—"to concentrate all his attention on the animal . . . giving it what he no longer has difficulty calling by its proper name: *love*" (219). But this gift of love, this service to the dogs that does them "honor," is so peculiar that it comes in the form of giving them death: "he has learned by now to concentrate all his attention on the animal they are *killing*, giving it what he no longer has difficulty calling by its proper name: love" (219). What kind of madness is that, in which the gift of love becomes at the same instant the gift of death?

Whatever it could all mean seems to be related to yet another woman in the text, Bev Shaw, the makeshift veterinarian who tends to all unwanted animals, mostly by ushering them out of this world. A final irony would therefore consist in the way that Professor Lurie turns his back in the end on his life-long commitment to European romanticism, and above all else, on his investment in the power of subjective irony he seems always to have associated with it. Lurie himself will suggest as much at one point, when he returns to his university in chapter 20, only to find that the department of literary studies has now become a department of applied language studies, a place where there are mostly specialists in language learning. "So much for the poets," Lurie sighs to himself, "so much for the dead masters. Who have not, he must say, guided him well" (179). *Disgrace,* among the many other stories it

appears to recount, also hints at the possibility of telling a story about the slow
but sure repudiation of a romantic tradition complicitous with precisely those
ideologies, policies, and institutions from which a character like David Lurie
received his education, his *Bildung*, his entire cultural and intellectual formation. By going to school with Bev Shaw at the end, David Lurie might also
be cutting himself off from that tradition of European romanticism—though
it is certainly not clear exactly how we should understand the postromantic
kind of "love" he seems to be learning from his new mentor to bestow upon
those poor dogs.

   Nonetheless, when Lurie finally realizes that the romantic poets have failed
him, in other words, have not guided him very well, there appears a slight but
decisive hesitation or pause in the text, one that bends the story yet again
in a new direction. That the romantic poets "have not, he must say, guided
him well" is therefore not the last word here. The judgment pronounced on
romanticism is followed by another, and very different, possibility: "*Aliter*, to
whom he has not listened well" (179). *Aliter*, of course, is a Latin term, and
simply by virtue of its formal quality *as* Latin it constitutes a rather *recherché*
way of bringing back into play the type of privileged education Lurie has
received from the romantic poets at the very moment he is calling such an
education into question.[7] Moreover, the meaning of *aliter* is "otherwise," "or
else," "differently," and so it marks an alternative, a turn away from whatever
judgment on romanticism preceded it. Lurie seems at this moment to glimpse
the possibility that it was not so much the writing of European romanticism
that failed, but rather the reading to which romanticism has so far been subject, that is, the canonical reception of European romanticism, including the
dominant reception of the concept of irony that remains indissociable from it.
It could be, then, that Bev Shaw does not represent a simple rejection of European romanticism, but is, perhaps, its most legitimate heir, a more advanced
and better reader of romantic irony than Lurie has so far shown himself able
to become.[8] This possibility certainly doesn't make the conclusion to *Disgrace*
any more clear or understandable—on the contrary. However, it does remind
us that what David learns from Bev has to do above all with letting go, with
giving up and setting free as distinct from holding on. "I thought you would
save him for another week," Bev admits when she sees David bringing into the
surgery the dog to which he has become especially attached, "bearing him in
his arms like a lamb." Then she asks him: "Are you giving him up?" (220). The
enigmatic nature of that dog David is carrying in his arms, like a lamb, would
be all too tempting to interpret and understand along lines that have been

amply marked out in romanticism and ever since. What possible meaning, after all—familiar or novel—could be exchanged against the figure of that sacrificial lamb-dog? In a book where much is made of being a "dog-man," an ending that speaks of the dog as a kind of lamb and asks at the same time about the possibility of "saving" it, nearly begs to be recontextualized within a pattern of salvational narratives, no matter how travestied or inverted the pattern has become in this case. All the more so given that God's most visible representative in the text is named Mr. Isaacs. "May I pronounce the word *God* in your hearing?" Mr. Isaacs asks David. "As for God," Lurie replies, "I am not a believer, so I will have to translate what you call God and God's wishes into my own terms" (172). What bizarre act of translation into his own terms might David Lurie be performing at the end of *Disgrace* when it comes to the word *God*? Would such a translation be able to make sense out of and thus *save* this lexicon of badly broken fragments—God, salvation, Isaac, sacrifice, lamb—that makes its appearance in the text only once David begins to learn a thing or two from his new teacher, Bev Shaw?

Before jumping to any conclusions about what it is that David might in fact be giving up by deciding not to save it for one more week, it might be prudent to pause—one last time—in order to note again that whatever else Bev is trying to teach him—about the dogs, about romanticism, about writing or reading, or about irony, for that matter—it has to do with putting a stop to holding on for just a little longer.[9] In refusing to shed more light on where Melanie might have gone, on where Lucy may be heading, on how David can eventually translate the name of God into some other language, or on what manner of gift Bev will have taught David to give in giving up the dog and finally the lamb, *Disgrace* insists upon its own dark freedom, as a literary fiction, to keep silent before our most aggressive and demanding gestures of interpretation and thus reappropriation of its own secrets. Strange freedom of fiction, which is always able to pretend to be and to do what it is not and what it does not. It always pretends, though, only in order to resist the pretense to act and to know in ways that could ever be considered proper only to it. Whether we—like David in the end—could ever learn to abandon, to give up and thus interrupt our own insatiable need to hold fast to whatever most tenaciously eludes our grasp, would of course not be a question we are even yet free to ask ourselves.

INTRODUCTION: *IRONY ON OCCASION*

1. The Greek word for which *occasion* can be used as a partial translation in English and the romance languages is σκανδαλίζει, *skandalizei*, and it could occasion an infinite commentary all on its own. Suffice it to say here that the noun from which the verbal form is derived, *skandalon*, refers to the part of a snare or trap on which bait has been placed and which springs to close the trap when the bait is taken. The same term, with some reference to Hebrew, can also be translated by *stumbling block*, *hindrance*, *impediment*, or, more elliptically, as *offense*. In every case, the term refers to that which can trigger, or occasion, a fall. It can be used pejoratively, as seems to be the case in Matthew 5:29, or more affirmatively, as in Romans 9:33, where Christ is referred to as both "a rock of offense" and "a stumbling block" for those lacking in faith. In that sense, God's "testing" of Abraham by asking him to give up Isaac could also be considered a *skandalon*, or an occasion of falling for him. For readers familiar with the standard Bible translations of the original Greek, the translations provided here may appear strange. For example, the King James Version of this verse reads: "And if thy right eye offend thee, pluck it out, and cast it from thee." In this book, where the vast majority of texts under consideration were not written originally in English, I have as a general rule and for the sake of convenience provided references to English translations when I had them readily at hand. However, also as a general rule, I have not hesitated to modify these translations when I felt the original allowed for (or sometimes required) it. All citations of published English translations that are given here should therefore be considered either as already having been modified or as eminently modifiable in the future. In this book, as should become clear especially in chapter 5, "faithfulness" could itself be translated as κίνησις or *change*.

2. The trace of this moment in de Man's 1980 seminar can be found in Paul de Man, "Sign and Symbol in Hegel's *Aesthetics*," in *Aesthetic Ideology*, ed. Andrzej Warminski (Minneapolis: University of Minnesota Press, 1996), 97.

3. The majority of these essays were written as a result of invitations I have received over the years either to deliver a conference paper or a lecture, or to contribute an essay to a journal or a volume. I would like to thank all those who kindly made those invitations and thus contributed enormously to the writing of this book. I have always been fascinated by the stunning confession Descartes makes in the first of his six *Meditations on First Philosophy*. He admits that several years—read "many"—had passed since he first realized he should be writing his book, but due to the size of the task he had continued to procrastinate. How did he know when it was time to write? He procrastinated so long, he says, that ultimately he was forced to decide that he could spare no more time to brooding over the book rather than writing it. Mostly thanks to occasional invitations, I have been made to realize by others what Descartes seems to have been able to realize all on his own.

4. Søren Kierkegaard, "The First Love," in *Either/Or*, tr. Howard V. Hong and Edna H. Hong (Princeton: Princeton University Press, 1987), 1:231–79. Further references to this book appear in the text, identified by the abbreviation *EO*. It could be argued that Carl Schmitt's decision to call romanticism "subjektivierter Occasionalismus," a subjectified Occasionalism, was itself prompted by Kierkegaard's use of the term in this fragment of *Either/Or*—although, as Schmitt points out, it can also be found in certain fragments of Novalis. It is also probable that Schmitt's entire understanding—and rejection—of romanticism was occasioned in large part by his reading of Kierkegaard. Schmitt's critique of political romanticism follows so closely the outline sketched by Kierkegaard in *The Concept of Irony* that it could be taken as an indirect and unacknowledged gloss on Kierkegaard's text. Schmitt's sustained effort to articulate the link between "occasionalism" and a romantic theory of irony confirms the soundness of his reading, though with at least one crucial qualification. In Kierkegaard, the critical reflection on romantic irony is conducted from the inside. The philosophical critique of ironic self-consciousness carried out by Kierkegaard's writing is equally attentive to the vulnerability of its own language to irony—an irony that would no longer be accessible to philosophical categories of critique and cognition, including that of the subject and the kind of consciousness proper to it. See Carl Schmitt, *Politische Romantik* (Munich and Leipzig: Dunker and Humblot, 1925); *Political Romanticism*, tr. Guy Oakes (Cambridge, Mass.: MIT Press, 1986).

5. "Causa, casus, gehört zum Zeitwort cadere, fallen, und bedeutet dasjenige, was bewirkt, daß etwas im Erfolg so oder so ausfällt." Martin Heidegger, "Die Frage nach der Technik," in *Vorträge und Aufsätze* (Tübingen: Neske, 1954; 1990), 12; "The Question Concerning Technology," in *The Question Concerning Technology and Other Essays*, tr. William Lovitt (New York: Harper, 1969), 7. Further references to this essay appear in the text, identified by the abbreviation "QT" for the English translation and "FT" for the German original.

6. Although Heidegger makes a point of displacing the etymological root of causality—*Kausalität, Ursächlichkeit*—from the substantive *causa* to the verb

cadere, he is equally careful in this essay to restrict the resonance of the German word for *cadere—fallen*—to the role it plays in the compound verb *ausfallen*: "Causa, casus, gehört zum Zeitwort cadere, fallen, und bedeutet dasjenige, was bewirkt, daß etwas im Erfolg so oder so ausfällt" ("FT" 12; "QT" 7). At the beginning of Kierkegaard's essay "First Love," the Greek concept of *poiesis* is present in the form of the Danish word *Productivitet*: "Anyone who has ever had leanings toward productivity" are the first words of the essay. But the occasion that Kierkegaard, like Heidegger, will go on to associate with *poiesis* is one that is characterized right from the start as accidental, or *tilfældig*: "Anyone who has ever had leanings toward productivity has certainly also noticed that it is a little *accidental* external circumstance that becomes the *occasion* for the actual producing" (*EO* 1:233; emphasis added). The German word closest to *tilfældig* would of course be *zufällig*, from the verb *zufallen*. Bypassing the Latin word *occasio* in order to translate the Greek term *aition*, Heidegger is able to propose the German term *Veranlassung* as a more essential (and more Greek?) translation of the concept "occasion." This is possible, however, only by ignoring the ineluctable role played by *Zufall*—the word and the occurrence—in all of this.

7. The tension at issue here becomes readable in the first *Critique* as the juxtaposition of the Second Analogy of Experience with the Third Antinomy of Pure Reason. The Second Analogy considers the law of causality as a necessary rule for all experience, and the Third Antinomy distinguishes causally determined phenomena of nature from transcendentally determined acts of free will. The space, or gap, that is thus opened between natural causality and practical freedom will become the occasion for Kant to develop his theory of the aesthetic in the third *Critique*. See Immanuel Kant, *Kritik der reinen Vernunft*, vols. 3 and 4 of *Werkausgabe*, ed. Wilhelm Weischedel (Frankfurt am Main: Suhrkamp, 1978), 3:226–42; 4:426–33; 4:488–506; *Critique of Pure Reason*, tr. Norman Kemp Smith (New York: St Martin's Press, 1929), 218–33; 409–15; 464–79.

8. See the last sentence of the introduction to Søren Kierkegaard's *The Concept of Irony: With Constant Reference to Socrates*, tr. Lee M. Capel (Bloomington: Indiana University Press, 1968), 50.

9. Maurice Blanchot, "Comment la littérature est-elle possible?" in *Faux Pas* (Paris: Gallimard, 1943; 1971), 92.

10. Kierkegaard, at the moment in his exposition alluded to here, is talking about Socrates and the way his irony comes to interrupt the course of world history; the irony of Socrates happens only by interrupting that which otherwise would be historically seamless, unchanging, and therefore wholly empty. Socrates can begin the history of philosophy—without which there would be no history for thought—only to the extent that he interrupts what is nonhistorical about history itself. See *The Concept of Irony*, 222.

11. Near the beginning of his two-volume book on Nietzsche, Heidegger appears to quote from this letter, though without giving the reference and, even more interestingly, without including what Nietzsche himself goes on to say

about the *Gedankenstriche*: "Was Nietzsche zeit seines Schaffens selbst veröffent-
licht hat, ist immer Vordergrund [What Nietzsche himself published during
his creative life was always foreground]." For Nietzsche's letter, dated May 20,
1885, see *Nietzsche Briefwechsel: Kritische Gesamtausgabe*, ed. Giorgio Colli and
Mazzino Montinari (Berlin and New York: Walter de Gruter, 1982), part III,
3:53; *Selected Letters of Friedrich Nietzsche*, tr. Christopher Middleton (Chicago:
University of Chicago Press, 1969), 241. For Heidegger's unacknowledged and
truncated citation of this letter, see Martin Heidegger, *Nietzsche* (Pfullingen:
Günther Neske, 1961), 1:17; *Nietzsche: Volumes One and Two*, tr. David Farrell
Krell (New York: HarperCollins, 1991), 9.

I. FRIEDRICH SCHLEGEL AND THE MYTH OF IRONY

1. Geoffrey Hartman, "Criticism, Indeterminacy, Irony," *Criticism in the
Wilderness* (New Haven: Yale University Press, 1980), 280.
2. Friedrich Schlegel, *Lyceum Fragment* 115, in *Philosophical Fragments*, tr.
Peter Firchow (Minneapolis: University of Minnesota Press, 1991), 14; *Friedrich
Schlegel: Kritische Ausgabe seiner Werke*, ed. Ernst Behler, with Jean-Jacques Anstett and Hans Eichner (Munich: Ferdinand Schöningh, 1958–), 2:161. Further
references to these editions, identified by the abbreviations *PF* and *KA* respectively, will appear in the text.
3. See also *Athenaeum Fragment* 56: "Since these days philosophy criticizes
everything it can get its hands on, a criticism of philosophy would be nothing
more than a just reprisal" (*PF* 25; *KA* 2:173).
4. Philippe Lacoue-Labarthe and Jean-Luc Nancy, *L'Absolu littéraire: Théorie
de la littérature du romantisme allemand* (Paris: Seuil, 1978). The analysis, minus
the presentation and translation of the German texts in question, is available
in English as *The Literary Absolute: The Theory of Literature in German Romanticism*, tr. Philip Barnard and Cheryl Lester (Albany: SUNY Press, 1988). Further
references to the translation, identified as *LA*, will appear in the text.
5. These comments are made in a section of *The Concept of Criticism* titled
"System and Concept," in which Benjamin broaches the question of whether
and to what extent Schlegel and the early romantics can be taken seriously
from a philosophically systematic point of view. Benjamin's own treatment of
romantic irony is anything but straightforward, as is suggested in the way irony,
which names a dissolving power of displacement (*verschieben*), becomes itself in
this passage a displaced name for the absolute. See Walter Benjamin, "System
und Begriff," in *Der Begriff der Kunstkritik in der deutschen Romantik* (Frankfurt:
Suhrkamp, 1973), 39; *The Concept of Criticism in German Romanticism*, in *Walter
Benjamin: Selected Writings*, ed. Marcus Bullock and Michael W. Jennings (Cambridge, Mass.: Harvard University Press, 1996), 1:137–38.
6. Peter Szondi, "Friedrich Schlegel and Romantic Irony," *On Textual Understanding and Other Essays*, tr. Harvey Mendelsohn (Minneapolis: University of
Minnesota Press, 1986), 65–66; emphasis added.

7. Mme de Staël, *De l'Allemagne* (Paris: Garnier-Flammarion, 1968) 3:3, chap. 11, 162; cited by Lacoue-Labarthe and Nancy in *L'absolu littéraire*, 22.

8. Paul de Man, "The Resistance to Theory," *The Resistance to Theory* (Minneapolis: University of Minnesota Press, 1986), 19.

9. Jacques Derrida was the first to raise this question with respect to *L'Absolu littéraire* in his essay "La Loi du genre," now collected in *Parages* (Paris: Galilée, 1986). Derrida refers to his own essay, which was first presented in July 1979 at a Strasbourg colloquium organized in part by Lacoue-Labarthe and Nancy, as "a modest annotation in the margins of *L'absolu littéraire*" (256). The problem, we are reminded by Derrida, has to do with the enigma of "citing" an example of the literary performance, the actual *ré-cit* of which literature is always composed, without simply occulting it, and thus replacing it by a systematic theoretical exposition: "What is at stake, in effect, is exemplarity along with the entire *enigma*—in other words, as the word *enigma* indicates, the *récit*—that traverses and undermines [qui travaille] the logic of the example" (*Parages*, 256). It would not be irrelevant in this context to cite another marginal annotation made later in the text by Derrida about the kind of re-mark the theoretical re-citation of literature always entails: "[H]ere, then, is the *irony*, which cannot be reduced to a subjective attitude or consciousness" (264; emphasis added).

10. This is confirmed by the further statement: "Purely theoretical completion is impossible . . . because the theoretical infinite remains asymptotic. . . . But it is indeed in this not being there, this never yet being there, that romanticism and the fragment *are*, absolutely. *Work in progress* henceforth becomes the infinite truth of the work" (Lacoue-Labarthe and Nancy, *LA* 48).

11. Gérard Genette, *Mimologiques: Voyage en Cratyle* (Paris: Seuil, 1976).

12. Interestingly enough, Lacoue-Labarthe had himself already considered this possibility in an earlier essay examining Hegel's critique of Schlegel's infamous novel, *Lucinde*. In that essay, irony is nearly identified with the literary as that which resists and disrupts philosophical speculation. However, neither *Lucinde* nor its purported ironic dimension is actually submitted to textual analysis by Lacoue-Labarthe, and irony is still understood there according to Hegel's determination of it as subjective self-reflexivity. See Lacoue-Labarthe,"L'Imprésantable," in *Poétique* 21 (1975), 53–95; "The Unpresentable," tr. Claudette Sartiliot, in *The Subject of Philosophy*, ed. Thomas Trezise (Minneapolis: University of Minnesota Press, 1993).

13. The "Rede über die Mythologie" forms the second part of the *Gespräch über die Poesie*, and can be found in the second volume of Schlegel's *Kritische Ausgabe*. An English translation, titled "Talk on Mythology," is available in Friedrich Schlegel, *Dialogue on Poetry and Literary Aphorisms*, tr. Ernst Behler and Roman Struc (University Park: Pennsylvania State University Press, 1968). Further references to "Talk on Mythology" will appear in the text with the page number from *Dialogue on Poetry*, abbreviated *DP*. I have often modified the translation.

14. Jean-Luc Nancy, *La Communauté désoeuvrée* (Paris: Christian Bourgeois, 1986); *The Inoperative Community*, ed. Peter Connor (Minneapolis: University of Minnesota Press, 1991); Philippe Lacoue-Labarthe, *La Fiction du politique: Heidegger, l'art et la politique* (Paris: Christian Bourgeois, 1987); *Heidegger, Art, and Politics: The Fiction of the Political*, tr. Chris Turner (London: Blackwell, 1990); and Lacoue-Labarthe, *Heidegger, la politique du poème* (Paris: Galilée, 2002); *Heidegger and the Politics of Poetry*, tr. Jeff Fort (Urbana and Chicago: University of Illinois Press, 2007). Further references to *Heidegger, Art, and Politics: The Fiction of the Political*, identified as *Fiction*, appear in the text. To these works should be added an exposé prepared together by Lacoue-Labarthe and Nancy in 1980, which has subsequently been published in English under the title "The Nazi Myth," tr. Brian Holmes, *Critical Inquiry* 16 (winter 1990): 291–312. A slightly modified French version of the text was subsequently published as *Le Mythe nazi* (Paris: Seuil/Editions de L'Aube, 1991).

15. The hyperbolic version of this litotes is provided by Paul de Man in his reading of Schlegel's irony: "It would hardly be hyperbolic to say (and I could defend the affirmation) that the whole discipline of *Germanistik* has developed for the single reason of dodging Friedrich Schlegel, of getting around the challenge that Schlegel and that *Lucinde* offer to the whole notion of an academic discipline which would deal with German literature—seriously." See Paul de Man, "The Concept of Irony," *Aesthetic Ideology*, ed. Andrzej Warminski (Minneapolis: Universty of Minnesota Press, 1996), 168.

16. See, especially, the chapters titled "National-aestheticism," "Mimetology," and "Myth" in *La Fiction du politique*, as well as the entirety of *Heidegger: La Politique du poème*. Also essential, in this respect, is the chapter titled "Myth Interrupted" in Jean-Luc Nancy's *The Inoperable Community*, where Schlegel's text is inscribed in the following way: "The notion of a 'new mythology' . . . contains both the idea of a necessary innovation in order to create a new human world on the ground of the finished world of ancient mythology, and at the same time the idea that mythology is always the obligatory form—and perhaps the essence—of innovation. A new humanity must arise from/in its new myth, and this myth must be (according to Schlegel) nothing less than the totalization of modern literature and philosophy, as well as ancient mythology, revived and united with the mythologies of the other peoples of the world. The totalization of myths goes hand in hand with the myth of totalization" (51). Nancy seems in this passage at least to align the concept of "totalization" with the way the term *absolu* is used in *L'Absolu littéraire*: the literary absolute that must also become absolutely literary as well as absolutely philosophical, historical, and political.

17. See, in particular, the chapter titled "*Il faut*" in *Heidegger and the Politics of Poetry*, where Lacoue-Labarthe relies heavily on Walter Benjamin's reading of Hölderlin, precisely in order to distinguish the "prosaic sobriety" of Hölderlin's poetry from the "mythological" tendencies shared by Jena romanticism and Heidegger alike. A first version of "*Il faut*" was published, in French, in the German issue of *MLN* of April 1992.

18. See "Das älteste System-Programm" in *Hegel-Studien*, ed. Rüdiger Bubner (Bonn, 1973), 9:263–65; translated as "The Earliest System-Program of German Idealism," tr. H. S. Harris, in *Miscellaneous Writings of G. W. F. Hegel*, ed. Jon Stewart (Evanston, Ill.: Northwestern University Press, 2001), 110–12.

19. At issue here is the always vexing question of the relation between a constellation of discrete works and the philosophical or political ideology subsequently arising from it, which is also a version of the relation between individual textual details and the systematic exposition that would encompass and thus understand them. In "The Nazi Myth," Lacoue-Labarthe and Nancy recognize and state this problem with all possible rigor: "There is no doubt whatsoever that the German tradition, and in particular the tradition of German thought, is not at all foreign to [Nazi] ideology. But that does not mean that the tradition is responsible for it, and because of that fact, condemnable as a whole. Between a tradition of thought and the ideology that inscribes itself, always abusively, within it, there is an abyss" (295). To draw as precisely as possible the lines of the particular abuse and the depths of the particular abyss constantly dogging our own efforts to understand Schlegel's irony would be a legitimate reason for extending an analysis of his "new mythology" beyond the limits of *The Literary Absolute*.

20. Schlegel's question here offers a clear echo of the crucial turn that is made in the eighth letter of Schiller's *On the Aesthetic Education of Man*: "Should philosophy then retire, dejected and despairing, from this field? While the dominion of forms [die Herrschaft der Formen] is being extended in every other direction, should this, the most important good of all [soll dieses wichtigste aller Güter], remain the prey of formless chance [dem gestaltlosen Zufall preisgeben sein]?" Schlegel's "Talk on Mythology" should thus be read as a direct response to Schiller's theoretical project of aesthetic education, a social and political *Erziehung* that depends on the fullest extension of the concepts of *Bild* and *Bildung*. However, what Schlegel's text—precisely on account of irony—will do with the question of chance, *Zufall*, remains entirely incompatible with the dynamics of Schiller's treatise. See Friedrich Schiller, *On the Aesthetic Education of Man*, ed. and tr. Elizabeth M. Wilkinson and L. A. Willoughby (Oxford: Clarendon Press, 1982), 48–49.

21. The sociopolitical underpinnings of *Dialogue on Poetry*, of which "Talk on Mythology" is but one part, are sounded most clearly at the end of the section titled "Epochs of Literature," which comes just before and serves to introduce "Talk on Mythology." After emphasizing how philosophy and literature are for the first time, here in Germany, in a position to stimulate and develop each other, the text concludes: "Nothing more is lacking than that the Germans [Es fehlt nichts, als daß die Deutschen] use these means to go further, that they follow the example [Vorbilde] established by Goethe, retracing the forms of art back to their origin in order to be capable of reanimating or combining them, and that they return to the sources of their own language and poetry, and once again set free the original power, the lofty spirit that even now lies dormant

and unrecognized in the documents of the fatherland's prehistory" (*DP* 74; *KA* 2:303). It is therefore precisely the status of what is "lacking"—in a name, a *Vorbild*, a *Gebilde*, a *Bildung*—that remains crucial for a reading of Schlegel's "mythology" as well as his irony.

22. There is a common misunderstanding that Schlegel had no use whatsoever for "intention" (*Absicht*) and simply dispensed with it. A careful reading of those fragments concerning intentionality, however, would show that it is never the unintentional or purely arbitrary as such that interests Schlegel, but rather the possibility of resolving the tension generated, in irony for instance, between intention and accident (see, for instance, *Lyceum Fragments* 42 and 108, and *Athenaeum Fragments* 51 and 305). A reading of the "Talk on Mythology" becomes crucial precisely to the extent that it brings this tension to the fore and makes it an object of critical analysis in its own right.

23. Friedrich Schlegel, *On the Study of Greek Poetry*, ed. and tr. Stuart Barnett (Albany: SUNY Press, 2001), 21; *KA* 1:223.

24. The romantic commonplace of constructing an artfully ordered and symmetrical chaos is a topos to which Schlegel returns throughout his writings, and it functions as a hypothetical synthesis of the antithetical relation between *Absicht* and *Willkür*. For other pertinent examples, see *Lyceum Fragment* 103 and *Athenaeum Fragment* 389.

25. Here, once again, it would be imperative to read as patiently as possible Heidegger's texts in their overdetermined relation to what Schlegel does in "Talk on Mythology" with the concept and term *Bild* and with that which, ultimately, must (not) "shine" through it. In a lecture from 1999 that was published only after his death, Lacoue-Labarthe, though without mentioning either Schlegel's "Talk on Mythology" or his irony, sketches the beginning of such a reading. See Philippe Lacoue-Labarthe, *La vraie semblance* (Paris: Galilée, 2008), especially 62–71. Other relevant remarks can be found in his "Epilogue: The Spirit of National Socialism and Its Destiny" in *Heidegger and the Politics of Poetry*, especially 86–89. On *Schein* as well as *Form* and *Gebilde* in Martin Heidegger, see Heidegger's discussion with Emil Staiger, "Zu einem Vers von Mörike," *Trivium* 9 (1951), 1–16, published in English as "A 1951 Dialogue on Interpretation: Emil Staiger, Martin Heidegger, Leo Spitzer," tr. Berel Lang and Christine Ebel, *PMLA* 105, no. 3 (May 1990), 409–35.

26. In order to preserve the illusion, or *Anschein*, of the text's commitment to metaphorical patterns in which *Bild* and *Bildung* can always be brought back to a specularly determined model, like that of the body and soul relation, most translators take the *Schein* here to signify a merely figural, and therefore derived, "appearance" of madness: "quelque-chose d'originel . . . qui laisse transparaître l'apparence de l'absurde et de la déraison" is thus the rendering Lacoue-Labarthe and Nancy opt for in *L'Absolu littéraire* (316). Understanding *Schein* here as mere "appearance," rather than as the more literal, idiosyncratic, and original "light" of mythology, allows for its subsequent transformation, or *Umbildung*, into a more constructed, and thus socially acceptable, or *gebildete*,

form of madness. This is consistent with the related remarks Lacoue-Labarthe and Nancy make on "chaos" (as well as irony) in Schlegel: "Il y a cependant, si l'on ose dire, chaos et chaos. . . . [L]e chaos est bien aussi quelque chose qui *se construit*" (*L'Absolu littéraire*, 72–73). It should also be noted that Schlegel himself, in the 1822–25 edition of his works, tried to retranslate and thus soften the blinding light of the Athenaeum version of his text by qualifying it as "odd and even paradoxical" rather than outright "absurd and mad." But this attempt at self-censure only draws more attention to the inimitable and irreducible madness of the "original" *Schein* (*Gespräch*, *KA* 2:319).

27. This is the association such a philosophically informed critic of literature as Rodolphe Gasché, following closely in the footsteps of Lacoue-Labarthe and Nancy, would hesitate to concede: "It is indeed questionable whether the very concept of the Romantic fragment is ever enacted on the level of the signifier. . . . The Romantic notion of fragment would be reductionist when applied to contemporary literary texts." See Gasche's foreword to Schlegel, *Philosophical Fragments*, viii, xxx. It would be difficult to imagine how that least tautological, that is, most fragmented, of all definitions of "romantic" writing could ever have been written without enacting itself on the level of the letter: "Ein Roman ist ein romantisches Buch" (Schlegel, "Letter on the Novel," *DP* 101).

2. TAKING KIERKEGAARD APART: *THE CONCEPT OF IRONY*

1. Søren Kierkegaard, *Concluding Unscientific Postscript to the Philosophical Crumbs*, ed. and tr. Alastair Hannay (Cambridge: Cambridge University Press, 2009), 67; further references to this translation, abbreviated *Concluding*, will appear in the text. *Afsluttende uvidenskabelig Efterskrift*, in *Søren Kierkegaards Skrifter*, ed. Niels Jørgen Cappelørn, Joakim Garff, Johnny Kondrup, et al. (Copenhagen: Søren Kierkegaard Research Centre and G. E. C. Gads Forlag: 1997 ff), 7:80; all references to Kierkegaard in Danish will be to this edition, hereafter abbreviated *SKS*. *Concluding Unscientific Postscript* was published pseudonymously under the name of Johannes Climacus, though Kierkegaard's name also appears on the title page. Later on in the text, Kierkegaard has Climacus say: "Indirect communication makes communicating an art in a sense other than that ordinarily assumed in imagining the communicator as having to present the communication to a knower for him to judge it, or to a non-knower so as to give him something to know. . . . [I]t has sometimes occurred to me to wonder whether it might not be possible to communicate all this about indirect communication directly" (232; *SKS* 7:250–52).

2. See Sylviane Agacinski, "On a Thesis," in *Aparté: Conceptions and Deaths of Søren Kierkegaard*, tr. Kevin Newmark (Gainesville: Florida State University Press, 1988); originally published as "Sur une thèse," in *Aparté: Conceptions et morts de Søren Kierkegaard* (Paris: Aubier-Flammarion, 1977). Further references to the translation will appear in the text. I have often modified the translations provided by this as well as by other English-language editions cited in this

chapter. For Kierkegaard's thesis, see *The Concept of Irony: With Constant Reference to Socrates*, tr. Lee M. Capel (Bloomington: Indiana University Press, 1965). Further references to this work, abbreviated *CI*, will appear in the text.

3. Friedrich Schlegel, "Über die Unverständlichkeit," in *Friedrich Schlegel: Kritische Ausgabe seiner Werke*, ed. Ernst Behler, with Jean-Jacques Anstett and Hans Eichner (Munich: Ferdinand Schöningh, 1958–), 2:364; "On Incomprehensibility," in *Friedrich Schlegel's Lucinde and the Fragments*, tr. Peter Firchow (Minneapolis: University of Minnesota Press, 1971), 260.

4. To some extent, the Hegelian interpretation is a more historical and therefore more dialectical version of the way Aristotle had theorized irony in the *Nicomachian Ethics*, as a deviation from the adequate expression of the truth that is characterized by understatement as opposed to overstatement. In this respect, the *eiron* is to be distinguished from, and valorized over, the *alazon*, who boastfully makes claim to a greater understanding than he is entitled to. Accordingly, Schlegel plays *alazon* to the *eiron* of Socrates, though in both cases, for Hegel, the deviation from the truth will call for its own *Aufhebung*. At bottom both *alazon* and *eiron* are hyperbolic, in that the degree of their deficiency with respect to truth is excessive. See Aristotle, *Nicomachian Ethics*, 4.13.1 127b22–6.

5. Is it only because we know that Kierkegaard himself was sincere in the impatience he shared with Hegel about the romantics that we do not often suspect that this "decadent" lineage joining the irony of Socrates to that of Schlegel is being itself drawn in an ironic mode? "In relation to a foolishly inflated wisdom which knows everything," Kierkegaard's text points out, "it is ironically correct to go along with it, to be transported by all this knowledge, to goad it on with jubilant applause into rising ever higher and higher in an always greater and greater lunacy" (*CI* 266; *SKS* 1:288).

6. Agacinski refers to Jacques Derrida, "La Double Séance," in *La Dissémination* (Paris: Editions du Seuil, 1971); "The Double Session," in *Dissemination*, tr. Barbara Johnson (Chicago: University of Chicago Press, 1981).

7. Given the paucity of texts that have managed to make genuine progress in understanding—never mind explicating—what is entailed in Kierkegaard's term *repetition*, as well as the text, *Repetition*, titled after it, one could do worse than consider Derrida's *iterability* to be a translation into Derrida's idiom of what, in the context of Kierkegaard's text, constitutes the singular event of repetition. See Jacques Derrida, "Signature événement contexte," in *Marges* (Paris: Minuit, 1972); "Signature Event Context," in *Limited Inc.*, tr. Samuel Weber (Evanston: Northwestern University Press, 1988).

8. Kierkegaard's understanding of the narcissistic pleasure involved in ironic consciousness is yet another of the legacies he inherits from Hegel's critique of the romantic interpretation and use of the Fichtean absolute ego. The eye that recognizes itself by looking into the face of the Napoleonic image can thus be considered a version of Fichte's "I = I," whose ultimate aim, at least on a first look, would be to recuperate the negativity implied in Napoleon's death by resituating all of the imperial power in the self-recognition of the conscious

subject. It is hardly an accident that Kierkegaard the ironist chose to illustrate the Socratic origin of ironic self-consciousness with the image of Napoleon, the same Napoleon who for Hegel was something like the "soul" of world history, the concrete appearance of the Idea—riding into Jena on horseback, no less!—though, ironically enough, perhaps without "knowing" all that himself.

9. For a similar formulation of the nonsymmetrical distinction between positing and meaning, and one that goes a long way toward suggesting the place Kierkegaard should occupy in a wider examination of the period from Kant to Marx and beyond, see Paul de Man, "Sign and Symbol in Hegel's *Aesthetics*," in *Aesthetic Ideology*, ed. Andrzej Warminski (Minneapolis: University of Minnesota Press, 1996): "The philosophical I is not only self-effacing, as Aristotle demanded, in the sense of being humble and inconspicuous, it is also self-effacing in the much more radical sense that the position of the I, which is the condition of thought, implies its eradication, not, as in Fichte, as the symmetrical position of its negation, but as the undoing, the erasure of any relationship, logical or otherwise, that could be conceived between what the I is and what it says it is" (98–99). The "inconspicuousness" to which de Man refers would indeed name the "indirection" of an irony that is also elliptical, in the sense of Socratic "ignorance" and "self-effacement." What de Man's reading brings out is the way irony as ellipsis always tends toward irony as hyperbole: the positing that makes meaning possible also deprives it of the power to maintain its equilibrium as meaning; the self-effacing "I" that irony posits eventually effaces its "own" meaning to an excessive degree.

10. Kierkegaard does not hesitate, along with the rest of the European philosophical establishment, to criticize Schlegel in the most severe terms for linking the ironic consciousness with a flight from historical actuality for the sake of a "new mythology." "Irony," Kierkegaard writes, having just suggested that Schlegel was its philosophical incarnation in the age of romanticism, "looked with special favor on the mythical aspect of history, saga, and fairy-tale. . . . Irony dispensed with historical actuality; with a flick of the wrist, all history became myth, poetry, saga, fairy-tale [I en Haandevending var al Historie bleven til Mythe—Digt—Sagn—Eventyr.]" (*CI* 294; *SKS* 1:313). Neither Hegel nor Kierkegaard has any patience with Schlegel and his ironic mythologizing. Kierkegaard has only little more patience with Hegel's replacement of Schlegel's irony with the image of the speculative thinker who, in the blink of an eye, masters historical actuality by "mediating" himself out of it. Kierkegaard will therefore replace Hegel's system with the image of the Christian who eschews both irony and dialectical speculation in the name, and in the instant, of faith. The degree to which faith can itself be construed as a peculiar type of "image" for both Schlegel's irony and Hegel's speculation is suggested by other chapters in this book.

11. Kierkegaard is no doubt recalling a famous moment in Kant's *Critique of Pure Reason*, section 7 of "The Antinomy of Pure Reason," where Kant argues that the world as a possible object of cognition cannot be considered as sim-

ply given—*gegeben*—to experience, but rather must be considered as a task—*aufgegeben*—to be taken up by philosophical thought. The reference to Kant in this context is not without significance, since what is ultimately at stake in Kierkegaard's interrogation of irony is the relation between knowledge and freedom; it therefore leads directly (back) to Kant and the problematic status of the aesthetic as a possible means of articulation between the first and third *Critiques*.

12. To the other more-or-less legitimate translations of *aparté* we might as well add this more-or-less ironic one. Translating the French word *aparté* into English as "taking (words) apart" is ironic since it simultaneously names and repeats the aparté of irony. As such, it is an interruption of determinate meaning that occurs on the level of *lexis* rather than *logos*, or on the level of the letter rather than the word. The "specific context" from which the French word *aparté* is borrowed is that of the theatrical "aside" or parabasis that interrupts the flow of action that is being staged. In that context, it is already a (scenic) translation of the nonscenic, nonrepresentational, nonmimetic element within irony. In the same spirit, *anacoluthon*, which names a disruption, indirection, or turning aside on the level of grammar—as distinct from representation—would perhaps offer a more adequate translation of *aparté*.

13. It is no mere accident that the echoing play between *Gave* and *Opgave* will reappear in *Fear and Trembling* precisely at the moment when faith—the most serious task to be left to the future by the gift of irony—is compelled to acknowledge its incompatibility with all understanding, and therefore all mediation in the universal: "The knight of faith knows that it is inspiring to *give up* himself for the universal, that it takes courage to do it, but that there is also a security in it precisely because it is for the universal. . . . This he knows, and he feels as if bound; he could wish that this was the *task* that had been set to him. In the same way, Abraham now and then could have wished that the *task* were to love Isaac as a father would and should, understandable to all." Søren Kierkegaard, *Fear and Trembling / Repetition*, vol. 6 of *Kierkegaard's Writings*, tr. Howard V. Hong and Edna H. Hong (Princeton: Princeton University Press, 1983), 76; emphasis added. "Troens Ridder veed, at det er begeistrende at opgive sig selv for det Almene, at der hører Mod dertil, men at der ogsaa er en Tryghed deri, netop fordi det er for det Almene. . . . Dette veed han, og han føler sig ligesom bunden, han kunde ønske, at det var denne Opgave, der var sat ham. Saaledes kunde Abraham vel af og til have ønsket, at Opgaven var at elske Isaak som det sig en Fader hør og bør, forstaaelig for Alle" (*SKS* 4:167). Abraham will have to *give up* himself in Isaac for the sake of the *task* to which he has been called by the absolute—which first of all gave Isaac as the promised gift to Abraham.

3. MODERNITY INTERRUPTED: KIERKEGAARD'S ANTIGONE

1. Collections appearing in English over the past few years include Martin J. Matustik and Merold Westphal, eds., *Kierkegaard in Post/Modernity* (Bloomington: University of Indiana Press, 1995); Jonathan Rée and Jane Chamberlain,

eds., *Kierkegaard: A Critical Reader* (Oxford: Blackwell, 1998); Alastair Hannay and Gordon D. Marino, eds., *The Cambridge Companion to Kierkegaard* (Cambridge: Cambridge University Press, 1998); and Elsebet Jegstrup, ed., *The New Kierkegaard: Studies in Continental Thought* (Bloomington: Indiana University Press, 2004).

2. *Søren Kierkegaard's Journals and Papers*, tr. and ed. Howard V. Hong and Edna H. Hong (Bloomington: Indiana University Press, 1975), 3:653. Further references to this work, identified as *Journals*, appear in the text. I have often modified the translations provided by this as well as by other English-language editions cited in this chapter.

3. Søren Kierkegaard, *Philosophical Fragments*, tr. David Swenson, revised tr. Howard V. Hong (Princeton: Princeton University Press, 1962), 11; further references to this work, identified as *PF*, appear in the text. *Søren Kierkegaards Skrifter*, ed. Niels Jørgen Cappelørn, Joakim Garff, Johnny Kondrup, et al. (Copenhagen: Søren Kierkegaard Research Centre and G. E. C. Gads Forlag, 1997 ff), 4: 218. All quotations from Kierkegaard in Danish will be from this edition, identified as *SKS*.

4. Theodor W. Adorno, "On Kierkegaard's Doctrine of Love," in Harold Bloom, ed., *Søren Kierkegaard: Modern Critical Views* (New York: Chelsea House, 1989), 20–21. For an excellent study of Kierkegaard that begins by taking seriously this aspect of his writing and thinking, see Peter Fenves, *"Chatter": Language and History in Kierkegaard* (Stanford: Stanford University Press, 1993).

5. Theodor W. Adorno, *Kierkegaard: Construction of the Aesthetic*, tr. Robert Hullot-Kentor (Minneapolis: University of Minnesota Press, 1989). Clearly, Adorno is much indebted to Walter Benjamin's unorthodox understanding of the allegorical mode distinctive of certain writers. Still, it is no accident that Adorno would have found fertile ground for this type of allegorical approach in the texts of Kierkegaard, just as Benjamin himself developed many of his most remarkable insights while working on the French poet Charles Baudelaire. Adorno had a clear sense of the close affinity between Baudelaire and Kierkegaard. But to date no substantial work has been done treating the two writers together.

6. There exists not only one scholarly book on this topic, but another book that extends and refines the scholarly information and findings of the first. See Niels Thulstrup, *Kierkegaard's Relation to Hegel*, tr. George L. Stengren (Princeton: Princeton University Press, 1980), and Jon Stewart, *Kierkegaard's Relations to Hegel Reconsidered* (Cambridge: Cambridge University Press, 2003).

7. A concise formulation occurs in *Concluding Unscientific Postscript*: "Reality itself is a system—for God; but it cannot be a system for any existing subject. System and finality correspond to one another, but existence is precisely the opposite of finality. It may be seen that system and existence are incapable of being thought together; because in order to think existence at all, systematic thought must think it as sublated, and hence as not existing." *Kierkegaard's Concluding Unscientific Postscript*, tr. David F. Swenson (Princeton: Princeton University

Press, 1968), 107. Further references to this work, identified as *Postscript*, appear in the text.

8. Søren Kierkegaard, *Fear and Trembling / Repetition*, vol. 6 of *Kierkegaard's Writings*, tr. Howard V. Hong and Edna H. Hong (Princeton: Princeton University Press, 1983), 28. Further references to this translation of *Fear and Trembling*, identified as *FT*, appear in the text.

9. For a contemporary "listener" who took Kierkegaard's text seriously enough to consider its threat in a thoroughly nonmetaphorical mode, see Jacques Derrida, *Donner la mort* (Paris: Editions Galilée, 1999); *The Gift of Death*, tr. David Wills (Chicago: University of Chicago Press, 2008).

10. Emmanuel Lévinas, "Existence et éthique," in *Noms propres* (Paris: Fata Morgana, 1976), 104.

11. Paul Ricoeur, "Two Encounters with Kierkegaard: Kierkegaard and Evil; Doing Philosophy after Kierkegaard," in Joseph H. Smith, ed., *Kierkegaard's Truth: The Disclosure of the Self* (New Haven: Yale University Press, 1981), 313–42; further references to this essay, identified as "KE," appear in the text. The response begun by Ricoeur can be only partial since he replaces the Kierkegaardian disjunction between philosophy and existence with their possible unity in "a new way of doing philosophy . . . a genre of conceptual thought, which has its own rules for rigor, its own type of coherence, and which requires its own logic" (341). This new genre would be a form of hermeneutic interpretation whose questions and answers eventually tie thought and existence meaningfully together in what Ricoeur characterizes as "representations." The logic referred to would apply simultaneously to literary, philosophical, and religious modes of representation. In this respect, Lévinas's insistence on the enigmatic, incognito, and thus nonrepresentational relation between the self and the absolutely other comes closer than Ricoeur to Kierkegaard's own nondialectical, and risk-laden, understanding of the relation between philosophy and existence.

12. For a reading of Kierkegaard that tends in this direction, see Georg Lukács, *The Destruction of Reason*, tr. Peter Palmer (Atlantic Highlands, N.J.: Humanities Press, 1981).

13. Søren Kierkegaard, *The Concept of Irony: With Constant Reference to Socrates*, tr. Lee M. Capel (Bloomington: Indiana University Press, 1965). Further references to this work, identified as *CI*, appear in the text.

14. Søren Kierkegaard, *The Concept of Anxiety*, ed. and tr. Reider Thomte and Albert B. Anderson (Princeton: Princeton University Press), 1980, 67. Further references to this work, identified as *CA*, appear in the text.

15. Johannes de Silentio, the pseudonymous voice of *Fear and Trembling*, puts it this way: "As for me, I do not lack the courage to think a complete thought. Up to now I have feared none, and if I should encounter such a one, I hope at least that I will have the honesty to say: This thought makes me afraid, it shocks me, and therefore I will not think it" (30).

16. Sylviane Agacinski, *Aparté: Conceptions and Deaths of Søren Kierkegaard*, tr. Kevin Newmark (Tallahassee: Florida State University Press, 1988), 172.

17. That the self is never anything but a derived relation to itself by way of the other is something that Kierkegaard also stated clearly: "The human self is such a derived, established relation, a relation that relates itself to itself and in relating itself to itself relates itself to another." Søren Kierkegaard, *The Sickness Unto Death*, ed. and tr. Howard V. Hong and Edna H. Hong (Princeton: Princeton University Press, 1980), 13–14. What complicates the issue—and therein lies its richness as well as its potential for misunderstanding—is the fact that, although Kierkegaard never wavers on this point, the way it is mobilized in different texts is highly volatile. Thus, the irreducible requirement that the self relate itself to itself through the other is not consistent with respect to the "other's" attributes. Sexual (man/woman), existential (Christian/non-Christian), ontological (human/nonhuman), and metaphysical (divine/human) differences account for some of the more important narrative strategies adopted by Kierkegaard. The sentence that states the definition of the self can also always be read in such a way that the "other" through which the self relates itself to itself is its own "self" in the very first place. The originality of the relation that conditions the self is such that the self is always already wholly "other" . . . for itself.

18. Only a slight shift is required to notice that the peculiar nature of this synthesis that so interests Kierkegaard in his theorization of *passion* bears an uncanny resemblance to what he excoriated in Friedrich Schlegel's linking of the finite and the infinite, or body and spirit, in his novel *Lucinde*. The "scandal" in Schlegel's text may not share the register and tone of the scandal in Kierkegaard's, but beyond all their differences, there remains the principle of mutual interference that, for both writers, interrupts any seamless articulation between thought and being, finitude and the infinite. Ultimately at stake here would be the "scandal" of thinking history as interruption rather than transition.

19. Agacinski, *Aparté*, 172.

20. For a text that in these terms closely approximates Kierkegaard's writing on passion and the disaster of thought, see Maurice Blanchot, *L'Écriture du désastre* (Paris: Gallimard/NRF, 1980); translated as *The Writing of the Disaster*, tr. Ann Smock (Lincoln: University of Nebraska Press, 1995). For an elaboration of the way passion, faith, and testimony function in another key text by Blanchot, *L'Instant de ma mort* (Paris: Fata Morgana, 1994), see Jacques Derrida, *Demeure: Maurice Blanchot* (Paris: Galilée, 1998); translated as *The Instant of My Death / Demeure: Fiction and Testimony*, tr. Elizabeth Rottenberg (Stanford: Stanford University Press, 2000).

21. This is the gist of the short text entitled "Either/Or" contained in *Either/Or*. It concludes with the following example: "Hang yourself, and you will regret it. Do not hang yourself, and you will also regret that. Hang yourself or do not hang yourself, you will regret it either way. Whether you hang yourself or do not hang yourself, you will regret it either way. This, gentlemen, is the sum and substance of all philosophy." Søren Kierkegaard, *Either/Or*, tr. Howard V. Hong and Edna H. Hong (Princeton: Princeton University Press, 1987), 1:38–39. Further references to this work, identified as *EO*, appear in the text.

For Kierkegaard, death is not susceptible to being integrated in what he calls the "successive dialectic," that is, a dialectic of *Aufhebung* in which any difference, including death, can be mediated into a higher unity of understanding and knowledge. Adorno is one of the few to appreciate how powerfully Kierkegaard's insistence on death can also function as a mode of "protest against a world which is determined by barter and gives nothing without an equivalent" ("On Kierkegaard's Doctrine of Love," 32). In a very strict sense, death cannot be economized on—it has no equivalent.

22. One recognizes in this formulation the curious task that is assigned to Abraham in *Fear and Trembling*.

23. *Philosophical Fragments*, 128. For an extended treatment of this figure, see Peter Fenves's "Autopsies of Faith: *Philosophical Fragments*" in his book "*Chatter*."

24. For more detailed treatments of this aspect of Kierkegaard's concept of irony, see Birgit Baldwin, "Irony, That 'Little, Invisible Personage': Reading Kierkegaard's Ghosts," *MLN* 104:5 (1989), 1124–41, and chapter 2, "Taking Kierkegaard Apart."

25. "The Tragic in Ancient Drama Reflected in the Tragic in Modern Drama," in *Either/Or*, 1:137–64. Further references to this work appear in the text, identified as "Tragic," *EO*. The Danish title is "Det Antike Tragiskes Reflex I det Moderne Tragiske." Further references to this work appear in the text. The very choice of Antigone for such a subject is both entirely predictable and incalculably overdetermined. Useful points of reference for the specificity of this choice include Jacques Derrida, *Glas*, tr. John P. Leavey, Jr. and Richard Rand (Lincoln: University of Nebraska Press, 1986); Luce Irigaray, *Speculum of the Other Woman*, tr. Gillian C. Gill (Ithaca: Cornell University Press, 1985), Irigaray, *Sexes and Genealogies*, tr. Gillian C. Gill (New York: Columbia University Press, 1993), and Irigaray, *An Ethics of Sexual Difference*, tr. Carolyn Burke and Gillian C. Gill (Ithaca: Cornell University Press, 1993); George Steiner, *Antigones* (New Haven: Yale University Press, 1984, 1996); Sylviane Agacinski, "Le Savoir absolu d'Antigone," *digraphe* 29 (March 1983), 53–70; Carol Jacobs, "Dusting Antigone," *MLN* 111:5 (1996), 889–917; and Judith Butler, *Antigone's Claim* (New York: Columbia University Press, 2000).

26. As is often the case for Kierkegaard's allegorical rewriting of classical or Christian narratives, a necessary intertext is provided by Hegel's philosophical commentaries. With respect to this text on the "reflection"—which is also a repetition and a haunting—of the ancient in modern tragedy, it is helpful to recall not only the treatment of ancient and modern tragedy in Hegel's *Lectures on Aesthetics*, but this brief affirmation from his *Philosophy of Right*: "The right of the subject's particularity, the right to be satisfied, or in other words the right of subjective freedom, is the pivot and center of the difference between antiquity and modern times. This right in its infinity is given expression in Christianity and it has become the universal effective principle of a new form of civilization." G. W. F. Hegel, *Hegel's Philosophy of Right*, tr. T. M. Knox (Oxford: Oxford University Press, 1967; rpt.), 84. Up to a certain point, named here by the word *pivot* (*Wendepunkt*),

Kierkegaard would be in complete agreement. But by occupying this pivot in a very particular way, Kierkegaard's Antigone gives a radical twist to the movement of philosophical and historical mediations narrated by Hegel's texts.

27. In this respect, one cannot fail to notice how Kierkegaard seems to "ignore" the political side of Antigone. How is it that Antigone's relation to Polyneices and to Creon, that is, her relation to the interference between the family and the state, is not addressed by Kierkegaard? Kierkegaard's own political "views" are well known and not very helpful in this context. More to the point would be a consideration of the political in the light of what role Kierkegaard assigns to the secret and the silence to which it pledges Antigone (and Abraham). To think the political in Kierkegaard would ultimately be to ask about a kind of political thought that would not economize on the essential secret at the heart of consciousness—a secret that separates the self not only from all others but from itself as well. For a reading of Antigone that focuses on the political in a way that would make Kierkegaard's version all the more challenging—and fruitful—to read, see Butler, *Antigone's Claim*.

28. In the Danish, "føler hun sig fremmed for Menneskene" (*SKS* 2:159). This is the gloss the text gives to the citation from Sophocles's *Antigone* on the following page, which in the translation reads, "alive to the place of corpses, an alien still,/never at home with the living nor with the dead" ("Tragic," *EO* 1:159). Antigone's solitude is all the more absolute to the extent that it occurs only through her separation from a densely populated universe: "She, too, does not belong to the world in which she lives; although healthy and flourishing, her real life is nevertheless hidden. . . . [S]he feels her own significance, and her secret sinks deeper and deeper into her soul, ever more inaccessible to any living being" (1:157). The curious insistence of the narrator that Antigone be a "bride" despite the fact that she "knows no man" can be slightly better understood when one recalls that the Danish word for bride (*en Brud*) echoes the word for break (*et Brud*) that inaugurates this essay on the ancient and the modern (*SKS* 2:139–40). *Bride* to her secret, Antigone necessarily *breaks* with the world. For several of Kierkegaard's own references to this play of the letter in his language, see Søren Kierkegaard, *Stages on Life's Way*, ed. and tr. Howard V. Hong and Edna H. Hong (Princeton: Princeton University Press, 1988), 79, 664.

29. In the text on Antigone it is written, "she carries her secret under her heart" ("Tragic," *EO* 1:158), but Kierkegaard was much more explicit elsewhere in characterizing such "carrying" as a moment within the process of term pregnancy. The editors of *Either/Or*, vol. 1, refer to a relevant *Journals* notation: "a similar expression is to hide a secret; she is a mother; it stirs under her breast" (*EO* 1:543). But even more to the point is Kierkegaard's enigmatic use of the mother and child imagery in *Fear and Trembling* to introduce the story of the "secret" that also serves to link and separate father and son, Abraham and Isaac: "When the child is to be weaned, the mother, too, is not without sorrow, because she and the child are more and more to be separated, because the child who first lay under her heart and later rested upon her breast will never again be so close" (*FT* 13).

314 Notes to pages 90–97

30. Kierkegaard often confronted the question of what it means to be a father, and whether in fact being a father, if it actually ever had taken place as such, would still be possible in anything other than a mode of *delusion*: "I believe that it is the most sublime to owe one's life to another person; I believe that this debt cannot be settled or discharged by any reckoning. . . . What does it mean to be a father? I must indeed smile when I think of myself as a father. . . . The contradiction here is something both to laugh over and to weep over. Is being a father a delusion?" *Stages on Life's Way*, 44–45. The text on Antigone is thus written in a very peculiar temporality: between the father of the past, who is no longer there ("Oedipus is dead"), and the future perfect mother—the modern Antigone to whom this text points, though only as the possibility of a future reflection, repetition, and thus transformation of that past.

31. To my knowledge, no one has drawn attention to the way this Greek word includes a subtle allusion to Abraham and his faith. In Romans 4:19, Abraham's faith is put in direct but inverse relation to his body: "And being not weak in faith, [Abraham] considered not his own body now dead, when he was about an hundred years old . . . " The Greek term used here to characterize Abraham's body is νενεκρωμένον, *nenekrōmenon*—a passive past participle indicating that the body's having become dead coincides with the moment that faith in God's promise can be first subjected to a test or ordeal. Both Abraham and A's Antigone are alone with their secret—separated absolutely in their entombment or encryption from all others. The Symparanekrōmenoi to whom this fragment is addressed come together each time, on Friday, only in order to experience—if one can still use that term here—their own separation and encryption from every community. I am grateful to Dan Harris-McCoy for drawing my attention to the echo, or re-flex, that joins Kierkegaard's use of the term *Symparanekrōmenoi* in *Either/Or* to the reference to Abraham in Romans 4:19.

32. The tension, and play, between the construction and its interruption, between coherence and fragmentation, is a critical topos in some of the main texts of German romanticism, and the text on Antigone is undoubtedly one of the places Kierkegaard enters the fray. Adorno shows his own sensitivity to the issue by using this particular passage to conclude his book on the "construction" of the aesthetic in Kierkegaard (*Kierkegaard: Construction of the Aesthetic*, 139–40). However, he takes the fragment in an entirely different direction from the one being proposed here. More relevant would be de Man's use of the term *anacoluthon* to characterize Friedrich Schlegel's use of the term *parabasis*. See Paul de Man, "The Concept of Irony," *Aesthetic Ideology*, ed. Andrzej Warminski (Minneapolis: University of Minnesota Press, 1996), 178–79.

4. READING KIERKEGAARD: TO KEEP INTACT THE SECRET

1. Sylviane Agacinski, *Aparté: Conceptions et morts de Søren Kierkegaard* (Paris: Aubier-Flammarion, 1977); published in English as *Aparté: Conceptions*

and Deaths of Søren Kierkegaard, tr. Kevin Newmark (Tallahassee: Florida State University Press, 1988).

2. "How far does the truth admit of being learned? With this question let us begin." Søren Kierkegaard, *Philosophical Fragments,* tr. David Swenson, revised tr. Howard V. Hong (Princeton: Princeton University Press, 1962), 11; *Søren Kierkegaards Skrifter,* ed. Niels Jørgen Cappelørn, Joakim Garff, Johnny Kondrup, et al. (Copenhagen: Søren Kierkegaard Research Centre and G. E. C. Gads Forlag: 1997 ff), 4:218. All references to Kierkegaard in Danish will be to this edition, abbreviated *SKS.*

3. Maurice Blanchot, "Le 'Journal' de Kierkegaard," now collected in *Faux Pas* (Paris: Gallimard 1943; 1971), 25–30. Further references appear in the text, identified as "Journal." The translations are mine.

4. *Les Temps Modernes,* of course, is the title of the Parisian postwar review founded in October 1945 with Sartre as director. Other board members included Raymond Aron, Simone de Beauvoir, Michel Leiris, Maurice Merleau-Ponty, Albert Ollivier, and Jean Paulhan.

5. Indeed, Agacinski's own sketch of a possible "solution" for piercing this secret relation is one feature of *Aparté* that seems to have left a genuine impression on its readers. Such a solution, however, depends in the final analysis on making Kierkegaard's conception of "existence" a consequence of his biographical origins and therefore sidesteps the way Blanchot inscribes both the father and the fiancée within the image—rather than the other way around. A reader as sensitive to the poetic dimension of Kierkegaard's writing as Louis Mackey is thus able to use Agacinski's text to argue that the peculiar motifs of the father/fiancée relationship in Kierkegaard were "required by his upbringing." See the last chapter, "Points of View," in Louis Mackey, *Points of View* (Tallahassee: Florida State University Press, 1986).

6. The figure for this incognito, as for so many others in Kierkegaard, is also Abraham: "'If he at least could explain why he wants to do it. . . .' But Abraham could not explain further, for his life is like a book under divine sequestration and never becomes public property." Søren Kierkegaard, *Fear and Trembling,* in *Fear and Trembling / Repetition,* tr. Howard V. Hong and Edna H. Hong (Princeton: Princeton University Press, 1983), 77; *SKS* 4:168. Further references to *Fear and Trembling* appear in the text, identified as *FT.* Kierkegaard mentions the invisibility of religiosity in *Concluding Unscientific Postscript*: "True religiosity is distinguishable by invisibility, that is, is not to be seen." In the "First and Last Explanation" appended to the *Postscript,* he describes how the pseudonymous writings were conditioned by "poetic" requirements. See Søren Kierkegaard, *Concluding Unscientific Postscript,* tr. Howard V. Hong and Edna H. Hong (Princeton: Princeton University Press, 1992), 1:475, 625–26.

7. Louis Mackey's fine contribution to Kierkegaard studies, *Kierkegaard: A Kind of Poet* (Philadelphia: University of Pennsylvania Press, 1971), would be an example of a very useful commentary on Kierkegaard's rhetoric that nonetheless

takes for granted the stability of its own understanding of what constitutes the *literariness* of Kierkegaard's writing in the first place.

8. "La Philosophie à l'affiche" was one of two lectures Agacinski gave in Copenhagen in September 1981. It was published under that title in *Revue des Sciences Humaines*, no. 185, (1982), 13–24. It was then retitled "La Philosophie s'adresse-t-elle? Réception et déception de Kierkegaard à Derrida" for its inclusion in Sylviane Agacinski, *Critique de l'égocentrisme: L'événement de l'autre* (Paris: Galilée 1996), 47–72. The translation is mine.

9. Søren Kierkegaard, *Either/Or*, tr. Howard V. Hong and Edna H. Hong (Princeton: Princeton University Press, 1987), 1:32; *SKS* 2:18. Further references to this work in translation appear in the text, identified as *EO*.

10. Søren Kierkegaard, *Repetition*, in *Fear and Trembling/Repetition*, tr. Howard V. Hong and Edna H. Hong (Princeton: Princeton University Press, 1983).

11. *Fear and Trembling* is a particularly spectacular recounting of just such an experience/experiment of the ordeal (*Prøvelse*). God puts Abraham to the test (*Prøve*) in order that Abraham might for the first time enter into history as the promise of his own infinite future in Isaac. *Faith* is another name for the repetition by which Abraham will have been able to receive Isaac for a second time, though only after he has been exposed to the mortal peril of losing both himself and Isaac in the process.

12. Agacinski, *Aparté*, 96–105.

13. "The Tragic in Ancient Drama Reflected in the Tragic in Modern Drama," *EO* 1:154; *SKS* 2:147.

14. Sylviane Agacinski, "Nous ne sommes pas sublimes," *Cahiers de la Philosophie*, nos. 8–9 (*Kierkegaard: Vingt-cinq études*), 167–85; reprinted as "Nous ne sommes pas sublimes: L'amour et le sacrifice, Abraham et nous," in *Critique de l'égocentrisme: L'événement de l'autre* (Paris: Galilée, 1996). Translated as "We Are Not Sublime: Love and Sacrifice, Abraham and Ourselves," in Jonathan Rée and Jane Chamberlain, eds., *Kierkegaard: A Critical Reader* (Oxford: Blackwell, 1998). Further references to the English translation appear in the text.

15. There is in fact a passage in *Fear and Trembling* which invites a reading that would be very close to the one Agacinski is suggesting here—and it will always be tempting to imagine that, in its very indirection as a passing "example" within *Fear and Trembling*'s meditation on Abraham and Isaac, it was addressed directly to Regine Olsen by Søren Kierkegaard, imagining or even praying that he and Regine could somehow share a "sublime" perspective on their own broken engagement: "These two will in all eternity be compatible [Disse Tvende vil da i al Evighed passe for hinanden], with such a rhythmical *harmonia praestabilita* that if the instant ever came—an instant, however, that does not concern them finitely, for then they would grow old—if the instant ever came that allowed them to give love its expression in time, they would be capable of beginning right where they would have begun if they had united in the beginning" (*FT* 45; *SKS* 4:139).

16. Agacinski's invention of an ironically skeptical response to the call from the Absolute—"I just don't believe it"—dovetails curiously with Thomas Mann's version in *Joseph and His Brothers*, discussed in chapter 7. In Mann's novel, Jacob imagines that, if called by the Absolute to sacrifice his son, Joseph, he would refuse. Like Mann, Agacinski seems to interpret a refusal to respond "Here I am" to a call from the Absolute as a sign of superior love and, ultimately, superior understanding. Far different would be the irony characterizing Abraham in Kafka's parable by the same name, which, like Agacinski's and Mann's texts, is also a response to Kierkegaard's Abraham. Kafka's fictional narrator imagines for himself several new Abrahams, the last of whom would possess "true" faith: "Ihm fehlt nicht der wahre Glaube—he is not lacking in true faith." This Abraham, who shows no lack of faith in the Absolute and its call, lacks faith rather in his own capacity to "hear" for whom the call of the Absolute is actually meant. Always and forever ready to respond "Here I am," this Abraham also believes in the possibility of hearing by mistake the call of the Absolute meant for another, and thus the possibility of responding in perpetual error. See Franz Kafka, "Abraham," in *Parables and Paradoxes* (New York: Schocken Books, 1961).

5. FEAR AND TREMBLING: "WHO IS ABLE TO UNDERSTAND ABRAHAM?"

1. Søren Kierkegaard, *The Concept of Irony: With Constant Reference to Socrates*, tr. Lee M. Capel (Bloomington: Indiana University Press, 1965), 285. Further references to this work, abbreviated CI, will appear in the text. *Søren Kierkegaards Skrifter*, vols. 1–55, ed. Niels Jørgen Cappelørn, Joakim Garff, Johnny Kondrup, et al. (Copenhagen: Søren Kierkegaard Research Centre and G.E.C. Gads Forlag, 1997 ff.), 1:284. All further references to Kierkegaard's works in Danish are to the *Søren Kierkegaards Skrifter*, abbreviated SKS.

2. Søren Kierkegaard, *Fear and Trembling/Repetition*, tr. Howard V. Hong and Edna H. Hong(Princeton: Princeton University Press, 1983), 148–49; *SKS* 4:34. Further references to these translation of these works, identified as *FT* and *R*, appear in the text.

3. Maurice Blanchot, *The Writing of the Disaster*, tr. Ann Smock (Lincoln: University of Nebraska Press, 1995), 47; *L'Écriture du désastre* (Paris: Gallimard/NRF, 1980), 79.

4. Søren Kierkegaard, "The Point of View for My Work as an Author," in *The Point of View*, tr. Howard V. Hong and Edna H. Hong (Princeton: Princeton University Press, 1998), 31.

5. This comment and the following entry from Kierkegaard's *Journal* are cited by the Hongs in the historical introduction to their edition of the text. See *The Concept of Irony, with Continual Reference to Socrates*, tr. Howard V. Hong and Edna H. Hong (Princeton: Princeton University Press, 1989), xiv.

6. See *Concept of Irony*, 98–115, for Kierkegaard's critique of the *Phaedo*, where he describes Socratic irony as a "longing for death" that is insufficiently Christian precisely to the degree that it is excessively intellectual.

7. This reference is provided by Lee Capel in a note to Kierkegaard's use of the same pun within his thesis: "[Hegel] is not fond of a lot of fuss [Ophævelser], and not even Schliermacher's attempt to arrange the dialogues so that one great Idea moves in successive development through them all finds grace in his eyes" (*CI* 243–44, 403). Jean-Luc Nancy has pointed out that a similar instance of the term can be found in Hegel's own language. See his *La remarque spéculative* (Paris: Editions Galilée, 1973), 49.

8. The link between *Fear and Trembling* and *Repetition* is made in a concrete way by Kierkegaard's insistence on the necessity of rethinking historical κίνησις—kinesis, motion, change. In each text, Kierkegaard proposes a name— faith, repetition—for that which would be capable of breaking the "standstill" to which historical actuality is brought by merely formal conceptions of thought. For this reason, in the very last lines of *Fear and Trembling* Kierkegaard ironizes the Eleatic thesis that denies motion (*FT* 123); and then he "repeats" the same gesture in the first lines of *Repetition* (*R* 131). Another way of understanding the relation between these two texts would be to consider them as only slightly veiled but complementary addresses from Søren Kierkegaard to Regina Olsen on the occasion of the second anniversary of their broken engagement, which occurred on October 11, 1841. But the recourse to empirical facts of biography to explain these two texts would always beg the question to the precise extent that both texts understand the actuality of historical existence primarily through the concepts of repetition and faith, rather than the other way around. In this respect, one has a better chance of understanding what must have constituted the historical actuality of Søren Kierkegaard and Regine Olsen by reading *Fear and Trembling* and *Repetition* than of understanding *Fear and Trembling* and *Repetition* by knowing something about the biographies of Søren Kierkegaard and Regine Olsen.

9. Later in the text, de Silentio will put both verbs in the same sentence to emphasize how Abraham is subject to them simultaneously—and to suggest the state of mind in which this double burden may finally result: "It takes [Abraham] seventy years to get what others get in a hurry and enjoy for a long time. Why? Because he is being *tested and tempted*. Is it not madness! [Hvad Andre faae hurtigt nok og længe have Glæde af, det bruger han Aar til; og hvorfor? fordi han prøves og fristes. Er det ikke Afsindighed!]" (*FT* 77; *SKS*, 4:168). See also this passage: "It is an ordeal [Prøvelse], a temptation [Fristelse]. A *temptation*— but what does that mean? [En *Fristelse*; men hvad vil dette sige?]" (*FT* 60; *SKS*, 4:153).

10. This passage in de Silentio's text, which emphasizes the challenge to understanding that this repetition constitutes for thought, is itself a repetition of a similar but nonidentical passage just two pages earlier: "By faith Abraham emigrated from the land of his fathers and became an alien in the promised

land. He left one thing behind, took one thing along: he left behind his worldly understanding, and he took along his faith. Otherwise he certainly would not have emigrated but surely would have considered it unreasonable. By faith he was an alien in the promised land, and there was nothing that reminded him of what he cherished, but everything by its newness tempted [fristede] his soul to sorrowful longing. And yet he was God's chosen one in whom the Lord was well pleased! As a matter of fact, if he had been an exile, banished from God's grace, he could have better understood it—but now it was as if he and his faith were being mocked [nu var det jo som en Spot over ham og over hans Tro]" (*FT* 17; *SKS* 4:113–14).

11. See G. W. F. Hegel, *Enzyklopädie der philosophischen Wissenschaften*, in *Werke in zwanzig Bänden*, E. Moldenhauer and K. M. Michel, eds. (Frankfurt: Suhrkamp, 1969–71), 8:71–75.

12. See G. W. F. Hegel, "Der Geist des Christentums und sein Schicksal," in *Werke in zwanzig Bänden*, 1:274–81. Hegel takes Abraham to represent a preliminary moment in the necessary passage (*Übergang*) from Nature to Spirit, or from Adam to Christ. As such Abraham is both a breaking point (*Trennung*) and an origin (*Stammvater einer Nation*). In other words, he plays the anthropomorphic role of what Constantin Constantius, in *Repetition*, treats under the Hegelian terms *mediation* and *transition*.

13. For a compelling and moving example of this reading of *Fear and Trembling*, see Sylviane Agacinski, "We Are Not Sublime: Love and Sacrifice, Abraham and Ourselves," in Jonathan Rée and Jane Chamberlain, eds., *Kierkegaard: A Critical Reader* (Oxford: Blackwell, 1998). Certain elements of such an interpretation are also legible in Emmanuel Lévinas's remarks about Kierkegaard. Unwilling to challenge the authority granted to Abraham by the Bible, Lévinas finds a subtle but highly effective way around it: he suggests that Abraham's willingness to offer Isaac as a burnt offering is merely a device that allows God to forbid such an act for the future. In the Lévinasian version, it is almost as though Abraham had at first suffered from a temporary hearing or attention disorder. For Lévinas, Abraham seems to be listening or paying attention to God's voice only at the moment it forbids him to lay a hand on Isaac: "the most important moment of the drama is when Abraham pays attention to the voice that returns him to the ethical order by prohibiting human sacrifice. That he would have obeyed the first voice is surprising; what is essential is that he kept enough distance from this obedience to be able to hear the second voice." It is of course precisely that "surprising," or rather, shocking and even *mad*, dimension of Abraham's faith, which Lévinas passes over rather quickly, that Kierkegaard's de Silentio identifies as the essence of Abrahamic faith. See Emmanuel Lévinas, *Noms propres* (Paris: Fata Morgana, 1976), 113 and 108–09, translated as *Proper Names*, tr. Michael B. Smith (Stanford: Stanford University Press, 1996), 76–77 and 74.

14. The paradox, according to de Silentio, is that Abraham can buy historical time only at the price of repeating at each instant the movement of faith, of

enduring the unthinkable temptation, and of raising the knife over Isaac and the future of his meaning: "at every instant that he lives he [Abraham, the one who has faith] buys the opportune time at the highest price [kjøber han hvert Øieblik, han lever, den beleilige Tid til den dyreste Priis], for he does not do even the slightest thing except by virtue of the absurd" (*FT* 40; *SKS* 4:135). The "highest price," the text makes clear in another passage, is that Abraham be compelled "every instant to see the sword hanging over the beloved's head [hvert Øieblik see Sværdet svæve over den Elskedes Hoved]" (*FT* 50; *SKS* 4:144). *Fear and Trembling* joins *Repetition* at precisely this point, since in both repetition and faith, what is being contested is the possibility of a historical "movement" that could occur by means of dialectical "mediation." Thus, in a footnote to his insistence that the movement of faith (i.e., raising the knife over Isaac) must be repeated at every instant, de Silentio adds: "no reflection can produce a movement [ingen Reflexion kan tilveiebringe en Bevægelse]. This is the incessant leap into existence that explains the movement, whereas mediation is a chimera [Dette er det idelige Spring i Tilværelsen, der forklarer Bevægelsen, medens Mediationen er en Chimaire]" (*FT* 42; *SKS* 4:137). The other side of what Abraham must at each instant repeat in order to be Abraham is the evasion thanks to which, at every instant, he could otherwise find rest in the universal—and drop out of his own existence: "At every instant [I ethvert Øieblik], Abraham can stop; he can repent of the whole thing as a spiritual trial; then he can speak out, and everybody will be able to understand him—but then he is no longer Abraham [men da er han ikke Abraham mere]" (*FT* 115; *SKS* 4:202).

15. See, for instance, Problema I: "It is an ordeal, a temptation. A temptation—but what does that mean? As a rule, what tempts a person is something that will hold him back from doing his duty, but here the temptation is the ethical itself, which would hold him back from doing God's will. But what is duty? Duty is simply the expression of God's will. Here the necessity of a new category for the understanding of Abraham becomes apparent [det er en Prøvelse, en Fristelse. En Fristelse; men hvad vil dette sige? Det, der ellers frister et Menneske, er jo det, der vil holde ham tilbage fra at gjøre sin Pligt, men her er Fristelsen selve det Ethiske, der vil holde ham tilbage fra at gjøre Guds Villie. Men hvad er da Pligten? Pligten er jo netop Udtrykket for Guds Villie. Her viser Nødvendigheden sig af en ny Kategori for at forstaae Abraham]" (*FT* 60; *SKS* 4:153). *Temptation* is used in the same sense again in Problema III: "it is an ordeal such that, please note, the ethical is the temptation" (*FT* 115).

16. See Søren Kierkegaard, *Concluding Unscientific Postscript*, tr. Howard V. Hong and Edna H. Hong (Princeton: Princeton University Press, 1992), 267; *SKS* 7: 242–43. Emphasis in the original.

17. The ram appears at several key moments in *Fear and Trembling*, and always in a curious way. It appears twice in the short prefatory material, before the philosophical development of the text in the Problemata. It enters Kierkegaard's text for the first time in the "Exordium," in version 2 of the four versions of Abraham's story retold there, presumably by the anonymous reader who is

thinking more and more about Abraham, though understanding him less and less. "They rode along the road in silence, and Abraham stared continuously and fixedly at the ground until the fourth day, when he looked up and saw Mount Moriah far away, but once again he turned his eyes toward the ground. Silently he arranged the firewood and bound Isaac; silently he drew the knife—then he saw the ram that God had selected. This he sacrificed and went home.—From that day henceforth, Abraham was old; he could not forget that God had ordered him to do this [Fra den Dag af blev Abraham gammel, han kunde ikke glemme, at Gud havde fordret det af ham]. Isaac flourished as before [trivedes som forhen], but Abraham's eyes were darkened, and he saw joy no more" (*FT* 12; *SKS* 4:109). What is missing from Kierkegaard's text here is an overt reference to how Abraham sacrifices the ram *in place of* Isaac, and thus in exchange for Isaac's safe return to his father. Even more surprising is the way the demonstrative pronoun, "this," in the phrase "he could not forget that God had ordered him to do this," does not determine its antecedent with clarity or precision. It could of course be most reasonably understood to refer here to the entire ordeal, test, temptation. But since, after all, Isaac does come home again and "flourish as before," it could also be taken to refer to the ram that God had selected, and which Abraham did in fact put to death and burn there—for no good reason after all. The second time the ram appears is in the "Eulogy on Abraham," where it is mentioned twice: once in passing, and once in a manner that is as unsettling as its earlier appearance in the Exordium: "if irresolute Abraham [hvis Abraham raadvild] had looked around, if he had, before drawing the knife [inden han drog Kniven], happened to spot the ram, if God had allowed him to sacrifice it instead of Isaac—then he would have gone home, everything would have been the same [da var han dragen hjem, Alt var det Samme], he would have had Sarah, he would have kept Isaac, and yet how changed! [han beholdt Isaak, og dog hvor forandret!]" (*FT* 22; *SKS* 4:118). How can de Silentio imagine a contrary-to-fact scenario in which "God had allowed Abraham to sacrifice the ram instead of Isaac," when *in fact* that is exactly what God does allow Abraham to do in Genesis 22:13? Obviously, the only "reasonable" interpretation is that Abraham is not allowed to sacrifice the ram *before* he draws the knife on Isaac and proves his faith. But since the power of "reason" is precisely that which is interrupted at the very moment Abraham does draw his knife, the possibility of maintaining a causal logic of "before" and "after" as the ground of any meaningful relationship is also interrupted for this single instant. And in this instant—the only instant that matters for de Silentio—Kierkegaard's text imagines that the ram is *not* allowed to be sacrificed.

18. The ram appears for the last time in *Fear and Trembling* at the end of the "Preliminary Expectoration." Here, de Silentio makes it abundantly clear that the ram always functions as a defensive strategy that is used to deprive Abraham's faith of the "ordeal"—the test and temptation—that constitutes its most essential element. To the extent that "we see the ram," de Silentio insists, "we forget Abraham" (*FT* 52; *SKS* 4:146).

6. SIGNS OF THE TIMES: NIETZSCHE, DECONSTRUCTION, AND THE TRUTH OF HISTORY

1. A partial list of the many relevant publications, both from the recent past as well as from the so-called culture wars of the 1980s and 90s, might include Anthony T. Kronman, *Education's End: Why Our Colleges and Universities Have Given Up on the Meaning of Life.* (New Haven: Yale University Press, 2007); Andrew Hacker and Claudia C. Dreifus, *Higher Education? How Colleges Are Wasting Our Money and Failing Our Kids—And What We Can Do About It* (New York: Times Books, 2010); Mark C. Taylor, *Crisis on Campus: A Bold Plan for Reforming Our Colleges and Universities* (New York: Knopf, 2010); Richard H. Hersh and John Merrow, eds., *Declining by Degrees: Higher Education at Risk* (New York: Palgrave, 2005); Drew Gilpin Faust, "The University's Crisis of Purpose," *New York Times*, September 6, 2009; Martha C. Nussbaum, *Not for Profit: Why Democracy Needs the Humanities* (Princeton: Princeton University Press, 2010); Allan Bloom, *The Closing of the American Mind* (New York: Simon and Shuster, 1987); Dinesh D'Souza, *Illiberal Education: The Politics of Race and Sex on Campus* (New York: Free Press, 1991); Donald Kagen, "The Role of the West," *Yale Alumni Magazine*, November 1990; Roger Kimball, *Tenured Radicals: How Politics Has Corrupted Higher Education* (New York: Harper and Row, 1990); and David Lehman, *Signs of the Times: Deconstruction and the Fall of Paul de Man* (New York: Poseidon Press, 1991). *Signs of the Times* will be examined in some detail in this chapter. Further references to the book, identified as *ST*, will appear in the text.

2. See section 6 of Friedrich Nietzsche, *On the Genealogy of Morals*, tr. Douglas Smith (Oxford: Oxford University Press, 1996), 7–8. Nietzsche's own considerations of the value of higher education—which are neither simple nor straightforward—can be found in *On the Future of Our Educational Institutions*, in *The Complete Works of Friedrich Nietzsche*, tr. J. M. Kennedy (New York: Russell and Russell, 1964), vol. 3.

3. Friedrich Nietzsche, *Twilight of the Idols*, tr. R. J. Hollingdale (London: Penguin, 1968), 21.

4. Paul de Man, "The Rhetoric of Persuasion," *Allegories of Reading* (New Haven: Yale University Press, 1979), 119–131. Further references to this work, identified as *AR*, appear in the text.

5. Søren Kierkegaard, *Fear and Trembling/Repetition*, tr. Howard V. and Edna H. Hong (Princeton: Princeton University Press, 1983), 27; emphasis added.

6. One of the necessary effects of such a definition would be the interrogation and testing of the ways such terms as *truth* and *history* have been thus far understood by tradition, and to what extent such traditional modes of understanding remain adequate to their own historical production and effects.

7. In itself, then, *Signs of the Times* has little or nothing whatsoever to recommend it; its own "value" is therefore of extremely limited proportions. Lehman's book, and others like it, can be of interest to us only for what they might *occasion*. Such writings are aptly described by what Kierkegaard said about all such "occa-

sions": "The occasion, then, is nothing in and by itself and is something only in relation to that which it occasions, and in relation to that it is actually nothing." For both Nietzsche and Kierkegaard, it is the "nothing" of the occasion that occasions the critical analyses which constitute the event of their own writing (and the irony of that writing). Søren Kierkegaard, *Either/Or*, tr. Howard V. Hong and Edna H. Hong (Princeton: Princeton University Press, 1987), 1:238.

8. Friedrich Nietzsche, section 361 of *The Gay Science*, tr. Walter Kaufmann (New York: Vintage, 1974), 316–17; *Die Fröhliche Wissenschaft*, in *Werke in drei Bänden*, ed. Karl Schlecta (Munich: Carl Hanser, 1981), 2:234–35. Further references to the translation, identified as *GS*, appear in the text. I have often modified the translations provided by this as well as by other English-language editions cited in this chapter. This fragment is referred to, described, and annotated in an exemplary way by Jacques Derrida in *Éperons: Les Styles de Nietzsche*, tr. Barbara Harlow (Chicago: University of Chicago Press, 1978), 66–71. Other pertinent discussions of the fragment can be found in Pierre Klossowski, "Nietzsche, le polythéisme et la parodie," *Un si funeste désir* (Paris: Gallimard, 1963), 216–218; and in Gilles Deleuze, "Plato and the Simulacrum," *The Logic of Sense*, ed. Constantin V. Boundas (New York: Columbia University Press, 1990), 253–65.

9. For a consideration of the relation of Nietzsche to the Western metaphysical tradition, see Martin Heidegger's four-volume study, *Nietzsche*, tr. David Farrell Krell (New York: Harper and Row, 1991). *Verstellung*, or dissimulation, is of course another term for *irony* within the philosophical tradition. Whether knowingly or not, Nietzsche's fragment reinscribes itself within the romantic reception of Socratic irony as it was carried out by both Schlegel and Kierkegaard in their writings. One of Schlegel's best-known fragments, *Lyceum Fragment* 108, begins this way: "Die Socratische Ironie ist die einzige durchaus unwillkürliche, and doch durchaus besonnene Verstellung." (Socratic irony is the only entirely involuntary, and yet entirely deliberate, dissimulation.) See *Friedrich Schlegel: Kritische Ausgabe seiner Werke*, ed. Ernst Behler, with Jean-Jacques Anstett and Hans Eichner (Munich: Ferdinand Schöningh, 1958–), 2:160; *Philosophical Fragments*, tr. Peter Firchow (Minneapolis: University of Minnesota Press, 1991), 13.

10. De Man also wrote a number of articles for a Flemish newspaper, as well as for other publications, during the same period. The most complete documentation to date on this question is provided by Werner Hamacher, Neil Hertz, and Thomas Keenan, eds., *Wartime Journalism, 1939–1943* (Lincoln: University of Nebraska Press, 1989). To appreciate the misogynistic aspects of Nazi ideology, one need only consult the contemporary text by Alfred Rosenberg, *The Myth of the Twentieth Century* (Newport Beach: Noontide Press, 1993). For a concise overview, see Rita Thalmann's chapter entitled "L'Ordre Masculin" in her *Être femme sous le troisième Reich* (Paris: Robert Laffont, 1982).

11. Stéphane Mallarmé, *La Musique et les letttres*, in *Oeuvres complètes*, ed. Bertrand Marchal (Paris: Gallimard, 2003), 2:71–72. Further references to this work, identified as *ML*, appear in the text. The translations are my own.

12. Max Nordau, *Degeneration*, tr. George L. Mosse (New York: Howard Fertig, 1968). A typical sentence: "It is precisely in France that the craziest fashions in art and literature would necessarily arise . . . precisely there that the morbid exhaustion of which we have spoken became for the first time sufficiently distinct to consciousness to allow a special name to be coined for it, namely, the designation of *fin-de-siècle*" (43). What is of interest from the critical perspective of a Mallarmé or a Nietzsche, as opposed to the polemical stance of a Nordau, is neither simply coining (*erfinden*) names nor encouraging and maintaining their unquestioned circulation. Rather, it is the unremitting labor of verifying to what extent such "names" are adequate, in given situations, to the distinctions of consciousness, knowledge, and behavior that they are supposed to reflect.

13. A more extended selection of the French reads: "Tel un avis; et, incriminer de tout dommage ceci uniquement qu'il y ait des écrivains à l'écart tenant, ou pas, pour le vers libre, me captive, surtout par l'ingéniosité. Près, eux se réservent, ou loin, comme pour une occasion, ils offensent le fait divers: que dérobent-ils, toujours jettent-ils ainsi du discrédit, moins qu'une bombe, sur ce que de mieux, indisputablement et à grands frais, fournit une capitale comme rédaction courante de ses apothéoses." Given other pronouncements by Mallarmé, it is possible that he actually meant to say that writing is *more* effective than bombing: *mieux* qu'une bombe. For example, in an interview of May 27, 1894 given to *Le Soir*, he said, "And it is my opinion that there is no arm more effective than literature itself"; *Correspondance*, ed. Henri Mondor and Lloyd James Austin (Paris: Gallimard, 1981), 6:287; my translation. See also the statement quoted by Jean-Paul Sartre, "the only true bomb is a poem," in *Mallarmé: La Lucidité et sa face d'ombre* (Paris: Gallimard, 1986), 157. Maurice Blanchot quotes the same statement in *The Writing of the Disaster*, tr. Ann Smock (Lincoln: University of Nebraska Press, 1995), 7.

14. Martin Heidegger, *What Is a Thing?* tr. W. B. Barton, Jr. and Vera Deutsch (Chicago: Henry Regnery, 1967), 43; *Die Frage nach dem Ding* (Tübingen: Max Niemeyer, 1987), 33. Further references appear in the text, identified as *WT* and *FD*, respectively.

15. See Friedrich Nietzsche, "On the Vision and the Riddle" and "The Convalescent," in part 3 of *Thus Spoke Zarathustra*, tr. Walter Kaufmann (New York: Penguin, 1966). The difficulty of coming to terms with Nietzsche's thought of the eternal return—a thinking of history as the gateway under which past and future collide with and affront each other, *sie stossen sich gerade vor den Kopf*—without turning it into a mere platitude is aptly rendered by Martin Heidegger's commentary on Zarathustra's animals, the eagle and the serpent. It is much easier, according to Heidegger, to repeat the knowledge of the eternal return in mere prattle—by mindlessly deriding or celebrating it—than to think it: "Precisely this knowledge is the weightiest and most difficult; all too easily it flies off or slithers away in evasions and equivocations, in pure foolishness." See Heidegger, *Nietzsche*, ed. David Farrell Krell, 2:47–48; *Nietzsche* (Pfullingen: Neske, 1961), 1:301.

16. The problem of the actor or artist and the dissimulation proper to him is also the problem of the aesthetic as such, and it leads from this fragment by Nietzsche directly back to Schiller and his concept of the aesthetic as a possible mediation between nature and history. Thus, it is not without interest to note the way Schiller will himself refer to women at a key moment in his essay "On Naïve and Sentimental Poetry": "The feminine need to please strives after nothing so much as the *appearance of being naïve* [Nach nichts ringt die weibliche Gefallensucht so sehr als nach dem *Schein des Naiven*]; proof enough, if one had no other, that the greatest power of the sex depends on this property [daß die größte Macht des Geschlechts auf dieser Eigenschaft beruhet]." What is natural or proper—*eigen*—to woman, and what grants her effective power, *Macht*, according to Schiller, is her need not for nature but for *Schein*—the aesthetic attribute par excellence as it is articulated throughout his *Letters on the Aesthetic Education of Man*. Further on in this fragment, Nietzsche will not fail to address the concept of *Schein*, though in a manner that is much closer to Schlegel and his irony than to Schiller and his unpardonable "good-naturedness." See Friedrich Schiller, "Über Naïve und Sentimentalische Dichtung," *Sämtliche Werke* (Munich: Carl Hanser, 1980), 5:705; "On Naive and Sentimental Poetry," *Friedrich Schiller: Essays*, ed. Walter Hinderer and Daniel O. Dahlstrom (New York: International Publishing Group, 2005), 190.

17. The German reads: "die Lust an der Verstellung als Macht herausbrechend den sogenannten 'Charakter' beiseite scheibend, überflutend, mitunter auslöschend." Fragment 316, in *Werke in drei Bänden*, 2:234.

18. On the status of rhetorical figures within the philosophical argument of Nietzsche's text, see Andrzej Warminski, "Towards a Fabulous Reading," *Graduate Faculty Philosophy Journal* 15, no. 2 (1991), 93–120. On rhetorical figures within philosophical argument in general, see Jacques Derrida, "La Mythologie blanche," *Marges de la philosophie* (Paris: Minuit, 1972), 247–324.

19. The expression, "to turn one's coat to the wind," is not, to my knowledge, an idiomatic equivalent in English for the concept of "adaptability," and this makes the task of commentary and exegesis even more challenging in this instance. Translating the German into something like "to trim one's sails to the wind," of course, would be more recognizable, but for that very reason less demonstrative from a philosophical and rhetorical point of view. *Translation*, then, would be another name for the radical dissimulation of Nietzschean appearance and its infinite potential to become literalized in aberrant ways.

20. Nietzsche says, in fact, that the figure of the coat becomes *almost* a coat, *fast zum Mantel werdend*; the figural potential to dissimulate is thus never totally erased or neutralized by a final, definitive, and truly literal understanding here, although this critical insight is in turn blurred by the text's own straightforward naming of "Jews" and "women" at its conclusion. Therefore, the example of the coat—which, as pertaining directly and irreducibly to language, is a genuinely rhetorical example—is not, in the end, exactly the same as the example of the Jews and women, which are not strictly speaking, or exclusively, rhetorical

326 Notes to pages 175–80

figures. Between the rhetoric and the anthropology of the fragment, then, there is all the same the slightest gap—a gap of similarity, of which Nietzsche says elsewhere: "Precisely between what is most similar, illusion lies most beautifully; for the smallest gap is the most difficult to bridge." See "The Convalescent," in part 3 of *Thus Spoke Zarathustra*, 217.

21. See the last chapter of *Ecce Homo*, "Why I Am a Destiny," in *The Anti-Christ, Ecce Homo, Twilight of the Idols, and Other Writings*, ed. Aaron Ridley and Judith Norman. (Cambridge: Cambridge University Press, 2005), 144. Nietzsche also refers to himself in this section as a *Hanswurst*, an idiomatic term which is difficult to translate into English. This dynamite that is Nietzsche's text explodes the way a joker or a clown interrupts and tears asunder whatever happens to be taking place when he is allowed to enter the scene. Friedrich Schlegel, in a similar vein, hit on another term for characterizing the interruptive force of such ironic interventions. In texts that are thoroughly infused with irony, Schlegel said, "there lives a real transcendental *buffoonery*. Their interior is permeated by a mood that surveys everything and rises infinitely above all limitations, even above its own art, virtue, or genius; and their exterior is marked by the histrionic style of an ordinary good Italian *buffo*." Friedrich Schlegel, *Dialogue on Poetry and Literary Aphorisms*, ed. Ernst Behler and Roman Struc (University Park and London: Pennsylvania State University Press, 1968), 126.

7. *DEATH IN VENICE*: IRONY, DETACHMENT, AND THE AESTHETIC STATE

1. Thomas Mann,"Irony and Radicalism," in *Reflections of an Unpolitical Man*, tr. Walter D. Morris (New York: Ungar, 1983), 429; "Ironie und Radikalismus," in *Betrachtungen eines Unpolitischen*, in *Gesammelte Werke in Zwolf Bänden* (Oldenburg: S. Fischer Verlag, 1960), 12:582. Further references to "Irony and Radicalism" appear in the text, identified as "IR," *RUM*. Further references to the *Gesammelte Werke* are identified as *GW*.

2. Thomas Mann, *Joseph and His Brothers*, tr. John E. Woods (New York: Alfred A. Knopf, 205), 79; *Joseph und seine Bruder*, in *GW* 4:104. Further references to the translation appear in the text, identified as *Joseph*.

3. The interpretation of Abraham that is offered here to Jacob by his son Joseph was anticipated—and rejected—by the pseudonymous "author" of *Fear and Trembling*, Johannes de Silentio. "But just suppose," de Silentio proposes, "that someone listening to Abraham's story is a man who suffers from sleeplessness—then the most terrifying, the most profound, tragic, and comic misunderstanding is very close at hand. He goes home, he wants to do just as Abraham did, for the son, after all, is the best. If the preacher found out about it, he perhaps would go to the man, and he would muster all his ecclesiastical dignity and shout, 'You despicable man, you scum of society, what devil has so possessed you that you want to murder your son'"; Søren Kierkegaard, *Fear and Trembling and Repetition*, tr. Howard V. Hong and Edna H. Hong (Princeton: Princeton

University Press, 1983), 28. By splitting the interpretation of Abraham's faith between two types of "truth"—Jacob's suspicion that he lacks Abraham's faith, and Joseph's assurance that such faith is no longer relevant—Thomas Mann mobilizes an "alternative" that is patently missing from Kierkegaard's text. For Kierkegaard the alternative, if there is one, is not between two types of truth: it is between historical actuality—only that which happens in a historical mode, that is, the repetition of Abraham's faith, is true—and that evasion of historical reality that merely pretends to take the true challenge Abraham's story seriously.

4. An early novella by Mann, *Tonio Kröger*, contains at its center a virtual lesson on how ironic detachment can be defined and described in these terms. See Thomas Mann, chapter 4 of *Tonio Kröger*, in *Death in Venice and Other Tales*, tr. Joachim Neugroschel (New York: Penguin, 1998), esp. 186–95; *Tonio Kröger*, in *GW* 8:295–305.

5. Thomas Mann, "The Art of the Novel," in *The Creative Vision*, ed. Haskell M. Block and Herman Salinger. (Gloucester, Mass.: Peter Smith, 1968), 88; "Die Kunst des Romans," in *GW* 10:353.

6. Thomas Mann, "The Artist and Society," in *The Creative Vision*, 100; "Der Künstler und die Gesellschaft," in *GW* 10:394. Further references to the translation appear in the text, identified as "Artist," *CV*.

7. Tellingly enough, when Mann revised his talk for publication in Germany, he expanded this passage a bit, making its comments about social consciousness considerably harsher than the comments written for the American audience at Princeton. For the German version, he also spelled out how irony is implicated in what he now qualified as the artist's "impatient" relation to social reality: "It is the position the intellectual occupies in opposition to an innate human propensity to be stubborn, stupid, and rotten that has always guided the fate of the literary author, and that has had the furthest-reaching effects on his attitude toward life [Es ist die Stellung des geistigen Menschen gegen ein obstinates, dumm-schlechtes Menschenwesen]. . . . Wherever knowledge and form [Erkenntnis und Form] are missing, there is stupidity, the quotidian stupidity of humanity [da ist Dummheit, die alltägliche Menschendummheit], which by the same token expresses itself as a lack of both form and knowledge [die sich zugleich als Form- und als Erkenntnislosigkeit äußert]—and the literary writer wouldn't be able to say which of the two is more annoying for him. Here also, if anywhere, lies the ground for that intellectual—and I would say even moral— feeling of superiority [*Überlegenheitsgefühl*] over bourgeois society that the artist develops early on and above all through a practice of self-ironization [Selbstironie]" (my translation; *GW* 10: 391–92).

8. Friedrich Schlegel, "Talk on Mythology," in *Dialogue on Poetry*, tr. Ernst Behler and Roman Struc (University Park: Pennsylvania State University Press, 1968), 86.

9. Thomas Mann, *Death in Venice*, ed. Naomi Ritter, tr. David Luke (Boston: Bedford Books, 1998); *Der Tod in Venedig*, in *GW*, vol. 8. Further references

to this translation appear in the text, identified as *DV*. I have often modified the translations provided by this as well as by other English-language editions cited in this chapter. Numerous commentators have noted how chapter 2 of the novella retraces Aschenbach's literary career and attributes to his authorship a number of literary and critical works that Thomas Mann himself either wrote or planned to write. *Death in Venice* is in this respect a *mise en abyme* of the relationship between referential author and fictional character. In this case, the author becomes a character in the fiction he is writing, while the character becomes the author of the author's other writings. By crossing from fictional to referential context and back again, Mann's technique unsettles the one-sidedly "fictitious" dimension that characterizes, at least on the surface, André Gide's use of *mise en abyme* in such texts as *Paludes* and *Les Faux-Monnayeurs*. *Death in Venice* is therefore not only "about" the artist and society; it is itself an example of the uneasy relationship between art and reality that conditions the identity of every real artist.

10. Not much is told regarding Aschenbach's social existence in Munich. However, there is no indication that the Munich of *Death in Venice* is anything like the Munich portrayed in "Gladius Dei," another of Mann's texts where the relation between art and society is thematized and interrogated. In "Gladius Dei," it is the window of a Fine Arts boutique, *Kunstmagasin, Schönheitsgeschäft*, that allows the interior world of the aesthetic to communicate with and pass into the external world of social and economic reality. In *Death in Venice*, in a city of glass and water, the reflective surfaces that allow for light to pass across and therefore through all such borderlines are everywhere to be found.

11. In fact, the question of what exactly constitutes the main "subject" of the *Phaedrus* itself has a rather complex and unresolved history. Perhaps the philosophical concept of the aesthetic (beauty) as a means to a particular kind of knowledge is itself a mere example of the larger and more troublesome question of how any knowledge is possible at all. In this case, the seductions associated with beauty and beautiful bodies would have to be inscribed within a more general problematic concerning nonaesthetic and thus nonsensuous seductions of the mind. Hence the question of rhetoric that is also treated by the *Phaedrus*. One of the most dangerous seductions of the mind, Socrates is trying hard to teach Phaedrus, is the one that results from the use of *writing* as opposed to *speech*. For a reading of the *Phaedrus* occasioned by these questions, see Jacques Derrida, "La Pharmacie de Platon," in *La Dissémination* (Paris: Seuil, 1972); "Plato's Pharmacy," in *Dissemination*, tr. Barbara Johnson (Chicago: University of Chicago Press, 1981).

12. The reference to the candlesticks, like the other references to Schiller mentioned here, can be found in chapter 2 (*DV* 30; *GW* 8:452). The "same" candlesticks that Aschenbach uses to write also appear in a description of Schiller's study at the beginning of "Schwere Stunde" (*GW* 8:372); "Harsh Hour," in *Death in Venice and Other Tales*, tr. Joachim Neugroschel (New York: Penguin, 1998), 244.

13. See the extensive and well-documented introduction to Friedrich Schiller, *On the Aesthetic Education of Man*, ed. and tr. Elizabeth M. Wilkinson and L. A. Willoughby (Oxford: Clarendon Press, 1982), esp. lxviii–lxxiii. Wilkinson and Willoughby refer there to Schiller's "addiction to the figure of antithesis" (*Aesthetic Education*, xxix), while Aschenbach's treatise, *Intellect and Art*, is characterized by its "antithetical eloquence" (*DV* 28). Another conspicuous instance of the chiasmic principle underlying the aesthetic theory that Aschenbach inherits from Schiller furnishes the occasion for Aschenbach to convert Tadzio's physical "beauty" into the inner "spirit" of his well-wrought prose. The theory of chiasmus is here illustrated by the use of chiasmi within the narrator's own prose: "The writer's joy is the *thought* that can become wholly *emotion*, the *emotion* that can wholly become *thought*. At that time the solitary Aschenbach took possession and control of just such a pulsating *thought*, just such a precise *emotion*: namely that *nature* trembles with rapture when the *spirit* bows in homage before *beauty*. He suddenly desired to *write* . . . from Tadzio's *beauty* he gave form to his brief essay—that page and a half of exquisite *prose*" (*DV* 62, emphases added; *GW* 8:492).

14. No feature of the novella has proven to be more of an interpretative crux than the status of its narrator. In particular, the question of the narrator's relationship to both the character in the story, Gustav von Aschenbach, and the author of the story, Thomas Mann, functions as the litmus test for whether and to what extent *Death in Venice* is to be considered an ironic text. For a useful discussion of the problem as well as the relevant bibliography, see Dorrit Cohn, "The Second Author of 'Der Tod in Venedig,'" in Benjamin Bennett, Anton Kas, and William J. Lillyman, eds., *Probleme der Moderne* (Tübingen: Max Niemeyer Verlag, 1983), 223–45. Cohn's self-professed assumption "that *Tod in Venedig* is a flawless work—flawless in the sense that it perfectly achieves its author's intentions" (242) leads her to a very different reading of the text's irony than the one offered here.

15. As soon as Kant introduced the principle of "disinterest"—*ohne alles Interesse*—to characterize aesthetic reflective judgments of taste, he also opened the way to a possible transgression of the line that should separate the genuinely human from a mere imitation of it. The coherence of Schiller's aesthetic theory depends entirely on being able to maintain that line without disruption. By drawing attention to the way Tadzio resembles the *Dornauszieher*, or Spinario, *Death in Venice* also relates itself directly back to Heinrich von Kleist's well-known text *Über das Marionettentheater*. In the middle episode of *Marionettentheater*, a fifteen-year-old boy catches sight of himself in a mirror and is reminded of a copy of the Spinario he has just seen in Paris—where he was visiting in the company of an adult male. His newly acquired self-consciousness is accompanied by a simultaneous loss of his natural gracefulness. Kleist's text is, like Mann's, an allegorical critical analysis of romantic aesthetic theory. *Death in Venice* redoes Kleist's version from the point of view of the adult observer—the artist/educator—rather than of the adolescent. Kleist's text emphasizes the

instability that is introduced when humans try to measure themselves against works of art—puppets, statues, fencing bears—and come up short. Mann's text seems to go one step further and ask what happens when a human being is turned into a statue through a "successful" process of aesthetification. Both texts can be taken to ironize key aspects of Schiller's ideal of aesthetic education. What remains to be seen, however, is the degree to which the ironic standpoint of such texts can itself become subject to irony. For a reading of Kleist's text that would suggest that, at least on the level of narrative voice, Kleist's irony is not the same as Thomas Mann's irony, see Paul de Man, "Aesthetic Formalization: Kleist's *Über das Marionettentheater*," in *The Rhetoric of Romanticism* (New York: Columbia University Press, 1984).

16. The structure is not unique to *Death in Venice*, moreover, since it can also be seen to inform Mann's novel *Doctor Faustus*. The change in perspective from the detached and anonymous narrator in *Death in Venice* to the sympathetic and highly personalized narrator of *Doctor Faustus*, Serenus Zeitblom, cannot conceal the same hermeneutic pattern that is operative in both fictions. It would be of considerable interest to examine these two works—both of which serve to interrogate a supposedly romantic conception of the aesthetic and its potential to mediate between *Geist* and *Leben*—from a historical and political point of view. Whereas *Death in Venice* can only hint at the political threat that inheres in all aesthetic ideologies by inventing an allegorical epidemic of cholera that devastates the aesthetic, financial, and political economy of Venice, *Doctor Faustus* is able to return to the same issues from the far side of World War I, the Nazizeit, and World War II. What is at stake in and is played out by both of these literary texts is the possible recovery of understanding and self-understanding in the wake of historical and political disasters in which philosophical (and therefore aesthetic) thought is also implicated.

17. See especially *Lyceum Fragment* 42: "Philosophy is the true home of irony, which might be defined as logical beauty. . . . In this respect, poetry alone can rise to the height of philosophy, since it is not, as oratory, based upon ironic passages. There are ancient and modern poems that breathe, in their entirety and in every detail, the divine breath of irony. In such poems there lives a real transcendental *buffoonery*. Their interior is permeated by a mood that surveys everything and rises infinitely above all limitations, even above its own art, virtue, or genius; and their exterior form is marked by the histrionic style of an ordinary good Italian *buffo*." In Friedrich Schlegel, *Dialogue on Poetry and Literary Aphorisms*, ed. Ernst Behler and Roman Struc (University Park and London: Pennsylvania State University Press, 1968), 126. For a reading of this fragment in the context of a sustained critical analysis of romantic irony, see Paul de Man's lecture "The Concept of Irony," in *Aesthetic Ideology*, ed. Andrzej Warminski (Minneapolis: University of Minnesota Press, 1996), 177.

18. "Détaché de tout, y compris de son détachement"; Maurice Blanchot, *L'Écriture du désastre* (Paris: NRF/Gallimard, 1980), 25; *The Writing of the Disaster*, tr. Ann Smock (Lincoln: University of Nebraska Press, 1995), 12. Blanchot

has some interesting remarks of his own about Thomas Mann and his irony in "La Voix narrative," *L'Entretien infini* (Paris: Gallimard, 1969), esp. 560–62.

1. Maurice Blanchot, "Comment la littérature est-elle possible?" *Faux Pas* (Paris: Gallimard, 1943 ; 1971); Jean Paulhan, *Les Fleurs de Tarbes, ou, La Terreur dans les lettres*, ed. Jean-Claude Zylberstein (Paris: Gallimard, 1941; 1990).

2. The most economical indication of the way politics, philosophy, and literature are inextricably conjoined for Schlegel is no doubt the terse affirmation, "The French Revolution, Fichte's *Theory of Knowledge*, and Goethe's *Wilhelm Meister* are the three greatest tendencies of the age." Friedrich Schlegel, *Athenaeum Fragment* 216, in *Dialogue on Poetry and Literary Aphorisms*, tr. Ernst Behler and Roman Struc (University Park: Pennsylvania State University Press, 1968), 143. For Blanchot's own reference to this fragment by Schlegel, see Maurice Blanchot, "L'Athenaeum," in *L'Entretien Infini* (Paris: Gallimard, 1969), 521.

3. Indispensable in this regard is the book by Philippe Lacoue-Labarthe and Jean-Luc Nancy, *The Literary Absolute: The Theory of Literature in German Romanticism*, tr. Philip Barnard and Cheryl Lester (Albany: SUNY Press, 1988). To an important degree, this is also the path followed by Simon Critchley in his treatment of Blanchot together with Schlegel in his book, *Very Little . . . Almost Nothing: Death, Philosophy, Literature*. (London and New York: Routledge, 1997). Since Critchley makes use of Blanchot's essay "Comment la littérature est-elle possible?" he refers in passing to *The Flowers of Tarbes*, without, however, pursuing the extent to which Paulhan's text contributes to an understanding of Blanchot with Schlegel—that is, an understanding of the reception and transformation of German romanticism by certain twentieth-century French writers.

4. The texts by Paul de Man referred to are, respectively, *Allegories of Reading: Figural Language in Rousseau, Nietzsche, Rilke, and Proust* (New Haven: Yale University Press, 1979), 301; *Aesthetic Ideology*, ed. Andrzej Warminski (Minneapolis: University of Minnesota Press, 1996), 179, 184; and *Critical Writings, 1953–1978*, ed. Lindsay Waters (Minneapolis: University of Minnesota Press, 1989), lxxiii.

5. An obvious omission from this list is the name Jacques Derrida. What is the relation of the writings of Derrida to all these issues and all these proper names? A straightforward account of irony in Derrida would be overly cumbersome and finally inconclusive. Derrida's own remarks about irony, responsibility, and seriousness in response to Richard Rorty would constitute one possible point of departure for such a question. As Derrida himself says there, "There is irony and there is something else." To the extent that one could say that irony always speaks more than one language, one could say that in Schlegel, Kierkegaard, Nietzsche, Mann, Paulhan, Blanchot, de Man, and Coetzee as well, there is irony and there is "something else." Perhaps the most economical way

to name the "something else" in all these writers would be to call it *the irony of irony*. See Jacques Derrida, "Remarks on Deconstruction and Pragmatism," in Chantal Mouffe, ed., *Deconstruction and Pragmatism* (London and New York: Routledge, 1996), 77–88.

6. The quotation is from the first chapter of the first part of *Les Fleurs de Tarbes*, in a sub-section entitled "Défaut de la pensée critique" (A shortfall of critical thinking, a falling-short of critical thought), 33. Further references to the book, identified as *Fleurs*, appear in the text. All translations into English are my own. Since the first version of this chapter was published, a translation has appeared: Jean Paulhan, *The Flowers of Tarbes, or, Terror in Literature*, tr. Michael Syrotinski (Urbana: University of Illinois Press, 2006). For the sake of convenience, I will also provide references to pages of the translation (identified as *Flowers*) that correspond to my citations from Paulhan. For this passage in the translation, see *Flowers*, 5.

7. As mentioned in n. 6, *Les Fleurs de Tarbes* appeared in English translation only in 2006, though without the collateral material ("Notes et documents" and "Dossier") that accompanies the French edition. For an excellent sustained study of Paulhan, see Michael Syrotinski, *Defying Gravity: Jean Paulhan's Interventions* (Albany: SUNY Press, 1998).

8. "There are some *solutions* stranger than the problems. . . . In truth, it seems that we have limited ourselves to substituting a new paradox for the old one, and to displacing the difficulty more than resolving it." Jean Paulhan, "La Demoiselle aux miroirs," in *Oeuvres complètes* (Paris: Cercle du Livre Précieux, 1966), 2:171; emphasis added. Further references to *Oeuvres complètes* are identified as *OC*. An English translation of this text is now available; see "Young Lady with Mirrors," in Jean Paulhan, *On Poetry and Politics*, ed. Jennifer Bajorek and Eric Trudel, tr. Jennifer Bajorek, Charlotte Mandel, and Eric Trudel (Urbana: University of Illinois Press, 2008), 57.

9. The French text reads: "Je préfère, devant l'agression, rétorquer que des contemporains ne savent pas lire—." Stéphane Mallarmé, "Le Mystère dans les Lettres," in *Oeuvres complètes*, ed. Bertrand Marchal (Paris: Gallimard, 2003), 2:234. An argument could also be made that a similar rebuttal of the dominant critical response, or resistance, to the mystery in literature, or what both Mallarmé and Paulhan call "letters," is what motivates Friedrich Schlegel's curious essay "On Incomprehensibility," available in *Friedrich Schlegel's Lucinde and the Fragments*, tr. Peter Firchow (Minneapolis: University of Minnesota Press, 1971). Clearly, de Man's essay "The Resistance to Theory" puts itself in the same constellation of texts when it states the problem in somewhat more technical language: "The resistance to theory is therefore a resistance to language itself or to the possibility that language contains factors or functions that cannot be reduced to intuition. But we seem to assume all too readily that, when we refer to something called 'language,' we know what it is we are talking about, although there is probably no word to be found in the language that is as over-determined, self-evasive, disfigured and disfiguring as 'language.'" Paul de Man,

The Resistance to Theory (Minneapolis: University of Minnesota Press, 1986), 12–13.

10. "'What is literature?'—a childish question, but one that an entire life is spent avoiding" (*Fleurs*, 38; *Flowers*, 8). One of the ways the question has been evaded most effectively since Paulhan asked it in this form has been by conveniently replacing the difficulties of his text by the very clear and understandable response to the same question that was soon afterwards proposed by Jean-Paul Sartre. For the lack of critical reception and commentary devoted to *The Flowers of Tarbes*, and the near-total invisibility that has descended upon its inaugural formulation, "What is literature?" is neatly reflected in inverted manner by the universal familiarity with Sartre's *What Is Literature?* published in 1948, or a mere seven years after Paulhan's text.

11. "One judges less the work than the writer, less the writer than the man. . . . Criticism thus acquires a righteous violence, which it hardly even imagined before. For it is so much easier, or at least more pleasant, to rage against a person than against a book. Moreover, it is more effective; since with the person it becomes possible to capture fifty books at their very source" (*Fleurs*, 60–61; *Flowers*, 23).

12. *The Flowers of Tarbes* first appeared in several installments of the *Nouvelle Revue Française* between June and October of 1936, and it was reprinted in one volume in 1941. As one recent critic puts it, the extension of Paulhan's term *terror* from rhetoric to politics is overdetermined from the start: "[T]his invocation of the 1793–94 revolutionary period pointed to a secondary discourse of connotation whose force increased over the five years between the two versions of the essays." See Steven Ungar, *Scandal and Aftereffect: Blanchot and France since 1930* (Minneapolis: University of Minnesota Press, 1995), 117, 118. To the extent that there can be no "flower," or trope, without a specifically referential vector, or supplement, included along with it, the "exceptional" nature of the supplementary force Paulhan's use of the word *terror* was to achieve in fact under Nazi occupation should be understood as exemplary of every text, all the time and anywhere. What is truly exceptional about *The Flowers of Tarbes* is the way this tropological force is theorized and accounted for there.

13. G. W. F. Hegel, "Die absolut Freiheit und der Schrecken" (Absolute Freedom and Terror), *Phänomenologie des Geistes*, in *Werke in zwanzig Bänden* (Frankfurt: Suhrkamp, 1970), 3:431–41, esp. 436; *Hegel's Phenomenology of Spirit*, tr. A.V. Miller (Oxford: Oxford University Press, 1977), 355–65, esp. 360. The convergence of Hegel and Paulhan around the question of the Terror, self-conscious subjectivity, and language also helps to situate Blanchot's own reflections on the relation between literature, death, and terror in his essay "La Littérature et le droit à la mort," in *La Part du feu* (Paris: Gallimard, 1949).

14. At issue here is the tension between figuration and disfiguration that is involved in the constitution as well as the operation of all tropological systems. Some helpful treatments of this tension and its consequences include Jacques Derrida, "La Mythologie blanche," *Marges de la philosophie* (Paris: Editions de

Minuit, 1972); Paul de Man, "Autobiography as De-facement," *The Rhetoric of Romanticism* (New York: Columbia University Press, 1984); and Andrzej Warminski, "Prefatory Postscript," *Readings in Interpretation* (Minneapolis: University of Minnesota Press, 1987).

15. See also the passage in which Paulhan recognizes the radical impossibility of an absolute metalanguage: "[I]t is as though there were no *pure* observation of language, but rather a play of reflections and mirrors that constantly displayed in this language (and in literature, too) the very reflection of the movement through which we approach it" (*Fleurs*, 163; *Flowers*, 91).

16. Jean Paulhan, "La Rhétorique renaît de ses cendres," in *OC* 2:160; emphasis added. Further citations of this work appear in the text, identified as "La Rhétorique." An English translation of this text now exists; see "Rhetoric Rises from Its Ashes," in Paulhan, *On Poetry and Politics*, 48. Further citations of the translation appear in the text, identified as "Rhetoric," *PP*.

17. "And so, if the Terror is not only the state into which Rhetoric propels us, but also the state that Rhetoric announces to us ahead of time, this is no doubt also because the Terror, even more than its result or effect, is Rhetoric's *intention*. . . . The rhetorician is able to *anticipate* the next move (as we say in a chess game) better than the terrorist. In short, the real merit of Rhetoric might be this: it *indulges itself* in the Terror [c'est qu'elle *se permet* la Terreur]" ("La Rhétorique," *OC* 2:165–66; "Rhetoric," *PP* 54–55; emphasis added).

18. For a discussion of Paulhan's grammatical model and the limits of its application to the concept of an extraliterary, or referential and political, model of "justice," see Allan Stoekl, "Paulhan and Blanchot: On Rhetoric, Terror, and the Gaze of Orpheus," in *Agonies of the Intellectual: Commitment, Subjectivity, and the Performative in the Twentieth-Century French Tradition* (Lincoln: University of Nebraska Press, 1992).

19. The French text reads: "Mal informé celui qui se crierait son proper contemporain, désertant, usurpant, avec impudence égale, quand du passé cessa et que tarde un futur ou que les deux se remmêlent perplexement en vue de masquer l'écart." Stéphane Mallarmé, "L'Action restreinte," in *Oeuvres complètes*, ed. Betrand Marchal (Paris: Gallimard, 2003), 2:217. See also Maurice Blanchot: "We are not contemporaries of the disaster: that is its difference, and this difference is its fraternal threat"; *The Writing of the Disaster*, tr. Ann Smock (Lincoln: University of Nebraska Press, 1995), 6.

9. ON PAROLE: LEGACIES OF SAUSSURE, BLANCHOT, AND PAULHAN

1. See Maurice Blanchot, *The Writing of the Disaster*, tr. Ann Smock (Lincoln: University of Nebraska Press, 1995), 10. *L'Écriture du désastre* (Paris: Gallimard, 1980), 23. Further references to the translation appear in the text, identified as *WD*. Blanchot is in fact rewriting something he had himself already read in the writing of Mallarmé: "Strictement j'envisage la lecture comme une pratique désespérée." ("Strictly speaking, I consider reading a desperate practice,

a practice of despair.") In the same text, a page or so before associating reading with desperation and despair, Mallarmé had asked the famous question about literature's (non)existence: "Quelque chose comme les Lettres existe-t-il?" ("Does something like Letters, something like literature, actually exist?") See Stéphane Mallarmé, "La Musique et les Lettres," in *Oeuvres complètes*, ed. Betrand Marchal (Paris: Bibliothèque de la Pléiade, 1998–2003), 2:67, 65. The association of reading and writing with anguish and despair will become more evident further on in this chapter.

2. One of the possible sources for Blanchot's attentiveness to the word *désastre* may be traced back to its use by another perhaps even more shadowy figure in twentieth-century French thought, Jean Paulhan. In an obscure corner of a little-known text by Paulhan, *Alain, ou la preuve par l'étymologie*, one reads: "L'écart de *désastre* à *catastrophe* et à *calamité* n'a plus rien à voir avec les étoiles, le bouleversement, la paille." ("The distance that separates *disaster* from *catastrophe* and from *calamity* no longer has anything to do with the stars, or with overturning, or with *calamus*, straw.") *Alain*, in Jean Paulhan, *Oeuvres complètes* (Paris: Cercle du livre précieux, 1966–70), 3:277. Further references to this work, which will be discussed at more length later in this chapter, appear in the text. Another possible source is better known: Mallarmé's "Le Tombeau d'Edgar Poe." The last stanza of the sonnet begins with this line: "Calme bloc ici-bas chu d'un désastre obscur" ("Calm block fallen here below from an obscure disaster"; *Oeuvres complètes*, 1:38).

3. Among the most compelling proofs is provided by the way that *langue* and *parole* have actually become part of the English language. When one consults *Webster's Unabridged Dictionary of English* for the existence of the word *langue*, one finds the following entry: "language that is a system of elements or set of habits common to a community of speakers—contrasted with PAROLE." The corresponding entry for the word *parole*, sense 6, reads: "a linguistic act: linguistic behavior—contrasted with LANGUE."

4. Louis Hjelmselv, "Langue et parole," in *Essais linguistiques* (Paris: Minuit, 1971). Further references appear in the text.

5. Ferdinand de Saussure, *Course in General Linguistics*, tr. Wade Baskins (New York: McGraw Hill, 1959), 9, 14. Further references appear in the text. Saussure also wrote, "Langue, in distinction to parole, is an object that can be studied separately. . . . Not only can the science of langue do without consideration of the other elements of language, it is possible only on condition that these other elements not be mixed with it" (*Course*, 15). To appreciate just how vexed Saussure's institution of the distinction langue/parole has been from the very start, one should begin by reading the long note to the critical edition of the *Cours de linguistique générale*, ed. Tullio de Mauro (Paris: Payot, 1976), 420–22.

6. Paul Ricoeur, "Structure, Word, Event," in *The Conflict of Interpretations* (Evanston: Northwestern University Press, 1974), 85; "La Structure, le mot, l'événement," in *Le Conflit des Interprétations* (Paris: Seuil, 1969), 85–86. Ricoeur's

stated aim is to prevent Saussure's linguistic model from putting human subjectivity at risk of being "torn apart"—*déchiré* (*Conflict*, 88; *Le Conflit*, 89).

7. This unknowable power is first of all and most importantly the power of *change*: "C'est dans la parole que se trouve le germe de tous les changements"; "It is in parole that the germ of all change is found" (Saussure, *Cours*, 138; *Course*, 98). As such, and as we shall see, it is also the most unforeseeable and unstoppable power of what can actually occur as *history*.

8. Jacques Derrida, "Sémiologie et grammatologie," in *Positions* (Paris: Editions de Minuit, 1972), 39–40.

9. In *The Writing of the Disaster*, Blanchot writes: "Beyond the serious, there is play, but beyond play, on the lookout for what puts out of play: the gratuitous, from which there is no hiding" (12). This fragment on the alternative serious/play is itself based on the gratuitous play of the letter that Blanchot emphasizes when he writes, "mais au-delà du jeu, cherchant ce qui déjoue: le gratuit" (*L'Écriture du désastre*, 25). There would be no hiding from this play of the letter, which lying beyond the serious, also undoes mere play as well—ce qui déjoue le jeu. Paronomasia, the play beyond the seriousness of any system, and thus *la langue* freed on parole from all systematic constraint, is also what remains at stake in Blanchot's writing of the disaster.

10. See *Writing of the Disaster*, especially pp. 85–86, 92–95, 104, and 107. What works (*travaille*) in Heidegger's text is thus also interrupted, or put out of work (*désoeuvré*) by Blanchot's reading of it. Or, as Blanchot himself writes in *La Communauté inavouable*, "la lecture—le travail désoeuvré de l'oeuvre" (Paris: Minuit, 1983), 42.

11. Heidegger's exegesis of the word *aletheia* and its relation to truth is complex and differentiated, and it evolves over the course of some thirty years or more. Starting out as a straightforward case of etymological derivation, it ends up coming much closer to a free-standing paronomasis. Two concise but thorough considerations of what is at stake in Heidegger's insistent thinking of *aletheia* as *a-letheia* are Robert Bernasconi, "*Aletheia* and the Concealment of Concealing," in *The Question of Language in Heidegger's History of Being* (Atlantic Highlands, N.J.: Humanities Press, 1985), 15–27; and John Sallis, "At the Threshold of Metaphysics," in *Delimitations: Phenomenology and the End of Metaphysics* (Bloomington and Indianapolis: Indiana University Press, 1995), 170–85.

12. *Alain, ou la preuve par l'étymologie* dates from 1953, and is available in volume 3 of Paulhan's *Oeuvres complètes*. Blanchot refers explicitly to Paulhan's text when he considers Heidegger's "etymology" of *aletheia* (*WD* 93–97), and Paulhan includes a reference to Heidegger in his comments on the use of etymology by philosophy (*Alain, OC* 3:267). And then there is the specific example of the word *désastre* given by Paulhan: "L'écart de *désastre* à *catastrophe* et à *calamité* n'a plus rien à voir avec les étoiles, le bouleversement, la paille" (*Alain, OC* 3:277). Another useful point of reference would be Gérard Genette's study of poetic cratylism in *Mimologics*, tr. Thaïs E. Morgan (Lincoln: University of Nebraska

Press, 1994). However, what makes Genette's examination of etymology different from those of both Paulhan and Blanchot is a lack of attention to its properly philosophical dimension. It is this dimension, the seriousness beyond which play acquires genuine philosophical import, that is necessitated by Heidegger's thinking of *aletheia* and Blanchot's writing of the disaster. Without keeping this horizon in mind, Blanchot says, one risks falling prey to a "facile complacency" (*WD* 103).

13. In this respect, and still in the context formed with Heidegger and Blanchot, Paulhan's considerations on language and truth could be fruitfully compared to those of Nietzsche.

14. Such would be the "mystery" of literary language in general and poetry in particular: a capacity to work according to a law lying beyond and interfering with the reach of epistemological laws. Blanchot, in an essay tellingly entitled "Mystery in Literature," says that Paulhan aims at "finding a law whose legitimacy would be grounded in mystery, which is to say, a law in conformity with that which escapes the law." See "Le Mystère dans les lettres," in *La Part du feu* (Paris: Gallimard, 1949), 59. Michael Syrotinski cites this passage in his excellent study of the relation between Blanchot and Paulhan. See his "Blanchot Reading Paulhan," in *Defying Gravity: Jean Paulhan's Interventions in Twentieth-Century French Intellectual History* (Albany: State University of New York Press, 1998), 77–104.

15. The reference is to the famous passage in Mallarmé's "Crise de vers": "Les langues imparfaites en cela que plusieurs, manque la suprême. . . . le vers, lui, philosophiquement rémunère le défaut des langues" (*OC* 2:208). Paulhan includes a reference to this passage, though without citing it directly, when he uses some of Mallarmé's examples in his own discussion of onomatopoeia (*Alain*, *OC* 3:273–75).

16. See Jean Paulhan, *Petite Préface à toute critique* (A Short Preface to All Criticism): "If ever there were someone who, by his very vocation, seemed to us a perfect candidate to be exempt from a reproach of *verbalism*—by that I mean an excess reliance on words to the detriment of thought—it would have to be the philosopher. For there is someone who seeks truth, and who is ready to sacrifice everything for what he seeks. But it so happens that there is no philosopher who doesn't find himself everywhere vulnerable to being taxed with verbalism. . . . Moreover, this is precisely the objection at the center of every criticism leveled against philosophers. It commands and contains all the others" (*OC* 2:285). An analogous argument about linguists is made in *Clef de la poésie* (A Key for Poetry), in the section entitled "Les Linguistes en défaut" (The linguists fall short; *OC* 2:258–62). An English translation of this text is now available; see *Key to Poetry* in Jean Paulhan, *On Poetry and Politics*, ed. Jennifer Bajorek and Eric Trudel, tr. Jennifer Bajorek, Charlotte Mandel, and Eric Trudel (Urbana: University of Illinois Press, 2008), 86–90.

17. "It consists in a projection thanks to which the sense, and indeed even the idea itself, shared by any number of individual sounds and words, and which

we are only now able to discover, appears to us suddenly as though it had been, at the very origin of the words, their own reason for being as well as the link between them. That *cult* and *culture* are one and the same term is an idea that required a great deal of effort for Alain to bring to light, a rigorous method of reflection—or, if one prefers, an entire philosophical system" (Paulhan, *Alain, OC* 3:284). Once again, a "knowledge" of the "true meaning," or *etumon*, of the word functions as both the means and the end of the philosophical system to be built here: by uncovering and then respecting the word's root—*cult*—one forges the tools for eventually constructing an entire world of meaning—*culture*. When all due allowance is made for the differences of idiom and context, Paulhan's reference here to "culture" might be fruitfully considered in its relation to all that lies sedimented for German romanticism in the word and concept of *Bildung*.

18. The example is the one that, following Paulhan, is used by Blanchot, *WD* 92–94, 103–04. See especially, "Did the Greeks think *alètheia* on the basis of *lèthe*? This is doubtful. . . . And that we might say it by substituting ourselves for them . . . would make philosophy dependent upon a philological mode of knowledge" (*WD* 104).

19. See Jean Paulhan,"Lettre aux *Nouveaux Cahiers* sur le pouvoir des mots" (Letter to the Directors of the *Nouveaux Cahiers*: On the Power of Words) in *Les Fleurs de Tarbes*, ed. Jean-Claude Zylberstein (Paris: Gallimard, 1990), 235. It is in this context that a comparison between Paulhan and Friedrich Schlegel on the one hand and Roland Barthes on the other would be of relevance. In many respects, Barthes provides a convenient link between German romanticism and twentieth-century French theory since, in the case of Barthes, the treatment of myth stems from a highly combustible mix of Saussurian semiology and German ideology critique. As Barthes will clearly state in his preface to the 1970 edition of *Mythologies*, there can be no effective political analysis that does not recognize its dependence upon semiological principles, and no consistent semiology that bypasses its own political dimensions and implications. The main difference between Paulhan and Barthes consists in the way that myth is, or is not, treated in relation to *irony*. Barthes, at least at this stage, is more utopian than Paulhan in his belief in the possibility of cleansing his own discourse of a rhetorical, epistemological, and political authority that remains suspect and in need of critical analysis in its turn. See Roland Barthes, *Mythologies*, tr. Annette Lavers (New York: Noonday Press, 1972), 9.

20. This is exactly what Saussure had argued regarding the necessary relation between parole and langue: in order for the signifying functions of langue to become established as the seat of intelligibility, parole, in all its randomness, had to come first.

21. Saussure tends to use etymological examples precisely when he needs to argue for the necessary exclusion of parole from langue, or of diachronic from synchronic linguistics. Some of the more memorable examples occur in the section on onomatopoeia, itself a subcategory of paronomasis (*Course*, 69).

The fact that he will attempt to make etymological "proof" indiscriminately illustrate *both* the arbitrary *and* the motivated nature of parole indicates a certain lack of control over his own examples of etymology. Parole, like etymology and paronomasis, is a fiction capable of motivating every relation, though without ever being able to escape its own radically arbitrary elements. One of the most unforgettable examples of etymology, paronomasia, and parole to be found in Saussure's *Course* (175) is picked up by Paulhan in his text on literature, knowledge, and politics, *De la paille et du grain* (*OC* 5:316). It is the example of what comes between France and Germany in a particularly overdetermined way, that is, Alsace: *Choucroute* is an attempt to grant parole to a foreign and intruding langue, Sauerkraut, by re-endowing the sound of its German letters with French meaning. Saussure calls this an example of those "crude attempts to explain refractory words by relating them to something known" (*Course*, 173). On the uncertain status of etymology in Saussure, see Jacques Derrida, *Glas* (Paris: Galilée, 1974), esp. 103–112.

22. The *Petite Préface à toute critique* dates from 1951. The two critics to whom Paulhan responds at the end of his text on etymology are Maurice Nadeau and Aimé Patri. The original edition of *Alain, ou la preuve par l'étymologie* (Paris: Editions de Minuit, 1953) contains two paragraphs at the beginning of "Notes et Observations" that are not reproduced in the *Oeuvres complètes*. They are written under the heading "Je dois l'avouer" (I have to admit it, I have to confess), and they concern Paulhan's feeling that critics have missed the point of his earlier text. "I have to admit it," Paulhan begins, "it seems to me that I don't deserve certain of the criticisms that have been made about *Petite Préface à toute critique*. That wouldn't be so bad: but I also wonder if I even deserve the praise it has earned me." Because neither the negative nor the positive reception of Paulhan's text seems to have gotten its point, he promises to make it clearer in the responses that follow; or, rather, he says he will have to *confess* better this time what he was trying to say before: "De toute manière, il me faut avouer, mieux que je ne l'ai fait jusqu'ici, quel était mon propos." The response to Maurice Nadeau will be about "critical method," the one to Aimé Patri will be about "critical value" (*Alain* 1953, 87–88). All of these reflections are very close to ones Paulhan included under the title "Trois pages d'explication" (Three Pages of Explanation), which he appended to *The Flowers of Tarbes* in 1945 (*OC* 3:143–45). In several places Paulhan even repeats the very same paragraphs, but substitutes a reference to *Petite Préface à toute critique* where he had earlier written *Les Fleurs de Tarbes*. In both instances, these appendices offer abbreviated versions of Paulhan's constant reflection on the epistemological imperative to seek truth, on the possibility—or impossibility—of determining linguistic laws in the formation of critical method, and on the way the problems of language made accessible by way of literary study offer a reliable means of confronting universal social and political problems.

23. Paulhan's position here is not without analogy to that of Paul de Man as it is articulated, for instance, in "The Resistance to Theory." This is not surpris-

ing to the extent that de Man, like Paulhan, is addressing the problem of critical method, or "theory," from a post-Saussurian point of view that emphasizes those factors and functions of language—and de Man will refer both to etymological proof ("Cratylism") and paronomasis in this context—that cross between and eventually cross up a neat division between rhetoric and epistemology, langue and parole, literature and philosophy, fiction and referentiality. Just as Paulhan in *Alain, ou la preuve par l'étymologie*, de Man will examine the rhetorical element in etymology, or paronomasis, as a "trope that operates on the level of the signifier and contains no responsible pronouncement on the nature of the world—despite its powerful potential to create the opposite illusion." The power at work is one of illusion or dissimulation, and it necessarily operates on every referential discourse of knowledge as well as of power. See Paul de Man, "The Resistance to Theory," *The Resistance to Theory* (Minneapolis: University of Minnesota Press, 1986), esp. 9–10.

24. *Les Fleurs de Tarbes* (1936) in *Les Fleurs de Tarbes*, ed. Jean-Claude Zylberstein (Paris: Gallimard, 1990). Here and following, the pages in question, which treat the problem of critical method in terms of failure, hope, and solution, are 247–50.

25. Maurice Blanchot, "Comment la littérature est-elle possible?" in *Faux Pas* (Paris:Gallimard, 1943; 1971), 100. For a deceptively powerful and beautiful meditation on this move in both Paulhan and Blanchot, see Ann Smock, *What Is There to Say?* (Lincoln: University of Nebraska Press, 2003), especially the section entitled "Getting Across," 30–44.

26. No one has done a more thorough job of interrogating despair than Søren Kierkegaard. It would be of considerable interest, from the standpoint of irony, to examine Kierkegaard's existential despair together with Paulhan's rhetorical despair. Such an examination would go a long way toward bringing out the rhetorical dimension in Kierkegaard and the existential dimension in Paulhan. The "pas au-delà" to which Blanchot refers in his reading of Paulhan's text is of course called *faith* in Kierkegaard's text. See Søren Kierkegaard, *Sickness Unto Death*, ed. Howard V. Hong and Edna H. Hong (Princeton: Princeton University Press, 1983).

27. *To hope against hope* is an idiomatic expression that in general means to hope despite being deprived of any grounds for hope. From the moment such a possibility is taken seriously, it becomes a stumbling block for the rational mind and all its operations. The expression, *to hope against hope*, is an elliptical version of the phrase that is used in Romans 4:18 to characterize Abraham's *faith*: "Who against hope believed in hope, that he might become the father of many nations, according to that which was spoken, So shall thy seed be." That Abraham, against hope, believed in hope, or that, in hope, he believed against hope, or that he more simply believed in hope against hope, or against hope in hope—all such formulations point to how difficult it is to determine with precision the relation between his belief, that is, his faith, and his (lack of) hope. Paulhan's text on

etymology can thus be considered another version of Abraham's story, though one that, like Kierkegaard's, is ironic inasmuch as the *desperate* nature of faith— its essential relation to *dés-espoir*—is never allowed to fade from view.

28. Such is the proposition that motivates Paulhan at the beginning as well as the end of his meditation: "for want of a rigorous investigation, incessantly pursued, into the words we use, we are at great risk of becoming duped by them and of thus becoming slaves to them" (*Alain, OC* 3:285). See also the beginning: "one has to wonder how often it happens (if not always) that instead of expressing our thought, we are merely thinking our language" (*Alain, OC* 3:263).

29. Such is the privative "law" of all language: it forever separates us from any direct access to light (*astre*) and hope (*espoir*) by making it always necessary to pass first through disaster and despair (*l'écriture du désastre*; *une solution de dés-espoir*). In this respect, it is also a "bridge" (*pont*) that can be "crossed" (*traversé*) only in the mode of an impassable obstacle (*à la traverse*). See Paulhan's récit "Le Pont traversé," in *Oeuvres complètes*, 1:85–100. Another way to put this is found in Paulhan's "conclusion" to *The Flowers of Tarbes*. Since the illusions of language are constant and permanent, we are forever condemned to a critical method of dis-illusionment: "Où l'illusion forge le fait, la désillusion le ruine" [Where illusion creates the thing, disillusion ruins it] (*OC* 3:80). But since the "dis-illusion" must itself work by means of an etymological play present in all language, this necessarily de-lusive search for truth is also necessarily endless. See also "Lettre aux *Nouveaux Cahiers* sur le pouvoir des mots," in the 1990 Gallimard edition of *Les Fleurs de Tarbes* (235), for a slightly modified version of this predicament in the search for all truth.

30. In fact, this very formulation is, more or less, a mechanical repetition taken from the "Three Pages of Explanation" following *The Flowers of Tarbes*: "No doubt the Terrorists made their judgments without rhyme or reason [Les Terroristes certes jugaient à tort et à travers]; but they made them so *constantly* without rhyme or reason [mais ils jugaient si *constamment* à tort et à travers] that for want of a critical method, that is, for want of knowing what they were talking about, they themselves became laws [qu'à défaut d'être savants ils devenaient eux-mêmes lois]" (*OC* 3:145). More *and* less mechanical: for the later version does repeat the cliché that the original version was itself repeating verbatim—à tort et à travers; but it now "repeats" the cliché with a difference. First of all, it extends the law of the fall, the *défaut* that characterizes all knowledge, *le savoir*, by applying it to Rhétoriqueurs as well as to Terroristes. Secondly, Paulhan now dissolves the most mechanical aspect of the *lieu commun*, its recognizability as a pat phrase—the adverbial qualification *à tort* turns into the actual errors of *des torts*, and the adverbial qualification *à travers* turns into the very real aberrancies of *des travers*. Paulhan therefore displaces the cliché by putting its signifying potential back into play in a slightly altered and more "pronounced" manner. Blanchot draws attention to the way this process resembles Paulhan's theory of "translation" as it is articulated in *La Demoiselle aux miroirs* (The Young Lady in

the Mirror; *OC* 2:171–83). The result of such a model of translation, for Blanchot, would be "des paroles déchirées par l'éclair"—paroles that have been torn apart by lightning (*Faux Pas*, 101). Paulhan's "solution de désespoir" could indeed be read as one such bolt of lightning: the only hope is to resolve the word, to dip the word—*désespoir*—into a critical *solution* capable of separating it into its constituent parts—*dés-espoir*. Another term for such a "desperate solution," of course, would be *irony*.

10. "WHAT IS HAPPENING TODAY IN DECONSTRUCTION"

1. See Jacques Derrida, "Some Statements and Truisms about Neologisms, Newisms, Postisms, Parasitisms, and Other Small Seismisms," in David Carroll, ed., *The States of 'Theory': History, Art, and Critical Discourse* (New York: Columbia University Press, 1990), 85. The French version of this lecture was published in 2009. See Jacques Derrida, "Some statements and truisms about neologisms, newisms, postisms, parasitisms, and other small seisms," in Thomas Dutoit and Philippe Romanski, eds., *Derrida d'ici, Derrida de là* (Paris: Galilée, 2009), 243. In their note to the title, the editors of the French text point out that the text was written in French by Derrida, though with this English title and in order to be translated and delivered in English at a conference held at the University of California, Irvine, in April of 1987. They also point out that the English translation differs in some places from the French version, which is faithful in every respect to Derrida's manuscript. In the citation included here, for instance, I have adopted the punctuation of the French text, since it includes the quotation marks around the word *statement* as well as around the "statement" as a whole and within the "statement" where reference is made to "what happens." Leading up to this "statement," the lecture contains some highly relevant remarks about the use of quotation marks and their relation to "irony" ("Some Statements," 73–78; "Some statements," 232–37).

2. Over and over again, Kierkegaard repeats, varying its expression only slightly each time: "If this paradox is not faith, then Abraham is lost, then faith has never existed because it has always existed." See Soren Kierkegaard, *Fear and Trembling/Repetition*, tr. Howard V. Hong and Edna H. Hong (Princeton: Princeton University Press, 1983), 55. For the repetitions that punctuate the rest of the text, see 56, 81, 113, 120.

3. See Jacques Derrida, "Letter to a Japanese Friend," in David Wood and Robert Bernasconi, eds., *Derrida and Différance* (Evanston, Ill.: Northwestern University Press, 1988). This letter, written to Toshihiko Izutsu, was first published in French in 1985. It can now be found, titled "Lettre à un ami japonais," in *Psyche: Inventions de l'autre* (Paris: Galilée, 1987).

4. The unspecified reference is probably to the use Heidegger makes of both terms, *Destruktion* and *Abbau*, in a lecture course he gave during the summer of 1927. The lectures have been published as *The Basic Problems of Phenomenol-*

ogy, tr. A. Hofstadter (Bloomington: University of Indiana Press, 1982); see esp. 20–23.

5. See Jacques Derrida, *De la Grammatologie* (Paris: Editions de Minuit, 1967), 21 ; *Of Grammatology*, tr. Gayatri Chakravorty Spivak (Baltimore: The Johns Hopkins University Press, 1997), 10; I have often modified the translations provided by this text as well as by other English-language editions cited in this chapter. It is worth remarking that a first version of *Grammatology* was published in essay form in the French journal *Critique*. Derrida himself mentions this in a note to the "Avertissement," the prefatory note or notice, that precedes the text (*Grammatologie*, 7; *Grammatology*, 323). What was to become only the first part of the book, "L'Écriture avant la lettre" (Writing before the Letter), appeared in condensed form over the course of two issues of *Critique* under the titles "De la Grammatologie (I)" and "De la Grammatologie (II)." While there are numerous changes that Derrida makes from the earlier version to the later, the sentence that will be under consideration presently is retained verbatim with two exceptions, one of which is telling. In *Critique*, Derrida writes of the "rationality" that rules "writing *in a sense* thus extended and radicalized," whereas in *De la Grammatologie* he removes the qualification put on writing by its relation to sense or meaning, that is, to logos; "l'écriture au sens ainsi élargi et radicalisé" in *Critique* thus becomes "l'écriture ainsi élargie et radicalisée" in *Grammatologie*. See Jacques Derrida, "De la Grammatologie (I)," *Critique* 223 (December 1965), 1023.

6. For one relevant text in which Derrida addresses *chance*, see Jacques Derrida, "Mes chances: Au Rendez-vous de quelques stéréophonies épicuriennes," *Cahiers Confrontations* 19 (1988); "My Chances/Mes Chances: A Rendezvous with Some Epicurian Stereophonies," in *Taking Chances: Derrida, Psychoanalysis, and Literature*, ed. Joseph H. Smith and William Kerrigan (Baltimore: Johns Hopkins University Press, 1984). For Derrida's treatment of chance, dice, and falling in Mallarmé, see "La Double Séance," in *La Dissémination* (Paris: Seuil, 1972); "The Double Session," in *Dissemination*, tr. Barbara Johnson (Chicago: University of Chicago Press, 1981). Other helpful references include Jacques Derrida, *La Carte Postale: De Socrate à Freud* (Paris: Flammarion, 1980), *The Post Card: From Socrates to Freud and Beyond*, tr. Alan Bass (Chicago: University of Chicago Press, 1987), and his "La Main de Heidegger (*Geschlecht* II)," in *Psyche: Inventions de l'autre* (Paris: Galilée, 1987), "*Geschlecht* II: Heidegger's Hand," tr. John P. Leavey, Jr., in *Deconstruction and Philosophy: The Texts of Jacques Derrida*, ed. John Sallis (Chicago: University of Chicago Press, 1987).

7. See Maurice Blanchot, *L'Écriture du désastre* (Paris: Gallimard, 1980), 25; *The Writing of the Disaster*, tr. Ann Smock (Lincoln: University of Nebraska Press, 1995), 12.

8. This sentence also appears in *On Grammatology*: "There is nothing outside the text" is the translation given on p. 158 of the English-language edition for the French, which appears on p. 227 of *De la Grammatologie*. This sentence has

often, though mistakenly and misleadingly, been taken as a denial of referential reality when, on the contrary, it affirms and extends the reach of referential reality and its effects to include the writing of texts, such as *Of Grammatology*, as well as the reading—or nonreading—of such texts.

9. See Paul de Man, "The Resistance to Theory," in *The Resistance to Theory* (Minneapolis: University of Minnesota Press, 1986), esp. 11.

11. BEWILDERING: PAUL DE MAN, POETRY, POLITICS

1. Paul de Man, "Aesthetic Formalization: Kleist's *Über das Marionettentheater*," in *The Rhetoric of Romanticism* (New York: Columbia University Press, 1984), 289. Further references to *The Rhetoric of Romanticism* appear in the text, identified as *RR*.

2. Paul de Man, "Hegel on the Sublime," in *Aesthetic Ideology*, ed. Andrzej Warminski (Minneapolis: University of Minnesota Press, 1996), 107. Further references to *Aesthetic Ideology* appear in the text, identified as *AI*.

3. "An Interview with Paul de Man by Stefano Rosso," in Paul de Man, *The Resistance to Theory* (Minneapolis: University of Minnesota Press, 1986), 121; emphasis added. Further references to *The Resistance to Theory* appear in the text, identified as *RT*.

4. Stefano Rosso makes a point of emphasizing how "de Man had agreed to try to be as 'perspicuous' as possible, since he had to be understood by listeners and not by professional readers" ("Interview," *RT* 115). The degree to which the contractual agreement of the interview depends here on the transparency of an "understanding" that would not be subject to the constraints of "professional" reading is already a symptom of the uneasy relation between critical epistemology and ideology.

5. Originally announced under the title, "Kant on the Sublime," the published version of the lecture is entitled "Phenomenality and Materiality in Kant." See de Man, *Aesthetic Ideology*. Further references to the lecture appear in the text. For the work on which the lecture primarily focuses, see Immanuel Kant, *Kritik der Urteilskraft*, vol. 10 of *Werkausgabe in 12 Bänden*, ed. Wilhelm Weischedel (Frankfurt am Main: Suhrkamp, 1978); *Critique of Judgment*, tr. Werner S. Pluhar (Indianapolis and Cambridge: Hackett, 1987). Further references to this work by Kant appear in the text, identified as *Kritik* and *Critique*.

6. "Kant and Schiller," *AI* 132, 133. Further references to this lecture appear in the text.

7. Now entitled "Anthropomorphism and Trope in the Lyric," the lecture is published in de Man, *The Rhetoric of Romanticism*. Further references appear in the text.

8. For an elaboration of the way this aporia between the singularity of the event and the iterability of the trace it will as such have left on the world is legible in Paul de Man's writing, see, inter alia, Jacques Derrida, "Typewriter

Ribbon: Limited Ink (2) ('within such limits')," in Tom Cohen et al., eds., *Material Events: Paul de Man and the Afterlife of Theory* (Minneapolis: University of Minnesota Press, 2001), especially 329–36.

9. De Man's actual sentence, not atypically, is syntactically and grammatically loose enough to require explication: "Our question, then, becomes whether and where this . . . becomes *apparent* in the text, at a moment when the aporia of the sublime is no longer *stated*, as was the case in the mathematical sublime and in the ensuing general definitions of the concept, *as* an explicit paradox, but *as* the apparently tranquil, because entirely unreflected, *juxtaposition* of incompatibles" ("Kant," *AI* 79; emphasis added). The parallel construction, "the aporia of the sublime is no longer stated as . . . an explicit paradox"/"but [rather stated] as the . . . juxtaposition," cannot be completed in a satisfactory way here, since a "juxtaposition," unlike a "paradox," cannot really become a "statement" in the strict sense of the term. This is nevertheless consistent with the fact that whatever material trace the passage to history leaves in a text, it could not become "apparent," or better *legible*, as either an explicit "statement" or a "conceptual definition." It appears then that the theoretical consistency of de Man's thinking, at least in this passage, can be maintained only at the cost of its own grammatical coherence.

10. The specification of nature, in the sublime, as both an art and techné of the "building" is not, properly speaking, part of de Man's argument in the fourth Messenger Lecture, but comes instead from an earlier paper that he delivered at the MLA in 1981. The paper is entitled "Kant's Materialism," and it can in many respects be considered another or preliminary version of "Phenomenality and Materiality in Kant." "Kant's Materialism" is published in *Aesthetic Ideology*; for the reference in question, see *AI* 125–27.

11. The key word in this formulation is the pronoun *es*, it, for what exactly the poets "do" in constructing the experience of the sublime remains impossible to say properly, since it is in fact the condition of possibility for saying anything. De Man offers his own highly compact version of this undecidability in his paper "Kant's Materialism," when he traces out the architectonic of the sublime in the following "juxtaposition of incompatibles": "What is [the erection of the architectonic] for Kant? We receive a hint in a passage which tells us how *to look* at the sublime, how *to read* judiciously, like the poets ('wie die Dichter es tun'): 'If we call sublime the sight of a star-studded sky . . . '" (*AI* 126; emphasis added). For an elaboration of what lies compacted in de Man's juxtaposition of "looking" and "reading" here, see (read) Andrzej Warminski, "'As the Poets Do It': On the Material Sublime," in Cohen et al., eds., *Material Events*, 3–31.

12. There is an irony in the way that de Man distinguishes here between Kant's (wild) "poet" and the more familiar image of Wordsworth, one that perhaps only de Man would indulge in so good-naturedly. Just as nothing has happened in the reception of Kant—until "this" reading by de Man?—so, too, nothing would have happened in the reception of Wordsworth—at least noth-

ing that would have made a dent in the overwhelmingly aesthetic reception of his poetry. And so this de Man, like everybody else—*wie ein anderer*—reads Wordsworth here as though another (*ein ganz anderer und wilder*) de Man had not already read him as Kant's poet in so many other essays! The passage in Kant can be found in the *Logik*, in *Werkausgabe* 6:457.

13. "Die Stimmung des Gemüts zum Gefühl des Erhabenen erfordert eine Empfänglichkeit desselben für Ideen. . . . [W]as man mit dem gesunden Verstande zugleich jedermann ansinnen und von ihm fodern kann, nämlich in der Anlage zum Gefühl für (praktische) Ideen, d.i. *zu dem* moralischen" (Kant, *Kritik*, 189, 190; *Critique*, 124, 125). See also section 7 of the introduction. On the role of affectivity in an aesthetic judgment of the beautiful, see Jacques Derrida, "Le Parergon," in "Parergon," in *La Vérité en peinture* (Paris: Flammarion, 1978). For an excellent account of what remains in play in the philosophical reception of Kant's sublime "feeling," which however does not mention either de Man or Derrida, see Peter Fenves, "Taking Stock of the Kantian Sublime," *Eighteenth-Century Studies* 28, no. 1 (1994), 65–82.

14. De Man made this remark in the earlier paper on Kant's sublime referred to in n. 10 above; see "Kant's Materialism," *AI* 123.

15. It would hardly be an exaggeration to say that de Man's abiding interest in romanticism as a crux for literary theory as well as for literary criticism and history stems from his attentiveness to the peculiar structure and occurrence within it of "shock." For de Man's most extended considerations of the textual occurrence of shock, interruption, and fragmentation, see *The Rhetoric of Romanticism* and *Romanticism and Contemporary Criticism: The Gauss Seminar and Other Papers*, ed. E. S. Burt et al. (Baltimore: Johns Hopkins University Press, 1993).

16. And this characterization recalls a still earlier description, in section 14, of the affect of the sublime and the standard of measure (*Maßstab*) peculiar to its judgment: "Rührung, eine Empfindung wo Annehmlichkeit nur vermittelst augenblicklicher Hemmung und darauf erfolgender stärkerer Ergießung der Lebenskraft gewirkt wird, gehört gar nicht zur Schönheit. Erhabenheit (mit welcher das Gefühl der Rührung verbunden ist) aber erfordert einen andern Maßstab der Beurteilung, als der Geschmack sich zum Grunde legt . . ." (Kant, *Kritik*, 142; *Critique*, 72). Yet another passage, in section 27, compares the shock affect of the sublime to a shaking, shuddering, or trembling motion: "Das Gemüt fühlt sich in der Vorstellung des Erhabenen in der Natur *bewegt*. . . . Diese Bewegung kann (vornehmlich in ihrem Anfang) mit einer *Erschütterung* verglichen werden" (*Kritik*, 181; *Critique*, 115). For a consideration of the way Kant's text on the sublime is organized by the intersecting lines of all these questions, see Jacques Derrida, "Le Colossal," in *La Vérité en peinture*.

17. *Verwundern*, to amaze or astonish, has no semantic tie to *verwunden*, to wound. The shock of the "Wunde" in *Verwunderung* therefore occurs and can only occur at the level of the inscribed signifier, which is also to say that, like the erection of the "wide vault" under which the wild poet always stands, it can happen neither as cognition nor perception. The English word *wound*, moreover,

does not appear in de Man's reading of the third *Critique* in this lecture. Rather, it becomes legible in the way he characterizes the "shock" of *Verwunderung* variously as "suffering," "pain," "mutilation," and "dismemberment" ("Kant," *AI* 86, 88, 89). Nonetheless, all the wounding implications of *Verwunderung* in the Kant lecture emerge in the Kleist lecture, where the word *wound* is made to play a key role in de Man's treatment of the philosophical and historical category of the aesthetic as it developed in the wake of the third *Critique* ("Kleist," *RR* 275–80).

18. It would be pertinent to ask whether and to what extent an "equivalent" political moment can be documented in all the Messenger Lectures. The question could be developed by following the way Kant's analysis of the sublime necessarily relates measurement (*Messung*), freedom (*Freiheit*) and justice (*Gerechtigkeit*) directly to the question of *equality*. Sections 25–27, on the mathematical sublime, refer at key moments to the need for a standard of comparison and equality, *ein Maßstab der Vergleichung*, an obligation which by extension would also hold for the practical realm of law and politics. The possibility of establishing "Gleichheit" as equality, parity, and equivalence is of obvious importance in the first lecture (the "correspondances" in Baudelaire) as well as in the last lecture (the individual "fragments" of a vessel that, according to Benjamin, without having to equal each other, "nicht so zu gleichen haben," nonetheless allow themselves to be articulated together, "sich zusammenfügen zu lassen"). In each case, it would be necessary to demonstrate the precise ways in which de Man's critical analysis of textual models leads to the disclosure of the historical and political systems that come into existence only as their correlate. The overtly political dimensions of the lectures on Kleist, Schiller, and Hegel are of course more clearly pronounced, though they too stand in need of being traced back to the rhetorical and epistemological configurations from which they also have to result. In this way would be disclosed what we might call the "law" of Paul de Man's own writing: a repeated response to the irreducible differences— linguistic, epistemological, economic, political, and ideological—that always lie concealed in the usurped, and therefore illusory, authority of equivalence. "The law," de Man writes in an economical summary, "is always a law of differentiation (*Unterscheidung*), not the grounding of an authority but the unsettling of an authority that is shown to be illegitimate" ("Hegel on the Sublime," *AI* 115).

19. For if the affect of shock is truly prerequisite to "feeling" the sublime in the first place, then what could ever prevent the sublime feeling of admiration from repeating this inaugural shock in its very attempt to recover from and move beyond it? Kant himself comes close to sketching out the mutually interruptive relationship that is involved here when he writes: "A [sublime] cast of mind can be called noble . . . only if it provokes not so much *amazement* [*Verwunderung*] (an affect in which the representation of novelty exceeds all expectation) as *admiration* [*Bewunderung*] (an amazement [*Verwunderung*] that does not cease once the novelty has passed)" (*Critique*, 133 [translation modified]; *Kritik*, 199; also see section 62, *Kritik*, 311; *Critique*, 243). In other words, *Bewunderung* is itself nothing but (ceaseless) *Verwunderung*—the uninterrupted, though now

dissimulated, shock that necessarily accompanies the rational fiction of the mind's capacity to attain tranquil admiration, respect, nobility.

CODA: DARK FREEDOM IN J. M. COETZEE'S *DISGRACE*

1. J. M. Coetzee, *Disgrace* (New York: Viking Press, 1999). Further references to this work appear in the text. Unless otherwise noted, all emphases in quoted passages have been added by me.

2. David's comportment during the hearing provides an excellent illustration of the kind of subjective detachment and superiority that is often associated with romantic irony. He appears there as vain as well as "evasive," exhibits a "subtle mockery" with respect to the entire procedure, refuses to state his position unequivocally, and ultimately resists any effort "to pin him down"—especially the attempt to have him make "his own words" coincide with his "sincere feelings." Lucy will use the term *irony* later on to qualify the same attitude that she has experienced in her dealings with David: "[C]an we have some relief from that terrible irony of yours?" she asks, and then adds: "For years you used it against me when I was a child, to mortify me" (200). From the subjective perspective of this type of ironist, others seldom if ever grow out of childhood.

3. David's stubborn refusal to give in, to go slack, to give up the position of subjective mastery is the other side of his repressed knowledge—and terror—about what it must have been like for Melanie to undergo a radical loss, a privation of self. Later on, in chapter 11, and before David is made to endure his own violation at the hands of the three intruders, he has a haunting vision of Melanie: "He sees himself in the girl's flat, in her bedroom, with the rain pouring down outside and the heater in the corner giving off a smell of paraffin, kneeling over her, peeling off her clothes, while her arms flop like the arms of a *dead person*" (89). This vision recalls what David had already registered without comprehending it at the time of his intrusion: "He has given her no warning; she is too surprised to resist the intruder who thrusts himself upon her. When he takes her in his arms, her limbs crumple like a marionette's" (24).

4. At one point, at the marriage celebration for Petrus, David believes he "knows" something about the dark trio: "From the far side of the fire someone is staring at him. At once things fall into place. He *knows* that face, *knows* it intimately. . . . 'I *know* you,' he says grimly. . . . 'Do you *know* who this is,' he asks Petrus. 'No, I do not *know* what this is,' says Petrus angrily. 'I do not *know* what is the trouble'" (131, 132). In one of the novel's most strained and remarkable sentences, it becomes clear that the only thing one knows for sure is how much one does not yet know about the "new" South Africa: "It is hard to say what Petrus is, strictly speaking. . . . It is a new world they live in, he and Lucy and Petrus. Petrus knows it, and he knows it, and Petrus knows that he knows it" (116–17).

5. The desire to know the whole story, the desire to make the woman speak and tell her story, is one that punctuates the entire novel. When David is left

in the dark by Soraya in chapter 1 of the novel, he hires a detective to "track her down" (9). More importantly still, in chapter 3, the first time David will see Melanie after the encounter that is described as "not rape, not quite that," she is distraught, and David tries to get her to tell him what it is all about. "Is there something the matter?" he will ask her, "Do you want to talk? . . . Will you tell me now what this is all about?" (26, 28). Melanie promises to tell David her story later on, but this particular later on, of course, will never come for David.

6. David exhibits a remarkable proclivity for inventing just such stories, especially about women, and they always serve to reinforce his own self-image as a self-conscious and knowing subject. He thus imagines that he is in a "reciprocal" relationship with Soraya, one based on mutual "affection" and a shared recognition that they are equally "lucky" to have found each other. He imagines a fiction for Melanie: because she doesn't like to cook, she will have to marry a husband who does all the cooking. More seriously, he will tell himself that Melanie could not have been the one to have brought charges against him, but rather that she must have been "talked into it" by her father, "the little man in the ill-fitting suit," and cousin Pauline, "the plain one, the duenna" (39). By resisting the impulse to tell such stories, Melanie and Lucy retain a right to keep what one might call the secret of their secret. In other words, neither Lucy nor Melanie attempts to reveal that which, in the alienating "experience" of having been violated, cannot be brought into the light and narrated for the sake of claiming knowledge, understanding, and power.

7. For instance, *aliter* is part of the well-known quote from book 1 of Vergil's *Aeneid*: "Dis aliter visum"—The gods thought otherwise. At the end of chapter 19, another famous phrase from book 1 of the *Aeneid* is quoted by Lurie: "*Sunt lacrimae rerum, et mentem mortalia tangunt*"—"These are the tears of the world, and what it means to be mortal touches the heart." Robert Browning wrote a poem entitled "Dis aliter visum; or, Le Byron de nos jours."

8. At one point before David has learned that he has much to learn from Bev, he compares her to a romantic figure one might be least inclined to consider an example of irony: Emma Bovary (150). However, it may be that in Emma's case, too, one has not yet learned to read very well what is actually written into the "romanticism" of Flaubert's text. To the degree that Emma, like Flaubert, puts her faith wholeheartedly in fiction, in other words, to the degree that she takes literary fictions with the utmost seriousness, and that she responds unconditionally to their appeal, without regard for preserving control over her own interests and understanding, she may in fact—at least in part—exemplify an irony of irony, an irony beyond a merely subjective and self-controlled ironic consciousness. Of course, Flaubert's treatment of Emma has another side to it as well, and David, especially before he meets Bev Shaw and begins his own process of melanization, shows his sensitivity to it. "He thinks of Emma Bovary," the text reads, "marvelling at herself in the mirror" (5–6). The figure of a self marvelling at itself in the mirror of its own self-consciousness corresponds to a type of

subjective irony that characterizes David—as well as David's understanding of romanticism—only at the beginning of the novel.

9. It would always be possible to avoid or parry the difficulty that is posed by the ending of this text by turning it into a formalistic trick or device of fictional autoreferentiality and thus self-reflexivity. Considered from the point of view of stylistic features that become even more prominent in later novels by Coetzee, such as *Slow Man* and *Diary of a Bad Year*, it could be argued that the ending of *Disgrace* is merely about . . . the ending of *Disgrace*: the "dog" in question at the end of chapter 24 of the novel is, after all, the one that comes after the other twenty-three dogs have been "put down" and therefore disposed of before it (219). However, rather than resolving the question of whether and how this text is itself ironic, such a reading would merely take for granted its own understanding of where fiction ends and extratextual reference begins.

Abraham
  Agacinski on, 116–17
  Derrida on, 310n9
  faith of, 112–20, 316n11
  and hope, 340–41n27
  Kafka on, 317n16
  Kierkegaard on, 86, 99–100, 314n31
  and repetition in history, 127–28
  secret at heart of, Kierkegaard on, 99,
    113–20, 136–37, 315n6
  sublimity of, 113–14
Abraham and Isaac story
  contemplation of, as turn away from
    rational thought, 129–31, 133–35
  de Man on, 2
  Hegel on, 133–35, 144
  incomprehensibility of, 128–29
  Kierkegaard on, 72–73, 143, 326–27n3
  Lévinas on, 319n13
  Mann on, 179–81, 317n16, 326–27n3
  ram in, Kierkegaard's treatment of, 2,
    142–45, 320–21nn17–18
  ram in, Mann's treatment of, 180
Abraham's response to God's call, Kierkegaard on
  as irony, 145–46
  as moment beyond ethics, 135–36
  as moment beyond rational thought and
    language, 129–31, 135–36, 140–41,
    143–45
  as moment of absolute isolation,
    136–37
  as ordeal, 128

as point of fear and trembling, 129–31,
  133–35
and source of meaning and existence
  of history, 131, 132–33, 134, 136,
  137–40, 141
as test and temptation, 131–33, 138,
  140–41, 318n9, 320n15
as uninterrupted repetition, 137–44,
  319–20n14
L'Absolu littéraire (Lacoue-Labarthe and
  Nancy)
  on *Bild* and *Bildung* in Schlegel, 33
  on chaos and *Schein* in Schlegel,
    304–5n26
  on irony, 17–18
  Paulhan and, 331n3
  on relationship between literature and
    philosophy, 17, 19–20
  on the romantic fragment, 22–25
  on romanticism of Schlegel, 18–21
  and *Schein* underlying Schlegel's new
    mythology, 37
  on Schlegel and National Socialism,
    25–26, 33
absolu littéraire of Schlegel, 20
  and National Socialism, 26–29, 33,
    303n19
  theoretical resistance to, 22
academic community
  appropriation of philosophical figures,
    96
  crises of the humanities in, 149–50
  economic incentives and truth in, 102

de Man on history
  as emergence of language of power out
    of language of cognition, 267–72
  history *à la lettre*, conditions for,
    271–72
  history *à la lettre*, leaving of mark by,
    272–75
  progress and, 268–69
  reinscription within tropological sys-
    tem, 275
  relapse into ideology, inevitability of,
    269–70, 271
  as wounding, 278–81, 346–47n17
de Man on history and politics, passage
  from language to, 261–63, 265
  and articulation, 265–67, 270–71
  in Kant's *Critique of Judgment*, 265,
    266–67, 272–73
  necessity of synechdochal tropes in,
    266–68
  as passage from cognitive to performa-
    tive models of language, 267–72
  reinscription within tropological sys-
    tem, 275
Deleuze, Gilles, 323n8
"La Demoiselle aux miroirs" (Paulhan),
  206–7
Derrida, Jacques
  L'Absolu littéraire and, 301n9
  and deconstruction, efforts to increase
    precision of, 251–53
  on deconstruction, definition of,
    243–44
  deconstruction and *dé-sédimentation* in,
    251–53
  and deconstruction as term, adoption
    of, 249–51
  and deconstruction as term, efforts to
    increase precision of, 253
  De la Grammatologie (Of Grammatology),
    249, 251, 253
  on de Man, 261
  La Dissémination, 54, 328n11
  Donner la mort, 118–20, 310n9
  Donner le temps, 118–20
  Éperons, 323n8
  relation to Heidegger and Mallarmé,
    243

  on irony, 331–32n5
  Kierkegaard and, 310n9
  on law of iterability, 55–56, 306n7
  "Letter to a Japanese Friend," 249
  "La Mythologie blanche," 325n18,
    333–34n14
  Nietzsche and, 323n8
  Parergon and, 346n13
  Plato's *Phaedrus* and, 328n11
  on play of language, 158
  on representation, 54
  on Saussure, 228
  "Some Statements and Truisms about
    Neologisms, Newisms, Postisms,
    Parasitisms, and Other Small Seis-
    misms," 243–44
Descartes, René, 298n3
La dé-sédimentation, Derrida on, 251–53
despair
  Kierkegaard and Paulhan on, 340n26
  and possibility of epistemologically
    legitimate language, in Paulhan,
    234–41
Dialogue on Poetry (Schlegel), 32–33,
  303–4n21
Diapsalmata, radically fragmented mean-
  ing of, 101–4
"The Diary of the Seducer" (Kierke-
  gaard), 77
Disgrace (Coetzee)
  and dark freedom of silence, 289–90,
    296, 348–49n5–6
  Lucy, and dark freedom of silence,
    289–90
  Lucy's "darkening," 287–88, 291
  Lurie as figure of colonial exploitation,
    286, 293, 349n6
  Lurie's commitment to European ro-
    manticism, 283–84, 287, 294–95
  Lurie's "darkening," 287–88
  Lurie's efforts to freedom of action and
    knowledge, 286
  Lurie's ironic detachment, 282–84,
    288, 294, 348n2
  Lurie's subconscious identification with
    Melanie, 348n3
  Lurie's veterinarian service, significance
    of, 294–96, 349–50n8

imagination and reason, interplay of, in
Kant's *Critique of Judgment*, 275–81
The Inoperative Community (*La Communauté désoeuvrée*; Nancy), 26, 302n16
intellect and life, Mann on relationship
between, 181
intention, authorial, Schlegel's new mythology and, 32
intention, Schlegel on, 304n22
interrogation of history
Heidegger on, 167–68
Mallarmé on, 165–67
Nietzsche's eternal return and, 169–70,
324n15
Irigaray, Luce, 312n25
ironic detachment, in Mann, 181–83
ironic indirection
Hegel on, 43–46
and limits of speaking subject, 44–45
and self-consciousness, 44–45
timeliness of, 47
ironic indirection, Kierkegaard's theory of
Agacinski on, 42–43
central importance of, 41–42
The Concept of Irony and, 42–44, 47–48
as dialectical, 47–48
and faith of Abraham, 116–20
as general theory of language, 55–58
generation of meaning within ironic
negativity, 52–59
incorporation into historical process,
46–48
irony as attribute of linguistic self, 60
and irony as divergence of *logos* and
lexis, 42
irony's undermining of laws of philosophical grammar, 48–52, 58–60
and Kierkegaard's poetic style, 100–101
Napoleon's grave engraving as figure
for, 52–59, 306–7n8
and possibility of direct speech, 43
and recurrence of ironic disruption,
64–65
and truth value of words, 101–2
ironic indirection, negativity of
generation of meaning within, 52–59
incorporation into historical process,
45–47

and self-consciousness, 44–45
ironic interruption, in Kierkegaard's *The
Concept of Irony*, 43–44
ironic understanding, limits of, in *Death in
Venice*, 197–202
ironist *vs.* Christian, Kierkegaard on
subjectivity in, 60–62
irony
as always occasional, 3
as coming apart of word and context,
61–63
as death of thought and identity, Paulhan on, 208, 211–15
definition of, Szondi on, 19
inescapable awareness of, in Nietzsche,
175–76
neutral, Blanchot on, 202
as permanent parabasis, Schlegel on,
38
philosophical status of, Schlegel and,
15–17
resistance to theory, 25, 301n12. *See
also* Kierkegaard's theory of ironic
indirection
irony, eruptions of in literature
Lacoue-Labarthe and Nancy's *L'Absolu
littéraire* on, 17–18
Schlegel on, 18
irony, negativity of, 8–9, 44–46, 53–54,
58–60, 121
generation of meaning within, 52–59
incorporation into historical process,
45–47
Kierkegaard's engagement with,
100
and self-consciousness, 44–45
irony and history
Benjamin on, 10–11
incorporation of ironic indirection into
historical process, 45–47
irony as dash in history, 11–12
Kierkegaard's reinscription of history
of irony into salvational narrative,
11–12
irony and occasion, relationship between,
7–12
irony and truth, and tension between
literature and philosophy, 16–17

Kierkegaard, Søren (*continued*)
on fatherhood, 314n30
father's influence on, 99, 100, 113,
315n5
fiancée's influence on, 99, 100, 119,
315n5, 318n8
on guilt, 89
and Hegel, influence of, 69–70, 72,
125, 213–14n26
on Hegel, 70, 106
on historical reality and sin, 6–7
images, subtle complexity of, 101
importance, elusiveness of, 66
influence, need for research on, 112
influence on Schmitt, 298n4
intellectual reception, types of, 96–98
on invisibility of irony, 7–8
and irony, philosophical status of, 15
on irony as dash in history, 11–12
on irony as telling of death, 85–86
Lévinas on, 74–75
on occasion and cause, 3, 5–6
on original sin, 78–81
on passion, 82–83, 87, 88–90, 311n18
political commentaries, dubious nature
of, 77
on professors and academics, 66–67
reinscription of history of irony into
salvational narrative, 61–62
resistance to commentary, 66–68
on Schlegel, 18, 307n10, 311n18
on secret, keeping of, and existence,
88–92, 107–8
on self, ability to discover new truths
about, 68–69
separation as motif in, 98
and Socratic irony, 45
and subjective existence in Kierkegaard,
106
on truth, discovery of, 67–68
on twofold relationship between
subjectivity and historical actuality,
62–64
Kierkegaard, works by
"The Ancient Tragic Reflected in the
Modern Tragic," 86–94, 109–12,
313nn27–29
The Concept of Anxiety, 78, 86, 109, 122

The Concept of Irony, 42–44, 47–48,
52–59, 65, 77, 85, 86, 122, 123, 124,
125, 283
Concluding Unscientific Postscript,
140–41, 309n7
Diapsalmata, 101–4
"The Diary of the Seducer," 77
Either/Or, 85, 101–4, 109, 311n21
Fear and Trembling, 86, 139, 143,
318n8, 319–20n14
"The First Love," 3, 299n6
Journals, 67, 125
Philosophical Fragments, 67–68, 83, 85,
86, 87, 123
The Point of View, 48
Repetition, 77, 107, 122–23, 127, 139,
318n8, 319–20n14
Works of Love, 119
"Kierkegaard and Evil" (Ricoeur), 75
Kierkegaard's theory of ironic indirection
Agacinski on, 42–43
central importance of, 41–42
The Concept of Irony and, 42–44, 47–48
as dialectical, 47–48
and faith of Abraham, 116–20
as general theory of language, 55–58
generation of meaning within ironic
negativity, 52–59
incorporation into historical process,
46–48
irony as attribute of linguistic self, 60
and irony as divergence of *logos* and
lexis, 42
irony's undermining of laws of philosophical grammar, 48–52, 58–60
and Kierkegaard's poetic style, 100–101
Napoleon's grave engraving as figure
for, 52–59, 306–7n8
and possibility of direct speech, 43
and recurrence of ironic disruption,
64–65
and truth value of words, 101–2
kinesis, Hegel's transition (mediation)
and, 122–23, 318n8
Kleist, Heinrich von, 264–65, 329–30n15
Klossowski, Pierre, 323n8
knight of faith, Kierkegaard on, 100, 136,
138, 308n13

self-conscious suffering and, 87

subjective truth, in Kierkegaard
  and death, thinking of, 83–85
  entry through subject into existence, 70
  as product of opposition of thought and existence, 70, 71, 75
  and suffering, 82

subjectivity
  and emptiness of ironic positing, 58–60, 306–7n8
  as gift and task, in Kierkegaard, 63–64, 307–8n11, 308n13
  interruption of by encounter with death, 93–94
  ironic indirection and, 44–45
  in ironist *vs.* Christian, Kierkegaard on, 60–62
  language as public grammar and, 55–58, 58–60
  as product of opposition of thought and existence, in Kierkegaard, 70, 71, 75

sublime in Kant's *Critique of Judgment*, de Man on, 266–67, 272–81

suffering, self-conscious, and truth of subjectivity, 87

Symparanekromenoi, in Kierkegaard, 92–94

Symposium (Plato), on occasion, 4

Syrotinski, Michael, 332n7, 337n14

Szondi, Peter, on Schlegel, 19

"Talk on Mythology" ("Rede über die Mythologie"; Schlegel), 25, 28–29, 32–33, 34–39, 301n13, 303n20

"The Task of the Translator" (Benjamin), de Man on articulation in, 265

terror of ironic disjunction between language and thought, Paulhan on, 211–19

text, space between formal coherence and referential force in, 158

theory, resistance to, theory itself as, 21–22

thought
  ironic disjunction between language and, Paulhan on, 211–19
  irony and death of, in Paulhan, 208, 211–15

thought and existence, opposition of in Kierkegaard, 70–72, 75, 309n7

and existence as alien to thought, 71–72

and limits of reason, effort to establish, 76

and problems of free will and evil, 75

and radical fallibility, 74

and repetitive rediscovery of truth of subjective existence, 76

Ricoeur on, 75

and risk of descent into meaninglessness, 75–76

serious implications of, 71–75

Thulstrup, Niels, 309n6

"The Tragic in Ancient Drama Reflected in the Tragic in Modern Drama." *See* "The Ancient Tragic Reflected in the Modern Tragic" (Kierkegaard)

transition, of Kierkegaard from philosophical scholar to religious witness, 122

transition (mediation) in Hegel
  Greeks' kinesis and, 122–23
  Kierkegaard's critique of, 122–25, 126–27
  Kierkegaard's repetition and, 122–23, 126–27

truth
  discovery of, Kierkegaard on, 67–69
  and error, distinguishing in language, Blanchot on, 229–30
  gap between history and, in language, 157–58
  and irony, and tension between literature and philosophy, 16–17
  in Kierkegaard, Agacinski's focus on, 98
  new mythology of Schlegel as revelation of, 35
  subject as vehicle for entry into existence, in Kierkegaard, 70
  of subjective existence, discovery of in Kierkegaard, 76
  vs. learning, Kierkegaard on, 97–98, 123

truth and history
  deconstruction in relation to, 157
  as defining poles in Nietzsche's philosophy, 157
  gap between, in language, 157–58
  Mann on, 181